ARCHAEOLOGY OF THE BIBLE: BOOK BY BOOK

ARCHAEOLOGY OF THE BIBLE: BOOK BY BOOK

Gaalyah Cornfeld
and
David Noel Freedman

HENDRICKSON
PUBLISHERS
PEABODY, MASSACHUSETTS 01961-3473

ARCHAEOLOGY OF THE BIBLE:
Book by Book

Copyright © 1976 by Gaalyah Cornfeld

Hendrickson Publishers, Inc. edition

ISBN: 0-943575-28-1

reprinted by arrangement with
Harper & Row, Publishers, Inc.

First Printing, April 1989

Printed in the United States of America

CONTENTS

INTRODUCTION

The Bible, unlike much religious literature, is not only an anthology of sacred books containing a series of theological and ethical teachings, but it is the story of the people of Israel who lived in the land of Israel. They had learned to confess their faith by telling their history and by seeing within it the hand of God, who rules history. God's own righteous ends in history provided the framework for the biblical understanding of both communal and personal history. This, however, is an interpretation by faith that is not subject to objective testing.

The surviving written records provide us with only glimpses of life in antiquity for the reconstruction of biblical history. Many periods remain obscure because of the silence of the biblical record. To reconstruct the record where it is silent and to illuminate it where it does speak, the modern student has turned to archaeology. The results of excavations may aid him through a study of the material remains and the ancient written sources that lay buried for thousands of years. He can gather from them all the data that throw a direct or indirect light upon the events related in the Bible and upon the background of the ancient Hebrews.

1. ARCHAEOLOGY AND THE BIBLICAL TEXT

The study of archaeology leads the student of the Bible, nevertheless, to an unavoidable risk. He may find that the biblical events did not occur in the way described or that many happened in different historical order, thus upsetting the chronological sequence set forth by the writers of the Bible. An example from the Bible concerns the Patriarchs and their appearance on the stage of history: Was there a gap of more than four centuries between these events and the Israelite invasion of Canaan, as is stated in the books of Genesis and Exodus? Similarly, we may ask whether or not the Israelite occupation of Canaan took place in a brief but violent campaign as recorded in the book of Joshua. Or, coming to the New Testament, although the resurrection of Christ was an inner certainty to the early Christians, it is something that archaeology cannot illuminate. Nevertheless, the discovery and analysis of the Dead Sea Scrolls and Jewish-Christian inscriptions have thrown an altogether new light on the beginnings of Christianity, thereby helping to explain much that is elliptical and foreshortened in the New Testament account of the mission of Jesus and his disciples.

While it is true that, for the most part, archaeology has substantiated and illuminated the biblical story, the biblical archaeologist must limit his deductive thinking by rigid scientific discipline. He cannot and does not set out to prove that "the Bible is true" in line with the traditionalist approach of the believer who accepts the biblical text literally, including the short antiquity of life and of man upon the earth; nor does this discipline include the enthusiastic and uncritical approaches expressed—too often in recent years—by popular books on the Bible and archaeology, which follow no set scientific discipline for lack of an understanding of the complex problems involved. The biblical archaeologist can illuminate the historical setting, the cultural background, and the events with which the biblical text is concerned. He thus plays a positive role in biblical exposition, but he avoids facile or biased conclusions. He is bound to test his conclusions through a constant examination of material remains, written and unwritten, and by continuing discussion with qualified specialists in the field. The discoveries of the past decades in the Holy Land, and especially in the last few years in Jerusalem, west and east of the Jordan, and in the south of Israel, call for a reassessment of positions and conclusions in many areas of biblical research. Long-cherished views of scholars have had to be discarded for lack of supporting evidence, while there has been unexpected confirmation of other opinions as a result of these new investigations.

In general we may cite the late E. A. Speiser: "Independent study helps to increase one's respect for the received material beyond the fondest expectations of the confirmed traditionalists" (*Genesis,* Anchor Bible 1, pp. xix-xx). At the same time it should come as no surprise that many scholars have reached revolutionary results through independent analysis of recent archaeological discoveries, as will be set forth in the following chapters. Many theories of biblical archaeology that have gained credence, even in the recent past, are now being discarded for lack of acceptable archaeological evidence.

2. THE FIVE BOOKS OF THE PENTATEUCH

The first section of the Bible consists of five books, headed by Genesis, and is called the Pentateuch ("five-volume work" in Greek), whereas the traditional Hebrew title is *torāh,* meaning "law" but also "instruction, a body of teachings." Despite the title of the works, they are not devoted exclusively to ritual or legal codes. Rather, the book of Genesis, the first part of Exodus, and sections of the other books are characterized by their marvelous stories, to which the Pentateuch owes its universal appeal.

A passage in the book of Deuteronomy (31:9) that related that Moses wrote the Torah gave rise to the doctrine of Mosaic authorship of the whole Pentateuch. Modern scholarship has long since disregarded this dogma. Instead of being entirely the work of Moses, the Pentateuch is a composite work of many hands and periods, including priestly editors and professional scribes. It is the result of a long history of growth, compilation, and transmission. Much of its narrative content derives from oral traditions that were subsequently reworked and expanded by revisers of various schools. This accounts for the fact that the five books of the Pentateuch contain so many duplications, inconsistencies, and even contradictions, not to speak of major stylistic differences, the result of the blending of diverse traditions and disparate points of view.

Overleaf:
Sennacherib receiving the booty
from the Israelite inhabitants of
Lachish who kneel before him.
One of the vast Assyrian reliefs
of Kuyunjik

Process of Transmission of the Biblical Traditions

More than a century of biblical research has been devoted to the analysis of the process by which the books of the Bible emerged from a welter of traditions, oral and written, and the determination of the main stages of transmission up to the present received text. The principal result has been the promulgation of the so-called documentary hypothesis, which is associated with the name of the great German scholar, Julius Wellhausen, who gave it its classic formulation.

In his literary analysis of the Hexateuch, Wellhausen distinguished four main sources in the Pentateuch. In the simplest form of the theory each of these was regarded as an independent "document" that had been composed or compiled by a single author or editor. It was understood that various editors had put these sources together with necessary modifications, bridges, and adjustments to produce a connected whole. Working from the same premises and with the same methods, other scholars have found additional basic sources and evidence of more extensive redactional activity in the course of accretion and transmission. The dating of these documents is: J and E (Yahwist and Elohist for their characteristic divine names) before the major prophets of the eighth to seventh centuries B.C.; D (Deuteronomist) in the century before the discovery of the document in the Temple in 622 B.C.; and P (Priestly) during or after the Exile (sixth century B.C.). Y. Kaufmann and others have defended effectively an earlier date for P, making it roughly contemporary with D. Various scholars have found in the J material two sources, an earlier one, J_1 (which O. Eissfeldt identified as L, for Lay Source), running from Genesis 2 to the end of Samuel, and a later one, J_2. The question of the separate status of E has been raised by several scholars and remains unsettled. Though the documentary hypothesis continues to command general acceptance, there have been serious reactions against it and, in some cases, an abandonment of the "source-critical" method.

Archaeological discoveries, on the other hand, have continued to have a very important if indirect impact on scholarly analysis and interpretation of the text. The net effect has been to support the general trustworthiness and substantial historicity of the biblical tradition where data are available. In general this means that all strata and parts of the biblical literature deserve a measure of credence, regardless of the date of final edition or publication, and unless direct evidence to the contrary exists. Archaeological information most often sheds light on the background and context of the biblical accounts. When literary materials are available, they offer assistance in the clarification of obscure passages—unusual terms and linguistic features. At times, it is necessary to reassess the biblical tradition when historical evidence supplied by extrabiblical sources is at variance with the record.

3

PART I

A. THE BOOK OF GENESIS*

The Book of Genesis consists of the primeval history in chapters 1–11 and the story of the Patriarchs, which takes up the remaining four-fifths of the book, in chapters 12–50.

The first book of the Bible, Genesis, refers to "beginnings." It comes from the Greek *genesis,* which means "origin, source." The Greek title is based upon the phrase *biblos geneseos,* the book of creation, which occurs at Genesis 2:4 and elsewhere in Genesis. The book of creation or beginnings may be divided into five sections, each marked by its own "genealogy" and accompanied by a long narrative of events: (1) the beginning of the world, chapters 1–4; (2) antediluvian man, chapters 5–6:4; (3) the Flood, chapters 6:5–9:29; (4) the renewal of man and repopulation on the earth, chapters 10:1–11:9; and (5) the ancestry of Abraham, chapter 11:10–26.

The first section describes the creation and the principal factors affecting the life of the first human generations. It consists of five narratives: (a) an account of creation, (b) a second account of creation, (c) the temptation in Eden and the Fall, (d) Cain and Abel, and (e) Lamech and his children.

The balance of the book is devoted to the story of the Patriarchs: Abraham and Isaac, chapters 11:27–25:18; Jacob and Esau, chapters 25:19–27:46; Jacob and Laban, chapters 28:1–32:3; Jacob's return to Canaan, chapters 32:4–36:43; Joseph and his brothers, chapters 37:1–50:26.

1. PRIMEVAL HISTORY

In accordance with the guiding principles of the biblical tradition, the primeval history has the whole world as its stage, its time span reaching back all the way to Creation. It serves as a prologue and provides a universal setting for the early history of the Hebrews, the particular story with which the rest of the Pentateuch and the Bible is concerned.

The account of creation and human prehistory, though couched in the language of biblical religion, did not originate with the Israelites. It contains elements drawn from the polytheistic myths of the Sumerians and Babylonians. This mythology is carefully adapted to the concepts of Israelite monotheism. The similarity in detail only serves to highlight the uniqueness of Israel's single God acting in the world.

a. *Literary Antecedents of the Primeval Sagas*

While the Hebrew version of primeval times had been adapted to biblical tradition and religion, much of the background material of these early

---

*Interested readers would be advised to read with a Bible in hand. Our quotations are taken from the American Revised Standard Version, 1952.

narratives comes from Mesopotamia. This is borne out by the archaeological discovery of ancient libraries containing collections of mythological texts. The process of remolding old traditions is common in the history of cultures. The same approach was followed by the Hurrians, who adopted Mesopotamian traditions and eventually brought them to Canaan.

The biblical genealogies before the Flood parallel the antediluvian dynasties of Sumer, the kings of which are credited with enormous reigns. The names of some of the antediluvian patriarchs reflect Akkadian (Babylonian) characteristics. The stories of Eden and the Tower of Babel are largely Mesopotamian in substance, as are other cycles of the primeval history. Modern research is delving deeper into the complex problems arising out of the early chapters of Genesis and their sagas. It is seeking to determine the extent and manner of the influence of the Mesopotamian and Canaanite epics on the early biblical sagas, as we shall see in the following pages.

b. *The Story of Creation*

Let us begin with the Mesopotamian version of cosmic origins in the *"Enuma elish,"* the Babylonian Creation Epic, which has much in common with the opening chapters of Genesis. Note the striking correspondence in details and, more significantly, the similar order of events as seen in the following tabulation:

Enuma Elish	*Genesis*
Divine spirit and cosmic matter are coexistent and coeternal	Divine spirit creates cosmic matter and exists independently of it
Primeval chaos, Tiamat (a mythological figure) enveloped in darkness	The earth a desolate waste, with darkness covering the deep (*tehom*)
Light emanating from the gods	Light created
The creation of the firmament	The creation of the firmament
The creation of dry land	The creation of dry land
The creation of luminaries	The creation of luminaries
The creation of man	The creation of man
The gods rest and celebrate	God rests and sanctifies the seventh day

The *Enuma elish*—Babylonian Creation Epic—inscribed on cuneiform tablets, relates the myths of creation from primeval chaos

Babylonian cosmogony and its theory of the origin of man, central to Sumero-Akkadian "science" or "wisdom," were basic to their religion. Such traditions found their way to Israelite scribal schools—either in a direct line from Mesopotamia or indirectly through later Canaanite sources. In their Israelite form these cosmogonic traditions underwent drastic alterations, occasioned by distinctive biblical theological views. Just as the normative religion of the Hebrews diverged from Mesopotamian myths, it expressed a corresponding departure regarding the master of Creation. It reflected a monotheistic concept in absolute terms, as opposed to the succession of mythical rival deities in the *Enuma elish*.

The Mesopotamian "serpent" monster was no ordinary serpent as implied in Genesis. It is depicted in the mosaic of the Gate of Ishtar, Babylon (6th c. B.C.)

c. *The Story of Eden*

The name of the garden itself is borrowed from the Sumerian (third to second millennia) *eden,* perhaps indirectly through the Akkadian *edenu,* which meant garden or paradise. Genesis names four rivers that were believed to have converged near the head of the Persian Gulf (present-day southern Iraq) in a rich garden that was the land of the blessed.

The biblical story includes special features such as the tree of life and the tree of knowledge of good and evil in the midst of the Garden, the serpent—a mythical monster rather than an ordinary snake—endowed with extraordinary faculties for trouble making, the temptation and Fall of the woman, Eve, and the man, Adam, and the subtlety of their relationship and their common bond in guilt, pleasure, and punishment. Such themes of sexual awareness, wisdom, and paradise are known from various ancient sources, as, for example, in a beautiful passage of the Babylonian Gilgamesh Epic (Tablet I, column 4, lines 16ff.) when the legendary hero Gilgamesh meets his rough friend Enkidu. The latter has been seduced by the courtesan goddess Ishtar, in a passage noted for its explicit language; he has lost his wildness for "he now has wisdom, broader understanding." As Ishtar tells him, "You are wise, Enkidu. You are like a god," and she improvises some clothing for him. The implied quest for immortality in the Hebrew version of the story is paralleled in other ancient literature. The Mesopotamian analogues to this theme are the Tale of Adapa and the Epic of Gilgamesh (Tablet IX), in both of which the attempts end in failure.

A Sumerian king-list enumerated the antediluvian kings of Sumer, who reigned a total of 241,200 "years" based on an unknown calendrical system

d. *From Eden to Flood*

There are two genealogies of the line of Adam in chapters 4 and 5, one through Cain to Lamech and his musically and mechanically minded children Jubal and Tubal-cain, the other through Seth to Lamech and his son, Noah, the hero of the Flood story. These are paralleled by Sumerian genealogical lists that bridged the gap between Creation and Flood. The most striking common features are the sharp diluvian divide and the abnormal life-spans attributed to the principal figures. The number of Hebrew prehistoric patriarchs is eight in chapter 4 and the number in chapter 5 is ten; in the Babylonian documents the number varies between nine and ten. The years in the Hebrew list (chapter 5) run into the hundreds (totaling 1656), while those of the reigns in the Babylonian list run from 18,600 to nearly 65,000 "years." The source and significance of these extraordinary numbers remain a puzzle of chronology in both the Mesopotamian and Israelite traditions.

e. *The Flood Story*

The biblical account of the Flood in Genesis 6:1–9:17 goes back to Mesopotamian cuneiform sources that contain a number of versions of the story. The most ancient is from the Sumerians, the story of Ziusudra, but it is incomplete. The most extensive and best-known prototype is found in Tablet XI of the Gilgamesh Epic, which also has most in common with the biblical story. In the Mesopotamian epic, Gilgamesh seeks the last survivor of the flood to learn from him the secret of survival and immortality. After many adventures, Gilgamesh finally meets Utnapishtim, the Babylonian hero of the flood. He tells Gilgamesh that he owes his life to Ea, the god of wisdom, who warned him of the coming deluge in a dream and granted him immortality. In both stories the hero leads a remnant in building an ark, riding out the flood, discovering dry land by sending out a series of birds, and giving thanksgiving offerings when the flood has fully abated. But while the Babylonian flood is the result of the spiteful actions of the gods, the Bible presents it as an indictment of mankind for its sinfulness. The Flood Story may ultimately derive from memories of a giant cataclysm actually experienced in recent geological times. Evidence of such an event has been uncovered by Lees and Falcon in a survey of Lower Mesopotamia. Waters from the Persian Gulf submerged a large coastland area, owing to a sudden rise of the sea level some thousands of years ago in one of the pluvial periods. Heavy rainfall

Right:
A series of clay tablets inscribed with the Babylonian account of the flood and the Gilgamesh Epic (Nineveh, 7th c. B.C.)

Below:
Presumed figure of the Mesopotamian hero and King Gilgamesh of Sumer (ca. 2700 B.C.) from Khorsabad, dating to the 8th c. B.C.

8

accompanied by undersea eruptions may well have left an indelible impression on the survivors.

In S. Loewenstein's opinion, the Flood Story, originally a Mesopotamian epic, was first recited as a Hebrew epic about the hero Noah and later turned into prose. It reached the Hebrew medium through Canaanite literature rather than as a Mesopotamian import. The evidence supporting this view is a pottery fragment of the Mesopotamian Epic of Gilgamesh found in a Canaanite stratum of Megiddo dating to the El Amarna period (fourteenth century B.C.) and a fragment of the Flood Story found in Ugarit (northern Canaanite kingdom).

Clay fragment of the Babylonian Epic of Gilgamesh found at Megiddo, dating to the 14th c. B.C.

f. *The Table of Nations*

The biblical list of nations (chapter 10), which provides a schematic arrangement of the major cultural divisions of mankind, specifying ancient nations and their great cities contemporary with early Israel, derives from Mesopotamian sources reflecting the world situation toward the end of the twelfth century B.C. According to E. A. Speiser, the figure behind the hero Nimrod, famed for his prodigious deeds, is not the Babylonian god, Ninurta, but the Assyrian emperor, Tukulti-Ninurta I, who reigned from 1234 to 1200 B.C. He was known for his military achievements, in particular, the conquest of Babylon, as well as his building projects at home. The genealogical lists, which actually reflect political and economic filiation, as well as cultural affinities, prominently feature the early *Aramaean* groups. These groups emerged from the wilderness toward the close of the second millennium, gained a foothold in the region of North Syria between the Assyro-Babylonians in the East and the Canaanites in the West, and gradually expanded their territory and their authority in that area.

The four registers of the restored stele of Ur-Nammu (ca. 2060–1955 B.C.) suggest that the subject was the building of a *ziggurat* (temple-tower). The king is seen carrying a basket and building instrument as a token of his devotion to the rising shrine

g. *The Tower of Babel*

The story in chapter 11 has the most explicit connection with Mesopotamian sources of any of the materials in Genesis 1–11. The Israelite author, however, used it to explain the scattering of human beings on earth and the multiplicity of languages, suggesting that there was increasing tension between God and man over the proper limits of the latter's activity. While the ultimate source of the biblical story is doubtless the great temple-tower of Babylon, the tradition has been mediated in literary form and the biblical writer was apparently influenced by the account of the building of Babylon and its temple, Esagila, given in lines 60–62 of the *Enuma elish* epic. Standard practice with respect to religious architecture in Mesopotamia included the year-long preparation of sacred bricks that preceded the solemn placement of the first one. The Akkadian text reads: "The first year they molded its bricks. And when the second year arrived they raised the head of Esagila toward Apsu [the boundless expanse of fresh waters above the heavens]." Moreover, the Sumerian name Esagila means "the structure with upraised head" while the Akkadian rendering for "they raised its [Esagila's] head" is a play on the same word. It appears that the biblical phrase "with its top [literally "head"] in the sky"

harks back to the Mesopotamian versions, as does the biblical expression "Let us make bricks," a reference to the building customs of Babylon. The Hebrews used this material to criticize man's folly and presumption in challenging the supremacy of God.

It is interesting to note that both W. G. Lambert and B. Mazar place this story around 1100 B.C. Lambert dates the Mesopotamian sources to this period, while Mazar, who believes that the bulk of the material in Genesis belongs to the same era, rather than the Middle Bronze Age, suggests that the Mesopotamian literary traditions reached Israel, not only through the medium of Canaanite culture, but more directly through the movements of caravaneers and merchants from east to west.

2. THE KENITE METALWORKERS OF THE SOUTHERN ARABAH

A startling reference in Genesis 4:22 emerges out of the context of the Mesopotamian image of the "beginnings" of mankind when it identifies the Kenites as the traditional "first" metalworkers. This has led to considerable scholarly theorizing in the past, but recent discoveries in the valley of Timnah, north of Elath, prove that the reference in question is actually grounded in the history of the land of the Bible and not in the enigmatic traditions of the early chapters of Genesis.

The Kenites, apparently a clan of the Midianite settlers in the southern Arabah, made their appearance in the Timnah valley in the fourteenth to twelfth centuries B.C., and they had close ties of kinship with the Israelites during the period of their settlement in Transjordan and Southern Canaan.

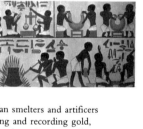

Egyptian smelters and artificers weighing and recording gold, blowing through tubes to heat the metal for casting, and fashioning the molded objects

Smelting furnace of the Kenites at Timnah, south of Canaan, showing the melting bowl and, before it, the tapping pit of copper ore between the flanking stones (14th c. B.C.)

Direct evidence of bronze- and iron-working methods in the Late Bronze Age is provided by excavations in the Timnah valley. Its vertical white sandstone walls were attacked with stone hammers and the copper nodules picked out of the heaps of shattered sandstone. By this method, about twenty kilograms of nodules could be "mined" by one man in a day's work, enough to produce two to four kilograms of copper. "Dressing" or winnowing of copper or iron took place in the saucer-shaped hollows on the slopes next to the actual mining works where many grinding implements were found. The winnowing operation could have utilized the strong north wind prevailing on the open horizontal surface or, alternatively, the local inhabitants could have mined the ore and the women and children ground it and sorted the ore from the gangue. The ore was then carried to smelting sites.

3. ABRAHAM'S GENEALOGY AND THE HARAN ANCESTRY

The end of chapter 11 resumes the genealogical record that was interrupted at the end of chapter 5 to accommodate the stories in chapters 6–10. The two genealogical segments once may have been part of a single document that incorporated the very old tradition of the Aramaean ancestry of Abraham into the larger framework of the primeval history of Genesis. The final genealogy of Abraham also serves as a bridge to the central narrative of the Patriarchs. Thus the name Nahor, attributed to both the grandfather and brother of Abraham, is identical with that of the city, Nahur, which is known from the Mari tablets of the eighteenth century B.C. It was in the region of Haran, situated west of the Balikh river, a tributary of the Euphrates. Another place name in the area was Serug, which was the name of Abraham's great-grandfather. This interchange between personal and place names is a common phenomenon in the ancient Near East; in this case it reflects the close cultural contacts between Abraham's family and the region and supports the tradition that this was their homeland for a long period of time.

The mention of Ur of the Chaldeans brings up a complex problem. Ur was an ancient and renowned Sumerian center, as demonstrated by thousands of cuneiform tablets, but was never connected with the Chaldean branch of the Aramaean peoples. They were late arrivals in western Mesopotamia, their appearance dating to the twelfth century B.C. In the Bible they are identified with the group that ultimately took over the Babylonian kingdom with Nabopolassar and Nebuchadnezzar as kings of that dynasty (625–562 B.C.; cf. II Kings 25, Jeremiah, Ezekiel). While the "Chaldean" references in Genesis 11:28, 31, and 15:7 remain an anachronism, the mention of Ur by itself may have some historical basis. Behind the settlement in Haran, which is supported both by tradition and the evidence of the names, there may have been an earlier sojourn in Ur, but beyond the mere mention of the place the Bible is silent and we have nothing to add. The historic homeland of the Patriarchs was the region of Haran. While this cannot be disputed—though it has not been attested by

Fragment of carved war scene from Ebla (Tell Mardikh) dating to the end of Early Bronze III (ca. 2400 B.C.)

Wooden feminine figure from the palace of Ebla (Early Bronze IV)

archaeology—the main question that remains to be considered is the true historical and archaeological setting of the story of the Hebrew Patriarchs.

Let us preface the study of the patriarchal period with a review of the Canaanite background before the appearance of the Hebrews.

4. THE RICH EARLY CANAANITE ARCHIVES OF EBLA

The excavations at Ebla (Tell Mardikh), thirty miles south of Aleppo, Syria, conducted by P. Matthiae, uncovered more than 15,000 inscribed cuneiform clay tablets dating to the latter part of the third millennium (Early Bronze IV). According to the epigrapher G. Pettinato, they were written in Sumerian and Canaanite (the ancestor of Hebrew). They contain references to the Canaanite cities of Hazor, Megiddo, Gaza, and 'urusalima' (Jerusalem) and also include stories recounting the creation of the world and a great flood that correspond to the biblical accounts of the world's beginnings.

Most of the documents are economic texts recording the receipt and shipment of goods to distant centers. Other tablets are literary, legal, diplomatic, historical, and geographic in content. They show that Ebla was the capital and cultural center of a great early Canaanite kingdom that shared in the civilization of the Near East. Myths known from ancient Mesopotamia circulated throughout the kingdom, and the laws of Ebla corresponded in many ways to those known in Mesopotamia from somewhat later sources.

Thus, long before the time of ancestors of the Patriarchs, Syria and Palestine shared in the mythic and cultural traditions of Sumer and Akkad. Wherever the remote ancestors of the Israelites may have lived or wandered, they would have had access to and been in contact with the traditions behind the *early* stories of Genesis.

5. CHRONOLOGICAL TABLE OF THE MIDDLE AND LATE BRONZE AGES IN CANAAN

Date	Archaeological Period		Historical Period
2200 to 2000 B.C.	Middle Bronze Age I	Middle Canaanite	
2000 to 1800 B.C.	Middle Bronze IIA	Urban Expansion in Canaan	
1800 to 1630 B.C.	Middle Bronze IIB	Middle Canaanite	Hyksos Period from 1720
1630 to 1550 B.C.	Middle Bronze IIC (the transition period to the Late Bronze)	Middle Canaanite	Hyksos Period to 1575
1550 to 1400 B.C.	Late Bronze I	Late Canaanite	Egyptian Rule in Canaan
1400 to 1300 B.C.	Late Bronze IIA		El Amarna Period and the Habiru
1300 to 1200 B.C.	Late Bronze IIB	Early Hebrew	
1200 to 1150 B.C.	Iron Age IA	Israelite Settlement in Canaan	Israelite I
1150 to 1100 B.C.	Iron Age IB		

B. CANAAN IN THE MIDDLE AND LATE BRONZE AGES

1. THE HYKSOS AND THE "400-YEAR STELE"

The period from the end of the eighteenth century to the middle of the sixteenth century (equivalent to the later part of MB-IIB and all of MB-IIC) was marked by the invasion of Egypt by Asiatic peoples called the Hyksos and the establishment of an empire including that country and Canaan (Palestine and Syria). In the list of kings and other notables are numerous Semitic names; some of these are similar to patriarchal names, like *ya'qob-har*. For a long time, some association between the patriarchal groups and the Hyksos has been taken for granted, and this view has been supported by reference to two chronological items preserved in the Bible. The first states that "Hebron was built seven years before Zoan (Tanis) in Egypt" (Num. 13:22) and is usually connected with the Hyksos conquest of Egypt and founding of the latter city around 1700 B.C. The other text states that the Israelite sojourn in the district of Tanis lasted for 430 years (Exod. 12:40). This figure has been linked with the Hyksos era of Tanis, symbolized by the "400 year stele" erected shortly before the accession of Rameses I around 1320 B.C., and commemorating the rule of the god Seth over Egypt. Seth is shown at the top of the stele wearing an Asiatic garment and headdress, which in other Egyptian representations are associated with Baal, the chief Canaanite deity. The stele reads: "Year 400, fourth month of the third season, day 4, of the king of Upper and Lower Egypt; Seth, the Great of Strength. . . ." If the ascendancy of the god Seth in Asiatic garb is related to the domination by these foreign kings, this

Bichrome pottery vessel of the Late Canaanite period (1500–1200 B.C. from Tell Nagila)

Jericho, the oldest city in Palestine, already lay in ruins in the Middle Bronze Age, before the days of Joshua

13

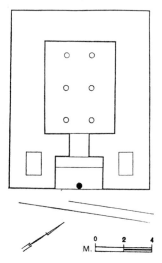

Ground plan of the Middle
Bronze temple-fort of Shechem

After the expulsion of the
Hyksos, Shechem expanded. An
outer wall was built of huge
boulders, thus meriting the term
"cyclopean." A new gate
complex was erected in the
northwest section

stele places the beginning of their rule around 1720 B.C. In any case, the 400-year anniversary marks the date of the refounding of Tanis by Rameses I. By adopting Seth, the pharaohs of the Nineteenth Dynasty established themselves as the official successors of the Hyksos rulers, whose ancient capital was Tanis. The Hyksos were expelled by native Egyptian chieftains who established the Eighteenth Dynasty and inaugurated a new era in Egypt, the New Kingdom.

2. THE HURRIANS

The widespread movement of peoples in the Near East during Middle Bronze IIB abated somewhat and the political situation in the northern tier was stabilized with the emergence of the major kingdoms of the Hittites in Asia Minor and of the Mitanni in northern Mesopotamia in the middle of the sixteenth century B.C. The principal groups in the latter were Hurrians and Indo-Iranians. As a result of these developments, Syria and Palestine came under the influence of these new groups and were infiltrated by representatives of all of them. They gained ascendancy over the native population, constituting an aristocracy governing from strongly fortified cities. They were known as *maryannu* and typically fought with chariots in contrast with the lower classes, who served as foot soldiers. Each city-state constituted a feudal fiefdom ruled by a prince or kinglet with the help of the noble warrior class. At the bottom of the pyramid were the native groups, the urban landless poor and the serfs or semislaves of the rural areas permanently attached to the landed estates. This period, Middle Bronze IIC, marks the transition to the Late Bronze Age.

3. MATERIAL AND SOCIAL CHANGE

The principal architectural change in this period was the construction of massive city walls, and unlike earlier structures of the Middle Bronze Age, these were made from squared and carved stones laid out in regular courses, topped by bricks. The wall was completed by a well-fortified gate suited to the passage of chariots. Striking examples are the massive cyclopean wall at Shechem and the glacis of Tell Beit Mirsim modeled on fortifications in eastern Anatolia. This type of construction eventually became standard throughout the coastal plain and in the hill country of Canaan.

Another important innovation of the period was the construction of fortified temples, termed "temple-forts" by B. Mazar. The best example is the rectangular two-story building in the walled city of Shechem. It had a long hall inside the thick outer walls with an entrance in the front. The statue of the deity was placed at the end of the hall facing the entrance. This temple was contemporary with a Canaanite temple at Megiddo. Both lasted through the Late Bronze Age II, and then were destroyed in the twelfth century B.C. The contemporary stratum of Megiddo (VII A) marks the last wealthy and fortified Canaanite city. In its treasury a hoard of about 200 carved ivories was found, representing Canaanite art at its best. Another temple of the same period is the fourteenth century sanctuary of

Hazor found by Y. Yadin. It consisted of a porch with two pillars, a hall, and then the Holy of Holies with a rectangular niche in the rear wall. Many elements, such as the tripartite division and the two pillars in the porch, have counterparts in the Temple of Solomon. It was destroyed by Joshua in the second half of the thirteenth century B.C.

Thutmose IV (early 15th c. B.C.) rides over wounded Canaanites and their chariotry on a battlefield

4. THE PEOPLE OF CANAAN

An indication of the social stratification of Canaan may be found in a double list of prisoners captured by Pharaoh Amenhotep II of the Eighteenth Dynasty in his second campaign into Canaan in 1443 B.C.:

First List		Second List	
550	*Maryannu* (chariot-riding knights)	127	governors of Retenu (the Egyptian name for Canaan)
240	wives of the above	179	brothers of the above
640	Canaanites	3600	*'Apiru*
232	sons of governors	15,200	*Shosu* (nomads)
323	daughters of governors	36,300	*Huru* or native Canaanites
		15,070	*Nuhašše*, natives of north Syria
270	concubines of all foreign provinces	30,652	wives of the above

The Canaanites in these lists were middle-class citizens, not serfs. The *'Apiru* (or *Habiru*, see discussion below) were a social group outside the official classification and lacked definite status. The *Shosu* were wandering Semitic clans who are known to have crossed into eastern areas of Egypt in periods of drought and famine. This situation, which conforms in many ways to the biblical portrayal of Canaan in the book of Genesis, persisted until the Israelite occupation of the land.

Canaanite man and woman painted on a jar (Middle Bronze). Note a resemblance to the Early Bronze Ebla carving shown earlier

5. THE PROBLEM OF THE HABIRU

Genesis 14:13 calls Abraham a Hebrew, *Ibri*. Scholars have undertaken an extensive investigation into the possible connection between the biblical *Ibrim* (Hebrews) and the landless *'apiru* or *habiru* mentioned in documents from Mesopotamia, northern Syria, and Egypt from the nineteenth century onward. There has been particular interest in the Amarna tablets that describe the *'apiru* activity in Canaan immediately preceding the biblical period.

These tablets were discovered in A.D. 1887 near Tell el-Amarna, site of the capital and royal residence of Pharaoh Amenophis IV (Akhenaten), and his father Amenophis III. They come from the royal archives, which contained approximately 385 tablets, including about 150 letters written by vassal kings of Canaan and western Asia to the Egyptian pharaoh.

In the Late Bronze I period (Late Canaanite), Canaan was under nominal Egyptian rule, with city-kings paying tribute to their overlords and providing wheat and other agricultural products. The gradual disinte-

One of the Tell el Amarna tablets (15th–14th c. B.C.), which mention the '*apiru* (*ḫabiru*) involved in disorders in Canaan before the Israelite invasions

Statue of Idrimi, a king of northern Syria, relating his seven years of exile among the '*apiru* of Canaan (ca. 1500)

gration of Egyptian rule is revealed in the tablets, which were written in Akkadian, the international language of the period. In them we see a confused political situation and a period of transition in Canaan. There are plots, counterplots, and conflicting accusations, but they vividly portray the conditions of life and the social structure of the local population in the Late Bronze Age (fifteenth to fourteenth centuries B.C.).

The '*apiru* were not an ethnic group, nor did they come from a single geographic location. Rather they were a loosely defined, constantly shifting, social class of people. This view is supported by a number of observations: (a) References to them are scattered throughout a millennium in lower and upper Mesopotamia, Asia Minor, Syria-Palestine, and Egypt; (b) Their names do not come from a single language but reflect the languages of the regions where they are met, whether Akkadian, Hurrian, or others; (c) When the homeland of individual '*apiru* is identified, they may be natives, or from neighboring or distant countries—there is no uniform pattern. In short, they are not necessarily members of the local population; they cannot be identified with any single social class of the population, and often are described as outcasts or residents without status or citizenship rights; they do not have common occupations in the communities where they dwell. The common denominator seems to be that they are associated with various ethnic groups, as clients or mercenaries, or in some other dependent relationship.

A possible link between the Amarna letters and the Bible may be found in the traditions concerning the fate of Shechem and the early history of Jerusalem. Nevertheless, there can be no direct identification of the Amarna '*apiru* (*ḫabiru*) with the biblical *Ibrim;* the intervening century or two alone would rule it out. Furthermore, the origin of the Hebrews does not accord with the description of the cuneiform '*apiru* who consist of a variety of wandering and landless groups, not clearly identifiable with any of the settled peoples among whom they lived.

Conclusions

Need one wonder that the anonymous Israelite historian described Canaan before the Israelite conquest as a land of many diverse peoples—seven, according to tradition, even more in fact? They possessed a material culture superior to anything the Israelites had experienced. In the words of those who spied out the land in the days of Moses: "The people who dwell in the land are strong, and the cities are fortified and very large" (Num. 13:28).

This is the land Abraham came to know when he travelled west in pursuit of his destiny, as may be determined on the basis of archaeological discoveries, including both written and unwritten material.

The traditional picture presented by the biblical writers finds substantial support in the available data, although in the light of scholarly investigation and evaluation, some adjustments in detail have proved to be necessary. It is remarkable how much of the tradition has withstood the test of time and scientific questioning.

C. THE STORY OF THE PATRIARCHS

1. THE SECOND SECTION OF GENESIS

In dealing with the historical narrative, beginning with the second part of Genesis and continuing through the Pentateuch and on into the books of Joshua, Judges, and Samuel, we have adopted the viewpoint of Professor B. Mazar, eminent biblical scholar and archaeologist, who believes that in its present form the narrative is a unified product of the early Monarchy and that it all bears the marks of that age.

To quote his words, which are of the utmost importance in understanding the position:

"Though it is undoubtedly true that the Israelites retained vague memories of the common origin and destiny of the tribes in the remote past, and traditions about the names and genealogies of their forefathers, of their origin in Mesopotamia and their connections with the 'sons' of Nahor, of their migration to Canaan, and of their descent to Egypt, a penetrating analysis of the accounts recorded in Genesis does not permit us to consider them as a faithful representation of the actual history of the Patriarchs and their exploits. Nor can we consider them to be ancient sources from which we may reconstruct, to any significant extent, the stages of the Israelite emergence against the background of general history, dwelling on the processes and developments relating to the lives of the Patriarchs over the generations, till the time of the formation of the 'amphictyony' of the twelve tribes of Israel.

"In my view, it is much more within reason that the way of life and the ethnic and socio-political picture reflected in the patriarchal accounts correspond to the end of the period of the Judges and the beginning of the monarchy. That is to say: the 'life-setting' (*Sitz im Leben*) of these accounts, part of which are certainly based on folk-legends from the time of the Israelite occupation of Canaan, derives principally from a time that preceded by only a generation or two that very period during which the great historiographic work was given its original written form. This hypothesis is supported by certain data which can be interpreted only against the background of their historic period" (*Canaan and Israel,* Hebrew ed., p. 136).

What this means for our study is that while the Israelite traditions concerning their ancestral heroes correctly identified them with the pre-Mosaic, pre-Israelite past, the stories as they have been preserved for us reflect, both in substance and in local color and detail, the events and circumstances of a much more immediate past, namely the period of early settlement, the Judges, that itself borders and blends with the contemporary situation. Certain memories of a more distant past have survived, and they can be illuminated by archaeological data of the Middle Bronze Age, chiefly from Mesopotamia, but the large bulk of recorded tradition belongs to a much later date, thus making the historical, social, and cultural traditions of Genesis 12–50 contemporary with those of the later books. Therefore we will draw on the archaeological riches of the early Iron Age to shed light on and to fill gaps in the biblical record, whether in Genesis or in Judges, books which, chronologically, belong together rather than apart.

No one would deny that in their present form the narratives from Genesis to Samuel are the literary product of the monarchic period. It should be recognized as well that any such narrative will combine traditional elements of great antiquity with others of lesser antiquity and some items that are close to, if not at, the time of the final author or chronicler. The question is where to draw the lines and how to be fair in dealing with the traditional material, editorial revisions, and complete rewriting. While all scholars recognize these points in principle, in practice they emphasize one factor more than another, or even to the exclusion of others. We would like to strike a balance, on the one hand conceding that there are many anachronisms in Genesis, too many to dismiss as accidental or incidental, and on the other hand that there are too many oddities and peculiarities that must reflect very distant times and places to rule out the survival of old materials or insist that it is mostly contemporary with the monarchy that produced the narrative.

When compared with Joshua-Judges, and certainly Samuel, Genesis stands in sharp contrast even after conceding all the similarities. When compared with Middle Bronze Age documents and artifacts, Genesis is also quite different, though there are familiar echoes here and there. Admittedly, there are too many Philistines, Aramaeans, and camels, not to speak of other major and minor points, for anyone to be comfortable with traditional views that relegate the Patriarchs to a background of the Middle Bronze Age.

2. CHAPTERS 12–50 OF GENESIS: THE PATRIARCHAL TRADITIONS AND THE FORMATIVE STAGES OF EARLY ISRAEL

The first three verses of chapter 12 describe Abraham's call and commission and the beginning of the continuous story that is the main concern of the Bible, in contrast with the earlier prehistory that provides a setting and serves as a backdrop for the all-important narrative. It opens with the story of Abraham and his family, then extends to his descendants and their descendants, and finally to the nation of which he was the ancestor. The narrative is not merely the story of individuals, of families, or a people, but the saga of a new religion and a new society, and its quest for identity and existence. Amazing though its impact was on world civilization, it is our responsibility to examine the historical aspects of the narrative and relate them to available archaeological or epigraphic evidence. Let us preface the study of the patriarchal period with a review of the Canaanite background before the appearance of the Hebrews.

The historical narrative, as distinct from the prehistory, begins with startling suddenness in Genesis 12. Nothing stated in the preceding chapters prepares us for the sudden appearance of Abraham and his descendants, the *Ibrim,* on the historical stage of Canaan in the Middle Bronze Age. This is the period to which many biblical scholars are inclined to assign Abraham and the other Patriarchs in accordance with traditional chronology, which specifies a period of more than five centuries between Abraham and the Exodus from Egypt. The difficulties will be discussed below.

Let us first remark that archaeology, despite great strides in understanding the Canaanite background of the Middle and Late Bronze Ages, has revealed no historical trace of the Hebrews to corroborate the patriarchal narratives *as a whole*. The reader must remember that archaeology cannot prove specific biblical stories to be literally true; it can only judge the accuracy of the backgrounds and customs found in the Bible. It is in this sense that archaeology bears on Genesis. It allows us to ask: When could this have happened and what is its historical background?

3. ABRAHAM AND THE PATRIARCHAL NARRATIVES

Leading scholars, notably W. F. Albright, Nelson Glueck, and G. Ernest Wright, have set a date for Abraham in the Middle Bronze Age or in the first part of the second millennium B.C. In this view Abraham lived in the Negeb (south), contemporary with the oldest settlements there. A closer examination of the biblical text in light of archaeological discoveries of the past decade tends to discount such theories. The Canaan of the patriarchal traditions proves to be significantly different from the Middle Bronze Age Canaan of the archaeologist. Abraham's Canaan is not a land of seminomads, but an area dotted with city-kingdoms, with a highly developed culture and building activity. He is the chief of a clan of herdsmen, warriors, and farmers, who lived in areas bordering on established cities such as Hebron, Jerusalem, or Shechem, even Gerar and Beersheba (the latter did not exist in the Middle Bronze Age).

The respect of Israeli scholars for the received text and their independence of the Documentary Theory (see Introduction) is not influenced by any orthodox interpretation but rather by a critical reassessment of the text in the light of archaeological and epigraphic findings. Their guide in dating the historical period of the persons and events of the Bible is primarily the *Sitz im Leben* or "life-setting" of the events in question. They contend that the patriarchal stories can best be understood in the setting of social and political conditions prevailing in Canaan when it had already been invaded by various groups. These invasions are hinted at by the traditions in Genesis 14 with Abraham as a charismatic chieftain, in chapters 20–21 when the ancestors of the Israelites were mingling with other occupants of the country, and in chapter 34 dealing with the Hebrew occupation of Shechem by Simeon and Levi, sons of Jacob, the ancestral names of early Hebrew clans.

Let us first examine these examples to see what bearing archaeology has on their historical content.

a. *Abraham, the Charismatic Hebrew Chieftain in Canaan*

The Abraham of chapter 14 is depicted in a far more realistic fashion than the familiar unworldly Patriarch of faith and kindly words and

Above:
Seven-cup offering vessel from a Late Canaanite sanctuary at Beth-Shemesh

Below:
Fragment of a ritual clay jar (early Israelite period)

deeds. He is a prosperous and powerful chieftain settled in southern Canaan, who can mobilize a sizable troop among his retainers and put foreign invaders to rout. This is a far cry from his image in the rest of Genesis, but, nevertheless, it is being substantiated by new discoveries. The narrative has all the ingredients of historicity. The first part, which deals with the expedition of Chedorlaomer, king of Elam, and his allies, contains elements familiar from ancient epics. W. F. Albright suggested the identification of Chedorlaomer with the Elamite Kudur-Nakhunte I, as the exploits of this monarch were widely reported in Akkadian annals and were retold often in later generations, when the story was localized in Canaan. It was a common device of the ancients to incorporate epic themes into historical accounts, or even into royal annals.

The setting of this story is international, the approach is impersonal, and the phraseology may be ascribed to a non-Israelite source. This is supported by the fact that Abraham is referred to as an *Ibri,* Hebrew, in verse 13. Elsewhere, the description of *Ibri* is applied to Israelites by, or for the benefit of, foreigners; they did not use it among themselves. If the non-Israelite origin of this passage is correct, it would tend to establish the "historicity" of Abraham, for an outside source would hardly make a charismatic figure of a foreign legendary hero. Commenting on this, E. A. Speiser states: "If Abraham was cited in a historical or quasi-historical narrative that was written not by Israelites but by outsiders, it necessarily follows that Abraham was not a nebulous figure but a real person who was attested in contemporary sources. Short of a non-Israelite text mentioning an Abram, son of Terah, or an Isaac, son of Abram, this is as close as we can as yet come to a direct epigraphic witness of the patriarch" (*Genesis,* Anchor Bible, p. 108). A parallel problem is the life-setting of Abraham.

b. *Abraham and Melchizedek*

The second part of the story relates the encounter between Abraham and Melchizedek, king and priest of Salem. The encounter has now been located by B. Mazar at 'En-rogel, the lower spring southeast of Salem (Jerusalem before the Israelite occupation) at the intersection of valleys leading to it from the south.*

B. Mazar attributes this chapter to the early days of the Monarchy in view of its two-fold purpose:

(1) To substantiate the Israelite right of possession over the land on both sides of the Jordan, from El-paran, which apparently is none other than Elath, all the way to the region lying south of Damascus, on the basis of the father of the nation's having acquired it by virtue of his victory over external enemies.

(2) To mention Abraham's relationship to Melchizedek, king of Salem,

---

*B. Mazar, D. N. Freedman, and G. Cornfeld, *The Mountain of the Lord* (New York and Jerusalem, 1975), p. 156.

and a priest of 'El-'Elyon, who had blessed the father of the nation and received from him a "a tenth of everything." The words of the poet in Psalm 110 may well testify that with the conquest of Jerusalem by David the genealogical tradition that had linked the rulers of the city of Melchizedek—and with it the right of possession over the city—was transferred to the House of David.

4. ABRAHAM'S COVENANT AND THE HISTORICAL "400-YEAR STELE"

The same tendencies of the Davidic Monarchy that we saw in Genesis 14 continue in chapter 15. We read in verses 18–19: "To your descendants I give this land, from the river of Egypt to the great river, the river Euphrates, the land of the Kenites, the Kenizzites...." The borders outlined here circumscribe a territory that extends from western Mesopotamia to the Wadi El-'Arish in the northern Sinai. There is a close correlation between these boundaries and those of the kingdom of David and Solomon, and the exact form of the promise in Genesis 15 seems to have been shaped by those who saw its fulfillment in the tenth century B.C. It was not until David that the Kenites and Kenizzites were incorporated into Judah and ceased to be separate ethnic entities. It was only in this period that Israelite dominion extended beyond Damascus, close to the Euphrates.

This chapter poses another interesting problem with its "400-year prediction" (15:13), which has been a foundation of biblical chronology for over two millennia. Taken literally, this would place the activity of the Patriarchs in the Middle Bronze Age, around 1700 B.C. There is a problem, however, in that it is agreed by many scholars today that this chronological item corresponds to and stems from an Egyptian source. It represents the 400-year anniversary of the rule of the god Seth over Lower Egypt, celebrated by the Egyptians and commemorated by the Tanis (Zoan) stele. There is the statement in Numbers 13:22 to the effect that "Hebron was built seven years before Zoan in Egypt." The coincidence between the figures, together with the Hebron-Zoan reference, does suggest that the Tanis area and its 400-year anniversary are somewhere at the root of the 400-year tradition of the sojourn in Egypt.

5. IN WHAT PERIOD ARE THE PATRIARCHAL NARRATIVES ROOTED?

With this reservation in mind, we must review pertinent episodes in Genesis to determine whether the patriarchal narratives are rooted in the period dating four or five centuries before the era of the settlement in Israel (thirteenth to twelfth centuries B.C.), or whether the episodes may be dated in the days when Israelites and Canaanites were coexisting in Canaan during the formative stage of the tribal federation. If the latter view is correct, this would be the time when the Philistines were already in the

Canaanite house at Gibeon. Its roof beams had rested over the row of stone pillars seen in the center

country (Genesis 20–21) around the twelfth century B.C. The early Hebrews were already mingling with the other occupants of the land (exemplified in Genesis 14, 23, and 34), buying and possessing property, and settling in various parts of Canaan before the disintegration of the top-heavy and oppressive feudal system of the Canaanites. In the narrative about a deed between Abraham and the sons of Heth (23), the legal details are indebted more to later patterns than those of the Middle Bronze. Hence the historical reliability of the narrative can be reassessed by attributing it to its proper historical setting, at the end of the second millennium.

This later dating is supported, in particular, by the poetic passages inserted in the patriarchal accounts, such as the Testament of Jacob (Genesis 49), which stresses Judah's ascendancy over the other Israelite tribes, Isaac's blessing of Jacob and Esau (Genesis 27), and Noah's curse on Canaan (Gen. 9:25–27). All of these are attempts to justify Israelite hegemony in Canaan and neighboring areas. B. Mazar has concluded: "That notion corresponds precisely to the national and religious spirit which surged within the Israelite people during the period of the United Kingdom (David and Solomon) and the extension of its borders far beyond the limits of the Israelite settlement. It is reasonable to assume that the traditions of Genesis were given their original written form during the time when the Davidic empire was being established, and that the additions and supplements of later biblical writers were only intended to help bridge the time gap for contemporary readers." When it was first written down, "the authors of Genesis had recourse not only to the national traditions then current, but also to various literary works, including Mesopotamian and Canaanite mythological and epic works. Some of them were embedded in Genesis . . . in the spirit of Israelite monotheism" (*Canaan and Israel*, p. 134).

D. BIBLICAL TRADITIONS AND CUSTOMS, AND ANCIENT NEAR EAST PARALLELS

1. SARAH GIVES HAGAR TO ABRAHAM

The tale recorded in Genesis 16:1–16 has long been compared to practices in Hurrian texts from the city of Nuzi in eastern Mesopotamia. One of them records the marriage of a certain Shennima to Giliminu. Their agreement provides that if Giliminu fails to bear children, she shall secure for Shennima a slave from the Lullu country as a concubine; in that case Giliminu shall have authority over the offspring. In assigning Hagar to Abraham to produce offspring, Sarah acted in conformity with Hurrian laws, the apparent source of many patriarchal practices.

2. THE *TERAPHIM* OR HOUSEHOLD DEITIES

The significance of the household deities that Rachel stole from the house of Laban is now well known (Gen. 31:19–55). They were figurines, at least sometimes in human form, that could be used for purposes of divination. More significant for this passage is the fact that possession of the *teraphim* could signify legal title to a given estate, particularly in the case of daughters, sons-in-law, and adopted sons. It was not just concern for piety, but threatened loss of real property that motivated Laban to pursue his daughters and the missing figurines.

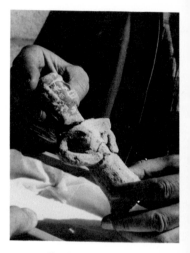

Clay figurine found in Jerusalem (7th c. B.C.)

Below:
The ubiquitous figurines in the *dea nutrix* attitude abound in Palestinian excavations. They bear a close relationship to the *teraphim*

Left:
Woman's interest in birth as expressed in an 8th c. Cypriot clay statuette. The woman in the middle "sits on the knees" of her companion while she is being attended by a midwife

3. ARE NUZI PARALLELS RELEVANT TO GENESIS?

These examples represent only a few of the many insights into ancient practices gained from the discovery of cuneiform documents from Mari, Nuzi, Alalakh, Boghazköy, and other centers of Near Eastern civilization. While these parallels are useful in explaining archaic biblical customs, they come from such diverse periods and places that they are less useful in pinning down a date for the biblical narratives. There are customs of people living east of the Tigris (Nuzi in the fifteenth century B.C.); a variety of documents from the Canaanite kingdom of Ugarit in northern Syria from the fourteenth to thirteenth centuries; royal archives from the upper Euphrates (Mari) from the eighteenth century; treaties of the Hittite kingdom from the thirteenth century; and correspondence of the Egyptian empire at Tell el-Amarna from the fourteenth century. Roland de Vaux points out the limitations of using these parallels in speaking of the customs of Nuzi: "If they are limited to this region and to this period, they cannot be used to enlighten the history of the patriarchs who were never east of the Tigris; if they are not limited to this region and this period they cannot be used to date the patriarchs." Moreover, although Hurrians had settled in Canaan, they did not become an important ethnic group there.

The Near East in the Middle Bronze Age; note the location of Ebla

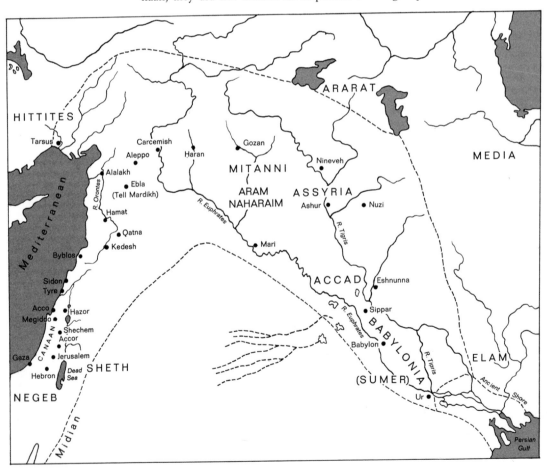

This leaves the question: When did the Hebrews become familiar with these Near Eastern traditions? Surely not when they were slaves in Egypt or when they were unorganized tribesmen struggling for existence in a hostile land. This acquisition of international "wisdom" traditions is more appropriate to the period of the early Monarchy or later, after Israel had become like the other nations.

4. TRADITIONAL SACRED SITES

A major theme of the book of Genesis is the association of the Patriarchs with sacred sites, with special emphasis on the erection of altars and the offering of sacrifices by them. It may be assumed that these accounts would date to a period when memories of events from the period of settlement of the tribes in the land were still fresh and when the traditions about their ancestors and their ties to sacred sites were still current.

In fact, most of the sacred sites associated with the fathers of the nation are located within the core of the original Israelite settlement, that is, in the Negeb, Judah, Mount Ephraim (Samaria), and Gilead, east of the Jordan. The biblical tradition identifies them with the major tribal shrines and cultic celebrations during the period of the Judges (twelfth to eleventh centuries B.C.) and the beginning of the Monarchy.

A related motif of the patriarchal traditions is the erection of *masseboth,* "pillars," at sacred sites near terebinth trees. Hebron is especially noteworthy in this connection: the terebinth of Mamre and the burial field and cave of Machpelah are central to the Abrahamic traditions. These associations with the Patriarchs made Hebron an ideal candidate as the first royal capital of Judah. The link between the founder of the new dynasty, David, and the ancient heroes would have enhanced the claims to legitimacy and prestige of the former and would have received appropriate emphasis if not specific literary formulation in contemporary documents.

A conical Phoenician *Bethyl* found at Paphos, Cyprus, bears a close analogy to the biblical *Beth-el* (sanctuary) and its sacred pillars (*masseboth*)

Right: A row of ten *masseboth* (sacred standing pillars) enshrined the Middle Bronze high place of Gezer

Left: Several *masseboth* face the Midianite shrine of Timnah (which replaced the Egyptian temple)

Beersheba, where Abraham dug his well in amity with the "Philistines," became a center of worship early in the days of the Israelite settlement, but not before. The accounts of the Patriarchs binding themselves to the inhabitants of the cities by treaties and protective arrangements seem to reflect a phase of coexistence with the native Canaanites before the latter were overcome militarily, integrated politically, and absorbed commercially during the period of the Judges. At Beersheba, a Hebrew sacrificial altar was found dating to the early days of the kingdom. Here again a site prominent in the traditions of Genesis plays a central role in the period of the Monarchy.

Until recent years biblical commentators have regarded references to the Philistines and the Aramaeans, whose appearance on the local scene dates to the twelfth century B.C., as anachronisms. There is a growing tendency, however, to re-evaluate their historicity in the patriarchal narratives.

a. *Abraham, Isaac, and the Philistine Kingdom of Gerar*

We have seen that Abraham's social and economic position was not that of a nomad or bedouin in the Beersheba wilderness during the first half of the Middle Bronze Age. Rather, power in the Negeb was divided among several city-kingdoms similar to those existing elsewhere in Canaan during the Late Bronze Age. We know that there was no large settlement between Gerar and Beersheba during the Middle Bronze Age. The close contacts maintained with Egypt in patriarchal times do not harmonize with what is known of the Middle Bronze Age, which is the only period in Palestinian history when no contacts worth mentioning are known to exist. The scant evidence of Middle Bronze settlements in the Negeb or the Sinai as tradeposts or way-stations on the caravan routes does not correspond with the description of settlement in the patriarchal period.

The progress of excavations at Tell Beersheba since 1975 has shed new light on biblical Beersheba prior to the monarchial period, before it became a walled city (identified with Stratum V of the dig). A fort dating to early Iron Age I has been uncovered below the ancient gate area, built apparently in the early days of the Monarchy (tenth century B.C.) The fort was protected by a casemate wall some 150 feet long, flanked by towers at the corners. It guarded the ancient well and the adjacent buildings dotting the tell, including some thin walls built on bedrock over the brow of the hill. Y. Aharoni deduces the great importance of Beersheba during early Iron I as a center of Israelite settlement in the days of Samuel: he had sent his two sons there to "judge" or govern the town (1 Sam. 8:1–2).

The fort and settlement are related to a chain of smaller forts extending over the Negeb as far south as Kadesh-barnea. The latter are connected with early settlements and roads dating to the early part of the eleventh century B.C. The question that arises is, who erected them? It is clear from recent surveys and excavations that they coexisted with the earliest Iron Age occupation in an unwalled town at Beersheba. The latter's

early fort already lay in ruins before the erection of the entire city wall in monarchial times (tenth century B.C., Stratum V), which covered it as well as the adjacent dwellings.

b. The "Well of Abraham"

A deep well, situated outside the city wall and already cleared up to a depth of 130 feet from the top of the tell, is linked with the three phases of settlement during early Iron I, which corresponds to the early strata (II and III) of settlement in neighboring Tell Meshash dating to the eleventh century B.C. The unbroken pottery found in the area near the Beersheba

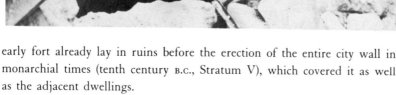

Left:
The deep well excavated outside the Israelite gate of Beersheba dates to an early period before the city was fortified, presumably in the days of Abraham. This represents one of the rare archaeological links with the story of the Patriarchs (Gen. 21:25; 26:25)

Above:
Stone altar found outside the gate entrance. The most intriguing problem raised by the excavation of Beersheba is that of its ancient cult and ritual hinted at in the patriarchal stories (Gen. 21; 26; 46). The later large altar of sacrifices found within the well-planned city constructed in the days of the United Kingdom, is described in Part VI: Amos

Left, below:
The earlier phase of Beersheba is represented by an unfortified settlement; but in one of its phases (Stratum VII of the excavation) a fortress about 165 feet wide overlooked the well
V—Section of solid wall
VI—Late 11th century house
VII—11th century fortress

27

well belongs to the transition period between the Late Bronze and the Iron Age. This new evidence leads to the following conclusions:

(1) This important well, dug so painstakingly from the top of the tell, close to the holy place of Beersheba, was invested with great importance in biblical tradition (Gen. 21:33; 26:23–24, 33–34, etc.). Y. Aharoni, B. Mazar, and other leading scholars believe it is probably the well associated with Abraham (Gen. 21:31), but not an Abraham of the Middle Bronze Age. Potsherds of the twelfth to eleventh centuries B.C., found in the deepest layer (Stratum VI), indicate that the mound was settled in the period of Judges, although it was apparently unwalled at that time. The well is adjacent to, but outside the wall.

(2) From early times there was a massive horned altar at the holy place. After its destruction, a non-Israelite sanctuary stood there until Hellenistic times. The stones of the Israelite altar had been removed and reused elsewhere on the tell. Nevertheless, the excavators were able to locate most of the pieces and to restore the original altar, which is the pride of the archaeological expedition and a witness to early Israelite cultic practice at Beersheba.

(3) The new data are of great historical importance, and if the proposed interpretation is correct, they tend to reinforce the theory advanced by B. Mazar and others that the patriarchal traditions connected with Beersheba relate to the historical period of Israelite settlement (Early Iron Age) and not to the traditional era of the Patriarchs (Middle Bronze Age).

6. THE PHILISTINES OF GENESIS

The Genesis accounts of the relations between Abraham, Isaac, and Abimelech, king of Gerar, are consistent with the conditions existing between the Israelite tribesmen of Judea and their subgroups in the Negeb and the Philistine kingdoms during the last quarter of the eleventh century. The background of Genesis is essentially the same as that of the books of Samuel. If Abraham belongs to the Late Bronze Age, there is no reason to consider the reference to the Philistines as a serious anachronism. The text may be more accurate than most modern scholars are willing to concede.

The political and social conditions existing in Canaan after the thirteenth century invasions of the Sea Peoples (a group that included the Philistines) were similar to those facing David and his mercenaries when they lived in the western Negeb as vassals to Achish, the Philistine king of Gath. Archaeological surveys in that area have turned up artifacts that are characteristically Philistine, dating to the second half of the twelfth and beginning of the eleventh centuries B.C.

7. ABRAHAM, ISAAC, AND THE HISTORICAL ARAMAEANS

The Aramaean people are known in the stories about Abraham, Isaac, and Jacob as natives of Aram, Haran, and Nahor, where the patriarchal families mingled with Aramaeans such as Laban and his clan (Gen. 22:20–24; 24; 29; 31). Though many scholars have argued vigorously for the existence of "proto-Aramaeans" before the twelfth century B.C., there is no convincing evidence to support that position. Cuneiform sources indicate that Tiglathpileser I (1116–1078 B.C.) was the first Assyrian king to fight the Ahlame-Aramaeans, seminomads of the steppes between the middle Euphrates and eastern Syria. They gained a foothold in western Mesopotamia in the course of the eleventh century at locations mentioned in Genesis. This may explain the historical importance of the genealogical lists of Aram as the younger branch in a federation of tribes of Nahor (Gen. 22:21). It also clarifies the important status accorded in biblical tradition to the figure of Laban, the Aramaean whose center was at Haran.

A brotherly pact between two parties. Middle Bronze engraving from Ugarit

We know that the Aramaeans absorbed the Hurrian culture in western Mesopotamia. They eventually spread south to the area of Damascus and into Transjordan or Gilead, where their territory impinged on that claimed by Jacob's clan. Genesis 31 explains that the name Gilead is derived from Hebrew *gal 'ed* (*yegar shahadutha'* in Aramaic), a mound of stones in a sacred high place that defined the boundaries between the two peoples. This reflects the state of affairs before the long wars between David and the more warlike Aramaeans of his day.

The Genesis stories accurately reflect the presence of the Aramaeans in the Near East during the second half of the eleventh century. This observation helps solve a geographical problem in the biblical account. We are told (Gen. 31:23) that Laban pursued Jacob and his livestock for seven days from Haran to Gilead; this is an impossible feat unless we take into consideration the fact that Aramaean territory lay much closer to Gilead than Haran proper. The encounter of Jacob and Laban is concluded by the erection of a pillar or *massebah* consecrated to the respective deities of the contracting parties in compliance with treaty practices throughout the ancient Near East.

8. CONDITIONS AT THE END OF THE SECOND MILLENNIUM

Transport, raiding, and warfare in the southern and eastern steppes were greatly facilitated by the domestication of the camel. This did not happen until the end of the second millennium. Until that time, transportation of people and goods was carried out by ass caravans. Their territorial range was limited by their greater need of water. The frequent mention of camels in the patriarchal narratives would have to be regarded as anachronistic if we dated them in the Middle Bronze Age. This is not the case, however, if we place them in the twelfth century B.C., or even later, when the camel had been domesticated in Palestine.

a. *Jacob-Israel and Esau-Edom*

In Genesis 36, which includes Edomite genealogies and stories, Esau-Seir is the ancestor of the Edomites just as Jacob-Israel is the eponymous ancestor of the Israelites. The prominence given to Esau in the patriarchal tradition suggests that during the formative stage of Israel, Edom played a very prominent role. Though they are linked with the Horites in Genesis 36:20–39, the Edomites were not Hurrians, who appear in the Bible as uncircumcised people dwelling in Shechem. The biblical glimpses of the Edomites, including the tantalizing lists of political leaders in chapter 36, may be illuminated and fleshed out as archaeology pursues this elusive people in its historical settlements from the late fourteenth or early thirteenth century B.C.

b. *The Capture of Shechem*

The account of the rape of Dinah (Genesis 34) and the capture of Shechem by her brothers, Simeon and Levi, presents the events as personalized history. This account may be rooted in traditions of certain ethnic relationships from the early days of the settlement of the Israelites in Canaan. The slender evidence it presents rests on a historical foundation. In Genesis 34:2 Hamor, chief of Shechem, is called a Hivite, but the Septuagint translation identifies him as Horite. We know that Shechem was inhabited at that time by Hurrian elements, because: (a) the Shechemites were still uncircumcised, whereas the Semitic Canaanites would have been circumcised, and (b) the Amarna letters dispatched to Egypt from Shechem show that Hurrians were active in central Palestine from about 1400 B.C. onward.

There is also an obscure reference to the capture of Shechem in Genesis 48:22; here, in what may be the oldest tradition of all, the antagonists are Jacob and the Amorites. A final story concerning Shechem in the period of Judges is found in chapter 9 of that book. It tells of the breaking of a treaty between the Israelites and the Shechemites and the destruction of the city by Abimelech.

A new city wall and eastern gateway were built in Shechem in the Late Bronze Age, consisting of two towers, each 23 × 42 feet, containing guard rooms. See the picture of Shechem's cyclopean wall, earlier

c. *The Story of Judah and Tamar*

Judah, we are informed, had left his kin and moved to Adullam, in the Canaanite lowlands to the west (cf. Genesis 38). There he married a Canaanite woman and had three sons by her. The significance of the story goes far beyond a mere narrative about one of the eponymous ancestors of the nation. It reflects a current tradition related realistically to the early settlement of the tribe of Judah, its relations of peaceful coexistence with the Canaanites in the coastal plain, its branching out into clans, and their expansion.

Let us mention one archaeological detail out of many, namely the seal-and-cord chosen by Tamar to confirm her testimony and guarantee the identity of the person by whom she was pregnant. The seal-and-cord were not chosen for their intrinsic value but for purposes of personal identification to be produced at the critical moment in the narrative. The seal mentioned here was of the well-known cylinder variety, found everywhere in the Near East, but especially in Mesopotamia. Numerous specimens have turned up in Palestinian excavations. These seals were often perforated vertically for threading with a cord, so that the seal-and-cord were worn around the neck as a unit. The seal served as the legal surrogate for the person wearing it. Its impression on a tablet signified the owner's acknowledgment of full responsibility with respect to the contents and was the equivalent of a modern document duly signed and sworn.

9. THE STORY OF JOSEPH

Genesis 37–50 is devoted to the story of Joseph. Its sustained human drama is unsurpassed in the whole Pentateuch. Despite its rich characterization, the novella lacks historical references that would help to pin down its date. It serves to close the patriarchal period and offers a rationale of the descent of the Hebrews to Egypt. It also provides a link to the eventual Exodus from Egypt. There are numerous problems that make its dating uncertain, though there are numerous details that derive from and are consistent with the traditions of the ancient Near East. The motif of an adulteress (Genesis 39) turning on a young man who spurned her was well known to the Egyptians from "The Tale of the Two Brothers." Joseph's tunic of many colors in 37:3 should properly be translated as an "ornamental tunic." Cuneiform records refer to a *ḳutinnu pishannu* (cf. Hebrew *ḳutonet passim*) as a ceremonial robe that could be draped around statues of divinities and had appliqué ornaments sewn onto it.

It was appropriate that Joseph was given the Pharaoh's signet ring in Genesis 41:42, for in Egypt the vizier was known as the "Sealbearer of the King of Lower Egypt." The gift of the gold chain is another authentic touch; it sanctioned a vizier's control over regulation of the food supply.

In Genesis 44:5 we read of Joseph's cup that he used for divination. There is ample evidence of the sort of divination whereby oil or water was poured into a bowl and interpretations and forecasts given on the basis of the liquids inside.

The land of Goshen (Gen. 45:10) is identified with the region of the Wadi Tumilat. "The region of Rameses," as it is called by the Egyptians in Genesis 47:11, is synonymous with it. It is often argued that the use of the name "Rameses" is an anachronism in Genesis since the royal name became popular only in the Nineteenth Dynasty, that is, not before the end of the fourteenth century. This is one more reason to date the contents of the book of Genesis much later than the traditional patriarchal period in the Middle Bronze Age, and much closer to the presumed date of its composition in the Iron Age.

10. THE TESTAMENT OF JACOB (GENESIS 49), ONE OF THE EARLIEST BIBLICAL WRITINGS

The poem in Genesis 49 is composed of short sayings about each of the twelve sons of Jacob. This format invites comparison between this poem and Deuteronomy 33, which contains the same form, as well as Judges 5, where most of the tribes are listed and praised or censured for their participation in the Israelite war against Sisera and the kings of Canaan. Because of careful linguistic analysis there is now a consensus that these poems are among the earliest pieces of writing in the Bible. In their present form they are authentic products of the premonarchic age of Israel, and being poems with a fixed structure, they are less likely than prose passages to have been changed by subsequent editors.

It is likely that the comments on Simeon and Levi in Genesis 49:5-7— "Simeon and Levi are brothers; weapons of violence are their swords"— relate an episode in the settlement of Shechem. Another verse that deserves comment is 49:13: "Zebulun ... shall become a haven for ships." The coastline of Canaan from south to north (Sidon) was dotted with small natural inlets serving as harbors where ships could take shelter at night, as they did not travel in the dark. This accounts for the closeness of these harbors to each other.

PART II

EXODUS, LEVITICUS, NUMBERS, DEUTERONOMY

A. EXODUS

Following Genesis, the book of Exodus pursues the traditions from the days after the clan of Jacob settled in Egypt and after the death of Joseph. It is the history of the departure of Israel from Egypt. The second half of the book gives an account of the encampment at Sinai under Moses' leadership, the establishment of the covenant bond with God, and the worship in a tabernacle.

Its contents may be grouped as follows:

Chapter 1:1–7	An introductory statement linking Genesis and Exodus
Chapters 1:7–2:22	Oppression of Israel; early life of Moses and flight into the desert
Chapters 2:23–13:22	The call of Moses; interviews with Pharaoh; the ten plagues; the Exodus from Egypt
Chapters 14:1–18:27	Crossing the Reed Sea and the wilderness journey to Mount Sinai
Chapters 19:1–20:26	The revelation of Yahweh to the people at Mount Sinai; the Decalogue
Chapters 21:1–24:18	The Book of the Covenant and the ratification or renewal of the covenant
Chapters 25:1–31:18; 35:1–40:38	The priesthood; the building of the sanctuary and its furnishings
Chapters 32:1–34:35	The story of the worship of the golden calf and the subsequent events. The last chapter includes a renewal of the covenant and the cultic Decalogue.

Exodus is one of the most familiar books of the Hebrew Bible, for the events of this book are central to Israelite history. We only need to list the central traditions of the book to see its importance for biblical thought:

The vision and call of Moses at Horeb: Exodus 3:1–4:17

The plagues: Exodus 7–11

The institution and law of the Passover: Exodus 12:1–13:10

The Song of the Sea: Exodus 15:1–21. This is very early poetry.

The Decalogue and the Book of the Covenant: Exodus 20:1–23:33; 24:7.

> The Ten Commandments are followed by the Book of the Covenant, the first and oldest statement of the Law of the Pentateuch.

The worship of the golden calf: Exodus 32

The critical reader of the Bible should be aware that the introductory statement (Exod. 1:1–7) linking the settlement of the descendants of Jacob with the amorphous peoples of the Oppression and Exodus is a secondary

addition in the view of most scholars. The traditions behind Genesis and
those of Exodus arose from different groups who banded together in Canaan to become Israel; only later were these traditions joined to make a
single history of Israel.

1. EGYPTIAN DATA ON ISRAEL IN EGYPT

There is still no direct evidence from Egyptian sources on the vital
story of the Bondage and Exodus, or of Moses, his encounters with Pharaoh, and the plagues. Few episodes in Israel's history have aroused as
many conflicting views among scholars in interpreting the biblical tradition
and its background.

Egyptian sources tell us that various wanderers from the east, including
families of herdsmen, would enter Egypt and settle in the pasture lands of
the Egyptian Nile Delta and its eastern approaches. The Egyptian papyrus
Anastasi VI tells of the permission that was granted to clans of Shosu
from Edom to cross over to the pools of Per-atum to get water for themselves and their animals. This is the earliest Egyptian reference to Edom,
and it describes the arrival of seminomadic Semitic clans that were then
settling in the hill regions of southern Transjordan. Papyri from the border fortress of Merneptah at Teku describe the careful watch kept on the
passage of nomadic clans through the network of forts along the desert
border, the biblical "Wall [shur] of Egypt." These nomads were often subjected to land taxes and to the corvée (forced labor) by their Egyptian rulers.

2. THE LAND OF GOSHEN

The clans of Israel were concentrated in the "land of Goshen," the
southern extension of the "region of Rameses," where Rameses I had re-
built Tanis (Zoan) and erected the "400-year stele." Tanis was renamed
Per-Rameses, the "house of Rameses." The land of Goshen extended from
Zoan-Tanis to the store-city of Pithom and to the depression of the Wadi
Tumilat east of the Delta. At the end of the last century E. Naville had

already identified the great mound of Tell el-Mashkuteh as Pithom, which Rameses II had built up and resettled as a border fortress in eastern Egypt. Several stelae and a temple were discovered there, consecrated to the god Atum, adding credence to its identification as Pithom (*Per-Atum,* "House of Atum"). Other inscriptions found there recently suggest the identification of the tell with Teku, probably biblical Succoth, the Israelites' first station after their flight from Per-Rameses. Some scholars believe that the city was known by both names, Per-Atum and Teku.

3. THE DATE OF THE EXODUS AND CONQUEST

Most scholars are agreed on dating the Israelite Conquest of Canaan, west of the Jordan, around the middle of the thirteenth century B.C. Support for this chronology comes from the following data: (a) The naming of "Rameses" as one of the cities built by the Israelites in Goshen (Exod. 1:11) at the beginning of the reign of Rameses II and its identification with Per-Rameses; (b) the Merneptah stele erected by Rameses' son Merneptah (1236–1223 B.C.) on one of his expeditions to Canaan, which mentions Israelites as one of the peoples that he defeated in Canaan about 1230; (c) the settlement of southern Transjordan in the thirteenth century. N. Glueck's archaeological surveys have shown that there was little settled occupation of the area in previous centuries. Therefore, Edom, Moab, and Ammon, mentioned in the narratives of the Conquest, could not have been in existence at an earlier time. These data, taken together, place the Exodus early in the reign of Rameses II (1304–1237), the two invasions of Transjordan either late in the fourteenth or early in the thirteenth century (see Numbers), and the major entrance into Canaan no later than 1230 B.C.

The historicity of the Exodus is undeniable, though it is not possible to establish from any outside source the name of the disparate elements or "mixed multitude" (12:38), or the size of the groups that gathered eventually at Kadesh-barnea before the invasion of Transjordan. But we do have contemporary documents that establish the historical background of the period of bondage and escape. In the reigns of Rameses and Merneptah,

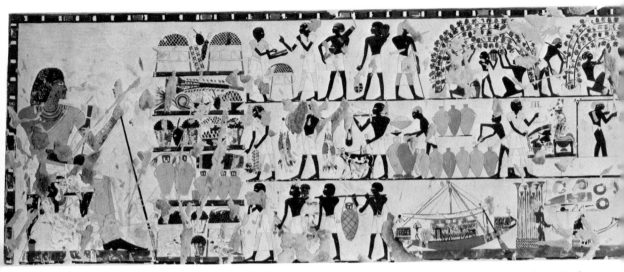

Egyptian landowner supervising
the produce—fruit, wine,
fish—gathered by slaves

Asiatics, including Habiru, were employed in various types of work for the king; some became officials, but most served in forced labor in the fields (mostly in fruit plantations or wineries), in mines, and in the construction of public buildings. This is in line with the biblical reference to the building of Pithom and Rameses, the royal city of the Nineteenth Dynasty, at Qantir, thirteen miles south of Tanis. The building of these cities was necessitated by the new Egyptian policy that shifted the main center of government to the north near the travel lanes that led to Canaan.

4. THE BIBLICAL CHRONOLOGY

Some scholars do not believe that Rameses II was the Pharaoh of the Exodus because his dates conflict with the biblical chronology in I Kings 6:1, which counts 480 years from the Exodus to the founding of Solomon's temple in 965 B.C. This traditional reckoning places the Exodus in the mid-fifteenth century or at the time of Thutmose III. This chronology is suspect, however, because it is based on the calculations of a later source. According to traditions stemming from a priestly source, the writer figured that there were twelve generations of priests from Aaron to Azariah of the House of Zadok, the first chief priest to officiate at the Temple, and that each generation was 40 years long. Thus he arrived at 480 years from the Exodus to the founding of the Temple. The artificial nature of this calculation militates against its use in reconstructing history. But, if we take 25–27 years for an average generation and count twelve generations (although this also may be an artificial figure) we arrive approximately at the beginning of the thirteenth century.

There is also skepticism about the total number of 600,000 men of military age given in the biblical tradition (Num. 1:46; 26:51). The consensus is that it must have been a much smaller group that eluded the Egyp-

Egyptian relief at Thebes
representing Rameses II
attacking fortified Dapur held
by the Hittites in Syria

tian army and crossed the wilderness. There have been several attempts at explaining the large figures given in Numbers. According to G. E. Mendenhall, following a suggestion by Flinders Petrie, the Hebrew word 'eleph (1,000) refers to the village or other population unit that provides troops from among its able-bodied men, and is not the number here. He arrives at a total figure of about 6,000 men as the maximum martial strength of the Israelite army during the period of the Judges. Albright believed that the figure reflected the total population of the United Kingdom in the time of David and his ill-fated census. There are other possibilities, but Mendenhall appears to be on the right track in recognizing the census roll as a military list. Hence, Numbers 1 refers to 600 small units.

5. A HISTORICAL CHAIN REACTION

While the biblical chronology is problematic here, it is possible that this central event took place as a result of the violent wars Rameses conducted against the Amurru of central Syria and his failure at Kadesh on the Orontes in 1286 B.C., which initiated a chain reaction. The decline of Egyptian power in Canaan allowed the recapture of Syria by the Hittites and their advance to the areas of Damascus and northern Transjordan, giving rise to a series of rebellions of the city-kingdoms throughout Canaan against the Egyptian overlords. The Hittite advance into Syria may be related to the biblical report of the rise of the Amorites in Transjordan and the founding of the kingdom of Heshbon in Numbers 21:26. Rather than resulting in a clear-cut victory, the struggle between the Egyptians and the Hittites for Canaan sapped the energy of both great powers, leaving both too weak completely to dominate the land. The power vacuum promoted the resurgence of local kings and of nomadic tribes from Seir (Edom) to Egypt's eastern border. This accounts for Rameses' frequent military expeditions to various regions including Edom and Moab. Egyp-

tian sources mention violent encounters in the lands of the Shosu bedouins and in the adjacent mountains of Seir, as well as the destruction of their settlements. An inscription found at Luxor tells of the capture of many fortified cities including Boterat in Moab, lying on the King's Highway east of the Jordan. Rameses left no stone unturned to regain control and ensure communications along this major trade route. Forts were built at strategic points along the way and the Egyptians began exploiting the copper mines at the south of the Arabah in the Negeb, as we learn from the discovery of the remains of an Egyptian temple near Timnah.

6. THE JOURNEY THROUGH THE WILDERNESS

The route of the Exodus and Wanderings remains a difficult and tantalizing problem. The location of the many encampments, and especially of Mount Sinai, seems to be beyond precise determination. Only the geography of the beginning can be established with some degree of certainty, as it is connected with names also known from Egyptian sources and located east of the Delta. The Israelites journeyed from Rameses to Succoth (Exod. 12:37), identified with *t-k-w* of Egyptian texts and modern Tell el-Mashkuteh. It was a border fortress on the Wadi Tumilat west of the Bitter Lakes, presently along the course of the Suez Canal. From there they

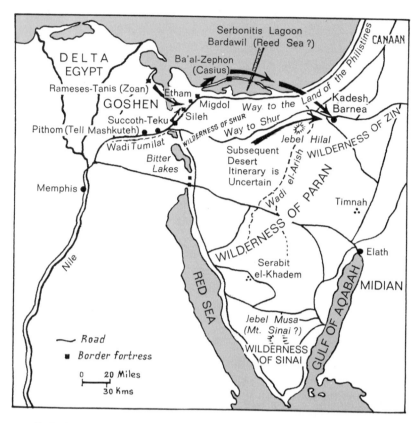

(Map labels:) Serbonitis Lagoon / Bardawil (Reed Sea ?) — Ba'al-Zephon (Casius) — CANAAN — DELTA EGYPT — Rameses-Tanis (Zoan) — Etham — GOSHEN — Migdol — Way to the Land of the Philistines — Kadesh-Barnea — Succoth-Teku — Sileh — WILDERNESS OF SHUR — Way to Shur — WILDERNESS OF ZIN — Pithom (Tell Mashkuteh) — Wadi Tumilat — Jebel Hilal — WILDERNESS OF ARISH — Bitter Lakes — Subsequent Desert Itinerary is Uncertain — Wadi el-Arish — WILDERNESS OF PARAN — Memphis — Timnah — Nile — WILDERNESS OF PARAN — Serabit el-Khadem — Elath — MIDIAN — RED SEA — GULF OF AQABAH — Jebel Musa (Mt. Sinai ?) — WILDERNESS OF SINAI — Road — Border fortress — 0 20 Miles — 30 Kms

travelled through Etam on the edge of the desert to Pi-hahiroth between Migdol and the Mediterranean Sea, in front of Ba'al-zephon (Exod. 14:2). Migdol is an Egyptian fortress northeast of Sile (modern Tell el-Heir) near Qantara, mentioned by Seti I and later Egyptian sources. Ba'al-zephon was a temple for mariners (Zeus-Casius of the Greeks) located on the narrow arm of land that embraces the Sabkhat-Bardawil lagoon (the ancient Gulf of Serbonis) and separates this lagoon from the Mediterranean (see map).

It was at Pi-hahiroth that the Egyptians overtook the fleeing Israelites, who were saved miraculously at the Reed Sea as described in the Song of

The narrow arm of land that embraces the Sabkhat-Bardawil lagoon (Gulf of Serbonis) or the "Reed Sea" is regarded as the northern route that the Israelites followed in their Exodus. Remains of an Iron Age I settlement were discovered at Casius

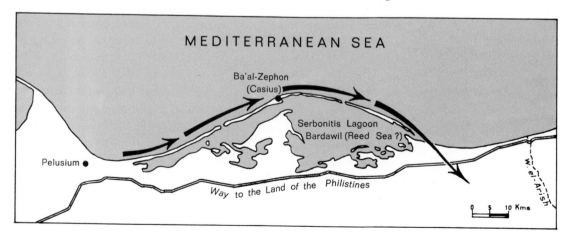

(Map labels:) MEDITERRANEAN SEA — Ba'al-Zephon (Casius) — Serbonitis Lagoon / Bardawil (Reed Sea ?) — Pelusium — Way to the Land of the Philistines — W. el-Arish — 0 5 10 Kms

the Sea (Exod. 15:1–18, 21). The familiar rendering, the "Red" Sea, derives from a mistranslation of the Hebrew, originally Egyptian, word *suph,* which means "reed." It probably refers to papyrus marshes near Rameses. Unfortunately, there are not enough data to say more than that the Reed Sea was a shallow body of water east of the Delta; perhaps it was the Gulf of Serbonis (the lagoon of Sabkhat Bardawil), which separated Migdol from Ba'al-zephon (see map).

Another reference to this stage of the journey comes from Exodus 13: 17–18: "God did not lead them by way of the land of the Philistines, although that was near.... 'Lest the people repent when they see war.'... But God led the people round by the way of the wilderness toward the Reed Sea." Because scholarly opinion holds that the Philistines did not precede the Israelites into the land, this reference must be an anachronism. The Philistines or "Sea Peoples" settled on the coast of southern Palestine in the twelfth century B.C. The coastal route, also called the "Way to the Land of the Philistines," would have been convenient, but it was precluded because it was guarded by a network of Egyptian forts.

7. THE NORTHERN AND SOUTHERN ROUTES

The route of Israel's journey through the wilderness is still open to question. The choice between the "northern" and "southern" theories rests primarily on the location of Mt. Sinai, which is problematic. According to the "northern" theory, Sinai should be close to Kadesh-barnea (see Exod. 15:22), the well-watered oasis that held a central place in the wilderness period, possibly Jebel Hilal, thirty miles to the west. The incident of the quails in Numbers 11:31–32 is consistent with a route along the Mediterranean coast where swarms of migrating birds drop exhausted after their flight across the sea. On the other hand, there are traditions that locate Sinai at a greater distance from Kadesh (Num. 33:16–36; Deut. 1:2) and support a southern route. This hypothesis rests on early Christian traditions that locate Sinai at Jebel Musa, Mount Moses, in the south of the Sinai peninsula. It is here that Justinian I dedicated a monastery to Saint Catherine of Alexandria in A.D. 527 to protect the hermits who lived in the Sinai wilderness from the fifth century on. Supporters of this theory point out that Jebel Musa, 7,497 feet high, is a more likely candidate for the awe-inspiring theophany than Jebel Hilal at 2,927 feet. If this identification is correct, however, it would imply that the Israelites made a long, difficult, and topographically unnecessary detour in the rough and waterless part of the peninsula. A third hypothesis would place Mount Sinai in or near Midian on the eastern, Asiatic side of the Gulf of 'Aqaba. The episode of the burning bush in Exodus 3 implies such a location, and other evidence tends to support it. The lack of a clear, continuous tradition about the location or even name of the mountain suggests that there may have been more than one such experience and that several traditions have been blended imperfectly.

Whatever the route, the Israelites ended at Kadesh-barnea, an important crossroads on the highways leading from Egypt. This was the central assembly point for forty years and the largest oasis in the Sinai wilderness. Only a few of the way stations can now be identified and those very hesitantly. At any rate, the identifications stem from several sources, some of which are very ancient, and were joined together only later. We should remember that only small numbers of people with cattle and scant food and water can move in the wilderness, especially in the southern part of the Sinai peninsula.

8. MOSES

The debate over the historicity of Moses, just like the quest for the historical Jesus, has led nowhere. Archaeology is generally unable to confirm the existence of a single individual, so we must rely on the biblical accounts. It is clear that certain legendary motifs have been added to the story, particularly in the narrative of Moses' birth and abandonment to the river. A similar legend was told of Sargon of Akkad and numerous other ancient heroes who were certainly historical figures.

It seems an inescapable conclusion that a certain personality, who completely dominates the traditions of the Exodus, initiated and directed the revolutionary events that bound Yahweh with a nation, Israel, through the Covenant. It was the heroic achievement of Moses to have rallied an amorphous agglomerate of slaves and outcasts and imbued them with the faith to adhere to a single god, Yahweh.

One must also consider certain realistic details in the life of Moses, such as his marriage to Zipporah, daughter of the priest of Midian. The early date of the tradition is unquestionable; by the time of the Judges the Midianites had become bitter enemies of Israel. A later description of Moses would not have included the marriage of the great lawgiver to an enemy. Even more, how could any tradition allow Moses to be guided by a Midianite priest unless it were early and authentic?

9. THE SANCTUARY AND ARK

The sources that describe the desert sanctuary (Exod. 26–31; 36–40) go into great detail about the construction of the Tabernacle, how it was set up, and what its furnishings were. This idealized description in its present form is a late priestly tradition. It has proved impossible to sort out all the data so as to produce a sequential picture of the stages of tradition, but broad lines can be determined. The original tabernacle was a portable tent of simple manufacture. The last, improved model doubtless served David in Jerusalem before the Temple was built, and the present description most likely reflects the latter rather than the former phase. The *mishkan* ("Dwelling") was a collapsible temple made of wooden frames of desert acacia wood. They were put together making a rectangular building 30 by 10 by 10 cubits (45 × 15 × 15 feet) that opened on the eastern side. It was

Right:
Detail of the background showing, on the white tell, a Judean fortress built there a few centuries after the Exodus

covered with bands of fine-woven material, sewn together to make two big pieces fastened with hooks and clips. They were embroidered with figures of cherubim. Goat skins covered the material "like a tent over the Dwelling." Lastly, skins of rams, dyed red, covered the whole frame, and were in turn covered by very light leather hides. A curtain covered the entry and an ornate veil was drawn across the innermost ten cubits and marked the division between the Holy Place and the Holy of Holies. The only object in the latter was the Ark of the Testimony (Exod. 26:33; 40:21), while the Holy Place contained only the lampstand and the table of shewbread. An altar, with the basin for washing, stood outside the entrance of the Dwelling (Exod. 40:30). An open court around the Dwelling (100 × 50 cubits) was formed by a barrier of bronze posts and silver curtain rods from which the linen hung to the ground. It was suggested on the basis of a bas-relief from Palmyra (as illustrated here) that the Dwelling was a tent like the people's dwelling places during their wanderings in the Sinai.

10. A MIDIANITE SANCTUARY AT TIMNAH

Recent excavations have been conducted by Y. Aharoni and B. Rothenberg at the Egyptian copper mining center in the Timnah valley, some eighteen to twenty miles north of Elath. Egyptian pharaohs from the days of Seti I to Rameses III, and later, Rameses IV and V (fourteenth to twelfth centuries B.C.) had maintained there large-scale primitive copper smelting facilities. They were manned by the indigenous Amalekites of the southern Negeb, as well as the Midianites and Kenites of the Arabah and Midian. The Kenites, it will be remembered, possessed metallurgical traditions going back to prebiblical times as recorded in Genesis 4:22. The Egyptians had erected at Timnah a sanctuary to the goddess Hathor, "The Lady of the Turquoise," who was also worshiped at the mines of Serabit el Khadim in Sinai, also worked by Semitic laborers. This temple was destroyed, then rebuilt between the fourteenth and twelfth centuries B.C. The actual maintenance of Egyptian mining enterprises is further attested by the papyrus Harris I, dating to the reign of Rameses III. Thousands of ar-

Midianite bichrome wheel-made juglet with an ostrich figure decoration

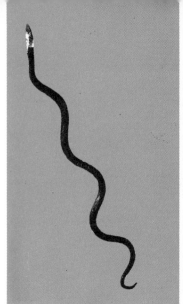

tifacts in clay or metal, of both local, probably Midianite, and Egyptian provenance, attest to the expansion and vitality of the Midianite culture, stemming from sedentary and semisedentary centers southeast of Elath and extending to the threshold of Arabia in the northern Hedjaz. They represent a witness to the history of the days roughly corresponding to the periods of Exodus and the wanderings of disparate Hebrew clans in the semiarid areas south of Canaan and Transjordan. They bespeak some cultural and social interrelations between the Midianites and Kenites and the early Hebrews. They serve to authenticate the tradition of the relationship between Jethro, the Midianite priest, and Moses, his son-in-law.

Toward the end of the twelfth century, the temple the Egyptians had rebuilt was destroyed, apparently by earthquake. Shortly thereafter all evidence of the former cult was displaced by the Midianites who kept up the exploitation of the mines. The excavations show that the shrine was roofed with a tent, presumably as a desert sanctuary, and its holy of holies contained a copper snake with a gilded head as a votive object. The other radical change in the character of the shrine was the erection of a row of *masseboth* or stelae facing the inner sanctuary and an offering bench built

Left:
The final Midianite phase of the former Egyptian Hathor temple at Timnah, seen from the east. It is situated beneath the rock overhang of the cliffs popularly known as "Solomon's Pillars." A row of *masseboth* (standing pillars) is seen at the edge of the court of the sanctuary (center of picture)

Above:
The Midianite copper serpent with a gilded head found in the holy of holies of the sanctuary. It is suggestive of the metal serpent fashioned by Moses (see Numbers 21:9)

Left:
Ore-crushing and grinding tools of the Timnah mining camp

Below:
The portable tent-shrine carved on a bas relief of the Temple of Bel in Palmyra (eastern Syria) is suggestive of the "Dwelling" in the desert

The Midianite offering bench built against the wall; in the foreground, one of the stone-lined post-holes for the tented sanctuary

against the sanctuary wall. The votive snake was found in the holiest spot of the sanctuary, and numerous other copper votive artifacts and decorated pottery attributed to the Midianite phase of the cult were found in the sanctuary.

These discoveries strongly confirm the interrelationships between early Israel and the Midianites-Kenites (cf. Exod. 18:12–17). The votive snake of the desert sanctuary of Timnah may furnish an actual background for the tradition of the serpent Nehushtan of Numbers 21:9. The excavations may cast some light on the nature of Moses' tent-sanctuary and lend support to those scholars who have proposed that the cult of the invisible El or Yahweh of the Exodus period, who tented among his people and whose proper dwelling was a tent, may have been of Midianite-Kenite origin. Regardless of the theological implications raised by the discoveries, it is clear that they provide a cultural and historico-geographical background of facts and data related to the obscure phases of the wilderness narratives.

The holy of holies of the Midianite sanctuary with three niches in the background, beneath the rock overhang

11. THE ARK OF THE COVENANT

The Ark of the Covenant contained the two stone tablets on which the ten words of the Law were inscribed. God had given them to Moses (Exod. 31:18), and he put them inside the Ark (25:16; 40:20; cf. Deut. 10: 1–5). The Ark, as described in Exodus 25:10–12 and 37:1–9, was a chest made of acacia wood, about four feet long by two and a half feet wide, and two and a half feet high. It was covered with gold plates and had rings attached through which poles were inserted for carrying. A plate of gold, the size of the Ark, called the *Kapporeth,* was laid over the Ark. Two cherubim stood, one at each end of the *Kapporeth,* overshadowing it with their wings. Like the description of the Dwelling, the traditions of the Ark were influenced by the memory of Solomon's Temple, where the Ark stood in the Holy of Holies, overshadowed by the cherubim (I Kings 8:6). It is also likely that the objects and arrangements in the Temple were influenced by the prior practice in the Tabernacle. Nevertheless, the passage in Numbers 10:33–36 that describes the Ark on its travels preserves a much older tradition and evokes the spirit of the earlier age when the Ark symbolized the immediate presence of the deity and accompanied the people into battle.

It is difficult to say how the Israelites envisioned God mounted on the Ark. The most likely picture has him seated above it on a throne formed by the cherubim (for such a cherubim throne, see drawing at right). The Ark itself would serve as his footstool. In an early psalm he is described as mounting a cherub, but this is figurative language reflecting the imagery associated with the Canaanite storm god. Many scholars believe that the *Kapporeth* over the Ark was a later tradition and became a substitute for the Ark in the post-exilic period after the destruction of the Temple by the Babylonians. Thus the *Kapporeth* filled the role formerly ascribed to the Ark as the sign of the divine presence (Lev. 16:2, 13).

Canaanite and Phoenician carvings of the 13th–10th c. B.C. depict the king as seated on his throne; its side consists of a lion-headed winged sphinx or "cherub." The king's feet rest on a footstool

12. THE PASSOVER PASCHAL SACRIFICE

One custom, the paschal sacrifice, ordained in the Book of the Covenant (Exod. 23:18) and in the cultic Decalogue (34:25), has been maintained throughout the long history of Israel. The descriptions in Exodus 12:27, Numbers 9:2, and Deuteronomy 16:6 speak more vividly than archaeological discovery. This sacrifice is still celebrated by a sect of Samaritan Jews according to the biblical tradition on the night of the 14/15th day of Nisan (the first month of the ancient calendar) and is accompanied by the eating of matzo (unleavened bread) for seven days.

The sacrifice was first offered by the Israelites on the night of their flight from Egypt so that the avenging angel would bypass their homes. The killing and roasting of the yearling lamb was done by every Israelite in his home, not in a sanctuary, and anyone could partake. The meat had

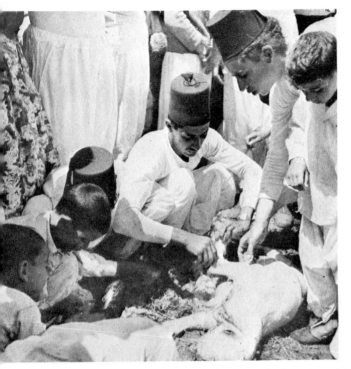

Left:
Lambs slaughtered by the Samaritan sectarian Jews on their Passover feast celebrated on Mount Gerizim above Shechem

Right:
The slaughtered lambs are roasted in fire pits, then consumed by the whole community to commemorate the Exodus from Egypt

to be eaten during the night, with any leftovers being burnt. The sacrificial blood was then smeared on the doorpost to mark each Israelite home and protect the first-born from being killed. The present-day festival commemorates the event and confirms the historical continuity between those who partake in the sacrificial meal and the Israelites who were saved from Egyptian bondage.

13. THE SAMARITAN SACRIFICIAL RITUAL

Passover is celebrated by Jews in drastically modified form on the Seder night. But the ancient customs are practiced to this day by the tiny Samaritan community in Shechem and Holon, who observe Judaism according to the literal ordinances of the Pentateuch (Torah) and disregard rabbinic or later norms of Judaism. Paschal lambs are slaughtered and skinned before nightfall; meanwhile the high priest conducts hymns and prayers. The lambs are skinned and roasted whole in deep pits fueled by brush; they are consumed by every member of the community; the extraordinary ceremony continues until late in the night.

14. ANCIENT CULT AND THE SOURCES OF THE BOOK OF EXODUS

Certain scholars, following the lead of J. Pedersen, regard the unit Exodus 1–15 as a kind of Passover *haggadah,* or book of ritual. In this view it was the celebration of the Passover that produced the narrative, which in effect explains the purpose and rationale of the celebration. The rest of the book then consists of descriptive notes and other helpful information relating to the central theme—deliverance from bondage in Egypt and the appropriate ways in which to worship God and praise him for his mighty deeds. While their methods are drastic and the conclusions are extreme, there is merit in the view that cultic celebration was central to Israelite faith and life, that the observance and re-enactment of the sacral event made each participant also a sharer in the original experience. The central events in Israelite ritual were historical and therefore unique and unrepeatable, unlike those of other religions. The tradition therefore could not be created by the cult, but rather was influenced and shaped by aspects of it. Because of the historical nature of the religion, the cult was dependent upon the tradition and not the other way around. We would deny that the celebration of the Passover was the only historical event; on the contrary, the event itself and the memory of it, however adapted and altered in transmission, were the factual basis on which celebration and observance were built. They were a re-enactment, not merely of previous celebrations, but of the event.

a. *The Oldest Materials in Exodus*

A great deal of attention has been paid over the last hundred years to the historical background of the three or four collections of laws in Exodus. On the basis of this research, W. F. Albright concluded that the Decalogue (Exod. 20:2–17), containing the oldest laws in the Pentateuch, parts of the Book of the Covenant (20:23–23:33), and possibly Exodus 24 can be traced back to the twelfth to eleventh centuries B.C. Probably the earliest piece of writing in the book, however, is the Song of the Sea (15: 1–18, 21), whose twelfth century date has been established by the linguistic studies of Albright and his students. While the law codes reflect social conditions and legal traditions of the days of the tribal confederation (Judges, Samuel), the Song of the Sea probably does not postdate the events it describes by very much and, along with Judges 5, is the oldest Israelite poetry in the Bible.

b. *The Character of Civic and Cultic Legislation of the Pentateuch*

In his classic form-critical studies of the legislation of the Pentateuch, A. Alt distinguished between case law, which was typical of all communities in the Near East, and "apodictic" law, which he regarded as unique to Israel. This type of law has the familiar form of the short imperative injunctions of the Ten Commandments, which are found in slightly altered form in Deuteronomy 5:6–21. Other laws couched in similar form may be found in Exodus 22:18, 23:19, Deuteronomy 14:21, and elsewhere. This form is rare in the ancient Near East, although there is a comparable pattern in the treaties between the Hittite emperors and vassal kings in the second half of the second millennium B.C.: "You shall keep the land which I give you, and shall not covet any territory of the land of the Hatti." That apodictic elements also occur in Assyrian vassal treaties of the first millennium (which are very different in other respects), indicates a common pattern of thought about the relationship between the suzerain and his vassals. The Israelites adapted the pattern from the diplomatic to the religious sphere, as they regarded the Covenant as a treaty between Yahweh, the God-king, and Israel, his vassal people, in which protection by the suzerain and obedience by the vassal are principal ingredients.

The group of "casuistic" (case) laws in the Bible reflects the principles of justice in ancient Israel. They begin with a conditional sentence that introduces a hypothetical case and then prescribe a certain action to settle the case. They served an exemplary purpose and offered guidelines for those who were entrusted with responsibility and authority in such matters. This is the common form of legislation in the Near East, dating back to the third millennium, and is well illustrated in Hammurabi's Law Code. Ancient law codes were not like their modern counterparts, which are deliberately set up as comprehensive codes in the form of statutory law, but rather were compilations of typical or representative cases intended to edify the faithful, admonish the faithless, and provide counsel for the local judiciary.

Mid-section of the stele of Hammurabi inscribed with his Law Code (282 laws), 18th c. B.C. Discovered at Susa. Some of its laws bear similarities to the codes of the Pentateuch

B. HISTORICAL BACKGROUNDS IN THE BOOKS OF LEVITICUS, NUMBERS, AND DEUTERONOMY

We have dealt thus far with the Patriarchs, the Bondage, the Exodus, and their historical backgrounds in so far as they are illuminated by extrabiblical sources. As the reader is aware, little can be said of Moses in this sense. Though he was no less historical than Rameses II, archaeology is silent in the case of Moses for he left no material witness behind. We must say the same of much of the rest of the other three books of the Pentateuch, in so far as they contain civil and cultic legislation and, only sporadically, historical narrative.

The reader of the Pentateuch must constantly be aware that the narratives and formulations of laws and customs of premonarchial times, as we have them, were modernized in succeeding periods. This is particularly the case for the period of the United Monarchy, when the royal courts and priestly schools in the Temple promoted the writing of historical annals and the formulation of legal and religious data. They probably revised some details of older traditions, in part to make them relevant to their audience, and added other pertinent details that reflected the thinking of their own times. Contrary to the assumption of older biblical scholarship, however, the use of a tradition by a later writer does not make the tradition itself late or inaccurate. Current research tends to show that the writers belonging to the priestly circles were both conscientious and careful in transmitting older tradition and, given the limitations of the era, were reasonably accurate.

1. BIBLICAL AND CANAANITE EPICS

Biblical scholars have been rewarded greatly in their search for material from early Israel by the studies of the form and language of early Hebrew poetry. These studies have been enormously advanced by the discoveries at Ras Shamra, ancient Ugarit, in northern Syria. Among the few thousand tablets found there, there are several Canaanite mythological epics and shorter hymns in a dialect very close to biblical Hebrew; they all date to the latter half of the second millennium (fourteenth to thirteenth centuries B.C.). This poetry shows that early Hebrew poets shared poetic style and diction with their Canaanite predecessors. Because these tablets can be dated archaeologically to the period immediately preceding the biblical period, they have aided in dating and understanding the early Hebrew poetry. By careful study of linguistic and poetic features, W. F. Albright concluded that the Song of the Sea (Exodus 15) was the earliest preserved Hebrew poem of any length, and that the Song of Deborah (Judges 5) is only slightly later from a stylistic point of view. The similarities with Canaanite poetry may be seen, for example, in Exodus 15:17, which reads: "Thou wilt bring them in and plant them on the mount that is thy possession, the place, O Lord, which thou hast made for thine abode." In the Baal epic from Ugarit, we find: "in the midst of my mount

..., in the holy place, in the mount of my inheritance" referring to Mount Safon, Baal's holy mountain, which has been identified as Mount Casius in Lebanon. There are many other close resemblances in vocabulary and style between Canaanite and Hebrew poems, though there are also marked differences, especially in terms of religious outlook and sense of history. Other old poetry in the Pentateuch includes Genesis 49 (see above) and its companion, Deuteronomy 33, and the Oracles of Balaam, consisting of the poetic passages in Numbers 23 and 24.

2. DATING THE PENTATEUCHAL LEGISLATION

In the Pentateuch we have a considerable body of legislation, carefully collected and arranged in later centuries. These laws and regulations are often recorded in more than one form, showing that there has been a long and complex history of transmission. They have been preserved in documents of different ages, which in turn have been edited and revised in the process of consolidation. Ultimately the communal and institutional background of Israelite law is to be found in the twelve-tribe system of the period of Judges. In the eyes of the Israelites, law is based on and rooted in the Covenant. Case law (see Exodus) reflects the impact of the Covenant, with its basic set of religious obligations, on the life of Israelite society.

Ugarit, a dynamic north Canaanite kingdom in Syria, preserved an important literature consisting of epic songs praising the deeds of gods and heroes. There is much in common, both in language and in content, between these epics and biblical poetry

C. LEVITICUS

Leviticus has the least amount of narrative of any of the books of the Pentateuch. It is limited to Aaron's priesthood (chapters 8–9), the punishment of Nadab and Abihu (10:1–7), the ritual error of Eleazar and Ithamar (10:16–20), and the stoning of a blasphemer (24:10–14, 23). The rest of the book deals predominantly with cultic matters, especially the Levitical priesthood, from which it derives its name. It is part of the Priestly corpus, which stretches from Exodus 25 to Numbers 10. Leviticus may be divided as follows:

Woman bathing. Clay figurine

1:1–7:38	Laws of sacrifice: burnt offerings, cereal offering, peace offering, sin offering, and supplementary material.
8:1–10:20	The consecration of the priests. This section follows Exodus 40, the completion of the sanctuary.
11:1–15:33	The laws of purification.
16:1–34	The Day of Atonement.
17:1–26:46	The Holiness Code.
27:1–34	Instruction concerning oaths and tithes.

Below left:
Bath (Lev. 15:12 on purifying earthen vessels)

Below:
Pan used for frying. Found at Lachish (Lev. 6:14 on the laws of the cereal offering before the altar)

1. RITUAL PURITY (LEVITICUS 11–15)

The ideas underlying this section go back to pre-Mosaic times. An unclean object was not simply dangerous in itself, but because it was repulsive to or prohibited by God, its presence endangered his continuing protection of the group. It was an important task of the priesthood "to distinguish between the holy and the common, and between the unclean and clean" (Lev. 10:10). Behind these laws of cleanness stands early hygienic experience coupled with broad, somewhat naive generalizations, ancient superstitions, simple prejudice, and deliberate avoidance of religious practices of the Canaanites, which were abhorrent to Israelite religion. Uncleanness was both a physical, that is, ritual, and a moral attribute, and in both senses it was considered contagious.

The abominable rite of child sacrifice to the Phoenician god Molekh is illustrated in this stela from Carthage, depicting a priest holding a child

a. *The Laws of the Holiness Code* (*Leviticus 17–26*)

These laws pertain to the life of the community as well as to public worship and the festal year. The code gets its name from the injunction in 19:1: "You shall be holy, because I, the Lord your God, am holy," which is repeated several times in this section.

b. *Idols*

One of the basic biblical ordinances prohibits the manufacture and worship of idols (cf. the Decalogue: Exod. 20:3–5; Deut. 5:8–10). A different form of the injunction appears in Leviticus 19:4: "Do not turn to idols or make for yourselves molten gods." This reference doubtless includes images of all kinds, not only the large statues located in pagan sanctuaries, but also the numerous figurines, whether metal or clay, that were pressed from a single mold, leaving the back as a flat background. These plaques, with representations of the chief Canaanite goddesses, including Asherah, Astarte, and Anat, were associated with the fertility cult. Among the thousands of figurines, as well as molds, found in excavations in the Holy Land, a characteristic type features a goddess with her arms encircling her breasts. She is depicted with full breasts in the stance of the nursing mother goddess (*dea nutrix*). Plaques in the form of a woman in labor, her hands clasped over her abdomen, may have been intended as an inducement to fertility or as a charm to ease labor pains. These anthropomorphic figures may be likened to the *teraphim* (household deities) in the story of Rachel (Gen. 31:34). There were small male idols as well, though they are comparatively rare in excavations.

The vast quantity and ubiquity of these figurines illustrate the persistence and success of pagan forms of worship in Israel. For the bulk of the people, some form of syncretism, combining faith in Yahweh, the God of Mosaic tradition, with an acknowledgment of the fertility figures, seems to have been prevalent through the centuries of the First Temple. The vehemence of the attack on such practices reflects how widespread they were and how difficult it proved to be to eradicate such blatant violations of the covenant code.

c. *The Sacrifice of Children*

The practice of human sacrifice has been demonstrated in the excavations of the Phoenician colony at Carthage and attributed to both the Carthaginians and the Phoenicians by numerous classical authors. The abolition of this barbarous sacrifice (Lev. 18:21) took place as a result of the reform of King Josiah (637–609 B.C.; cf. 2 Kings 23:10). The ban refers to the sacrifice of children to the Phoenician god Molekh, observed in the days of King Manasseh (698–642 B.C.) in the valley of Hinnom on the southern edge of Jerusalem. The place was named Tophet or the "place of burning."

2. ARCHAEOLOGY AND THE LEVITICAL CITIES

The rule laid down in Leviticus 25:32–34 (cf. Num. 35:1–8) that forty-eight Levitical cities be established throughout the conquered land has raised serious problems as to when they existed and what their function was. Scholars agree that these problems can be solved only through a study of the excavations in the various towns listed as Levitical cities. Parallel lists of the forty-eight cities appear in Joshua 21 and 1 Chronicles 6. Gezer, for example, was a Canaanite center that was annexed only in the time of Solomon. Other Levitical cities such as Gibbethon, Elteke, and Gath-rimmon were also annexed at that time. Others had been destroyed by Pharaoh Shishak or by Aramaean invaders after Solomon's time and were repopulated some centuries later. The excavations at Beth-Shemesh and Tell Beit Mirsim (Debir) show them to have been walled cities with typical casemate wall construction, containing royal stores and serving as administrative centers, for example, Strata B$_3$ and A at Tell Beit Mirsim.

B. Mazar concludes, therefore, that the establishment of this network of cities, which served the state by fulfilling secular, cultural, and administrative responsibilities, dates primarily to the time of Kings David and Solomon. The appropriation of state lands for the establishment of such centers goes back to the days of Egyptian rule in Canaan, when the pharaohs appropriated land and devoted it to their gods. Papyrus Harris (first half of the twelfth century B.C., in the days of Rameses III) mentions estates of the god Amun that include fortified Canaanite towns, containing stores for goods the people paid in taxes. Each city had a temple and a team of priests who were in charge of both the religious ritual and secular administration.

Female figurines in *dea nutrix* attitudes were common household possessions among Canaanites and Hebrews, who mingled for centuries before the former were assimilated

Left:
General view of the Canaanite sanctuary of Beth-Shemesh

Right:
A storehouse north of the settlement with utensils *in situ*

D. NUMBERS

The miscellaneous material that makes up the book is presented within the general framework of a record of the wanderings in the wilderness, beginning in the spring of the second year after the Exodus and ending in the events that followed the death of Aaron, the priest and brother of Moses, in the fortieth year after the Exodus (Num. 33:38). The concluding passages contain edicts issued to Israelites in the Plains of Moab east of the Jordan.

Geographically and chronologically, the book's material falls into five main sections:

Numbers 1:1–10:10	This section purports to deal with the departure from Sinai but actually contains supplements and appendices to the Priestly Code in Leviticus. At the heart of it is the census list (chapters 1–4). A second list appears in chapter 26.
Numbers 10:11–21:35	The wanderings in the wilderness from Mount Sinai to Kadesh-barnea, a period of about forty years.
Numbers 22:1–24:25	Balaam blesses Israel.
Numbers 25:1–33:49	The encampments and journeys in the wilderness and the Plains of Moab, including the recurrent themes of the danger of and rejection of idolatry.
Numbers 33:50–36:13	Miscellaneous laws; Levitical cities and female inheritance.

To be properly appreciated, the book's bewildering contents must be read for what they are, a miscellany of itineraries, lists, laws, and traditions that later editors preserved as part of the heritage of a past too distant to be distinct, but too vital to be forgotten. As we shall see, much of this material retains valuable information concerning the "setting-in-life" of certain historical events culminating in the conquest of Transjordan.

Netting quail on the northern shore of Sinai; after their flight over the sea, the birds fall exhausted into the nets

1. THE ASCETIC NAZIRITES

The law in Numbers 6:1–19 codifies a very ancient custom and adapts it to the Levitical (late priestly) ritual. To signify his special status as one dedicated to the service of God from birth, the Nazirite is separated from the world and its ways and adopts the ascetic vows of abstaining from all intoxicating drinks and leaving his hair unshaven. Nazirite vows could also be taken for briefer periods and specific occasions. There are historical reminiscences of actual Nazirites in the stories of Samson (Judges 13–16) and Samuel (1 Samuel 1).

Recent excavations conducted on Mount Scopus have uncovered an ornate tomb of a Nazirite dating to the last century B.C. or the first century A.D. This discovery shows that, by the end of the Old Testament period, a Nazirite was not necessarily a poor man who renounced worldly possessions. Nevertheless the tradition of pious poverty is preserved in early Christian writings; for example, James, brother of Jesus, was a pious Nazirite. The term must not be confused with "Nazarean," Hebrew *notsri*, meaning a citizen of Nazareth (also the Hebrew term for "Christian").

2. THE RED HEIFER

One of the most difficult passages in the priestly source describes the ritual of the ashes of the Red Heifer (Num. 19:2–10), which are used to prepare "the water of impurity, for the removal of sin" (verse 9). The rite originally was pagan and involved magical elements in putting evil spirits to flight: for example, the use of red as a protective color and the sevenfold sprinkling of blood, with its vital powers.

This ritual maintained its importance in the days of the Second Temple and is often mentioned in the Mishna and the Talmud in connection with the observances on the eve of the Day of Atonement, when the red heifer was taken out of the Temple courts and slain on the Mount of Olives, then burned with cedarwood, hyssop, and scarlet material. B. Mazar, in his excavations near the Temple Mount, investigated the whereabouts of the special path that led from the high Temple courts to the steep valley of Kidron and then up to the Mount of Olives. He noted, however, "that the purification rite of the Red Heifer was performed only five times throughout the whole period of the Second Temple, though the reason for its rarity is unknown. It is not likely that a permanent pathway had been constructed for these occasional rites; a temporary pathway was doubtless prepared for each occasion, and in the nature of the case, no evidence of it has survived" (B. Mazar, *The Mountain of the Lord*, p. 151).

3. ISRAEL AND MIDIAN

The Midianites, who later became enemies of Israel, played a vital role in Israel's earliest history. According to the tradition Yahweh first revealed himself to Moses in the land of Midian (Exodus 3), Moses was married to a Midianite woman (Exod. 2:21–22), and Israel's legal system was initiated with the help of Jethro, the Midianite priest (Exod. 18:13–27). According to Numbers 10:29–32, Moses requested the guidance of Hobab, a relative of Jethro, to lead Israel through the wilderness. This tradition has the ring of authenticity, for the Israelites were state slaves in Egypt, not seasoned veterans established in their own land like the Midianites. The latter were also involved in the earliest traditions of the priesthood and ritual known to Israel and were intermarried with clansmen of Judah and Simeon from the days of wandering onward. W. F. Albright has pointed out that the Midianites, the Kenites, who stemmed from Midian, and the ancestors of

Crushing enclosure for copper ore at ancient Timnah mining camp

Ore-grinding and crushing tools, Timnah

the Israelites belonged to the same or related groups. B. Mazar believes that the Midianites had established a sanctuary at Arad at the time the Israelites were settling in Canaan and that it was maintained later by the Israelites, reflecting a close relationship between the two groups. This is where the tenth century Judaean sanctuary and altar were discovered. A writhing serpent made of copper, five inches long, was found among hundreds of votice objects that had been brought to the Timnah sanctuary. This serpent is reminiscent of the account of a plague of poisonous snakes in Numbers 21:9. The ancient narrative would seem to imply that the copper snake that Moses raised on a pole had curative and cultic power, similar to that found in neighboring cultures.

4. WHENCE CAME THE MIDIANITES?

Midianite decorated pottery, such as that discovered in the metallurgical district of Timnah, had previously been found in smelting camps of the western Arabah valley and on the island of Fara'un (or Coral Island) in the northern part of the Red Sea, as well as in sites of the eastern Arabah and Edom; N. Glueck dated it to the thirteenth to twelfth centuries and called it Edomite ware. There is good archaeological evidence for its origin in northwestern Arabia, in the area traditionally known as Midian some hundred miles south of Elath-'Aqaba. A survey of Midian (1970) describes the site of a kiln at Qurrayah where the Midianite wheel-made decorated pottery had been produced, according to P. Parr. The Timnah pottery that originated in Midian provides the first solid dates for the Late Bronze sedentary and semisedentary sites of Midian, the seat of a Midianite civilization that expanded further north and inseminated early Israel.

5. THE SONG OF THE WELL

An interesting fragment from a poem, perhaps Moabite, appears in Numbers 21:17–18, though it is attributed to Israel:

> Spring up, O well—Sing to it!—
> Well which the princes dug,
> which the leaders of the people hollowed out,
> with their staff and their sticks.

This song, although we have only the opening lines, is among the oldest poetry in the Hebrew Bible, along with the Oracles of Balaam in chapters 23–24. Its setting and meaning are clarified by an understanding of the nature of the soil in the wilderness. In low-lying areas of Transjordan and in the valleys of the Negeb, one comes suddenly upon damp land in very dry surroundings, at times marked by clumps of vegetation. Such a place is known to the Arabs as a *temileh*. The earth can be dug easily and water is found at a shallow depth. This is the kind of well dug by the ancients "with their sticks."

6. THE BALAAM STORY

The narratives concerning Balaam (Numbers 22–24) contain four poems (23:7–10, 18–24; 24:3–9, 15–24) that were the basis of one of W. F. Albright's pioneering studies in early Hebrew poetry. Balaam was a seer from Pethor, south of Carchemish near the Euphrates, who was invited by the king of Moab to cast a curse on Israel, but found that he was able only to bless it. Albright explains the historical background as follows: The people of Moab and Midian invited the famous diviner to curse Israel, but he declined their offer and advised the Moabites and Midianites instead to make a covenant with Israel. They agreed to make the pact, which embodied matters relating to intermarriage and to syncretic religious observances that both the Israelites and their pagan neighbors could observe in amity. But some unyielding Israelites refused to compromise, regarding it as a prostitution of the sacred traditions and as blatant paganism; the plan miscarried and resulted in hostility between Israel and Midian.

7. THE DEIR 'ALLAH INSCRIPTIONS

J. Hoftijzer reports (1975) an astounding discovery of a dozen or so inscribed plaster panels that fell off the walls of a ruined Late Bronze temple at Deir 'Allah (biblical Succoth) near the Jordan river, in central Transjordan. Two or three of these short inscriptions, written in so-called

Ceramic receptacle found in the Deir 'Allah sanctuary inscribed with name of the Egyptian queen Tausert (1205–1194 B.C.)

One of the clay panels of Deir 'Allah sanctuary inscribed in an obscure script (end of 13th, or early 12th c. B.C.)

cursive Aramaic script in black and red ink, and couched in poetic style, purport—according to this Dutch scholar—to give an independent narrative of the prophecies of Balaam, his visions and experiences. The panels themselves date to the eighth to seventh centuries B.C.; the temple was destroyed by earthquake and fire. Hoftijzer believes that Balaam, named "seer of the gods" in the panels, enjoyed for a considerable time a prominent position in some specific religious tradition in Transjordan. Moreover, this is the first instance of a nonbiblical prophecy located in Transjordan. It will be noted that Balaam in the biblical text clearly belongs to an ancient tradition from Transjordan, and that the inscriptions discovered, in which he is presumed to play a central role, came from a Transjordanian sacred site. The biblical tradition relates that this non-Israelite prophet had been summoned to the locality by the king of Moab. The panels are currently being deciphered and analyzed by biblical scholars. Much more is yet to be learned from this discovery, and further elucidation may be expected.

8. THE LAND OF SHUTU AND ARCHAEOLOGY

There is reference in the fourth oracle (24:17) to the "sons of Sheth," who appear in poetic parallelism with Moab; these apparently are the tribe of Shutu known from Egyptian sources, which list three of its rulers. It is probable, according to Y. Aharoni and B. Mazar, that the land of Shutu is the ancient name for Gilead and the land of the Cushites, who appear along with Midian in Habakkuk 3:7. Evidently these passages preserve the names of the ancient population in these regions. Evidence from archaeolo-

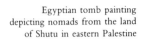
gy indicates that Gilead, southern Transjordan, and the Negeb did not have extensive settled populations in the later centuries of the Middle Bronze Age and in the Late Bronze Age. This area must then have been the homeland of nomadic tribes, such as Sheth (Shutu) and Cush, who have left few traces easily identifiable after 3000 years.

The picture of a caravan of Semites arriving in Egypt, perhaps via the King's Highway, is preserved in a wall painting from the early nineteenth century B.C. Egyptian tomb painting at Beni-Hasan. It depicts thirty-seven "Ammu Asiatics from the land of Shutu" (apparently Gilead in Transjordan) who are delivering black eye paint to Egypt. Their leader is named Ibsha, and he bears the Egyptian title "ruler of a foreign country."

But archaeology reveals, on the other hand, that somewhat later Egyptian sources from the days of Rameses II (early thirteenth century) describe strenuous campaigns that he led in the lands of the Shosu (Sheth), including Mount Seir (later Edom), and the destruction of many settlements. A contemporary Egyptian inscription from Luxor relates the capture of several walled cities, including Boterat along the King's Highway in southern Moab.

9. THE STELE OF BALUA

The stele featuring three figures discovered south of the Arnon river along the ancient highway is another Moabite remnant of sedentary occupation dating from the thirteenth century. Its mysterious inscription has not yet been deciphered, but that is also the case of other Transjordan inscriptions before the Canaanite-Hebrew alphabet prevailed. Finally, a temple of the late Canaanite period (thirteenth century), discovered by J. B. Hennessy at Amman, provides the first extensive corpus of pottery, local and imported, of that period, in the highlands crossed by the King's Highway. The existence of fortified cities there does not argue for the absence of sedentary settlements during the period, but neither does it provide definite evidence of the establishment of the kingdoms of Moab, Ammon, or Edom as early as the thirteenth century B.C.

The stele of Balua is a remnant of sedentary occupation in Moab in the 13th c. B.C.

Israelites, under the leadership of first Moses, then Joshua, effected the Conquest in stages and by various routes as suggested by different biblical traditions, namely Numbers 13; 14:44–45; 20:14ff.; 21:4–27; 33; 34:1–12. The time span, however, was not limited to a single generation, or just over forty years, as required by the biblical chronology. At different times, Israelites marched out of the oasis of Kadesh-barnea on the northern bor-

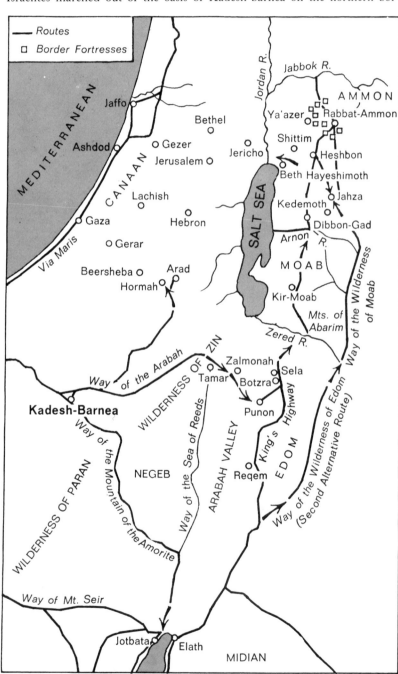

From their base at Kadesh-barnea, the Israelites invaded Transjordan by two different routes: First, in the late 14th or early 13th century B.C., by the Way of the Arabah and King's Highway, through territories later occupied by the kingdoms of Edom, Moab, and Ammon. A second invasion in the 13th century followed the roundabout route that controlled the Negeb via Elath and finally ended in eastern Transjordan. A former attempt to reach Canaan directly had failed. The land of Canaan was invaded later by groups of Israelite tribes. The final stage is described in the map

der of Sinai; but the course of conquest was far more complex than is indicated in the summary statements. It lasted from the fourteenth to the middle of the twelfth century B.C., as becomes evident from recent research.

a. *Two Routes from Kadesh-barnea to the Jordan*

A plausible reconstruction of the sequence of events follows:

1. Two traditions in Numbers preserve memories of journeys eastward and attempts to penetrate the less populated areas of Transjordan. One from chapter 33 lists a series of stations and settlements on the "Way of the Arabah" and the King's Highway, from Kadesh-barnea to the "plains of Moab." They crossed the areas of Edom and Moab and faced the Jordan on the east before these kingdoms, not to speak of that of the Ammonites, were organized by peoples culturally and linguistically related to the Israelites, and before they could offer any opposition. This movement may have occurred in the late fourteenth or early thirteenth century B.C. when the Israelites settled down in their camp at Abel-Shittim in the plains of Moab, after fighting the Midianites. In any case, the southern and sparsely populated portions of Transjordan, which were outside Egypt's sphere of control, served as the first objective for entry and conquest. Numbers 33:37–49 reflects the earliest traditions of various tribes that invaded Transjordan. (See map.)

2. The second invasion (Numbers 20:14ff.; Judges 11:17–18) occurred in mid-thirteenth century. When the Israelites encountered the opposition of the kings of Edom and Moab, who did not let them proceed along the King's Highway, they went up by way of a roundabout desert route (Numbers 21:4) that led south to Elath, then wound around the whole Negeb and continued through the wilderness east of Transjordan. The

Canaan remained within Egypt's sphere of control in the 14th century as is evidenced by Sethos I's punitive campaigns described in the reliefs from Karnak. In the upper register the king walks behind his chariot, carries prisoners under his arms, and leads rows of bound captives from Canaan. The lower register shows him returning to Egypt with captive *Shosu* nomads while he is met by officials at the border fortress of Sileh

A limestone figure of a king of Moab, or a deity, found in Amman; probably 10–9th c. B.C.

The seal of Adoni-nur the Ammonite

journey came to a halt away from the Jordan, between the kingdom of Moab and the new Ammonite state. There they were confronted by the forces of Sihon, the Amorite (Canaanite) king of Heshbon (21:21ff.), one of the few cities in Transjordan, and had to fight to make their way to the Jordan River. Sihon had extended his territory as far south as the Plains of Moab before the arrival of the Israelites, but the latter were victorious, and settled in the fertile areas of Gilead prior to their invasion of Canaan west of the Jordan. The tribe of Gad came in the first wave of Israelites, as attested in the Moabite Stone, a royal inscription of a later king of Moab, Mesha (ca. 850 B.C.): "The men of Gad had always dwelt in the land of Ataroth" as far as the river Jabbok. Another participant in the early invasion was Asher, full brother of Gad in the genealogies of Genesis. The biblical tradition goes on to relate the conquest of the land of Og, king of Bashan, and his sixty fortified cities (Deut. 3:5). The Amarna tablets refer to the presence of the 'Apiru in this area; while the equation of 'Apiru with Hebrew is not universally accepted, there may be some connection between the biblical traditions and the Amarna records concerning the earlier penetration of the 'Apiru into the territory. The different routes mentioned in the biblical stories and the archaeological evidence support the view that the Israelite Conquest was not carried out at one time, but over a period of time in several waves. These were later blended into the single narrative now preserved in the Bible.

The establishment of well-organized kingdoms in Edom and Moab during the thirteenth century, and in Ammon somewhat later, is abundantly attested by archaeology. The excavations in the copper mining settlements in the southern Arabah (north of Elath) show a peak of activity between the thirteenth and twelfth centuries B.C.; the high level of material culture they had reached by then is exemplified by a special type of decorated Edomite pottery. This illuminates the biblical traditions of the "border of Edom" in Numbers 20:14ff. and Deuteronomy 2:4ff. It also serves to explain Solomon's great interest in the area three centuries later, and his continuing efforts to exploit the possibilities of the Negeb and the Arabah and to stimulate trade with other wealthy population centers of the Arabian peninsula, such as Sheba.

b. *The Battle of Arad*

An attempt to invade the hill country of Judah from Kadesh-barnea was made early in the thirteenth century B.C., but it failed to penetrate the chain of fortified Canaanite cities in the Negeb. The Israelites were driven back by the king of Arad at nearby Hormah (Tell el-Meshash). Excavations at both of these towns have yielded no evidence of Israelite occupation for the next century and a half.

11. STAGES OF THE CONQUEST

We have come to realize from the assessments of the previous chapters that the traditional biblical picture of the wanderings of the pastoral patri-

archal clan in Canaan, followed by centuries of bondage in Egypt, does not jibe with the irrefutable historical and archaeological data of the Middle and Late Bronze Ages in Canaan or Egypt. Moreover, no extrabiblical references mention the existence of the Israelites in Egypt, Sinai, or Canaan if we except the references to 'Apiru (Habiru), who are not considered the biblical ancestors of the Hebrews, in the fifteenth or fourteenth centuries. But the Israelites were moving into Transjordan and Canaan and settling there from the early thirteenth century B.C., as indicated in Numbers, then in Joshua and Judges, but in different stages and at different times, unlike the consolidated biblical accounts. Moreover, the persistent and dynamic settlement of Israelites in Canaan in the thirteenth and twelfth centuries was no isolated phenomenon. It followed considerable 'Apiru agitation against the Egyptian and Canaanite feudal kings, and it is related to a great wave of Aramaean tribes exerting pressure on all the lands, from settlements in western Mesopotamia and northern Syria expanding into these areas all the way to the Jordan. The Edomites, Moabites, and Ammonites settled east of the Jordan in about the same period. The Israelite tribal migrations were activated by these broad moves, by the weakening of Egyptian power both in Goshen and Canaan, and finally by the concurrent invasion of the Sea Peoples (Philistines) of the coastland and western lowlands of Canaan. All of this hastened the process of settlement and occupation. In any case, the process was not the concerted plan of the whole federation of tribes under one chief, Joshua, but the achievement of isolated Israelite tribes or groups of tribes over a long period of time, as may be gathered from Judges.

Canaanite vassals in their typical ceremonial dress bringing tribute to the XVIII Dynasty Pharaonic court

E. DEUTERONOMY

The book of Deuteronomy, as we have it, is almost entirely from the hand of the Deuteronomist, the D source (see Introduction: The Documentary Hypothesis), whose editing is dated apparently to the end of the monarchial period. Much of the material the Deuteronomist incorporated, however, derives from Exodus and the older traditions that reflect the premonarchial period. What distinguishes this book from the rest of the Pentateuch is not so much its content, but its style. Unlike the Covenant Code where laws are succinctly stated in either "apodictic" or "casuistic" form, in Deuteronomy these laws are expanded with sermons or exhortations. These sermons are composed in long, complex sentences, often containing parenthetical remarks.

The book may be divided into four sections, as follows:

Deuteronomy 1:1–11:32	Introductory speeches that review the wanderings in the desert, the conquest of Transjordan, the meaning of the Law; then a preview of the Conquest of the country west of the Jordan. These discourses underscore the fundamental principles upon which the Law and the Covenant are based and call on the people to remain faithful to Yahweh and his Law.
Deut. 12:1–26:15	The Deuteronomic Code. This section lists some seventy laws pertaining to every aspect of the life of Israel in the promised land.
Deut 27:1–30:20	Closing speeches. At the heart of this section are blessings and curses, a blessing for those who are obedient to God and his Covenant, a curse upon those who are unfaithful.
Deut 31:1–34:12	The conclusion to the Pentateuch, including the appointment of Joshua, the "Song of Moses" (chapter 32), the "Blessing of Moses" (chapter 33). The last chapter tells of the death of Moses.

1. THE DEUTERONOMIC CODE

It has long been recognized that almost half of the laws of the Covenant Code (Exodus 21–23) reappear in Deuteronomy, though in modified form. It has been suggested that the new code of a later date was intended to replace the older laws, taking into account the social, political, and religious development that had taken place between the early centuries of settlement and the seventh century B.C. However, this hypothesis does not establish an adequate principle of selectivity governing the Deuteronomist's treatment of the older source. No explanation is given as to why the greater part of the Covenant Code was not incorporated into the book of Deuteronomy. It is possible that the Deuteronomist regarded those provisions as obsolete or no longer pertinent to existing conditions. Lacking this material, the Deuteronomic Code would have been an inadequate substitute for the earlier legislation. It is probably better to see both as being rooted in the same ancient traditions.

M. Weinfeld, a leading authority on Deuteronomy, points out that its fundamental distinction is not so much in the legislation it embodies, but in its characteristic homiletic style. One of the points of departure from the earlier legislation is the Deuteronomist's passion for social justice. This is particularly clear in the book's emphasis on the release of debtors and slaves. This quality is commonly attributed to the influence of the prophets. M. Weinfeld and S. Sandmel have found another source of this humanism in the "wisdom" circles that produced Proverbs and Job. Thus the Deuteronomist's work blends law, wisdom, and prophetic concern.

2. THE ALTAR OF SACRIFICE AND THE *BAMAH*

One of the most important innovations in Deuteronomy is the centralization of sacrifice ordained in the opening chapter of the Deuteronomic Code (Deuteronomy 12). This law reflects the religious reforms of King Josiah, which sought to neutralize the influence of Canaanite religion upon the people. The requirement runs counter to earlier Israelite practice, as the author recognized (verse 8) and as clearly established by archaeology.

Altars were the focal point of both high places, *bamoth,* and temples. The *bamoth* were essentially Canaanite sites of worship, but were acceptable also in earlier Israelite religion. They were usually open areas, with sacred trees and stone pillars, *masseboth,* associated with the altar, as well as buildings for the use of priests and the storage of garments and other equipment. These high places were often linked with sites of importance from the patriarchal period. The altars recently excavated at Arad and Beersheba in the Southern Kingdom probably belong to this category. Altars also were erected in conjunction with royal sanctuaries, such as those of Jeroboam of Northern Israel at Dan and Bethel.

The simplest altars were made of heaped earth or stones; a large, flat rock, often with natural or carved depressions at the top, could serve as an altar. These stones were not to be hewn, as the use of iron would defile the stone. More elaborate altars, despite the prohibition of steps in Exodus 20:26 (cf. Lev. 6:10), were built in tiers, though most were simply large cubes, such as the bronze altar of Solomon's Temple (2 Chron. 4:1), which measured twenty cubits long, twenty cubits wide, and ten cubits high. Other altars were made of hewn stone and provided with horns, as is the case with the large altar discovered at Beersheba and the numerous smaller incense altars that have turned up in excavations.

Seal ring depicting "Abomination" of Canaanite witchcraft (see Deut. 7:26)

3. MAGIC AND WITCHCRAFT

Although magic and witchcraft were practiced throughout the ancient world, in Israel they were forbidden by a law attributed to Moses (Deut. 18:10–14). While archaeological traces of the practice of witchcraft have been found in abundance in excavations in other Near Eastern countries, there is also evidence of certain superstitious practices among the Israelites. These include vessels impressed with snakes, fertility figurines to help in pregnancy or childbirth, and amulets and charms worn by women and children. The use of amulets was widespread and apparently persistent, although they were condemned by kings, lawmakers, priests, and prophets, as they involved trust in gods other than Yahweh. An amulet against night demons has been unearthed, dating to the period of the Monarchy. Archaeology has also uncovered other Canaanite fertility symbols that were used in Israel. Several Hathor-Ashtoreth figurines came from Israelite Gezer, and nearly two hundred of these objects were found in eighth century levels at Samaria. Indeed, almost every major excavation in Israel has produced numerous hand-size plaques depicting the nude fertility goddess, dating from the Bronze and Iron Ages to as late as the sixth century B.C.

One of the items in the list of women's finery in Isaiah 3:18–23 is an amulet or humming shell (*lahash*), which may have been connected with snake charming. Snake-deities are known to have been widely worshiped by the Canaanites and many vessels engraved or impressed with snakes have been discovered in excavations of levels dating to the Canaanite and Israelite periods. Bronze serpents were found in the Canaanite levels at Hazor, Megiddo, Gezer, and Shechem, and serpent-symbols have turned up in significant numbers in the Iron Age levels at Gezer, Beth-shean, Megiddo, and Tell en-Nasbeh. We have referred above to the tradition of Numbers 21:9 about Moses and the bronze serpent.

A *pazuzu* demon common in Mesopotamian witchcraft

PART III

A. THE BOOKS OF JOSHUA AND JUDGES

The book of Deuteronomy ends with the death of Moses, and the scribes and theologians responsible for the final ordering of the Hebrew Bible felt that this distinctive event marked the end of an era. They thus ended the Torah at that point. Working from the evidence of composition, we can safely say that this judgment was not a literary or historical one. Joshua, the sixth book of the Bible, is inseparable from the Pentateuch in outlook. On the one hand, its story line is directly connected to that of Numbers, chiefly chapter 33, which describes the first stage of the conquest of Transjordan; on the other, its world view is one with Deuteronomy's (cf. Deut. 29:8 and Josh. 1:8). More generally, the Pentateuch points forward to the promised possession of Canaan, and Joshua's book depicts the fulfillment of the promise. The editors of Joshua were motivated by the idea expressed repeatedly in Deuteronomy: God's presence in history is a palpable one.

As we shall often have occasion to remark, the historical matter in the Bible is not offered as a straightforward, mechanical record of the facts, but rather as an interpretation of them. Difficulties with the story of the Conquest in Joshua do not arise because the biblical tradition is obscurantist. Quite the contrary—they exist because the tradition was constantly seeking to understand and thus reinterpret itself. The narrative of Joshua may leave something to be desired as objective history-writing; nonetheless, it contains important factual data and its intrinsic value can hardly be questioned.

1. THE STORY OF THE BOOK OF JOSHUA

The book of Joshua is the epic story of its chief character's leadership of Israel. It begins with his divine call and ends with his death; the story of the Conquest is thus tightly bound up with Joshua's life.

According to tradition, Joshua crossed the river Jordan and captured the town of Jericho after the miraculous destruction of its walls (chapters 2–6). Recent excavations at Jericho have shown that the town was not occupied in Joshua's time. A close reading of the biblical text will reveal that the story itself is somewhat garbled. These two facts suggest at the outset that the Conquest as presented in Joshua is a literary reinterpretation of events the complexity of which later Israelites were unable to grasp fully. From Jericho, Joshua went on to capture Ai, thereby gaining a foothold in the central highlands (chapters 7–8). Joshua then moved into Judah (chapters 9–10) and Galilee (chapter 11), establishing Israelite enclaves throughout Canaan under his own leadership, within the first generation after Moses. Thus far are chapters 2 through 12; in chapters 13 through 22, the conquered territory is divided among the Israelite tribes.

The book ends with the solemn convocations at Shechem, where the Ark of the Covenant is established in the sanctuary, and with Joshua's farewell addresses (chapters 23–24).

2. AN UNCOMPLETED CONQUEST

Two significant sections in the book provide evidence that tends to correct, on the eve of Joshua's demise, the former picture of his sweeping conquest covering the whole land from Dan to Beersheba. One is the first verse of chapter 13, specifying that "there remains yet very much land to be possessed. This is the land that yet remains" either in Canaanite or Philistine possession. Furthermore, the opening chapter of Judges lumps together as a unit the various districts still unconquered by Joshua but which should be conquered and then divided among the tribes. In fact these territories are considered as already allotted piece by piece in Joshua 15–19. These conflicting statements are not deliberate falsifications but reflect different views of the Israelite settlement of the promised land; nor do we regard the book of Joshua as a work of fiction. Many stages of the Conquest are described realistically: the details of battle strategy and execution reveal an intimate and detailed knowledge of the area and times. It may be deduced, therefore, that the Israelite historiographer handed to posterity a *consolidated* biblical tradition. Recognition of the composite nature of the biblical record and the discoveries of archaeology, including epigraphic finds, oblige the historian to examine anew the biblical text and rethink its sequence, in order to disentangle the factual elements, that is, to determine which statements and data are part of an earlier tradition and which are of a later tradition. A classic example: The conquest of Hebron and Debir, originally by Caleb and Kenaz (Josh. 15:15; Judg. 1:12–15), was associated later with Judah (Judg. 1:10–11), then finally with Joshua leading all Israel (Josh. 10:36–39).

At this juncture, it must be pointed out, first, that the contents of Joshua must be read in conjunction with the book of Judges, which corrects sweeping generalizations and idealizations of fact. Traditions centered around Joshua were recorded in the book after his name, while traditions relating to the tribes were gathered in the book of Judges. Secondly, the two books, considered together as combined historical background material, are readily illumined by archaeological data and ancient nonbiblical epigraphic documents. What then was the sequence of events?

3. THE BOOK OF JUDGES

The first two chapters of the book of Judges list those territories conquered after Joshua's death as well as those that proved resistant to Israelite penetration. The bulk of the book (chapters 3–16) describes the exploits of local leaders who defended certain parts of the country against incursions of Israel's neighbors. The various wars described, except for the Song

of Deborah (chapter 5; compare the prose account in chapter 4), are local affairs limited to particular geographical regions, usually associated with only one tribal territory. These traditions culminate in the great Samson cycle.

Canaanite chariot-riding knights (*maryannu*) and foot soldiers. 13th-c. ivory carving from Megiddo

Major and Minor Judges: The framework of the book of Judges is later than its contents and seems to accord equal significance to all the judges. In fact, the actual traditions about the mighty deeds of the minor judges, Shamgar, Jair, Tola', Ibzan, Elon and Abdon, have not been preserved; it is only stated that they judged the people at a certain locality or, alternately, their wealth is emphasized (Judg. 10:4; 12:9, 14). Even the major judges, Othniel, Ehud, Deborah, Gideon, Jephthah and Samson, vary greatly in importance.

Sea Peoples invading Canaan by land

B. THE BIBLICAL TRADITION AND ACTUAL HISTORY OF THE CONQUEST IN THE THIRTEENTH CENTURY B.C.

The invasion of Canaan after the death of Moses, as related in the book of Joshua, began at Gilgal, the first Israelite camp and sanctuary west of the Jordan, and was followed by the capture of Jericho and Ai. Thereafter the book gives the picture of a rapid systematic conquest of the whole of western Palestine (Canaan). It is widely recognized that the Joshua narrative greatly oversimplifies matters and telescopes both time and circumstances to make it appear that all Israel under the single leadership of Joshua achieved the conquest of Canaan in a single generation (40 years). At the same time the basic tradition of violent conflict and many details have been confirmed by archaeological discovery. It is possible to recognize the data and reorder the sequence of events on the basis of careful attention to the biblical text and the archaeological evidence.

The stories of the capture of Jericho and Ai contain many legendary features, especially the sudden collapse of the walls of the former, when considered from a rigorous historical point of view. The capture of the two cities during this period has not been confirmed archaeologically. Jericho had lain in ruins for more than a century before the arrival of the Israelites, while the case with Ai is much worse. That city had been destroyed and abandoned in the Early Bronze Age a thousand years before Joshua. Many scholars believe that the tradition of Joshua 8:1–29 may relate to a small, unfortified village established at et-Tell on the acropolis of the Early Bronze city during Iron Age I (ca. 1200 B.C.) and that this site was biblical Ai. The men of Ai may have been the first inhabitants of the Iron Age village. However, Bethel appears to be one of the first Canaanite cities to be conquered in the mountains of Ephraim. It was destroyed toward the end of the thirteenth century (Judg. 1:22–26) as confirmed by archaeological excavation at the site.

1. THE CONQUEST

Abject humiliation of a defeated chief and his followers who are brought before the ruler amid celebration and music. Ivory carving from Megiddo

The complete picture of the gradual conquest and settlement of Canaan—the principal penetration took place in the early part of the thir-

An Israelite Iron Age house in
the new village built over
ancient Ai, with benches
constructed along the walls

The Lachish high place or
bamah, dating to the 13th c. and
consisting of the altar platform
and benches for offerings

teenth century—emerges from a process of combination and reconstruction
of events described in the books of Joshua and Judges. Although in the
present arrangement the narratives in the two books are sequential, actually they overlap, and together they describe the same general circumstances
from different points of view. Thus the account of the conquests of
Joshua, which were limited in extent, is only part of the picture and must
be supplemented by the stories of the incursions of the clans of Caleb,
Kenaz, and Judah (Josh. 15:13–14; Judg. 1:12–15), as well as by other
events in the saga of the settlement of the land. In the process of transmission and compilation, major traditions relating to the Conquest were consolidated around a nucleus of authentic data concerning Joshua, resulting
in the basic account of unitary invasion and overwhelming victory under
his aegis in the book of Joshua. Other accounts, including the exploits of
the separate tribes and of individual leaders, were collected in the book of
Judges, to be regarded as supplemental and subsequent to the main account. These fragmentary accounts of tribal activities in the early period of
settlement, found in the opening chapter of Judges, nevertheless have high

71

Ivory carving of a Canaanite
woman; from the Megiddo
treasury

Clay statuette of a Canaanite

historical value and require the most careful consideration in any reconstruction of the actual course of events. Certainly they convey a more realistic picture of what happened than the conventionalized military sweep portrayed in the book of Joshua. Archaeological excavations provide another mass of information bearing on the history of this period, sometimes confirming, sometimes challenging the tradition, sometimes shedding light on the circumstances and clarifying puzzling situations, sometimes raising new questions and posing problems to which new answers must be found.

On the basis of the extensive evidence for this period unearthed at numerous sites during the past decades, both scholarly analysis and synthesis have progressed to the point of providing a plausible and satisfying reconstruction of the sequence of events and the dates, or at least the chronological range, of their occurrence. Consideration of some of the more significant artifacts and the pertinent information on the date of the Conquest to be derived from them follows.

One of the most important of these consists of a clay bowl found in the destruction debris of the last Late Bronze city of Lachish. It bears an Egyptian inscription, including a date, the fourth year of an unnamed pharaoh. On the basis of typological and stratigraphic considerations, the bowl and the inscription must be dated in the later part of the thirteenth century; hence the most likely attribution is to the reign of Merneptah (ca. 1236–1223 B.C.), who is known to have conducted a military campaign in Palestine, or at least to have made the claim. This pinpoints the destruction of Lachish after 1233, perhaps a generation after the main Israelite invasion in the mid-thirteenth century. Excavations carried out at Lachish, Tell Beit Mirsim (Debir), and Tell el-Hesi (Eglon), have demonstrated that these cities suffered total destruction during the same period, at the end of the Late Bronze Age.

2. THE MERNEPTAH STELE

Another vital source of information is the stele erected by Merneptah (Nineteenth Egyptian Dynasty) at Karnak in the fifth year of his reign, ca. 1232 B.C. He boasts of many victories in the general area, specifically citing Israel, whom he claims he "laid waste, his seed is not." This is the first time the name Israel appears outside the Bible; here it is the designation of a people, though precisely what its composition or its structure was cannot be determined. Moreover, it provides us with a demarcation between the first and second waves of Israelite penetration in the thirteenth century. By then the Joseph tribes had moved into the area, taking some territory by force, but also establishing peaceful relations with key cities of that region such as Shechem, Tirzah, and Tappuah. The two peoples intermingled and shared in cultural and military alliances, even entering into formal treaties. We may find here an explanation of the fact that such cities as Shechem were not the target of Israelite attack at the time of the Conquest. Such a powerful concentration of forces in Canaan may have represented a threat to Egyptian suzerainty and prompted Merneptah to punish both the rebellious Canaanite cities and Israelite enclaves. This was presumably Egypt's last serious attempt to reclaim or capture lost territory in Asia; Merneptah's punitive raid probably stalled, for a time, the progress of the Joseph tribes in gaining control of their territory.

3. WAVES OF CONQUEST

a. *The House of Joseph*

The House of Joseph, including the tribes of Ephraim, Manasseh, and Benjamin, had penetrated the hill country in central Canaan by the thirteenth century B.C. and settled there permanently. This was followed several years later by the battle over Gibeon in the Benjamin area, between the Israelite tribes led by Joshua and a league of five Canaanite cities of the hill country, among them Lachish and Eglon, led by the king of Jerusalem. The flight of the Canaanites over the steep ascent of Beth Horon was recalled in a vivid figure preserved in an ancient corpus of Israelite poetry, the lost "Book of Jashar"; a brief extract from the victory ode is quoted in Joshua 10:12–13. This remarkable episode and the extraordinary role ascribed to Joshua probably constitute the nucleus of the tradition about his leadership, around which the historiographers of Israel then wove the whole story of conquest. Jerusalem itself fell after a short time into the hands of the Jebusites who held it for about two centuries until the time of David.

b. *Judah and Allied Southern Tribes*

The House of Joseph did not reap the fruits of this first victory over the Canaanite league. It was Judah and the other Leah tribes allied with it who gained the benefit. They apparently belonged to the later group that entered Canaan about the middle of the thirteenth century, as described in Judges 1:1–20. Moving down from the north, they captured Jerusalem, then relinquished it and gained a foothold in the hill country of Judah. The tribe of Simeon moved south and occupied Beersheba and Canaanite Hormah (Tell el-Meshash). At approximately the same time, the southern clans of Caleb and Kenaz settled in the region of Hebron and Debir, while the Kenite clans moved north to occupy the area of Arad where they established a sanctuary.

As Egyptian power waned toward the end of the thirteenth century, the southern Israelite tribes expanded into the Shephelah, the foothills and

The Merneptah (1236–1223 B.C.) stele from Thebes that contains in line 27 the only mention of the name *Israel* in all Egyptian records

Canaanite charioteers in battle

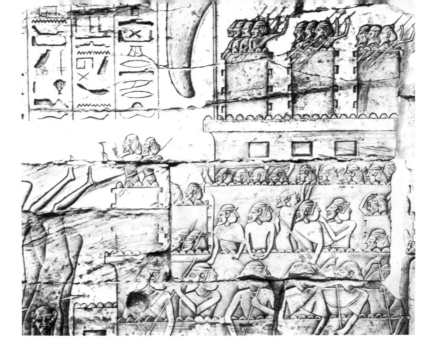

Battling over a fortified city in Canaan. Egyptain relief from Medinet Habu

the broad coastal plains, and defeated the Canaanite kings of Gezer, La-chish, and Makkedah (Joshua 15; follow the arrows on the left of the op-posite map.)

c. *The Conquest of Galilee*

Finally the other Leah tribes, along with Issachar, Zebulun, and Asher, who had moved from Transjordan during the first and second waves of invasions, separated from the main body and settled in various parts of Galilee and on the border of the remaining Canaanite cities of the north-ern coast (henceforth known as Phoenicia in accordance with Greek us-age). Archaeological evidence shows that the Israelites established themselves in the forested hill country and flourished from the beginning of the Iron Age (ca. 1200 B.C.). Lacking chariotry, field weapons, and siege engines, however, they were not yet ready to pit their strength against the prosperous fortified Canaanite city-kingdoms around Hazor.

There are separate biblical accounts of two crucial campaigns in Galilee that resulted in the end of Canaanite power. One is found in Judges 4–5, and consists of a prose narrative (chapter 4) and the well-known Song of Deborah (chapter 5), which celebrate the victory of Deborah and Barak over the Canaanite forces led by Sisera in the Valley of Jezreel. The other is in Joshua 11 and describes the battle of Merom and the destruction of Hazor, the chief city of the region. Though the sources assume a lapse of time between the two campaigns, Joshua preceding Deborah by several generations, B. Mazar believes that they represent two stages in the same war; on the basis of the biblical and archaeological data, it is possible to reconstruct the episodes and set them in the proper historical framework. The bulk of the Israelite tribes, including the powerful Joseph group, joined with Naphtali, Zebulun, and Issachar, who had settled in Galilee and were hard pressed by the Canaanites, against a coalition of Canaanite

Conquests and Battles

Areas of Continuous Settlement

Canaanite Cities, Unconquered

Tyre
Abel-Beth-Maacah   Dan
Beth-Anath
DAN
Achzib   Kedesh
Beth-Shemesh
Merom
ASHER
Gat'n   Hazor
Acco   Ramah
Aphek   Kinnereth
NAPHTALI   Adamah
GESHUR
Achshaph   Kedesh   Aphek   Ashtarot
Hannathon
ZEBULON
Shimron   Kedesh
Dor   Jokne'am   ISSACHAR
Jarmuth
HAVOT YAIR
Megiddo   Kamon
Aron   Ta'anach   Beth-Shean
Ible'am   Phahel   Ham
Gath   Rehob   Ramoth-Gilead
Hepher   Bezek   Jabesh-Gilead
Tirzah   Abel-Meholah
Mahanaim
Penuel
Adam
Aphek   Zeredah   EPHRAIM   GAD
Japha   Betonim
Timnath-Serah   Rabbath-Ammon
Lod   Bethel   Ja'azer
Jabneel   Beth-Horon   Ai   Jericho
Gezer   Mizpah   Abel-Shittim
Aijalon   Be'eroth   Beth-Horon   Heshbon
ASHDOD   Beth-Hoglah   Beth-ha-Jeshimoth
Ekron   Zor'ah   Jerusalem   Medeba
Beth-Shemesh   Bethlehem
Ashkelon   Adullam   GAD
Libnah   JUDAH   Ataroth   Jahaza
Gaza   Eglon   Hebron   Kiriathaim   Dibbon
Debir   Ziph   Aro'er
Gerar   Carmel
Eshtemoa   MOAB
Raphia
Sharuhen   Beersheba   Arad   Kir-Moab
SIMEON   Hormah
Aro'er

MEDITERRANEAN

PHILISTIA

Carmel

AMMON

DEAD SEA

Zoar

EDOM

kings. Confident in their superiority in equipment (chariotry) and numbers, the Canaanites boldly advanced in the plain. At the foot of Mount Tabor, however, sudden rains produced a flash flood in the Kishon river, swamping the iron-wheeled chariots, whereupon the Israelites attacked and defeated the immobilized Canaanite army. It is possible that those who escaped from this debacle attempted to regroup around Hazor but were pursued by the Israelites at Merom (Joshua 11:1–13), which is identified with Marun-er-Ras in northern Galilee. The remnant of the Canaanite forces was destroyed there, leaving the city of Hazor open to assault; stripped of defenders it fell into the hands of the Israelite army.

The excavations of Hazor, the largest city in Canaan, demonstrate beyond question that it was destroyed around the end of the thirteenth century B.C. A new population, presumably Israelites who had lived in modest villages in Galilee, settled over the vast ruins, as indicated by the distinctive types of pottery. Moreover, the fall of Hazor serves as a chronological marker for the northern military campaigns, indicating that they took place during the interregnum between the Nineteenth and Twentieth Egyptian dynasties (roughly 1200 B.C.). The decline of Egyptian power had opened the way for the decisive wars between Israel and Canaan.

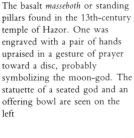

The basalt *masseboth* or standing pillars found in the 13th-century temple of Hazor. One was engraved with a pair of hands upraised in a gesture of prayer toward a disc, probably symbolizing the moon-god. The statuette of a seated god and an offering bowl are seen on the left

4. GRADUAL PROCESS OF SETTLEMENT DURING THE DAYS OF JUDGES

In the course of the twelfth century, in the period of the "Judges" (charismatic leaders of various tribes), the number and size of Israelite set-

tlements increased steadily, although the people lived in constant danger of invasion from without, and dissension and subversion from within. The biblical historian, appalled by the endless succession of near disasters, organized the traditional materials into a fixed moralizing pattern: When the Israelites were faithful to their God and obedient to his will, they were secure and prospered. When they rebelled against their Lord and quarreled among themselves, they fell prey to foreign invaders like the Moabites or Midianites, or finally to the Philistines, or local tyrants like Abimelech. In their distress and suffering, God took pity on them and raised up a deliverer, one of the Judges, who rescued them from their plight. Then for a while they enjoyed success and security, until they reneged on their obligations to God and the cycle of misfortune began again.

The Sanctuary of Baal-berith

History can survey developments of Judges 8–10 in terms of war and shifting boundaries, with an occasional glance at the details and circumstances that produced the changes. One especially significant sequence concerns the great charismatic judge, Gideon, who saved Israel at a moment of dire peril but was succeeded by a son, Abimelech, who brought ruin upon himself and near disaster to his people. He attempted to rule over all Israel after establishing a power base in Shechem. With his family connections and the memory of his father's great deeds, he was able to put together an alliance of Shechemites and Israelites centered around the sanctuary of Baal-berith, Lord of the Covenant. The remains of this temple-fort, called a *beth-millo* and built in the last phase of the Middle Bronze Age, were uncovered over the acropolis of Shechem. The great temple, 108 by 92 feet in size, had massive walls 18 feet thick and con-

The *beth-millo,* or platform, of the temple of Baal-berith (Lord of the Covenant) at Shechem with the great broken slab *massebah* re-erected in the forecourt. Two sockets for *masseboth* in the background (see arrows) marked the entrance to the most sacred area, where rituals were held

tained a large beaten-earth altar; its entrance was flanked by a pair of *masseboth* (sacred pillars). The city gates were originally of the triple type, consisting of parallel pairs of massive stone blocks. The temple had been reconstructed before the Israelite Conquest on a somewhat smaller scale; a huge *massebah* stood in front of the entrance. Shechem at this period (fourteenth century) is mentioned in the Amarna letters (see "Genesis"), when the ambitious Labayu ruled the district as an ally of the 'Apiru and a rebel against Egypt.

Shechem was destroyed after the Amarna Age, perhaps around 1300 B.C. Convincing evidence has been assembled by L. Toombs, one of the excavators of the site, to demonstrate this point. Whether this destruction can be associated with the traditions in Genesis 34 and 48:22 or should be attributed to a pharaoh of the Nineteenth Dynasty (Seti I or Rameses II) or some other invader, remains an open question. But there is no reason to doubt that from that time there were Israelites in or around the city. In any case these data provide the background of the story of Abimelech who was "made king by the terebinth [or oak] of the pillar at Shechem" (Judges 9:6), a sacred tree near the *masseboth*, after being supplied with money from the sanctuary of Baal-berith. Later, the Shechemites rebelled against Abimelech, who took revenge on them by razing the walls of the city. Many of the specific structures and places in the story have been identified by the excavators: the *beth-millo* with the ancient temple built on a platform (*millo*; Judges 9:20) associated with the terebinth of the pillar; the city gate with the fourteenth century east gate (Judges 9:35, 40,

44). The filling of pits beneath the temple with charcoal and early eleventh-century pottery supplies evidence of Abimelech's devastation of Shechem.

Finally, critical reading of the passages outlining the borders of the tribal territories in the book of Joshua (15–19) offers help in understanding the nature and gradual process of the Israelite occupation. The tribes settled first in the vicinity of the Canaanite cities; it was only at a later stage that the Canaanite centers fell into their hands. This is evident from the excavations at Bethel and the remains of Tappuah.

5. WERE THE TRIBAL TERRITORIES DIVIDED UP IN JOSHUA'S TIME?

Chapters 13 through 22 of Joshua detail the division and distribution of the whole land of Israel. While on the surface the scheme is a simple one, the text shows signs of editorial re-working, reflecting a long, complex history of development. This will also become apparent from the contradictions between the books of Joshua and Judges. The basis for the description is the administrative system in effect in the late period of Judges and early part of the Monarchy. This is most obvious from the fact that some of the land mentioned in the second part of the book was conquered not by Joshua, but by later Israelites.

A more accurate picture of Israel's land distribution and tenure at this time can be constructed from a critical evaluation of the text; rudiments of it are given in the map of Israelite settlement. Tribes and clans gradually established themselves in the shaded areas in the heartland of the country. Only after the long and often irregular process of preliminary settlement could firm territorial claims be made and ratified; the latter process generally required a strong central administration. It is only natural that the territorial boundaries of monarchial Israel of later centuries were projected back into Joshua's time, since those limits were the ultimate outcome of the exploits attributed to him, temporary fluctuations notwithstanding.

The more advanced stage of settlement, also accompanied by much insecurity, brings to an end one period of conquest and settlement and ushers in the traditional biblical *period of the Judges*. Actually, the periods of Joshua and Judges intertwine, as has been observed. In general the Hebrew tribal society infiltrated and broke down the Canaanite feudal system during the period of Joshua and Judges.

6. THE UNCONQUERED REGIONS

Two documents are preserved, however, that define the unconquered regions of historic Canaan:

(a) The list of some nineteen unconquered cities in Judges 1. They faithfully represent the historical situation during the later period of the Judges, namely the presence of several cities that separated Judah (and Jerusalem, then "Jebus") from the central part of Israel and a few cities on the coast, and those in the corridor (Megiddo, Beth-shean) that separated central and northern Israel. These cities appear in Judges 1, but for reasons explained above they are defined in the biblical tradition of Joshua 15 –19 as cities ordained for tribal inheritance (though the inheritance fell due closer to the time of the writing of the tradition, probably by an annalist of the court of David or Solomon.)

(b) The "land that yet remains" (Josh. 13:1 and Judg. 3:3; see map on p. 75). These areas were occupied in the south by the Philistines and in the north of Israel by the "Sidonians" (Phoenicians) and Aramaeans. All of them remained outside the limits of Israelite conquest, though a different outlook, reflected in later biblical traditions handed down in Numbers 34, regarded them as part of the land Yahweh promised Moses.

7. THE NEW PICTURE OF SETTLEMENT IN THE NEGEB

A new perspective on the settlement of the southern tribes, Judah, Simeon, and the allied Kenites (Midianites), in the eastern Negeb emerges from the excavations conducted by Y. Aharoni at Arad, Meshash, and Beersheba, as explained in the accompanying illustrations.

An Early Israelite Temple at Arad

One of the outstanding contributions was the discovery of an ancient temple at Arad in southern Israel. It stood on the grounds of an Israelite citadel and was the first Israelite sanctuary to be uncovered in an excavation. It is oriented westward, and its layout and contents recall, in many respects, Solomon's Temple in Jerusalem. It shows an even more striking resemblance to the biblical description of the Tabernacle in the desert (see "Exodus" to "Deuteronomy") and consists of a main hall from which three steps lead up to the *debir* (Holy of Holies), at whose entrance were found two incense altars. A small *bamah* (high place) and a *massebah* (stone stele) stood in the center of the Holy of Holies. In the outer courtyard stood an altar for burnt offerings: a square of five cubits (that is, approximately seven and a half feet on each side) conforming to the measurements of the Tabernacle altar in Exodus 27:1 and built of earth and unhewn field stones (Exod. 20:24–25). Other features of the sanctuary also bore a close resemblance to the biblical description of Solomon's sanctuary. But the early history of this high place and temple is even more intriguing because Arad had been settled before the days of the Monarchy by a Kenite clan akin to the Midianites and descended from Hobab the priest, a member of the same family as Jethro, Moses' father-in-law (Judg. 1:16). The Kenites built a high place and altar on the highest point overlooking the plateau of Arad. In the days of Solomon (tenth century B.C.) or shortly afterwards, a temple was built in this strategic center (Greater Arad), over the early Kenite high place, as shown in our pictures of the Holy of Holies and altar. Several high places had existed in Israel before and during the days of the Judean Monarchy, but this one may have been

destroyed by King Hezekiah (eighth century B.C.), or more likely by Josiah, who concentrated the religious ritual in Jerusalem in the seventh century B.C., as described in 2 Kings 22. The significant rich trove of ostraca found there will be described under 1 and 2 Kings.

8. OTHER DEVELOPMENTS IN THE PALESTINIAN WORLD

The changes that are associated with the central portions of southern Canaan at the end of the Late Bronze Age reflect historical processes that left no feature of the whole Canaanite sphere unaltered. The kingdoms of Moab, Ammon, and Edom arose at the same time Israel did. The military federation organized around the Philistine Pentapolis can hardly be later, and may well be earlier (see 2 Samuel). The technological developments of the Early Iron Age are better known. The development of slaked lime-plastered cisterns revitalized many of the area's potential centers of settlement, which had been dormant since the massive deforestation earlier in the Bronze Age. We will discuss some of these changes and related features in the pages that follow.

Archaeological research has proved that the Israelites did not bring a uniform tradition of material culture with them, but borrowed in the main from previous inhabitants, in building construction, weapons, art objects, and especially pottery. The Canaanite product was an excellent model to imitate. In the beginning, the imitation produced more primitive vessels in the same style. But unique vessels soon developed in a clearly

Model of the Arad sanctuary

81

definable style found among the Israelite tribes. In fact, the adoption of Canaanite culture coupled with rapid crystallization of independent forms is a familiar theme through all phases of Israelite tribal life.

a. *The Early Israelite House*

It has become evident from very recent excavations that the Israelite type of tripartite house as a homogeneous structure appeared for the first time in the period of the Judges (twelfth to eleventh centuries B.C.). It is generally built with an inner open court surrounded by rooms, as shown in our illustration. Early examples were found at Tell Far'ah south of Beersheba and at Tell el-Meshash, in a twelfth century settlement on virgin soil. It was believed at first that this type of house was of Late Canaanite or Philistine origin, but there is evidence to show that it may be an independent Israelite tradition that was realized in constructions even before the days of the Monarchy.

b. *Introduction of Slaked Lime-Plastered Cisterns*

Plastered and whitewashed water cisterns have been found in Canaanite Late Bronze strata in various excavations, including the deep water cistern of Hazor in Stratum XIV. The device was not original to the Israelites; it shows up in Canaanite cities, which proved very inventive in assuring emergency water supplies. The Israelites took to it very quickly, and it helped them to found small independent settlements, widely dispersed and unrestricted by the limited number of local springs and wells. The narrow confines and heavy concentration of the zones of occupation, first on the periphery of the Canaanites, then in their midst, affected the development of their society. As seen above, they first imitated, then improved on, their neighbors, both culturally and materially (see 2 Samuel and 1 Kings).

"Four-room houses" of the early Israelite settlement at Tell el-Meshash

PART IV

THE BOOKS OF 1 and 2 SAMUEL

A. SAMUEL

The Bible presents Samuel as a man who filled many different roles. According to Albright these should be considered as differences in emphasis and should no longer appear as hopeless contradictions but as contributions to a more complete historical picture.

At birth, Samuel was pledged to service at the temple at Shiloh by his mother, Hannah. As a *nazir,* he was devoted to an ascetic life and performed Levitical duties at the sanctuary. This may explain why 1 Chronicles 6:28 lists Samuel among the families of the Levites, unlike the more historical genealogy in 1 Samuel 1:1, which identifies Samuel as a Ephraimite.

We are told that early in his career Samuel became recognized throughout Israel as a prophet (1 Sam. 3:20). As such he was the prototype of the prophets, particularly of the Northern Kingdom, who announced Yahweh's election, favor, or displeasure with Israel's kings. In addition, Samuel is depicted as a local seer who could be consulted on small matters for a sum of money. There is the interesting footnote in 1 Samuel 9:9 that states that "the one who is now called a prophet was formerly called a seer."

1. THE CONTENTS IN HISTORICAL PERSPECTIVE

The Hebrew scribes regarded the two books as one, without interruption.

1 Samuel	*Parallels in 1 Chronicles**
Samuel's childhood and relationship to the Shiloh priesthood (chapters 1–3). The loss of the Ark, its wanderings, and return (4:1–7:2), which is continued in 2 Samuel 6.	
Samuel as judge and prophet (7:3–17).	
The accession of Saul (8:1–15:9)	1 Chronicles 8:33; 9:39; 40, 12:1
Conflict with Samuel (15:10–35).	
David's anointment (16:1–13).	
Beginning of David's adventures (17–20).	1 Chronicles 12
David as outlaw; Saul's defeat and death (21–31).	1 Chronicles 12

---

*The books of Chronicles contain passages of annalistic and factual material parallel to 1 and 2 Samuel, as indicated in the list of contents. This is also true of Chronicles and Kings; 1 Chronicles 1–8, however, is noteworthy mainly for its genealogical lists.

Iron sword discovered in Philistia

2 Samuel

Second account of Saul's death and his
elegy (chapter 1).

David, King of Judah (2:1–5:5).　　　1 Chronicles 11; 14:1–2

Jerusalem, the new capital (5:6–6:23)　　1 Chronicles 11:4–8

The growth of David's empire (8–10).
David and Bathsheba (11–12).
The rape of Tamar (13:1–39).
Absalom's rebellion and death (14–18).
Return to Jerusalem and revolt of
Sheba (19–20).

Various appendices (21–24).　　　　1 Chronicles 20–21

2. THE INVASION OF THE SEA PEOPLES

The first half of the twelfth century witnessed two related developments of great importance for the history of the Israelite settlement. One
was the invasion of the land by the Sea Peoples who came from the north
and west—from Asia Minor and the eastern Mediterranean, islands like
Cyprus and Crete, and the Aegean. These people spoke Indo-European
languages and belonged to that culture, in contrast with the local inhabitants, who spoke northwestern Semitic dialects. The other was the con-
comitant decline of Egyptian power in Canaan and the virtual
abandonment of the territory that had been held actually and nominally
for centuries.

The literary sources (both biblical and nonbiblical) convey a picture of
the Philistines as a vigorous, talented segment of the Sea Peoples, who left
not only their name but a permanent influence on the land they invaded
and settled: Canaan, which became Palestine. The Bible states that they
came from Crete, and this is doubtless true of some of them; others seem
to have come from the mainland. They belonged to the wave of "Sea Peoples," who, like the Norsemen in Europe millennia later, came by sea and
land to ravage and ransack the coastal regions of the eastern Mediterranean around 1200 B.C. They migrated from the Aegean Islands and Asia
Minor under pressure from the Dorians who invaded the Greek mainland,
a development that in turn is related to the events celebrated in Homer's
epic of the Trojan war.

In contrast to the Israelite invasion that began a little earlier and was
much more modest in size and impact, the Sea Peoples' campaign of destruction and conquest was much more extensive. Apparently they gave
the *coup de grace* to the great Hittite empire and very nearly overturned
the Egyptian state as well. At the same time, Mycenean power disintegrated on the Greek mainland. Some of the Sea Peoples, taking advantage of

Opposite page:
The great naval battle between
Rameses III and the Sea Peoples
(which included the Philistines).
Four Egyptian boats (right,
equipped with oars and sails)
engage five Philistine boats
(distinguished by a bird's head
on both prow and stern). The
Philistines are tall, shaven and
wearing feathered headdresses
and a breastplate or shirt. They
fought with round shields.
Reliefs in the temple of Rameses
III at Medinet Habu

the decline of the empires, had already invaded Palestine and Syria in the late thirteenth century. According to Egyptian documents, they attacked the Syrian and Egyptian coasts at the beginning of the reign of Rameses III (1196–1164 B.C.). Rameses III defeated them in Syria and repelled them finally from the Egyptian mainland, but only after fierce attacks on sea and land had threatened the survival of the kingdom. Nevertheless, an inscription of Rameses III from Beth-shean indicated that he re-established the Egyptian base there and rebuilt the temples. In fact, he settled some of the Sea Peoples as garrison troops in parts of Canaan, thus enlisting those aggressive warriors in his service as a mercenary border guard to prevent further invasions. Anthropoid coffins, containing the bodies of Philistines, have been found at Beth-shean, Tell Far'ah and elsewhere in Palestine. The Sea Peoples consisted of five groups: *p-r-sh-t* (Philistines), *t-k-r* (Sikel), *s-k-r-s, d-n-n* and *w-sh-sh*.

A warrior of the Sea Peoples wielding his battle axe

Rameses' victory and subsequent control over parts of Canaan did not deter the Philistines from occupying the southern coastal region, with Gaza, the former Egyptian provincial capital, as one of their major cities. An Egyptian source indicates that Dor (south of present-day Haifa) was occupied by the *t-k-r*. The story of the Egyptian priest, Wen-Amun, illuminates the situation in Canaan at the beginning of the eleventh century. He had been sent to Byblos to acquire cedar trees to construct a sacred barque for the god Amun. By that time there was no trace of Egyptian authority or influence, and although some memories of earlier contacts persisted along the Phoenician coast, Wen-Amun was confronted with a measure of contempt and the demand for cash on the line. His first stop

Right:
Core of the Philistine temple
uncovered at Tell Qasileh with
the altar and bases of three
masseboth (standing pillars)

Above:
Philistine pottery coffin found at
Beth-shean where the invaders
were eventually stationed by the
Egyptians

Below:
Philistine incense jar showing
man holding two pillars; found
in the temple at Tell Qasileh

was the Dor harbor where he was robbed; he elicited neither support nor sympathy from the chief of the *t-ḳ-r*. As he pursued his journey, probably to Tyre, he seized a boat belonging to the *t-ḳ-r,* thus recouping part of his loss. While eleven ships pursued him, he eluded them and sailed for Cyprus.

Philistine authority during the eleventh century extended as far as the Valley of Jezreel, while their influence and presence were everywhere in the land. They controlled the coastal towns of Ashkelon, Ashdod and Joppa (present-day Jaffa) and imposed their rule upon the local populace. They were also busily engaged in sea trade. They were organized into a confederation comprising five cities, each ruled by a *seren* ("tyrant" in Greek). They set about extending their territory, and in due course they became the dominant political force in Palestine. A few generations previously the Israelites had settled in Canaan, mainly in the hill country. With the collapse of the Canaanite military forces and city-states, the Israelites were left to bear the chief brunt of the Philistine drive for hegemony. With their monopoly of iron tools and weapons and their effective military organization, the Philistines proved more than a match for the Israelites and reduced them to the status of vassals (as reflected in the Samson stories, Judges 13–16, especially Judges 15:11). In this period the Philistines flourished as a political and cultural force, extended their control over the whole coastal plain of Palestine, and thereby threatened the political and economic future of Israel. They were the first to introduce the use of iron into the country, a new element that would ultimately revolutionize the way of life of the whole of civilization. They had brought it from the Hittite hinterland and maintained a monopoly of the product until the days of King Saul (1 Sam. 13:19–22). Philistine soldiers carried iron weapons and their farmers used iron tools. The description of their well-armed

champion, Goliath, seems to sum up this military superiority (1 Sam. 17:4–7).

Tell Qasileh

The excavation of Tell Qasileh on the northern bank of the Yarkon river has uncovered a small harbor founded by the Philistines, as indicated by the lowest levels of occupation (Strata XI–XII) of the twelfth century B.C. The findings show evidence of agricultural and industrial activities: granaries, baking ovens, oil and wine presses, a smelting furnace, and dyeing utensils. There are also remains of fortifications from the same period. The city served later as one of King Solomon's harbors. The most remarkable discovery was a Philistine temple from the twelfth century with a courtyard surrounding it. The altar of sacrifices and the steps leading to it appear in the center, surrounded by numerous ritual vessels and cult objects. It would be hard to separate the architecture of this sanctuary from the temple of Dagon at Gaza described in Judges 16:29. Two main pillars, whose bases were discovered in the excavations, seem just far enough apart to require the full extension of muscular athletic arms such as Samson's to reach around them and pull them down.

3. THEIR CITIES AND CULTURAL ATTRIBUTES

a. Ashkelon

We read in the famous elegy of David over Saul and Jonathan: "Tell it not in Gath, publish it not in the streets of Ashkelon" (2 Sam. 1:20). This actually refers to the bazaars of that storied city, which possessed the only safe harbor in southern Palestine and was a great trading center. Its importance as a center of crafts and arts is indicated by the temple of Ptah, the god of the city; we also find his name among the famous ivory

The excavation of Gerar (Tell Shera), the biblical city of the Negeb where Abraham had settled. The structure on the right is the Israelite 'four room' house. The older Canaanite complex is on the slope to the left

Figure of a female deity whose lower part merges with a throne

Part of a Philistine clay beer jug from Ashdod

carvings discovered in the royal treasure of Canaanite Megiddo of the thirteenth to twelfth centuries B.C. This Egyptian deity was identified with the god Chusor, or the older Kothar wa-Ḥasis, the craftsman god of the Canaanite pantheon. The culture of greater Canaan had permeated the Philistines.

b. *Gath*

The constant process of action and reaction between the Israelites and Philistines seems to have effected changes in the political structures on both sides. According to B. Mazar, Gath was raised in this period to supremacy over the Philistine cities, and its ruler, Achish, was king of the whole pentapolis. During this period David served as a vassal of the king of Gath (1 Sam. 27:5–6), exercising rule over a fiefdom of his own in the Ziklag region. It is identified with Tell esh-Sheri'ah, a prominent mound east of Gerar.

c. *Ashdod*

Excavations of Ashdod show continuous Canaanite occupation since the seventeenth century B.C. It was destroyed by the Sea Peoples at the end of the Late Bronze Age, and later occupied by the Philistines. It became one of the principal cities of the pentapolis. The Philistine levels reveal a rich material culture including a number of interesting objects: the figure of a female deity whose lower part merges with a throne, a musician's stand, and many offering tables, which attest to the local religious practices.

d. *Jaffa (ancient Joppa)*

The period of Israelite settlement begins with the fourth level (second half of the thirteenth century B.C.) of the excavations of ancient Joppa. Remains of the Israelite fortress have been uncovered; at the threshold was a bronze bar that supported the corner of the left gate. The Philistines attacked the city and destroyed it, leaving characteristic signs of their presence there. This action prevented the Israelites from using this seaport or the one further north at the mouth of the Yarkon river, where boats took shelter in the wintertime when the sea was stormy. The reference in Joshua 19:45 to the Yarkon river as the border of the tribe of Dan that "ran over against Joppa" is now dated by most scholars to the Davidic period when Israelite expansion was at its peak. In other words, Jaffa remained outside the boundary of Israelite settlement for most of the classical period. A link between Jaffa and the Greek world may be reflected in the so-called Andromeda rocks off the old harbor, which are associated in tradition with the legend of Perseus and the well-known princess of that name.

4. THE CANAANITE COASTLAND AND HINTERLAND

The territory north of Philistia and northwest of Israel is generally called Phoenicia, the Greek equivalent of Canaan. It was actually the northern part of Canaan and the last retreat of the Canaanites from the pressure of Israelite and Philistine expansion. It first achieved a distinctive identity in the Early Iron Age, although it had always been an important trading center. The great coastal city of the second millennium, Byblos, reappears in this period, but it is dwarfed by the great city-states, Tyre and Sidon. The greatest concentration of the Phoenicians outside Palestine was in North Africa; their language is called Punic, which is simply a Latin form of Phoenician. The great city of Carthage (Phoenician: *qart hadašt,* "new city") is well known from Roman tradition and records. Other major Phoenician colonies are known from Cyprus, Sicily, Sardinia, and Spain.

The first Assyrian empire under Tiglath-pileser I held the tribes of Syria in check, but, following his death in 1078 B.C., the hold of Mesopotamia on western Syria practically ceased. This stimulated the Canaanites north of Mount Carmel to establish independent states in Tyre, Sidon, and Byblos; it also allowed the Sea Peoples to plant themselves more firmly.

The Phoenician contribution to Israelite civilization best known from the Bible is architectural: Hiram of Tyre seems to have supplied Solomon with everything but the land for his temple. A greater contribution, the alphabet, is discussed below.

The north Canaanite hinterland in the Early Iron Age was apportioned among small kingdoms compounded of Aramaeans and Hittites. The latter had moved south from Anatolia as a result of the collapse of the Hittite empire and brought with them a knowledge of statecraft that they were able to adapt to their new home. These petty states appear frequently in the stories of David's imperial expansion, but their history is not otherwise well known.

Figurine of a Canaanite goddess cast in a mold (Nahariya)

5. EVIDENCE OF THE MARCH OF PROGRESS

The time was ripe for the expansion of sea trade along the coasts and the sea lanes established by the preclassical Greek Mycenean civilization. The decline of Egyptian sea power had left a vacuum that was rapidly filled by both the Phoenicians and the Sea Peoples, who opted for peaceful trade after their violent migrations of the preceding century. Philistine influence penetrated inland, as we gather from pottery finds in the towns of western Judah, Tell Beit Mirsim and Beth-shemesh.

Excavations have been conducted at many of the sites that are important in the books of Samuel, and the results have cleared up important points of detail about the role of Samuel in the successful transition from the federation to the Monarchy. Further light has been shed on this process by discoveries of two other sources of information: (a) the discoveries among the Dead Sea Scrolls of fragments of early recensions of the book of Samuel, found in Cave IV at Qumran and in the Ezra Synagogue in Cairo, and (b) the Aramaean treaty inscriptions at Sefire.

A proto-Canaanite inscription BŠLŠT painted on a pottery bowl from Lachish (13th c. B.C.)

Palaeo-Sinaitic inscription (15–13th c. B.C.)

B. EVOLUTION OF THE ALPHABET

The origins of the various arts and crafts figure prominently in the traditions of many peoples, and the book of Genesis comments briefly on the children of Lamech who devised agricultural tools and musical instruments (Genesis 4). But nothing is said about the invention of the alphabet, surely one of the most remarkable achievements of the human race. The oldest alphabetic writing extant in a Semitic language is to be found on a few inscriptions from the land of Canaan; they date from the seventeenth or sixteenth century B.C. Confirmation that this handful of characters actually belong to an alphabetic system was provided from an unlikely source, the turquoise mines of Serabit el Khadim in the western Sinai. In 1948 W. F. Albright restudied the inscriptions in a West Semitic dialect that had been uncovered in a series of expeditions to the site. He concluded that Sir Flinders Petrie had been correct in attributing them to the period of the New Kingdom, in the fifteenth century B.C. The date has now been fixed firmly by evidence of different kinds, and the Sinai inscriptions provide us with enough material to recover and reconstruct this oldest known Canaanite alphabet. Apparently the Semitic workmen there brought with them an alphabetic script developed in Canaan. Using modified forms of Egyptian signs, but interpreting and applying them to a West Semitic dialect, the Canaanites devised an extremely simple and extraordinarily effective system for transcribing the sounds of their language.

The two controlling principles were *acrophony* and *consonantism*. According to the first, each letter originally was a pictograph representing some common object, though in time they all became highly conventionalized. The sound of the letter was the same as the initial sound of the word that described the pictograph; that is, the letter *b* was originally a drawing of a house, which is called *bayt/bet* in West Semitic; the initial sound of that word is *b*, which is the value of the symbol. According to the second principle, only consonants were represented in the alphabet, not vowels. Since all syllables in proto-Semitic begin with consonants, the necessity for representing them is obvious. Vowels are another matter, especially if the vowel is regarded as originally attached to the consonant, as is the case in syllabic writing. The full separation apparently took place in two stages, with consonants being represented first and the vowels only in later stages of the alphabet. In the past decades numerous inscriptions in the proto-Canaanite alphabet have been found in Palestine; gradually all the letters have been identified and, with few exceptions, their true pictographic values established. By the early stages of the Iron Age, the Phoenicians had taken a final important step in normalizing their alphabet into twenty-two consonants and had given it to the world as the most efficient means of written communication.

By the end of the Late Bronze Age, the Canaanites had devised at least two alphabetic systems. One of these, the linear, was the ancestor of the Phoenician, Hebrew, Aramaic, Greek, and Roman alphabets; the other, written with cuneiform wedges, did not survive into the Iron Age.

The alphabet was developed by the Canaanites in the course of the Middle and Late Bronze Ages and the early years of the Iron Age. It was adopted, with suitable modification, by all of their neighbors, beginning in all likelihood in the eleventh century. Since Hebrew in its northern (Israelite) dialect is almost identical with Phoenician, we can hardly talk of borrowing; we would say they shared a common language and a common alphabet. In the case of other dialects and languages there can be no doubt that Phoenicia was the center of diffusion.

1. SIGNIFICANCE

The following description of the significance of the alphabet, by F. M. Cross, rightly focuses on the shift away from syllabic writing (in which each sign designates a syllable—in its simplest form, one consonant and one vowel) to a kind of pseudo-syllabary in which the sign designates one consonant and any vowel.

"This act of abstraction and simplification, absent from all previous syllable systems, created the alphabet: The step taken was unique. Once the alphabetic principle was discovered, it spread rapidly throughout the ancient world. The revolution may be compared with the invention of writing itself. High civilization was the creature of writing. The invention of the alphabetic principle put literacy in the reach of everyman, permitting the democratization of high culture" (F. M. Cross, Israel Explor. Soc. 10; 1972).

The importance of the alphabet in the economic and social development of Israel can hardly be understated, since it was the medium by which the biblical traditions were reduced to permanent form.

2. EXPANSION OF ALPHABETIC WRITING

Great strides were made in the use of Canaanite consonantal writing during the period of the Pax Philistia, namely the standardization of the twenty-two consonant alphabet and of writing from right to left. The trade relations between Philistia, Phoenicia, and Israel were an important factor in the rapid spread of this cultural medium.

The alphabet was carried to the early Greeks by Phoenician traders. Phoenician inscriptions from numerous Mediterranean sites testify to the extent of the Phoenician trading empire. They also enrich our evidence for the development of the alphabet adopted and adapted by the Greeks from the tenth century B.C. onward.

3. TRANSITION TO TRULY HISTORICAL WRITING

The books of Samuel cover a major transitional period in Israelite history, the rise of the Monarchy out of the tribal federation. As 1 Samuel opens, Israel consists of a loose organization of tribes struggling to maintain its existence; at the end of 2 Samuel, Israel is a national power, possessing all the benefits and drawbacks of central authority and commercial culture. These changes affected every aspect of Israelite life and religion and gave rise to traditions that remain central to Judaism to this day.

One of the changes that accompanied the rise of the Monarchy, illustrated in the books of Samuel, is the transition to truly historical writing in the modern sense. It is instructive to compare the treatment of the figures of Samuel and David. The picture of Samuel is drawn from several traditions that sometimes conflict and sometimes complement each other. On the other hand, the career and personality of David are presented in a single coherent narrative that begins in 1 Samuel and stretches to the beginning of Kings. The author of this narrative not only tells us the major events of David's life but also explains why and how they happened. They are told with such intimacy that we feel that we are reading an eyewitness report.

1	2	3	4	5	6	7	8	9	10
ʾ	alef						A	alpha	A
b	beth						B	beta	B
g	ghimel						Γ	gamma	G
d	daleth						Δ	delta	D
h	he						E	epsilon	E
w	waw						Φ	phi	V
z	zain						Z	zeta	Z
ḥ	heth						H	eta	H
ṭ	teth						Θ	theta	
j	yod						I	iota	I
k	kaf						K	cappa	K
l	lamed						Λ	lamda	L
m	mem						M	mi	M
n	nun						N	ni	N
s	samekh						Ξ	csi	
ʿ	ayin						O	omicron	O
p	pe						Π	pi	P
ṣ	sade								
q	qof								Q
r	resh						P	ro	R
ś	sin								
š	shin						Σ	sigma	S
t	tau						T	tau	T

Table showing the progress of the alphabet, from the Palaeo-Sinaitic to the Phoenician and Hebrew and, eventually, to the Greek and Latin:
1. Phonetic sound
2. Hebrew name
3. Palaeo-Sinaitic
4. Canaanite script, 12th c. B.C.
5. Phoenician, 9th c. B.C.
6. Hebrew cursive 8th c. B.C.
7. Modern Hebrew
8. Greek alphabet
9. Greek name
10. Latin alphabet

C. THE RISE OF THE MONARCHY

The most important aspect of Samuel's career was his decisive role in the introduction of monarchy into Israel. Under the threat of growing Philistine power, it became obvious to many in Israel that the voluntary confederation of tribes was no longer able to cope with the organized military power of the Philistines.

1. THE PRICE OF MONARCHIAL GOVERNMENT

In describing these important events, Hebrew historiographers, who were unwilling to tamper with old traditions, accepted different versions even if they were contradictory. For instance, two opposed opinions—one welcoming the establishment of the Monarchy, the other critical of royal practices—produced two conflicting accounts of Saul's accession; in the narratives in 1 Samuel 9:1–10:16 only the positive aspects of kingship are mentioned, while 1 Samuel 10:17–27 presents only the drawbacks of the monarchy. Samuel's warnings and arguments come under four heads, which reflect contemporary conditions:

(a) subjecting the people to service in the army; (b) appropriation of the peoples' property by the king; (c) the *corvée* tax, paid by physical labor on public projects; and (d) enslavement of the people, which actually took place under Solomon to support his great enterprises.

By convening the people to elect a *nagid,* Samuel bridged the gap between a charismatic and a monarchial government, the prevailing pattern in the ancient Near East.

2. THE SANCTUARY AT SHILOH

About the middle of the eleventh century B.C., the Philistines defeated the Israelites at the battle of Ebenezer (1 Samuel 4) and removed the Ark from the central sanctuary at Shiloh. Excavations indicate that they also overran and destroyed towns in Judah and Ephraim (central Palestine), including Shiloh, Tell Beit Mirsim (Debir), and Beth-zur, and achieved hegemony over most of Palestine for more than a century.

Excavations have revealed that the city of Shiloh enjoyed an era of prosperity in the period of the Judges when it was fortified. It perished in a violent conflagration, presumably set by the Philistines, which is alluded to by Jeremiah and the author of Psalm 78 (see verse 60).

3. END OF THE TRIBAL FEDERATION

The constant Philistine menace was the great challenge that forced the Israelites to face up to the problem of their survival as a distinctive religious community and a cohesive national entity. This marks the end of the federated tribal society during the period of the Judges and the begin-

Seal of "Jaazaniah servant of the king" found at Mizpah (2 Kings 25:23). The fighting cock was the high official's crest

ning of a united monarchy under King Saul, which established Israel as the dominant force in the country that would be designated the "land of Israel."

Samuel, the last of the charismatic judges, first won a victory over the Philistines at Mizpah in the land of Ephraim (Tell en-Nasbeh). Its main period of occupation was the Iron Age. The excavators uncovered the main part of the city, which contained many four-room houses typical of the period, some of which were unusually large and built with pillars to support roofs. On top of the tenth-century casemate wall, there are the outstanding wall and gate built by King Rehoboam in the ninth century. Hebrew seals and seal impressions were among the most abundant finds, one bearing the inscription "Jaazaniah servant of the king," dating to the seventh century B.C.

The biblical sources do not mention any of the cultural attributes of the Philistines, except to point out that they had enjoyed a monopoly of iron tools and weapons, which they used to subjugate the Israelites. As a result of this subjugation, a popular resistance movement developed. Though its primary motive seems to have been the removal of economic restrictions, it aimed ultimately at the expulsion of non-Israelites from the land and the unification of the tribes. This Israelite guerilla warfare was facilitated by the distances separating the Philistine garrisons and the difficulty in maintaining safe communications in the hill country, where the Israelites lived in large numbers.

4. KING SAUL. THE MODEST CAPITAL: GIBEAH OF BENJAMIN

The city of Gibeah was founded in the early days of the Israelite settlement and then destroyed before Saul's time in the fierce war waged by the other tribes against Benjamin because of the crime against the Levite's concubine (Judges 19–21).

Saul's citadel of Gibeah was in the form of a courtyard surrounded by a casemate wall (containing inner rooms) and strengthened by four towers, as shown in the diagram

94

Excavations have uncovered a rectangular citadel; its wall was made of undressed blocks, and there was a square tower in the excavated corner. It was apparently built by Saul and served as his modest royal residence. It was subsequently named after him, Gibeah of Saul (1 Sam. 11:4; 15:34). After his defeat at Gilboa, it was rebuilt in the time of David. It was rebuilt for a third time in the later days of the Monarchy, when it was surrounded by a feeble casemate fortification.

The struggle between the Philistines and Israel continued throughout Saul's reign in the lowlands of the Shephelah, but until the final battle he was able to achieve a stalemate and the enemy was kept out of the heartland and the hill country. In the end the Philistines attacked Saul from their bases (Megiddo, Beth-shean) along the *via maris* in the Valley of Jezreel and inflicted on Israel a crushing defeat at Mount Gilboa. Saul and his sons were impaled over the gates of Beth-shean. After Saul's defeat at Mount Gilboa, the balance shifted in favor of the Philistines. Though they had crushed Saul and helped to drive a wedge between Saul and David, their tactics failed in the end. The crisis in Israel proved to be temporary thanks to the emergence of David as a national hero.

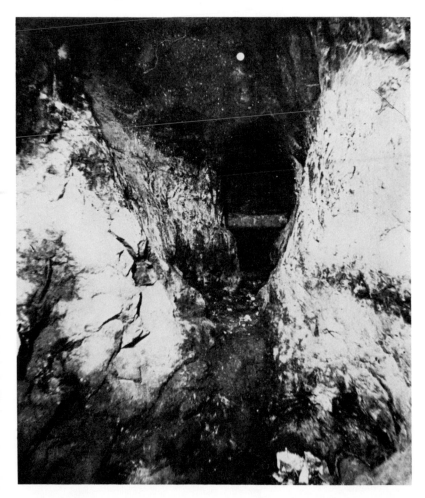

Part of the underground conduit or *sinnor* leading to the Gihon spring held by the Jebusites. Its damage by David led to the capture of Jerusalem (2 Sam. 5:8)

95

D. DAVID

As indicated above, the domination of the Philistines over Israel was a temporary phenomenon. In the end Israel was victorious, and it was David, the brilliant military leader and charismatic political figure, who turned the tide.

1. THE CAPTURE OF JERUSALEM

Unlike the siege of Jericho, where we have an elaborate description of the battle but no supporting archaeological evidence, the capture of Jerusalem by David is described in a single verse in 2 Samuel 5, but there is corroborative material data. Archaeologists have found part of a city wall built by the Jebusites in the Middle Bronze Age (ca. 1800) to protect the Gihon spring lying in the Kidron valley, as well as a system of shafts and tunnels to reach the underground source of water. According to the traditional interpretation of 2 Samuel 5:8, David's men were told to "go up the water shaft to attack. . . ." That would mean crawling up an almost perpendicular shaft to surprise the inhabitants of the city. While possible, it seems unlikely, and B. Mazar has proposed a different analysis of the passage and reconstruction of the event. In Hebrew the verse reads *wayyiga' bassinnor*, which means that "they struck [and damaged] the horizontal conduit" that brought the water from the source to the mouth of the spring shaft. According to the parallel account in 1 Chronicles 11:4–9, which doesn't mention the shaft, Joab was the first to go up against the city, possibly storming the wall at the lower end of the eastern fortification

Salient of the Jebusite wall of Zion (Jerusalem) ca. 1800 B.C., made of rough boulders, protected by another wall, seen on the right

close to the Kidron valley. A strategy combining an attack on the wall at one point and the disruption of the city's water supply at another offers a more logical solution to the problem of the capture of the city (B. Mazar, *The Mountain of the Lord*, p. 168).

2. THE PUZZLE OF THE MILLO TERRACES

The verse "and David built the city about from the Millo inward" (2 Sam. 5:9) has challenged comprehension, chiefly because the word *millo* was erroneously identified with a specific location in Jerusalem. Recent excavations have shown that the Millo consisted of supporting walls and stone terraces built in gradients, erected over the steep slopes of the southeastern hill of Zion, where the oldest city was established in pre-Israelite times. The houses of the town were then built upon these terraces, and in Solomon's time, the city began to expand westward, over the top of the hill. From that time on, great care was taken to keep the terraces in good repair to protect against erosion from rain water and to allow further expansion on the hillside.

3. DAVID'S EMPIRE

David consolidated the nation established by Saul; he united the tribes, along with several alien client groups, and conquered neighboring countries, under a stable system of government. Under his extraordinary leadership, Israel became for a time a major international force in the Near

The Canaanite or Jebusite wall made of large boulders (below) protected the underground Gihon spring, the main source of water of early Jerusalem. The wall above it is Israelite

East. As a result of his victories over the Philistines, Moabites, Edomites, Ammonites, and Aramaeans, he extended the boundaries of Israel as far as central Syria in the northwest and the approaches of the Euphrates in the northeast; the entire coast from Mount Carmel to south of Joppa became Israelite and the Philistines were reduced to paying tribute.

4. THE CHIEFS OF DAVID'S MIGHTY MEN

At the core of David's military organization were the thirty-seven leaders of his standing army, described as "the chiefs of David's mighty men who gave him strong support in his kingdom" (1 Chron. 11:10). They were recruited by him during his career as a vassal chieftain and remained personally loyal to him through his life. They were at the head of his troops when he was anointed king, first at Hebron and later in Jerusalem. These men served as the king's bodyguard and also as battalion leaders, commanding infantrymen and auxiliaries, much as did the *maryannu*, the chariot-riding knights of the Canaanite city-kingdoms of an earlier age. The most important sources on the subject are the two colorful lists in 2 Samuel 23:8–39 and 1 Chronicles 11:10–47 that identify the men and add details of their exploits.

5. THE MUSICAL GUILDS

Biblical tradition is consistent in acknowledging David as the father of Israelite music. His career began as a lute player in Saul's court. The memory of his contribution to the development of Israel's musical institutions was so powerful in later generations that practically everything in the way of liturgical music (including the Psalms) was attributed to him, much as all the laws were traced to Moses. However exaggerated these views may be, there can be little doubt that he was chiefly responsible for the establishment of the musical guilds and that the Temple services owe much to his inspiration and genius. We know from older sources that there was a rich tradition of Canaanite sacred music that was taken over and adapted by the Israelites. The names of the guilds recorded in Chronicles reflect the older pagan background: Asaph, Heman, Ethan, and Jeduthun; elsewhere we read of Heman, Khalkol, and Darda, "the sons of Mahol," that is, members of the orchestral guild (see "Psalms"). The creation of musical instruments is attributed to the gods or Titans (semidivine beings) in Near Eastern and Mediterranean mythology and, in the Bible, to the descendants of Cain, the eponymous ancestor of smiths, metalworkers and instrument-makers. The secrets of instrument-making and playing were guarded by the guilds and passed from generation to generation of those who were set aside for this service to the Temple and to the royal palace. There are many striking representations of musicians in finds from excavations (as for example, the remarkable incense altar from Ashdod, or the older ivories from Megiddo). In the list of prisoners captured by Sennacherib after the siege of Jerusalem in 701 B.C., musicians of the royal court, namely male and female singers, were mentioned prominently.

6. THE PAX DAVIDICA

Archaeological evidence reveals that there was a population explosion in Judah during and after the tenth century B.C. when the peace and prosperity David brought made it possible to build many new towns. This expansion was facilitated by two technological advances: the slaked lime cistern and the iron plow tip. The new cisterns allowed people to settle farther from water sources, and the plow tip greatly increased the yield from the soil. (The same phenomenon took place in Europe, after the Dark Ages, when the introduction of the large plowshare revolutionized agriculture.) These new developments were followed by the tremendous commercial and industrial expansion under Solomon, which accounts for the rapid growth of Jerusalem in his day.

7. JERUSALEM

Jerusalem thus became the new center of the traditional league of twelve tribes; its sacral character was emphasized by the transfer of the Ark of the Covenant there and the erection first of a shrine and then of the Temple in the city. The United Monarchy saw itself as heir to the ancient league that embraced both north and south Palestine and devoted its efforts to centralizing both political power and religious authority at the same place: the holy city of God, Jerusalem. In time the traditions and terminology associated with Yahweh's desert mountain sanctuary, Sinai, were appropriated for the Temple in Mount Zion, as the political traditions of the tribal league were assigned to the king and the royal entourage. God's Covenant of promise to Abraham was applied to the royal house and the royal city, and both were held to be inviolate and inviolable, eternally protected by the Deity. The Temple of Mount Zion, the holy city Jerusalem, and the dynasty of David were indissolubly linked in royal theology and hymnody and in the minds of both prophets and people, leaving a permanent legacy in the religious traditions of both Judaism and Christianity. Messianism was derived from the historical reality of David and Jerusalem; it projected into the eschatological future the hope of a restoration of a glorious past.

Left:
A musician playing the harp surrounded by friendly animals. Decoration on an 11th c. B.C. Megiddo vase

Center:
Iron plough from Tell Beit Mirsim (2 Sam. 12)

Right:
Iron pitchfork (10th c. B.C.)

99

The United Kingdom created
by David comprised Palestine
on both sides of the Jordan and
the various vassal states
bordering it on all sides

THE UNITED KINGDOM

PART V

A. THE BOOKS OF 1 AND 2 KINGS AND CHRONICLES

Originally the two books of Kings were one, as in the case of Samuel. They are a chronological continuation of the latter and are about the same length. Their historical narratives cover a period of about four centuries, from the tenth to the sixth B.C., and are paralleled roughly by 1 Chronicles 29 to 2 Chronicles 35 as shown in the table below. The history of the Monarchy in these books may be divided into three main parts:

1. 1 Kings 1–11 covers the United Monarchy. The first two chapters complete the history of David's reign, which is the main theme of 2 Samuel 9–20, and then describe the accession of Solomon. Chapters 3–11 present a dazzling picture of Solomon's rule over the United Kingdom of Israel, the climax of 1 Kings.
2. 1 Kings 12–2 Kings 17 deals with the schism of the United Kingdom and then gives parallel accounts of the separate kingdoms of Judah and Israel (Samaria) up to the destruction of the latter.
3. 2 Kings 18–25 continues the history of the kingdom of Judah, after the fall of the Northern Kingdom, up to the destruction of Jerusalem in 586 B.C. and the exile of the Judeans.

THE CONTENTS IN HISTORICAL PERSPECTIVE

Dates: It is important to recall that the first certain date in biblical history —the battle of Qarqar between the Assyrians and a coalition of western kingdoms in 853 B.C.—was established through archaeological findings. This has resulted in a more reliable and precise chronology of this period than has hitherto been available.

The United Kingdom

Date B.C.	Kings	The Event	Chronicles
970 – 968	1 Kings 1 – 2	The last days of David and the accession of Solomon to the throne	1 Chronicles 29:20 – 30
968 – 965		Coregency of David and Solomon	
965	1 Kings 3	The beginning of Solomon's sole reign	2 Chronicles 1
	1 Kings 4	(Extracts from the royal annals, a new and vital element of Israelite literature)	
	1 Kings 4 – 5	Solomon's ambitious building activities	2 Chronicles 2 – 4

Date B.C.	Kings	The Event	Chronicles
	1 Kings 8:1 — 9:9	The account of the dedication of the Temple	2 Chronicles 5 — 7
965 — 928	1 Kings 9:10 — 10:29	Miscellaneous data on the reign, especially concerning Solomon's economic activity	2 Chronicles 8 — 9
	1 Kings 11	His marriages to foreign princesses; the decline of his rule	

The Divided Kingdom

Date B.C.	Kings	The Event	Chronicles
928	1 Kings 12:1 — 24	The Schism	2 Chronicles 10
	1 Kings 12:25 — 14:20	Jeroboam, first ruler of the Northern Kingdom	
	1 Kings 14:21 — 15:24	Rehoboam, Abijah, and Asa, kings of Judah	2 Chronicles 11 — 16
	1 Kings 15:25 — 28	Shishak's campaign	2 Chronicles 12:1 — 12
907 — 882	1 Kings 15:25 — 16:28	Nadab to Omri (Northern Kingdom)	
871 — 851	1 Kings 16:29 — 22:40	King Ahab of Israel and the prophet Elijah story cycle. The battle of Qarqar (853 B.C.)	
867	1 Kings 22:41 — 50	Jehoshaphat of Judah	2 Chronicles 17 — 20
851	1 Kings 22:51 — 2 Kings 1:18	Ahaziah, the sixth king of Israel	
	2 Kings 2:1 — 25	Completion of the Elijah stories; prophet Elisha's succession	
851 — 843	2 Kings 3:1 — 8:29	The Elisha cycle; the reigns of Jehoram of Israel; Kings Jehoram and Ahaziah of Judah	2 Chronicles 21 — 22
842 — 815	2 Kings 9:1 — 10:36	Jehu of Israel	
	2 Kings 11 — 12	Queen Athaliah and King Joash in Judah	2 Chronicles 22 — 24
814 — 800	2 Kings 14:1 — 16	Jehoahaz and Jehoash of Israel	
799 — 787	2 Kings 14:17 — 29	Amaziah, eighth king of Judah; Jeroboam II of Israel	2 Chronicles 25
786 — 758 (sole reign)	2 Kings 15:1 — 31	Uzziah, ninth king of Judah; chaos in the Northern Kingdom	2 Chronicles 26
758 — 742	2 Kings 15:32 — 16:20	Jotham and Ahaz, tenth and eleventh kings of Judah	2 Chronicles 27 — 28
722/1	2 Kings 17	The destruction of the Northern Kingdom	

Judah Alone

Date B.C.	Kings	The Event	Chronicles
727 – 698	2 Kings 18 – 20	Hezekiah's reign; Assyrian King Sennacherib besieges Jerusalem; Hezekiah and the prophet Isaiah	2 Chronicles 29 – 32
697 – 640	2 Kings 21	Manasseh; his apostasy; Amon	2 Chronicles 33
640 – 609	2 Kings 22:1 – 23:30a	Josiah, the fifteenth king, and religious reformer	2 Chronicles 34 – 35
609 – 597	2 Kings 23:30b – 25:7	The last kings of Judah, from Jehoahaz, the sixteenth, until Zedekiah, the nineteenth; the last days of Jerusalem	2 Chronicles 36
586	2 Kings 25:8 – 30	Destruction of the State of Judah and the Exile. The last verses (22 – 30) recount the murder of Gedaliah and the release of King Jehoiachin in Babylon, after the death of the Babylonian King Nebuchadnezzar.	2 Chronicles 36:22 – 23, which is not parallel to 2 Kings (cf. Ezra 1:1 – 3) but mentions the decree of Cyrus that heralded the Restoration of the Commonwealth

Foundation Rock and presumed site of the Holy of Holies. The scars and markings reflect the vicissitudes of the site over four millennia. It stands now below the Islamic Dome of the Rock

103

B. SOLOMON

1. WHAT DID SOLOMON'S TEMPLE LOOK LIKE?

The Temple was oriented east-to-west, with its vestibule facing the rising sun. Solomon constructed the Temple of large rectangular stones and beams of valuable cedar and cypress woods brought from the forests of Lebanon and northern Syria. No traces of Solomon's Temple have been found on top of the Temple Mount. Any possible surviving remains of it, or of the palaces built nearby (the House of the Forest of Lebanon and the Porch of Justice), would lie buried beneath the seventh century A.D. Moslem sanctuary, Haram esh-Sherif, which is forbidden ground for archaeology. The most reliable archaeological evidence regarding the plan of this temple derives from a comparative study of contemporary sanctuaries at Tell Ta'inat on the Syrian coast, at Samal in northwestern Syria, and at Hamath in central Syria. The temple at Ta'inat is of special interest because of its close resemblance to the larger Jerusalem Temple. It is oblong and divided into three parts; compare the tripartite division of the Jerusalem Temple into the *'ulam* (entrance hall), the *heḳal* (main hall), and the

Ground plan of the palace (a) and the small shrine (b) of Ta'inat, which is strikingly similar in plan to Solomon's tripartite sanctuary: 1. the entrance hall; 2. the main hall, and 3. the *debir* (Holy of Holies)

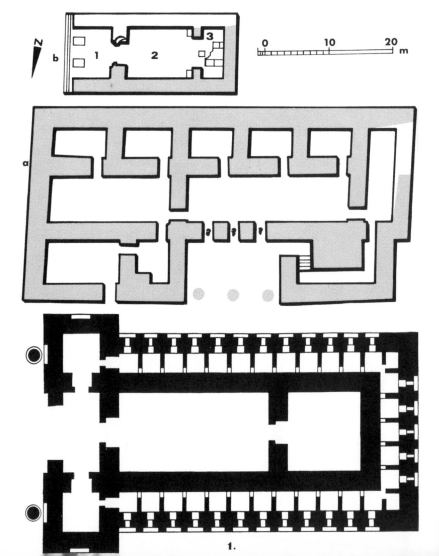

Plan of Solomon's temple showing two pillars facing the entrance, the three divisions of the sanctuary, and the outer chambers (*yazia*) flanking it on three sides

104

inner *debir* or Holy of Holies. An earlier prototype is the Late Bronze temple (sixteenth to thirteenth centuries B.C.) found at Hazor in Galilee or even Ebla (Tell Mardikh, Early Bronze IV) near Aleppo. Similar elements appear in Canaanite temples at Shechem, Megiddo, Beth-shean, and finally, the Israelite high place at Arad. Apparently all that is left of the Jerusalem Temple is the foundation rock on which the *debir* rested, now the heart of the Moslem sanctuary of the Dome of the Rock.

According to 1 Kings 6:31, olive wood doors separated the *hekal* and the *debir*. The whole temple was built on a platform and was 165 feet (100 cubits) long, 82 feet wide and 82 feet high. These measurements include the width of the wall and the storehouse, the *yazia,* a three-storied structure with numerous chambers that was built around the sanctuary on three sides.

2. THE FURNISHINGS OF THE TEMPLE

The sanctuary furniture and ritual objects were patterned after contemporary Phoenician equipment; most of the master craftsmen and skilled artisans also came from Phoenicia. The cherubim whose wings screened the Ark of the Covenant were winged sphinxlike creatures common to the mythological art and iconography of the ancient Near East. Numerous examples occur among the ivories of Megiddo and Samaria, as well as in pottery incense altars from Taanach and Megiddo.

The menorah, a candelabrum with seven branches, is known only from the period of the Second Temple; older antecedents in the form of lamps with seven spouts have been found.

Through archaeology we have an idea what the base and bronze lavers of the Temple looked like. There are parallels in the Megiddo openwork

A stand to wheel around large vessels in a sanctuary

stand and in a carriage base from Larnaca, Cyprus, whose large wheels are reminiscent of the base in the Bible.

The massive freestanding bronze pillars, Jachin and Boaz, flanked the outer entrance. They were elaborately decorated and crowned with bronze capitals. Similar columns have been discovered in Israel, and Phoenician temples are reported to have had them. Such pillars were outstanding achievements of bronze metalwork, as they had to be cast in special molds. Sennacherib of Assyria boasts of such a feat some 250 years later.

The Temple was in the center of a court surrounded by a thick wall. In the court stood the great Altar of Sacrifices, built of untrimmed stone, which was the focus of the daily sacrificial ritual. There was also the immense "sea" of bronze supported by twelve cast oxen. Its exact appearance remains a mystery; the nearest parallel may be the two huge cauldrons in an Assyrian relief depicting the temple at Musasir in Iraq (last quarter of the eighth century B.C.), or the large cauldron from Amatheus (although it is made of stone, not bronze).

3. SOLOMON'S FORTIFICATIONS

It was also during Solomon's reign that new methods and styles in the building of fortifications were introduced, including the extensive use of the casemate ramparts, consisting of a thick outer wall and a series of blind rooms filled with packed earth and rubble. At times they were sealed by a parallel inner wall; the blind rooms served as storage-chambers on occasion. In this way, the rampart was widened and strengthened, as is evident from the excavations at Megiddo, Hazor, Gezer, Tell Beit Mirsim, Beth-shemesh, and Tell Qasileh, all dating from Solomon's time. The first ramparts on the eastern flank of the City of David also were built in this period. This casemate wall was not abandoned after Solomon's time but continued in use as an inner defensive wall.

The terse biblical statement (1 Kings 9:15) that Solomon built Megiddo has been extensively amplified by archaeological excavations. They show that his plan covered three essential features of the ancient city: the fortified buildings, the gates, and the water supply. The Solomonic city gates at Megiddo, Hazor, and Gezer consist of two square towers and three pairs of buttresses with narrow passageways and chambers that served as guardrooms or armories. The approach to the gate was at an angle, running along the city wall. Any enemy chariots approaching along the wall in order to attack the gate were thus exposed to the defenders on the wall.

4. HYDRAULIC SYSTEMS AND TUNNELS

Solomon's underground hydraulic works, later enlarged by King Ahab, were found at Megiddo, Hazor, and Gezer. The one at Megiddo consisted of a vertical shaft lined with a masonry retaining wall. At its lower end, the vertical shaft became a steep passage that passed under the city wall

Casemate wall (with inner rooms) built by Solomon at Hazor. Seen in the foreground and left

Eastern side and upper level of Solomon's Gate of Megiddo. The entrance rests over a lower and older section (foreground)

Reconstructed site of the 8th c. B.C. self-contained water system of Hazor. It consisted of a shaft reaching 126 feet to the underground water table where it met a 67-foot horizontal tunnel lying outside the walls of the city, but beyond the enemy's reach

107

Above:
Underground water pool, Hazor

Right:
Reconstructed model of Israelite Megiddo. The governor's residence is in the background; the stables are to the left and the gate, in the foreground. The lower section to the right shows the older Canaanite city

and continued as a long tunnel with an arched ceiling. The tunnel ended at a cave and spring that lay outside the wall. The people could make their way unobserved to the cave, which was camouflaged. Inside the cave was found the burned skeleton of a guard who seems to have died when the cave was seized in a surprise attack and set afire. The Hazor tunnel was dug inside the city to reach the underground water level. Its shaft was 100 feet deep and the tunnel descended some 50 feet deeper, ending apparently in a pool. The Gezer tunnel, a shaft 27 feet deep with a sloping tunnel 132 feet long, led to a perennial spring at a depth of about 100 feet. It belonged to an older Canaanite type, probably of the Late Bronze Age.

5. A NEW TYPE OF ARCHITECTURE

The use of beautifully hewn and dressed stones in public buildings in the days of Solomon was a marked improvement over earlier building; it imitates the technique of stonecutting practiced in Phoenician cities. The external surface of the hewn stones is dressed with narrow borders, varying in width, on two or four sides, while the center of the ashlar block protrudes in a roughly rounded boss. Such stones were used in the foundations and lower courses, while those above ground were smoothed, with-

Below:
Reconstruction of citadel gate at Hazor (Ahab's reign, 9th c. B.C.)

Right:
Proto-Aeolian capital from the days of the Monarchy, Jerusalem

out protruding bosses. They were laid in header-stretcher fashion, successive courses alternating in orientation. Buildings constructed this way were provided with deep foundation trenches dug in bedrock to a depth of about ten feet.

Hewn stone pilasters stood as engaged columns at regular intervals along the walls and in the corners. They were usually crowned by capitals of a proto-Aeolian type. These architectural methods were used in Israel until the Exile.

6. REMAINS OF SOLOMON'S CITIES

Among the cities specifically mentioned as having been built or rebuilt by Solomon, several major sites, including Megiddo, Gezer, Hazor, and Lachish, have been excavated extensively. Some of their fortifications, monumental gates, public buildings, and stores have been preserved; one such building is the small palace of Baana ben Ahilud, the governor of Megiddo appointed by Solomon. It was his duty to provide food for the royal household one month each year; the large palace (see model opposite) was reserved for special ceremonies and royal visits.

7. SOLOMON'S INTERNATIONAL TRADE

Solomon took advantage of Israel's geographic location between Egypt, Syria, and southern Arabia to play an active role in international commerce, along with his Tyrian (Phoenician) allies. Important finds in Sardinia, Spain, and North Africa dating to the late eleventh and early tenth centuries B.C. have shown conclusively that the Phoenicians spread westward through the Mediterranean world as traders and colonists after David destroyed the Philistine confederacy and its maritime power around

Above:
Chariot and Syrian horse

Right:
Merchant ship in Solomon's
fleet, Tarshish type; 13th c. B.C.

Below:
Unloading logs from the boats
to the wharf

Right:
Phoenician boats transporting
logs in tow or aboard along the
shores of the Mediterranean; 8th
c. B.C. Assyrian relief

1000 B.C. This trans-Mediterranean shipping was led by the Sidonians and Tyrians, employing larger and stronger seagoing vessels than had previously been known. More ambitious ship designs could be realized by efficient use of the great cedars and firs of Lebanon and Cilicia (Asia Minor) and technological improvements in naval construction such as bands and spikes. This expansion attained its height in the ninth century and had passed its zenith by the middle of the eighth century B.C. when Greeks entered the seafaring competition in earnest.

Solomon's ships, built with Tyrian help in the port Ezion-geber, near Elath, took part in independent or joint expeditions to Ophir. The location of Ophis is still debated (South Arabia? East Africa? India?) but we have evidence that it was a source of gold in an ostracon found at Tell Qasileh on which was written "Gold from Ophir to Beth-horon—30 shekels." The Israelites went as far as Tarshish (probably in Spain), from which they brought precious metals, ivory, and other exotic products. The word *tar-*

shish apparently meant "metal refinery" in Phoenician and became the name of the sites where the Phoenicians established such installations, as in Sardinia and Spain.

The manner in which bulkier cargoes, such as timber, were carried to David and Solomon (2 Sam. 5:11; 1 Kings 5:1; 1 Chron. 14:1) is depicted in Assyrian reliefs. They show small riverboats, manned by Phoenicians, carrying logs stretched out on their upper decks, or tied to their sterns and trailing behind in the water. These cargo vessels moved down the coast from Cilicia or Lebanon by day and took shelter by night in the small coves and inlets of the eastern Mediterranean. The boats were unloaded at the mouth of the Yarkon river or Tell Qasileh (modern Tel Aviv) and the timber transported by ox-carts to Jerusalem for the great building operations of David and Solomon: the Temple, the royal palaces, and the elaborate homes of the nobility.

According to an obscure passage in the Bible, Solomon's merchants purchased horses from Ku'e (Asia Minor) and chariots from Egypt and bartered them to the Hittite kings in Syria (1 Kings 9:26–27; 2 Chron. 8:17–18). David, and to a greater extent Solomon, created chariot squadrons for their armies, and Solomon built special cities for his chariots. The famous stables found at Megiddo are, however, to be attributed to Ahab.

Clay figurine from Shikmona; Israelite period

a. *The Myth of Solomon's Mines*

Solomon's copper mining activity cannot be identified with the popular "Solomon's mines" near Elath, which are of Egyptian origin. There is no evidence of any copper mining or smelting in the Arabah valley between the twelfth and second centuries B.C. The credit given to Solomon belongs to Egyptians and Midianites a few centuries earlier. These negative results concerning mining are corroborated by the passages in 1 Chronicles 18:8 and 22:3 that indicate that David secured his metal from Syria. Furthermore, Solomon imported iron from the western Mediterranean in his boats of Tarshish. His fame in developing the Arabah emerged from his international seafaring enterprises based at the port of Ezion-geber, or Tell el-Kheleifeh, near modern Elath. Excavation there has revealed a small fortified center for warehousing, industry, and sea trade.

b. *Shikmona*

Another interesting aspect of Solomon's maritime expansion was revealed by recent discovery of a harbor city at Shikmona, south of Haifa, with the remains of four-roomed houses, oil presses, and a variety of artifacts dating from the tenth century. The place had previously been settled by Canaanites, but was taken over by David or Solomon as they consolidated their control of the country.

c. *Solomon and Arabia*

A Sabean kingdom was already established in Yemen (South Arabia) by the time of Solomon. Sedentary civilization and the use of writing

South Arabian (Sabean) scene of a queen and attendants. Late Iron Age

(derived from the Old Canaanite alphabet) have been traced back at least to the tenth century, and camels had been domesticated in Arabia before the eleventh century. Therefore, there is good reason to accept the biblical tradition that caravan trade between northern and central Syria, including Canaan, and southern Arabia began not later than the mid-tenth century B.C. The chief purpose of the Queen of Sheba's famous visit to the court of Solomon was probably to conclude a trade treaty, involving the exchange of the exotic spices of South Arabia for the agricultural produce of Israel, and a more complex deal for the manufactured products of third countries like Phoenicia.

8. THE CHARACTER OF KINGSHIP—PALESTINE AND PHOENICIA

Biblical tradition defines clearly the two functions of kingship in Israel: the king is chief executive, administrator, judge, also the commander in chief of the army and director of the nation's foreign policy. It was in the second role that David consolidated the tribes into a nation and built a standing army capable of defending it. The importance of royal justice was universally recognized in the ancient Near East. It is well illustrated in the inscription of Yehimilk, king of Byblos, a contemporary of Solomon. It says at one point: "May Baʿlshamem and the Lord of Byblos and the Assembly of the Holy Gods of Byblos prolong the days and years of Yehimilk in Byblos for [he is] a righteous and an upright king before the holy gods of Byblos!"

The Phoenician alphabet of the 10th c. B.C., derived from the Yehimilk and other inscriptions

𐤕 𐤔 𐤓 𐤒 𐤐 𐤍 𐤏   𐤎 𐤆 𐤋 𐤊 𐤉   𐤈 𐤇 𐤄 𐤅 𐤃 𐤂 𐤁 𐤀

In most countries the authority and power of the king were regarded as absolute and beyond challenge, though in practice his position rested on the support of army, priesthood, and aristocracy. In Israel the authority of the king was delimited by divine law. His role and power were carefully defined by a tripartite covenant involving the priesthood, the king, and the people, represented by the elders and army officers. The distinctive principle governing the Israelite monarchy was that all persons, including the king, were subject to the rule of law, namely the law revealed by God.

9. THE CLASSIC ERA OF BIBLICAL WRITING

It is commonly agreed that Solomon was a great patron of literature and the arts, and it is not accidental that his name was closely associated with the writing of songs and proverbs. The authorship of Proverbs, Song of Songs, and Ecclesiastes was attributed to him according to popular tradition, which was perpetuated in Scriptures in the same manner that David's name was attached to many Psalms, even if these books gradually crystallized into their present form later.

There is no doubt that royal secretaries and royal records proliferated in the days of Solomon and David; royal archives are often referred to in the books of Kings and Chronicles in such terms as "And the rest of the acts of King NN and all that he did are inscribed in the records of the royal chronicles of Israel and Judah." The term *sofer,* "scribe" or "secretary," had the same broad range of meaning in those days as it does today. Thus it might refer to the person who actually wrote at someone's dictation or who copied a text, like an office secretary. Or it might refer to a high official in the government, like cabinet members in the United States: Secretary of State, Treasury, Defense, and so on. So the "scribe" in the royal establishment of Israel had cabinet rank, was educated, skilled in writing, and widely read: such was "Jonathan, David's uncle . . . a counsellor, being a man of understanding and a scribe" (1 Chron. 27:32). Similar examples may be found in 1 Chronicles 2:55 and 4:9–10.

Israel's chroniclers had a literate audience that read and appreciated their writings, and it was the duty of the Levites scattered throughout the land to teach the people ritual, ethics, and letters. This literary and cultural level was not peculiar to Israel. The Phoenicians were equally literate, both peoples speaking and writing closely related Canaanite dialects. Scribal guilds were an institution in Canaan long before the Hebrew Conquest. As was the case in much of the ancient Near East, their members served not only in the royal courts but in every town, where they recorded official documents and served as public secretaries.

Overleaf:
The Northern Kingdom of Israel and Southern Kingdom of Judah after the division of David's and Solomon's United Kingdom

The king of Sam'al, in northern Syria, and his scribe, a high official (8th c. B.C. from Sinjirli)

113

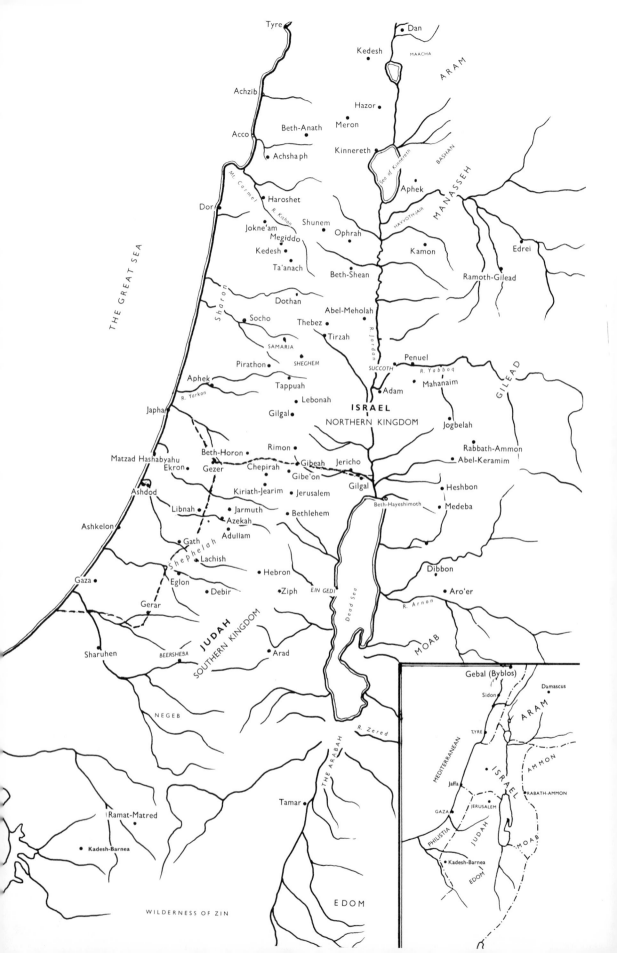

C. THE DIVISION INTO TWO KINGDOMS

The empire left by Solomon fell apart as a result of the opposition of the northern tribes to the heavy taxation and forced labor imposed by the king. Rather than speaking of the dissolution of a single nation, we may more accurately see the period of the United Monarchy as an interlude when two separate political entities were welded together by the personal power of David. We have observed that in the Song of Deborah (see "Judges") only the ten northern tribes are mentioned, implying that the southern tribes are isolated from them and constitute a separate group. Later, the numerous references to "the men of Judah and of Israel" in the stories of the time of Saul suggest that this distinction was already recognized before the time of David. It will be noted that on Saul's death the existence of separate states, north and south, was taken for granted when Ishbaal was made king of Israel and David king of Judah. In sum, even a centralized government was unable to overcome deep-seated differences and unify the separate groups permanently. This schism left two weak kingdoms, Israel (the Northern Kingdom) and Judah (the Southern Kingdom), which were soon attacked by Shishak, the Egyptian pharaoh, as recorded in an inscription in the Amon Temple at Karnak. It provides a long list of places in both Judah and Israel that were overrun by Shishak's army and details of his raid not mentioned in the Bible.

Fragment of an Egyptian stele marked *Shishak,* the pharaoh who invaded Palestine in Rehoboam's time

1. JEROBOAM, REHOBOAM, AND SHISHAK

Immediately after Shishak's campaign (the last quarter of the tenth century) radical changes were made in the construction of defensive walls to increase their strength. Solid walls, made of stone or a stone foundation with a brick superstructure, took the place of the casemate wall. This "off-set and inset" (slight salients and recesses) wall was further protected by superstructures. An outstanding example of the new type of work is seen in Megiddo's 11-foot-thick wall. Rehoboam, king of Judah, undertook to build fifteen such fortresses at Judah's most strategic points to guarantee the security of his kingdom and encourage its economic growth. There were large and flourishing cities, dating to the period following Jeroboam and Rehoboam, at Megiddo and Hazor as well as at Samaria. The famous stables at Megiddo also belong to this period.

Seal of "Shema servant of Jeroboam" (the second); 8th c. B.C., jasper, from Megiddo

Reconstruction of the stables of Megiddo built by King Ahab

Opposite page
First row left:
Monumental flight of steps
leading to the high place or
bamah of Dan, an open air
sanctuary

Right:
Characteristic Israelite masonry
of the sanctuary, showing
alternate "headers" and
"stretchers" in the wall

Second row, left:
The horned altar discovered at
Dan, measuring 16 × 16 inches
and 14 inches high

Right:
Bench at the right of the
entrance to the main gate,
where the elders sat in judgment

Third row, right:
The ashlar stone structure to the
right of the threshold of the
gate, and the paved street
leading into the city

Left: Detail

Jeroboam, first ruler of the Northern Kingdom, erected "golden calves" at the sanctuaries of Dan and Bethel after the schism of the United Kingdom (1 Kings 12:16 ff.). He meant both to rival Jerusalem as a cultic center and to establish parallel sanctuaries at both ends of his kingdom. The discovery of the high place at Arad, also founded during Solomon's days or shortly thereafter, indicates that kings established small royal sanctuaries (*miqdash melek*) in old cities on their borders to demonstrate their sovereignty in the region. In this way we can explain the presence of sanctuaries not only at Dan, Bethel, and Arad, but also at Beersheba on the edge of the desert that separated Israel from Egypt.

Judging by the change in pottery types after the destruction of Dan (Laish) in the middle of the eleventh century B.C., it was then settled by Israelites who migrated from the region near present-day Tel Aviv.

The excavations conducted by A. Biran since 1968 have uncovered a large structure from the Israelite period on the northwestern part of the tell (Area T). Its fine masonry, laid in headers and stretchers, resembles the monumental Israelite constructions found in Samaria and Megiddo. In fact it is a *bamah* or high place, that is, an open-air sanctuary. An almost square structure, roughly 60 by 62 feet, was discovered in the center. Its thick outer walls were made of dressed limestone except the northern side, which was built up of large basalt blocks. The area enclosed by the walls was filled with basalt stones, forming a wide, flat platform.

On the southern edge of the *bamah,* facing the town, a massive set of steps, 27 feet wide, was uncovered, built directly against the outer wall of the *bamah.* This stairway is built partially over earlier masonry. Pottery collected there dates to the ninth century. The first stage of the Israelite *bamah,* measuring 20 by 61 feet, probably comes from the reign of Jeroboam I (1 Kings 12:31). A second stage of the high place, with a still wider monumental stairway, is attributed to Ahab (1 Kings 20:34; 22:39).

a. *The City Gate*

After several seasons of excavation, a complete outer and inner gate complex, with a stone-paved square, a road, and a massive city wall, have emerged. The inner gate is built of large basalt blocks; it was about 97 feet long and had a width of 50 feet. It consisted of two towers and four guardrooms. The paved street leads westwards into the city, then turns toward the top of the mound.

A great deal of attention has been paid to an unusual structure and bench at the entrance to the gate. It is located along the outer wall of the northeastern tower. This is, according to biblical tradition, where the elders used to "sit at the gate" (Ps. 69:12) to deliberate and settle cases (cf. Ruth 4). The remarkable structure located near the bench is built of ashlars and originally had small columns with decorated capitals at each of its four corners (two of which were found *in situ*). The structure as a whole

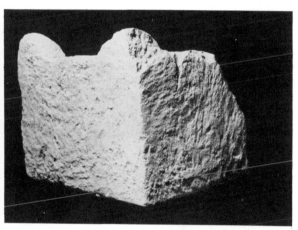

117

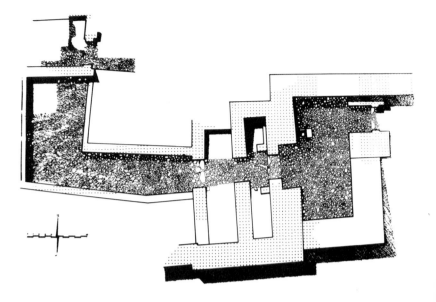

may have served as a throne or judgment seat, such as the one at the entrance of Samaria where the kings of Israel and Judah met on occasion (1 Kings 22:10).

Why then were the stone structure and the bench outside the inner city gate, facing the outer wall and gate? There is sufficient archaeological evidence to infer that a massive wall enclosed this plaza. It is an example of "the square at the gate of the city" mentioned in the Bible (Judg. 19:15–17; 2 Chron. 32:6). The gate complex was built at the end of the tenth century, probably by Jeroboam I (1 Kings 11:28).

b. *Standing Stones (masseboth)*

The *masseboth* were large stones or groups of them that were used for cultic purposes, usually found in Israel at sites associated with high places (e.g., 1 Kings 14:23; 2 Kings 17:10) and temples. They stood on a pedestal at the entrance to the "tower temple" of Shechem (see "Judges"). An elaborate group of ten of these stones, up to ten feet in height, was found at Middle Bronze Age levels of Gezer, lined up in three units, with an altar standing in the center. The temple at Hazor (thirteenth century B.C.) also had ten basalt *masseboth,* although they were much smaller. One was engraved with a pair of hands upraised gesturing toward the moon. Five stones stood near a temple at Timnah, center of the copper works near Elath. A *massebah* has also been found at the center of the high place of Arad (ninth century).

In the days of the United Monarchy these sacred stones were condemned because of the association with idol worship and particularly the Baal cult (1 Kings 14:23; 2 Kings 3:2; 17:10; 18:4). Their extensive use in Canaanite and Israelite rural worship stigmatized them and made them unfit for the religion of Yahweh.

The *massebah* or standing pillar set up in the Holy of Holies of the sanctuary of Arad

Royal ashlar masonry at
Samaria, capital of the Northern
Kingdom

3. THE DYNASTIES OF OMRI AND JEHU (882–745 B.C.) IN ISRAEL

The Northern Kingdom regained much of its earlier strength with the advent of the dynasty of Omri in 882 B.C. By then Israel had to face the ever-growing aggression of the Aramaeans of Damascus, who had displaced Israel's authority over Transjordan in the days of King Baasha (907 –882 B.C.). Omri, like David, abandoned the old provincial capital and moved to a new site, Samaria, that was free from any older tribal associations, making it a strictly royal city, the possession of the Omride dynasty. This remained the capital of the kingdom until its capture by the Assyrians in 722 B.C.

Excavations there have produced extensive evidence of the achievements of the northern kings during the ninth and eighth centuries and illustrated the material and cultural progress resulting from diplomatic alliance with the Phoenicians as in the days of Solomon. By then Tyre had become the mightiest sea power in the Mediterranean, and its colonies had spread as far as Spain and Africa. A vivid, detailed picture of Phoenician trade with Israel is given by the prophet Ezekiel (Ezekiel 27).

a. *Samaria's Remains*

Samaria was founded in 880 B.C. by Omri and enlarged by his son, Ahab. The former built his acropolis at the top of the hill, enclosing it by a wall of fine ashlar masonry and later enlarging it with a casemate wall. The lower town was protected by a massive wall of ashlar stones that surrounded the acropolis. On the acropolis two walls were found. The "inner wall," as it is called by the excavators, is five feet thick and encircled the summit of the hill, circumscribing an area of 194 by 106 yards. Its stones

Ivory carvings from the palace at Samaria. Mid-9th c. B.C.

were laid in header (perpendicular to the direction of the wall) and stretcher (parallel to the direction of the wall) formation. Several buildings were discovered within the walled area, among the remains of the Israelite palace, with its central court; the outside measurements are 89 × 79 feet. An "outer wall" was found to the north of the acropolis, apparently built by Omri. Ahab strengthened the defenses by adding a broad casemate wall about thirty-three feet wide, thus expanding the fortified area. The gateway seems to have been in the southwestern corner. On the eastern side of the acropolis proto-Aeolian capitals were found, suggesting that this was the main entrance to the inner area. In the west, between the "inner wall" and the casemate wall, there was a storehouse measuring 59 × 92 feet, labelled the "House of the Ostraca" because of the inscribed potsherds found there. In the northwestern corner a pool measuring 23 × 16½ feet was unearthed, and remains of the city gate were discovered on the eastern side of the summit.

Six phases of pottery and six corresponding periods of building, between 876 and 722 B.C., were decisive in dating the remains: Layer 1 (Omri); Layer 2 (Ahab); Layer 3 (Jehu and his successor); Layer 4 (Jeroboam II); Layers 5–6 (alterations and repairs). A layer of ashes over these levels is attributed to the Assyrian conquest and destruction. Furthermore, the lower strata of Layer 1 prove that there was already a small settlement on the hill of Samaria when Omri bought it from Shemer.

Two groups of small finds at this site deserve special attention. The first is the plaques found in the palace, mainly ivories of Phoenician and native workmanship in a style that is a symbiosis of Mesopotamian and Egyptian motifs. The palace was Ahab's "ivory house" (1 Kings 22:39), which the king had built for Jezebel, his highly sophisticated Phoenician consort. The ivories of Samaria, incidentally, supply a visual parallel to the ornaments of the Temple. The finds at Samaria also substantiate the biblical account of Phoenician influence at the court of Ahab and Jezebel. Even such a small detail as the horns of the altar (1 Kings 2:28) has now been confirmed by archaeological discoveries at Megiddo, Dan, and Beersheba. The prophetic strictures against idolatry can be better appreciated against the background of the numerous Astarte figurines found in the excavations at Samaria.

b. The Samaria Ostraca

In the western part of the acropolis were the royal storehouses, in which sixty-three ostraca (inscribed potsherds) were found. They record

the dispatch of wine and oil, giving the date, the place of origin, the recipient, and the commodity, followed by numerals. For example, Inscription Number 1 reads:

In the tenth year, to Shemaryahu, one jar of old wine

Pega (son of) Elisha	2	Ba'ala (son of) Elisha	2
Uzza (son of) Kabesh	1	Yedayahu	1
Eliba	1		

The written sources from the days of the Divided Monarchy, including the Samaria ostraca, the Siloam inscription, the Lachish letters, and those from Arad and Beersheba, and many other isolated finds, provide interesting sidelights on the political, religious, and military history of the period.

c. *The Abundance of Archaeological Finds*

There are indeed few periods in the history of the northern and southern kingdoms when the archaeological finds—written and silent—so accurately reflect the political events and the internal affairs as known to us from the literary sources. And the particular character of these finds fills in our knowledge of those regions that the biblical literary sources deal with very casually, such as districts in the north and the neighboring states in Transjordan. There is also a great abundance of seal impressions, weights and measures, and contemporary types of pottery that we illustrate in the margins of our pages.

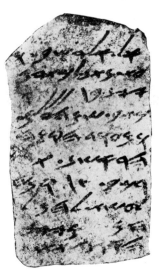

4. ISRAEL VERSUS ASSYRIA AND ARAM

The Northern Kingdom's expansion continued under Ahab (871–852 B.C.); Jehu (842–815) was forced to pay tribute to Assyria, but held his own among the neighboring nations and even gained a significant victory over the Aramaeans (816) besides quelling rebellions in Moab and Edom. Toward the end of the ninth century, the Aramaeans under Hazael overran both Israel and Judah, which were reduced to a state of helplessness. But their fortunes revived at the beginning of the eighth century. The Kingdom of Israel reached a third peak in the days of Jeroboam II (785–749 B.C.), while Judah prospered under the rule of Uzziah (Azariah: 786–758). In the latter part of the eighth century Israel's influence shrank and its position became increasingly precarious, owing to the growing power of

Assyria (which at least liberated Israel from the onslaughts of Aram). The death of Jeroboam II and his son Zechariah (748 B.C.) brought an end to the dynasty of Jehu. Between 748 and 722 B.C. five kings ruled over a much smaller Israel. It suffered a serious setback under the blows of Tiglath-Pileser III, who invaded in 733–732 B.C. Hazor was destroyed and rebuilt as an Assyrian town. When Sargon II invaded Palestine again, Samaria fell (722 B.C.), its inhabitants were deported, and the Kingdom of Israel came to an end.

a. *Shalmaneser III and the Battle of Qarqar*

In his campaign against the massed armies of the Aramaeans and Israel in 853 B.C., Shalmaneser enumerated on bronze tablets from Tell Balawat eleven countries that marshalled some 70,000 troops, 3,940 chariots (of which 2,000 were Ahab's and came partly from the famous stables at Megiddo that housed about 500 horses), and 1,000 camels from Arabia. We have noted that the first fixed date in biblical history, 853 B.C., was established through archaeological finds in Assyria. Thus, archaeology has helped to pinpoint events and to supply a wider view of the biblical past, discovering phenomena in ancient Israel not preserved in its literature.

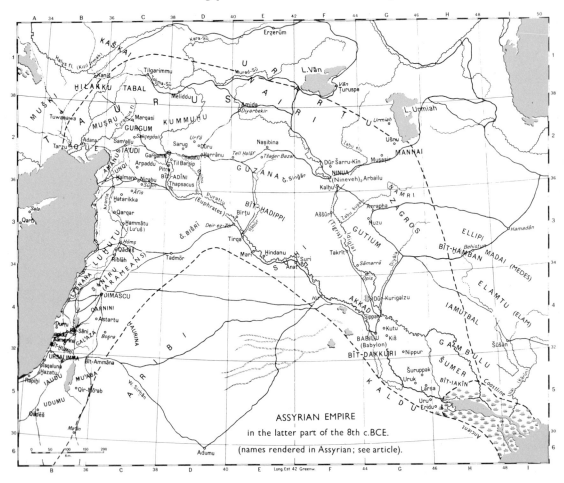

ASSYRIAN EMPIRE
in the latter part of the 8th c.BCE.
(names rendered in Assyrian; see article).

The battle of Qarqar proved inconclusive. Shalmaneser, however, invaded Palestine again twelve years later, this time winning a clear-cut victory over the "House of Omri" as the Northern Kingdom was known in Assyria, and exacting heavy tribute from Jehu of Israel and the king of Tyre. Though the Bible is silent on this, Shalmaneser III, in the "black obelisk" from Nimrud (now in the British Museum) described *ia-ú-a mar hu-um-ri,* "Jehu of the house of Omri." He is depicted bowing down to the ground in submission. This is the only extant representation of a king of Israel, but it is doubtless typical rather than specific. We owe a debt to the Assyrians for the fact that they were the only ancient people who left us faithful graphic descriptions of Israelite dress and weapons in their environment, from the time of Shalmaneser to that of Sennacherib. Nothing comparable has survived in Israel itself.

During the Omride period, Aramaean-Israelite hostility was resolved by a treaty (1 Kings 20:34) that granted the Aramaeans special economic privileges in Samaria. In return Israelites were given the right to open bazaars in Damascus.

b. *The United Aramaean Power: Damascus*

The unification of Aram and the rise of Damascus were mainly the work of Ben-hadad II. The new capital became the center of a large kingdom with an effective civil and military administration controlling all major lines of communication in western Asia. The Aramaic language spread as the international language of business and administration throughout the area, its script, also derived from Phoenician, being closely related to biblical Hebrew. At the battle of Qarqar, Aram and Israel were unified because of Shalmaneser's threat. When that danger abated, the alliance collapsed and Ben-hadad inflicted a decisive defeat on the combined forces of Israel and Judah at Ramoth Gilead east of the Jordan (851 B.C.; 1 Kings 22:1–35), in which Ahab lost his life. Ben-hadad's successor, Hazael, invaded both Judah and Israel. The representation of a king, "our lord Hazael," is found on an ivory plaque from Arslan Tash.

c. *The Mesha Stone*

Mesha, king of Moab, took advantage of Ahab's wars with the Aramaeans in order to rebel against Israel, whose rule extended into Transjordan. He set out to recover the independence of his ancient kingdom, then he rebuilt and fortified it. The stele, the Mesha Stone, in a typically boast-

Shalmaneser III and his attendants after the capture of Phoenician Hazazu. One of the many superb hammered bronze bands on the gates of the palace, Tell Balawat

Scenes from the Black Obelisk of Shalmaneser III showing him receiving tribute from kings and vassals, including King Jehu (second panel)

ful recital, credits victory to his military strategy. The Bible attributes the Israelite withdrawal to the horror and abomination felt when Mesha "took his eldest son . . . and offered him for a burnt offering upon the wall. And then came great wrath upon Israel and they withdrew" (2 Kings 3:27). The stele itself was discovered at Dibon in Transjordan in 1868. It was offered for sale to the French archaeologist Clermont-Ganneau, who refused to pay the price asked by the Arabs. They later broke it into pieces in order to get a better price by selling it piecemeal. Some of the larger fragments finally found their way to the Louvre in Paris where they were pieced together; thanks to an impression taken previously, many of the missing portions could be restored. When deciphered, the stele confirmed the historicity of the biblical record in the main, though it gave a variant account of the events. The thirty-four lines of the remarkable inscription are in Moabite, a dialect akin to biblical Hebrew. For a century this was a unique royal inscription from a Palestinian king of the period of the first Temple, but a few others have been reported found recently in Transjordan.

5. THE EARLY PROPHETS: ELIJAH AND ELISHA

Elijah and Elisha, in addition to Samuel's school of wandering ecstatic prophets, belong to the early or formative phase of Israelite prophecy, which is distinct in character and spirit from the prophecy of the eighth century B.C. These prophets of the early phase had much in common with the diviners or seers (Samuel: 1 Sam. 9:9; Balaam: Numbers 22–24) found elsewhere in Near Eastern antiquity, although a detailed comparison shows that there are many differences as well. Cuneiform tablets from Mari and texts from Egypt and Byblos illustrate how holy men divine while in states of frenzy. An idea that runs through both biblical and extrabiblical prophecy is that the prophet is the messenger of the god. For example, a sacrificial text from Byblos refers to a prophet with the following words: "Bring up the god! Bring up the messenger who is carrying him! It is Amon who has sent him."

Prophets during the early period are often mentioned in a context that suggests the existence of recognized groups specializing in invocations. So it is in the days of Elijah and Elisha (1 Kings 20:35 ff.; 22:6, 10; 2 Kings 2:3, 5; 4:1; 6:1). There is frequent mention of companies of prophets of the Lord, including groups located at Jericho, Bethel, and Carmel. The scene described in 1 Kings 18:20 ff. is typical of the activity of Elijah, the oracle of Carmel. As the contest between the prophets of Baal and the prophet of Yahweh reached its peak, sacrifices were offered at the top of the mountain, at a site now known as Muhraka or "burning place" (the site of the Carmelite Monastery of St. Elijah). B. Mazar is of the opinion that the Baal against whom Elijah contended was Baal Shamin (or Baal Shamem), the Lord of Heaven, a deity of cosmic significance among the Canaanites. Other scholars hold that it is Tyrian Baal, also known as

Melkart, the god of the underworld. Sanctuaries to Baal Shamem were situated mostly on the tops of mountains, notably Mount Carmel, as well as on peaks that dominated Phoenician settlements in Lebanon, at Carthage in Africa, and at Karatepe in northern Syria. Many scholars identify the deity with Zeus Olympios in the Hellenistic period. In fact, Baal Shamin is identified in the book of Daniel with the dominant deity of the Hellenistic Syrians who ruled Palestine in the second century B.C. on the eve of the Hasmonean revolt (cf. the books of Daniel and Maccabees). A temple to Baal Shamem was also discovered in the Nabatean religious center of Seia in the Hauran (northwest Transjordan).

Another characteristic of the earlier prophets was the transmission of their art from generation to generation. Elijah trained Elisha and named him as his successor (2 Kings 2, a truly dramatic narrative). Elijah and Elisha worked a variety of similar miracles. In the eighth century, however, divination and miracles played a much less important role in the activity of the prophets.

6. JEHOSHAPHAT—THE ALTAR AND CITY OF BEERSHEBA AND THE CITIES OF THE NEGEB

Several excavations and archaeological surveys have thrown light on the outstanding achievements of Jehoshaphat (867–851 B.C.). A contemporary of Ahab, he was one of Judah's best and most enterprising kings. He

Left:
A prince, or the god Melkart, out hunting as depicted on a Phoenician silver bowl. This brings to mind the taunts of Elijah addressed to the priests of Baal "Cry aloud, for he is a god . . . or he is hunting, or he is on a journey. . . ."

Right:
In his stele, Mesha, a king of Moab, tells of his wars with the kings of Israel (2 Kings 3). The inscription is in the Moabite dialect, which is close to biblical Hebrew (ca. 850 B.C.)

125

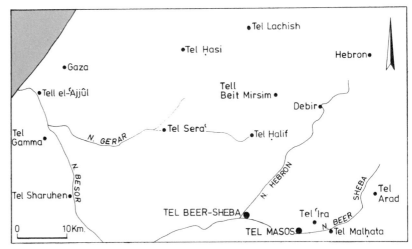

attempted to renew the commercial shipping from Ezion-geber but failed because a great storm wrecked his fleet. By then, Beersheba, founded in the twelfth to eleventh centuries B.C., had become the most prosperous city of the Negeb, as is shown by the extensive excavations conducted by Y. Aharoni. He uncovered the large altar of sacrifices that had stood in the sanctuary of Beersheba well known from biblical traditions.

Many new settlements established in this period have been discovered in the northern Negeb, east of Beersheba. For example, Tell Gharreh, located between Beersheba and Arad, was surrounded by a casemate wall. Tell Meshash, with its numerous four-room houses characteristic of Israelite architecture of the period, dates to the same time. Various other settlements were founded in the northern part of the Judean wilderness, "the fortresses and store cities" built by Jehoshaphat (2 Chron. 17:12). This has been confirmed by excavations of the "City of Salt," where the Essene community would be established several centuries later.

7. THE NEGEB FORTRESSES

From the tenth century onward, fortresses were built in the Negeb in the course of the southward expansion of the Judean kingdom. More than twenty have been located, but only a few excavated. Their outer defense is usually a casemate wall with rooms lining it and a courtyard in the center. Some of them, dating from the eighth to seventh centuries B.C., are rectangular (130 by 160 feet) with projecting towers, as at Kadesh-barnea, Khirbet Ghazza, and Arad. An earlier type (probably tenth century) consists of irregularly shaped buildings without towers, similar in size to the later ones. A third type, dating to the tenth century, was also a fort without towers, some 70 feet square, found on the roads to Kadesh-barnea and in the southern arid areas of the Negeb.

At Arad, six levels of fortresses were found covering a period from the tenth to the early sixth century B.C., each one built on the ruins of the preceding one. The walls were built of well-cut and bossed ashlar mason-

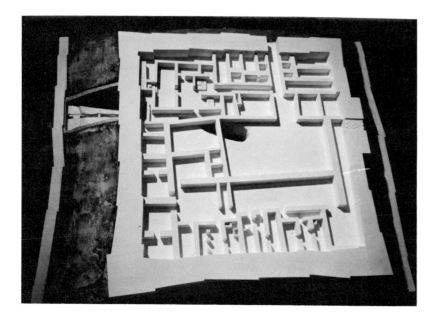

Model of the citadel of Arad in the Negeb (end of the 8th c. B.C.)

ry. The wall of the earliest fortress was of the casemate type; that of the succeeding five levels was solid and strengthened by a beaten-earth glacis and an outer wall; it was also strengthened by rooms built against the inside of the wall. The change in wall types was made to strengthen the defenses against improved methods of assault and more powerful siege engines. An Israelite high place was discovered on the northwestern side of the citadel and dated to the tenth or ninth century B.C.

8. THE ADMINISTRATIVE DIVISION OF JUDAH

Relationships between Israel and Judah had stabilized in the ninth century B.C. as the House of David finally accepted the separate existence of Israel. Jehoshaphat reorganized the administrative structure of Judah in the twelve-district pattern (2 Chron. 17:2). Most scholars agree that this is the source of the Judean town list incorporated in Joshua 15:21–62 by a later historiographer of the book of Joshua, though it is based on an earlier plan devised by David or Solomon.

Another of the great kings of Judah, Uzziah (786–758 B.C.), a contemporary of Jeroboam II, helped to enlarge Judah's domain over substantial areas of the Negeb, including parts of Philistia and Edom, with the idea of protecting and expanding the caravan trade. Large forts surrounded by casemate walls and defended by eight towers were erected at main highway junctions and on the borders. The same king carried out vast building projects and strengthened the fortifications of Jerusalem. Both he and his son, Jotham, increased the size of the Judean military forces. An ossuary, inscribed in Aramaic and purporting to contain the bones of Uzziah, was discovered not in the royal necropolis, but in the ancient cemetery at the foot of the Mount of Olives. It will be recalled that Uzziah had to resign the kingship because of his leprosy, and this fact may help to explain the curious disposition of his bones.

Inscribed tablet from Arad in the Negeb specifically identifying a sanctuary in the "house of Yahweh"

127

Above:
Seal of *Yehozerah ben Hilkiyahu servant of King Hezekiah*

Right:
The twelve regions of Israel in the reign of Solomon, plus Judah (later divided into twelve districts as well)

Below:
Top of a tomb comprising a square shaft that gave access to the burial chamber. The latter had a square opening in the ceiling, the *nephesh* or "memorial." The round hole was made by people who came accidentally on the tomb, or by grave robbers. Discovered west of the Temple Mount excavations, Jerusalem

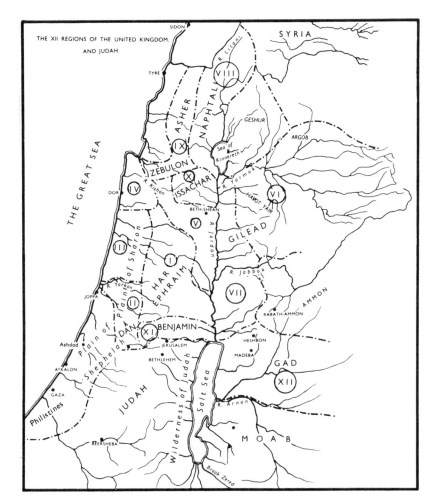

9. THE LAST TWO CENTURIES OF JUDAH

The Judean monarchy had to struggle continually for survival in the face of Assyrian and, later, Babylonian imperialism as well as periodic attempts by Egypt to sway the small Palestinian states from their allegiance to these northern empires.

The campaigns of Sennacherib, well known from Assyrian annals, are referred to in 2 Kings 18:13–35, 2 Chronicles 32:9, 21, and Isaiah 36 and 37. During Hezekiah's reign Judah suffered a devastating invasion by Sennacherib and lost dozens of cities and villages to the Assyrian army. At the end only Jerusalem and its environs were left, and they were under siege (701 B.C.). Through the payment of a huge tribute, the city was saved and the Assyrians lifted their siege. The Assyrians immortalized the siege and capture of Lachish, one of the fortresses guarding the approaches to Jerusalem, in a series of great wall reliefs, now collected in the British Museum. Archaeologists have discovered the broad wall Hezekiah built around the new Upper City quarters of Jerusalem, to protect the extension

A section of the "broad wall" built by King Hezekiah at the end of the 8th c. B.C. (2 Chron. 32:5) uncovered in the Western Hill (Upper City, or Mishneh) and over 20 feet wide

Lower left:
An inscribed sherd found in the Ophel (most ancient part of Jerusalem) bearing names such as *Yehezkiyahu, Abiyahu, Zephanyahu*

Lower right:
Inscription of the secondary burial of King Uzziah, carved in Second Temple times and found on the Mount of Olives, far from the royal necropolis, as he died of leprosy (2 Chron. 26:23)

129

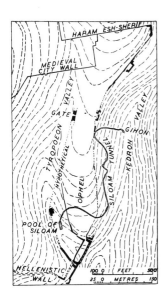

King Hezekiah had a long and somewhat winding tunnel dug under the lower Ophel. This brought the water of the Gihon spring directly to the Siloam pool situated within the city walls. It was covered and made impervious to Assyrian onslaught

of the city on the west side. A section of the wall has been uncovered in the Jewish Quarter of the Old City, revealing a broad rampart 23 feet thick and built of large unhewn stones, fitted together without mortar. The remains consist of two to seven courses of stone reaching a height of about 10 feet along a length of 128 feet. This represents only the foundations of the wall laid on bedrock; it served to reinforce and extend the original boundary of the city of David and Solomon.

a. *Hezekiah's Tunnel and the Siloam Inscription*

Hezekiah's greatest engineering achievement was a tunnel that has survived intact to this day. He decided to provide the city with a new reservoir of drinking water within the city walls and safe from Sennacherib's onslaught. He had a tunnel 1,750 feet long dug in the rock to bring water from the Gihon spring to the Siloam pool. The dramatic story is told in 2 Kings 20:20 and 2 Chronicles 32:30 ff., spelling out the accomplishment in detail. The feat is also commemorated in a Hebrew inscription carved in the side of the tunnel near its exit to the pool. It relates how the tunnelers, working with picks, started at opposite ends and finally met in the middle, completing their task.

b. *Recent Discoveries in Jerusalem*

Large quantities of pottery and other artifacts dating to the Monarchy were discovered in the excavations of the Ophel (the most ancient part of Jerusalem) and at the foot of the Temple Mount. Remnants of Israelite houses and a cave complex were uncovered by Kathleen Kenyon in the trench she dug below the upper Hasmonean wall and fortress. An interesting epigraphic item is the Ophel ostracon found in 1924, dating to the end of the Monarchy and bearing familiar names such as Yehezkiyahu

In 1976, the excavations at the Temple Mount uncovered the terraced area known as *Beth-millo* dating to the days of the Judean Monarchy. It is seen in the foreground, with remains of Herodian structures at a higher level

and Abiyahu. Numerous historical structures have also been discovered by B. Mazar since 1976 in the upper Ophel.

c. *Tombs*

A sizable cemetery of the eighth century B.C. has been discovered by Mazar on the slope of the valley facing the Western Wall of the Temple Mount. The tombs were carved in the rock, each comprising a square shaft or flight of stairs that gave access to a large burial chamber. The latter had a square opening in the ceiling, apparently the *nephesh* ("memorial"), covered with stone slabs or a gabled structure. This cemetery was used by the upper class population of Jerusalem. Because of the expansion of the city toward the upper (Western) hill, the cemetery was abandoned in the days of Manasseh (mid-seventh century B.C.). Another group of rock-cut tombs had been discovered previously and was attributed to the House of David by R. Weill, but the "royal" theory still lacks verification. One of the tombs has a shaft leading to a vaulted tunnel 54.4 feet long and 13.2 feet high, which ends at a stone bench in which a niche is carved, probably to hold a coffin. Numerous rock-cut tombs on the eastern side of the city have been discovered in recent years.

In 1927 J. W. Crowfoot uncovered masonry blocks that stood on cliffs overhanging the valley. He assumed that it was the Valley Gate of the lower city, but before this theory could be checked the land was built over by Arabs of the village.

The biblical tradition makes mention of the "King's Garden" located at the bottom of the valley near the Siloam Pool; it is irrigated by an overflow of that pool. The gardens are still there and flourish for the same reason, a living verification and reminder of the ancient tradition (B. Mazar, *The Mountain of the Lord*).

The Hezekiah tunnel near its outflow to the Pool of Siloam

Ancient Israelite tombs situated in the Ophel (the core of the Davidic city), truncated as a result of quarrying in Roman times

Upper right:
A royal tomb of the 8th c. B.C. uncovered west of the Temple Mount, with steps leading to the burial chamber

Upper left:
One of the underground halls, and inner burial chambers leading from it, constituting part of the northern necropolis of Jerusalem and situated in the courts of the St. Etienne Monastery (days of the Judean Monarchy)

d. *Royal Seal Impressions*

Hundreds of royal seal impressions have been found on various Judean tells in recent years. In the center of a typical impression there is a symbol, either a four-winged scarab or a double-winged sundisk, accompanied by the inscription *lmlk* "of the king," while below it is often written a place name: Hebron, Socoh, Ziph, or *mmsht*. Y. Aharoni has proved conclusively that the four-winged seal impressions were inaugurated by Hezekiah before Sennacherib's campaign; the double-winged symbol was adopted during the first half of the seventh century and was abandoned before the reign of Josiah (640 B.C.). The use of these seals corresponds to the reorganization and consolidation of Judah into four administrative cen-

Gate excavated west of the Ophel

ters for, among other purposes, the collection of taxes in the face of the impending war with Assyria. This explains the use of the names of the three Judean cities and *mmsht*, probably an abbreviation of "the state." The taxes, paid in agricultural produce, were collected in the four royal store cities. The figures in the seal impressions are based on foreign originals. Such pagan motifs on Judean seals disappeared later as a consequence of Josiah's religious reforms.

Jar handle bearing a seal impression with the word *lmlk*, belonging to the king/*Socoh*

10. JOSIAH'S REFORM AND THE DESTRUCTION OF JERUSALEM

Judah had a final period of political and religious resurgence during the reign of Josiah (640–609 B.C.) as Assyrian power disintegrated at the end of the seventh century B.C. The young king cast off the foreign yoke, expanding Judean authority over all Palestine. Simultaneously he removed the foreign cults associated with Assyrian influence and instituted a ritual purification throughout the land (2 Kings 22–23; 2 Chronicles 34). The biblical tradition associated the reform with a dramatic discovery, made in some dark recess of the Temple chambers, of a scroll of the Book of the Covenant or part of the Book of the Law we call Deuteronomy. This was impromptu archaeology with farreaching consequences. Though Josiah's reforms preceded the destruction of the state by the Babylonians in 586 B.C. by only thirty-six years, they had a lasting effect in focusing worship and ritual on the Temple Mount.

At the same time as the cult was being centralized, worship at the many high places (for example, Dan, Bethel, Arad, and Beersheba) was terminated by order of Josiah. The priests of the Judean high places "from Geba to Beersheba" (2 Kings 23:8) were transferred to Jerusalem. The elimination of the high places of the northern kingdom was far more drastic than in the south. The sanctuaries of Dan and Bethel were defiled by the burning of human bones on their altars, while the territory was annexed into the framework of the enlarged kingdom. The high places of Beersheba and Arad may already have been suppressed by Hezekiah, who is quoted as "saying to Judah and Jerusalem 'You shall worship before this altar in Jerusalem' " (2 Kings 18:22).

Winged scroll of *Ziph* on a jar handle bearing a *lmlk* seal impression. Such seals were presumably stamped by royal officials as a guarantee of the capacity of the store-jars so stamped

The wars of this period (2 Kings 24–25) and the events leading up to them are also reflected in extrabiblical sources. The royal annals and the reliefs of Sennacherib of the siege of Lachish (2 Chron. 32:4; Isa. 36:2) present textual and visual evidence of his campaign against Hezekiah. The defenses of Lachish represented in the Assyrian reliefs are similar to those uncovered in the excavation of the city. The famous Babylonian Chronicle contains a record of the events of the last years of the Judean kingdom, including an account of the capture of Jerusalem in 597 B.C. by Nebuchadnezzar. Other Babylonian inscriptions and an Aramaic letter from the king of one of the Philistine cities, probably Ekron, contribute further details.

Another piece of evidence of the time is an ostracon found at Mesad Hashavyahu, a small fort near Yavneh-Yam on the coast. It is a letter of a wronged peasant to the officer of the fort, and it shows how the social laws of the Bible were reflected in contemporary life during the reign of Josiah.

Y. Aharoni excavated a royal fortress and palace at Ramat Rahel, south of Jerusalem, which he dated to the last years of the realm. This is the only palace of a Judean king found in archaeological excavations. The walls were constructed of ashlar blocks like those at Ahab's palace at Samaria. The palace was decorated with proto-Aeolian capitals and had impressive window casements. Among other finds was a painted potsherd depicting the king, possibly Jehoiakim, seated on a throne (or a chariot).

11. ISRAELITE CLOTHING

Carved ivory inlays found in excavations at Megiddo (thirteenth to

Richer clothing of the period is illustrated by the woman who wears a cloak (*simlah*) and long veil and the priest in his long tasseled robe (from a Phoenician stele of the 4th c. B.C.)

eleventh centuries B.C.) and Assyrian murals of the seventh century give us a fairly good idea of dress styles and their evolution in biblical times.

From the earliest times, the basic undergarment was the kiltlike loincloth worn next to the skin, called the *ezor* (2 Kings 1:8; Isa. 20:2; Jer. 13:1 ff.) Many Egyptian paintings show such a garment wrapped around the loins and tied with a belt or girdle (*hagorah*). For religious functions, a shirt or apron was tied around the body (1 Sam. 2:18; 2 Sam. 6:14). The Hebrew term is transliterated as *ephod,* which refers also to an elaborate priestly garment (Exod. 28:6–12). The next most common outer garment was the tunic, the *ketonet* or *chiton.* This garment was made by simply folding a rectangle of cloth in half and sewing up the sides, leaving openings for the head and arms. This could be worn open or closed, with or without sleeves, depending on individual needs. The most frequent term for a top garment, possibly worn over the tunic, is the *me'il* (1 Sam. 2:19; 28:14; 1 Chron. 15:27), which in many English versions is wrongly translated as "coat" (as in the case of Joseph). Apparently it was worn also by people of high rank; such a costume is pictured on the borderstone of a Babylonian king (ca. 1100 B.C.).

Most people in the ancient Near East wore a shawl or cloak made of wool or linen draped around the body over the tunic. Biblical terms for this garment, variously translated, are *simlah* (Deut. 21:13; Ruth 3:3) or *salmah* (Mic. 2:8; 1 Kings 11:30). The *sa'ip,* a long veil (Gen. 24:65; 38:14), a woman's upper garment, is illustrated in a fourth century Phoenician carving of a woman and a priest. She is wearing the garment usually called a *himation* or *pallium.* Israelite law (Deut. 22:5) makes it clear that women's clothing differed from men's. According to S. Yeivin, however, the *saddin* (Judg. 14:12) was worn by both men and women; it was not an exclusively female garment, as had been assumed.

The earliest Israelite undergarment was the kiltlike loincloth, or *ezor* (left). The common tunic or *ketonet* was the outer garment worn by the three figures (right)

136

PART VI

A. THE CLASSIC PROPHETS

1. THE TRANSITION FROM THE EARLY TO THE WRITTEN PROPHETS

We have seen that traditions about the early prophets often included miraculous stories, and supernatural knowledge was attributed to them in many cases. Although divination was the target of constant attacks by the later prophets, it clearly played a role in stories about earlier figures such as Samuel and Saul.

Various examples of divination and ecstatic prophecy, known to us from the books of Samuel and Kings, have much in common with Canaanite, Egyptian, and Mesopotamian practices. The best-known examples attested by archaeological finds are the seers and diviners of Mari of the early second millennium B.C., known as the *apilum, muhhum,* or ecstatic prophets, and the *baru* priests, known from every period of Babylonian and Assyrian history, who specialized in liver omens. The similarity between the Mari prophets especially shows that prophecy was not unique to Hebrew culture but was well known in the ancient Near East. However, while Israelite experience gave rise to the great classical prophets, the phenomenon remained basically static in the rest of the ancient world.

In the period from Samuel to Saul, ecstatic prophets appear in groups, often under the leadership of a single seer. We have no record of such appearances in the period of the Monarchy, but during the reign of Ahab groups of independent prophets appeared throughout the land and may have helped in the struggle against Jezebel and her Phoenician acolytes (1 Kings 18:19–21:27).

Charismatic personalities such as Elijah and Elisha had a great impact on the prophetic tradition, and it was because of the respect in which they were held by their audience that these "men of God" were endowed with legendary accretions of magic and divination. Elijah was the leader of a prophetic group, one among many that flourished at that time. They were located in places hallowed by tradition, such as Bethel, Jericho, and Gilgal, where members lived a communal life. We learn that Elisha was a disciple of Elijah because he had "poured water on the hands of Elijah" (2 Kings 3:11). It seems that Elisha was instrumental in promoting Jehu's excessive cruelty in dealing with his Israelite enemies (2 Kings 9:1–10:36). While it may be true that pagan worship was eradicated from Israel, the ceaseless wars with the Aramaeans killed off multitudes of people and impoverished the masses, placing them at the mercy of the rich landlords and merchants. The later prophets became the mouthpiece of the downtroden.

In the eighth century B.C. the point of view in the biblical tradition shifted radically. In addition to stories about prophets the actual utterances of famous prophets were remembered and recorded. By this time prophets presented their messages to their fellow Israelites in the form of eloquent rhetorical compositions distinguished by their high artistic and theological standards. Underlying their prophecy was a sublime moral and religious experience as well as a broad understanding of the historical situation in which they lived.

2. A UGARITIC LEGAL TERM EXPLAINS THE TRANSITION TO WRITTEN PROPHECY

A study of Ugaritic legal documents written in a dialect of Canaanite has helped S. A. Löwenstamm to correct a crucial mistranslation of a well-known verse in Habakkuk (2:3), namely that the word 'od (the adverb "yet" or "still") should be read as 'ed (the noun for "testimony"). The line should therefore read "For the vision is a testimony of the appointed time." This explains the reason for the instruction in the preceding verse: "Yahweh answered me: Write the vision, make it plain upon tablets. . . ." It proclaims God's will that *prophecy should be recorded;* and when it is fulfilled, the written record will prove that the "word of God" has actualized itself in history. In the preface to the Song of Moses (Deut. 31:19) we find the same rationale: "That this song may be a witness [testimony] for me. . . ." Consequently, a proper understanding of the biblical data means that at this time, it was found imperative to record prophecy in writing, with momentous implications for Israel and the world.

The rhapsodic prophets who followed Elijah and Elisha were opposed to prophetic guilds, which practiced prophecy as a craft, and to the idea that any person could be taught by a master to prophesy. They were not professional prophets, nor were they connected formally with any shrine and its rituals. A new type of prophet had appeared who objected to the mistreatment of the poor and saw the lack of social justice as a fundamental violation of the Covenant between the people and their God.

3. PROPHECY RELATED TO HISTORICAL REALITY

It is important that the classic prophets set out to interpret Yahweh's commandments in terms of the historical reality of the day and therefore analyzed contemporary events with great insight. This separates prophecy clearly from the pagan practices of divination and magic that were dominant in the rest of the Near East. These Israelite prophets did not set out to divine the future, but rather sought to understand and improve the present. Divination rested on a deterministic belief that what was ordained by fate or by supernatural powers would certainly come to pass and that it was the diviner's task to discover it. The classic Hebrew prophet held that the future was not foreordained but depended in large part on the moral behavior of the people. Hence the current situation was of vital importance for its bearing on the future. Because of this the prophets are a reliable witness to the main events of their time, which biblical scholarship and especially archaeology can illuminate.

4. GENERAL THEOLOGY OF CLASSIC PROPHECY

The prophets proclaimed that the obligations inherent in the Mosaic Covenant and the commandments of the Law (Torah) were the essence of Israelite religion, but more than intellectual appreciation and assent was required to make them meaningful and significant. A commitment in faith to the God of Israel and the fulfillment in practice of his demands were the necessary ingredients. For instance, Isaiah (Isaiah 1) would not accept lip service as a substitute for active faith and an upright life. The prophets understood the Law as regulating the relations among human beings in the light of divine revelation and especially as restraining the exploitation of the weak, the poor, the downtrodden, and the defenseless. They spoke for God in behalf of the disinherited and disenfranchised. To them the viability of the state and the survival of the community depended on the response of all to the stipulations of the Covenant, but especially the rich and powerful whose behavior affected the lives of so many. All of the prophets gave warning of divine judgment that would come to pass in the context of historical events if the people as a whole failed to keep the terms of their commitment, and they summoned the people to repent before it was too late. They faced their task with a profound sense of divine vocation and an ultimate compulsion, for they had been called and commissioned by Yahweh to be his messengers.

There was a fundamental conflict between the prophets and the kings, which grew more intense toward the end of the Kingdom of Judah. Although the relationship went back to the beginnings of the Monarchy in Israel (Samuel and Saul and David), there were basic tensions and difficulties as royal policies and practices diverged more and more from prophetic standards of divine righteousness. Because kings necessarily were concerned with political decisions, both internal and external, designed to safeguard and promote the well-being of the nation and the dynasty, they therefore engaged in the international games of diplomacy and in military adventures; the prophets were more concerned with questions of ultimate morality and adherence to the religious requirements of the Covenant, both in relation to other nations and to internal matters. Modification or denial of the fundamental requirements in the interest of expediency met with radical rejection on the part of the prophets and denunciation of the monarch and his aides. The prophets were equally at odds with venal priests, who were mere sycophants and retainers of the crown. They easily misled many of the religious with assurances that faithfulness and continuity in the performance of the ritual were sufficient to meet the demands of the faith. The prophets insisted on a return to fundamentals, to a reaffirmation of Mosaic faith with its emphasis on commitment and compliance with the Law of God.

These prophets transmitted the divine message, "God's word," to the people or the king in highly personalized pronouncements. They were strong-willed men and kings listened to them whether they wanted to or not; priests came seeking them, never the reverse. Championing the rights of the downtrodden on the basis of the Covenant, the prophets risked abuse at the hands of those they attacked, as was the case with Amos and Jeremiah.

5. PROPHECY AND PREDICTING THE FUTURE

When read by later generations under altered circumstances, the prophetic message came to be interpreted in a way that the prophets themselves may not have intended. They were primarily concerned with their own generation and what the future held in store for it, especially if it failed to heed the words of warning and the call to repentance. Since many announcements of impending doom were fulfilled, the prophets were seen primarily as predictors of the future, whose words held meaning for later generations concerning their future. In other words, hidden in the prophetic oracles of the past were secret messages about the sequence of much later events, including destruction and exile and ultimate return and restoration of the people of God. What in the prophets had been conditional pronouncements about the future, consequences being affected by behavior and responses on the part of the people, became in later times explicit predictions fulfilled as evidence of their special powers and of God's overriding control and determination of the course of history. The early biblical scholars paid little attention to the context of the prophecies, namely the historical situation that was the object of their political analysis. Partly because of their literary merit, the prophets were read and increasingly investigated for hidden meanings relevant to the new age and situation. The eschatologists and messianists, concerned with the end of time, particularly the covenanters at Qumran, carried this practice to its extreme. Warnings of defeat or destruction that were related to the time of Isaiah or Habakkuk were reinterpreted in light of the tribulations of their own lives. Even greater was the temptation to find hidden promises of imminent redemption.

To be sure, the prophets believed that Yahweh would restore Israel to the land under the rule of a descendant of the House of David, who would be "Yahweh's anointed," but they saw this as resulting from the repentance of the people of their day. The Jews of the Roman and Byzantine periods, however, read into the prophets a prediction concerning the end of the post-Temple Exile and thought they would witness a third restoration in their days; this is particularly true in the time of Bar Kochba (second century A.D.) or Julian (fourth century). Similarly, the early Christians found in the Scripture predictions of the coming of Christ and his messianic role.

6. REFORMERS FROM WITHIN

The prophets should be considered conservative reformers, who wished to restore an earlier form of society, rather than as revolutionaries. They called for a radical return to, not a radical departure from, the traditions of Israel's earliest days. They sought to infuse ritual and legal regulations with spiritual integrity and a deep sense of moral justice and in this way to revitalize the existing order. They carried God's message to repent, to return to God's commandments to which Israel had bound itself at Sinai.

7. PARTICULARISM AND UNIVERSALISM

The prophets' concern did not stop with their own nation. They understood that Israel, as a small nation, was part of a large complex of nations that made up their world. They understood from the beginning that all the nations, the whole universe, was under the rule and power of the one God. Therefore the other nations served his purpose and played a role in his historical plans. On the one hand, this relationship could be seen in the use of the small and great powers as instruments of divine wrath in smiting Israel and Judah. On the other hand, here was an inherent universalism that became evident in later Israelite thought.

Thus, although their words were aimed at contemporaries, the prophets' message was perpetuated through the ages: the fundamental principles governing human society were for all, and all were equal before the Law and before God. The Covenant expressed the justice and mercy of God, qualities that were to be emulated by human beings in personal and social relationships. The words of Micah 6:8 sum this up: "What does the Lord require of you but to do justice, and love mercy, and walk humbly with your God?"

8. WHO WERE THE CLASSIC PROPHETS?

Limitations of space preclude detailed descriptions of the numerous prophets from Amos to Malachi whose writings are found in the Bible. They represent a pinnacle of Israelite tradition not only for their lofty ethical standards but also for the superb poetic quality of their writings. Moreover, the legacy of classic prophecy, its spirit, message, and style, has figured prominently in Judeo-Christian culture and is one of the foundations of western civilization.

We shall examine various prophets in brief, pointing out significant characteristics of the literary prophets with special attention to their historical background and context. This will include a discussion of the relevant archaeological information available for these periods.

The first of the classic prophets were Amos and Hosea, around the middle of the eighth century B.C., both of whom prophesied in the Northern Kingdom. They were followed shortly thereafter by Isaiah and Micah, who were active in Judah. Jeremiah's prophetic activity dates to a century later.

9. AMOS AND HOSEA

The great material progress under Jeroboam II (785–748 B.C.) resulted in a considerable rise in the standard of living of some and a growing disparity between the rich few and the poor masses. This is evident from the material wealth found in Samaria, dating to the days of Omri and Ahab. At the same time, Israel's religion seems to have been corrupted by the infiltration of pagan practices attacked by Hosea, Amos' contemporary, particularly the fertility cult with its immoral rites. The numerous figurines of the Lady Ashtoreth found in many Israelite cities provide archaeological evidence of this proliferation. Moreover, the Samaria ostraca (from the first half of the eighth century B.C.) show that names formed with Baal (like Yerubbaal, Ishbaal) were almost as common as names formed with Yahweh, or the short form Ya(h)u (like Shemaryau). This shows that Baalism and Canaanite customs, many of which were probably transmitted by the Phoenicians, had not been eradicated. This is the background against which we can appreciate the sayings of Amos and Hosea. Both were horrified by the selfish luxury, the oppression of the poor, and the immorality they saw around them.

The horned altar of sacrifices of the sanctuary of Beersheba, reconstructed from its scattered ashlar blocks. Now on view at Tell Beersheba

B. AMOS

The earliest of the recorded prophets was Amos. His career dates from about 750 B.C., during the reign of Jeroboam II. With Amos we have direct testimony of a creative individual in Israel's spiritual life, the like of whom is unattested earlier anywhere in the ancient world. What we know of the ministry of this rustic herdsman is limited to his visions and fearless preaching at Bethel and Samaria in the Northern Kingdom. His prophecy dwells on the impending judgment against the arrogant rich and the royal house. When challenged by the priest at Bethel, he defied him and asserted that regardless of other considerations, when a man is called by God and commissioned by him, he cannot submit to the rulings and restrictions of men.

1. CONTENTS

Like the other prophetic books, Amos is not a strictly coherent unity, but a series of oracles and addresses arranged in loose order. Therefore we will discuss the material according to subject matter rather than following the biblical sequence exactly.

The book of Amos opens with indictments against the neighboring nations, climaxing in 2:6–16 with an extended indictment against Israel. The next four chapters (Amos 3–6) contain oracles of judgment against Israel. Amos announces the punishment that will take place on the "Day of Yahweh" (5:18–20), a day of judgment when Israel will be oppressed, its land destroyed, and its people exiled (3:14–15; 5:3, 26–27). This material is followed by reports of five visions: the locusts (7:1–3), drought (7:4–6), the plumb line (7:7–9), the basket of summer fruit (8:1–3), and Yahweh announcing the destruction of Israel (9:1–4). Among these visions there is also the angry exchange between the prophet and the priest, Amaziah, at the shrine of Bethel (7:10–17). Finally there is the epilogue, which includes a final announcement of disaster for Israel (9:7–10) and a prediction of eventual restoration and prosperity which the inhabitants will enjoy (9:11–15).

2. AMOS' MESSAGE

Amos cries out against the oppression of the poor by the wealthy and powerful (2:6–7; 3:10; 4:1; 5:11), against those who pervert justice by bribery (5:7, 10–12), against dishonest merchants (8:4–6), and against the idleness and luxury of the rich of Samaria. No better description could be given of the exquisite beauty of the ivories discovered in the king's palace of Samaria and other rich homes of the capital. In retribution, the rich and their property would eventually be destroyed (3:11, 15; 4:3; 5:11; 7:11).

The famous passage in 5:21–25 censuring the popular sacrificial ritual is not a rejection of the formal cult *in toto,* but emphasizes that it is not the only or most important element in the worship of Yahweh; the criticism is based in part on the corruption of the cult, which was accompanied by drunkenness (2:7–8) and various Canaanite debaucheries and, more generally, on the performance of the ritual without regard to justice in everyday activity. Therefore Israel's shrines will be destroyed (3:14; 5:5; 7:9; and elsewhere).

Although Amos' prophecies of doom are often untempered with hope, he does include the idea that Israel will not be destroyed totally as a consequence of its sins. A "remnant" will be saved to enjoy the promises inherent in the Covenant (9:11–15). This concept, along with others such as the "Day of Yahweh" and the distrust of the formal cult practices, is echoed throughout the rest of Israelite prophecy.

3. THE DISCOVERY OF THE ALTAR OF SACRIFICES AND SANCTUARY OF BEERSHEBA

Until recently the high place at Beersheba denounced by Amos (5:5; 8:14) lay undiscovered, though biblical tradition stressed its importance from earliest times (Gen. 21:33; 46:1–5). We have seen above ("Kings") that it was customary to maintain sanctuaries at the boundaries of the

The city gate of Beersheba is situated to the right. The area to the left and the bordered streets date from Solomon's time

country. This is why Jeroboam chose Dan and Bethel as the sites of high places. Just as there was a sanctuary at Arad on the Edomite border of the Southern Kingdom, there was another at Beersheba, the last inhabited town bordering on the vast desert that divided the land of Israel from Egypt. It took Aharoni's expedition five years of excavation at Tell Beersheba to find the first evidence of its presence. Four ashlar blocks were found in a repaired section of the storehouse complex near the city gate (see picture); they had originally been part of a large horned altar that stood in the sanctuary. These ashlars, three of which were intact, had been built into the wall. Other similarly dressed ashlar blocks of a special sandstone were found above them and in other areas. The reconstructed altar

Aerial view of the gate area on the left (as in previous picture) with the storehouse area to the right

145

is similar in design to smaller incense altars from the period of the Monarchy. This altar is now on view at the expedition camp at Tell Beersheba.

4. LOCATING THE SANCTUARY OF BEERSHEBA

The first discovery confirmed the assumption that a sanctuary had existed at Beersheba, probably more elaborate than the isolated high place of Arad. Beersheba's altar was dismantled, apparently during the reign of Hezekiah. But where was the sacred high place? A large public building, some 65 feet square, was uncovered near the northwestern corner of the tell. West and south of the building were rows of basements connected by subterranean doorways. It had been built on bedrock and belonged to the latest Israelite city (Stratum 2). Various details of this structure were similar to that at Arad; their areas were the same, both were oriented east to west, and both had large courtyards to the east where an altar would stand. Support for the hypothesis that this was the sanctuary was provided by the discovery of a temple from the Hellenistic period. It was built nearby and consisted of one broad room, possibly with a central niche. East of it was a large courtyard with a series of ovens along its walls and the base of an altar of burnt offerings at its center. Though the later temple was pagan, it may have preserved the location of the earlier sacred site, a common phenomenon in the ancient world. Y. Yadin, on the other hand, argues that there was no real temple at Beersheba, but only a sacred high place, which was at a different location, with the horned altar nearby.

Ritual spouted bowl of faience from Beersheba

146

C. HOSEA

Hosea ben Be'eri came on the scene either at the end of Amos' career or shortly after, although the introduction to the book is not clear as to the precise dates of his ministry. Amos had lived in Jeroboam's prosperous and successful years; Hosea lived through the years of decadence and chaos that followed. The book of Hosea, after chapter 3, reflects the chaotic situation and the bewildering succession of plots and murders that brought six men to the throne within a score of years (Hos. 7:7; 8:4; 13:10 –11; 2 Kings 15). Hosea sneered at the dependence of these kings upon their fortified cities, impotent idols, or the protection of Assyria or Egypt.

Limestone statuette of a "Temple boy," one of the *qedeshim* of a sanctuary (from Cyprus)

1. THE NATURE OF CANAANITE CULTURE

The discoveries relating to Canaanite religion at Ras Shamra, ancient Ugarit, provide a panoramic view of Baalism, which would later be the target of Hosea's attacks. The extensive finds in the large tell have revealed, in addition to innumerable artifacts, a great collection of tablets containing mythic and ritual texts, historical, political, administrative, legal, and commercial data, as well as official correspondence. Examination of the tablets indicates a close relationship with the somewhat later Hebrew writings, especially poetry. Just as this classic Canaanite civilization contributed a major share to Israel's cultural heritage, we find it had a strong influence in Israelite religious ritual. The Canaanite cult included a highly developed sacrificial system, an extensive priesthood, and male and female servants. Early Israel was the heir of many Canaanite traditions and practices; it is clear that they persisted among the people of Israel in spite of the fierce hostility of the canonical prophets.

Clay fertility figurine from Tell Megadim

2. BAALISM

The struggles of nature formed the basis of the plot played out among the deities in the Canaanite cult drama. Priestly men and women enacted the major roles of gods and their consorts. Actual union of the male and female actors was believed to bring about, through mimetic magic, the union of the lord of nature, Baal, and mother earth to ensure great harvests and herds for the community. The use of wine and beer often turned the proceedings into bacchanalian festivals. Sacred prostitutes, both male and female, were designated by the same words in Ugaritic and Hebrew, *qedeshim* and *qedeshot*. In Hebrew the word for a temple attendant is different from that for a common prostitute, but the distinction is lost in tradition.

The prevalence of sacred prostitution called forth repeated invective from the prophets, particularly Hosea (e.g., Hos. 4:13–14). The prohibition against such practices was never totally effective. Even though Josiah later "broke down the houses of the cult prostitutes which were in the house of

Before the use of coins became current, metal silver was weighed to correspond to the amount of *shekels* agreed upon

The fertility goddess symbol bears a relation to the Hosea story

Yahweh" (2 Kings 23:7), these practices continued until the destruction of the Temple in the sixth century.

3. CONTENTS

The personal tragedy of the prophet's marriage runs through the book, which falls into two major sections. The first three chapters concern Hosea's marriage to Gomer and its significance as a paradigm or allegory of Yahweh's marriage to Israel.

(a) In chapter 1, written in third person, God tells Hosea to marry a harlot or an adulteress as a symbol of the apostasy of the people. He marries Gomer, and the son born to them is called Jezreel in token of the blood of innocent victims the ruthless kings of the dynasty of Jehu shed in Jezreel. The daughter is called "Not pitied," an allusion to the house of Israel. A second son is named "Not my people" to symbolize the people's breach of the Covenant with God and his rejection of them. Chapter 3 continues the story of his marriage from a point subsequent to that reached in 1:9 and is written in the first person. It records a similar story: God commands Hosea to love the adulteress, who has meanwhile sunk to the level of a slave, and to ransom her for fifteen pieces of silver and a generous measure of barley. (In Exodus 21:32 the price of a female is thirty shekels of silver, while archaeological records reveal that the price of a slave was around forty pieces of silver in contemporary Assyria.) Hosea orders Gomer to live in chastity for many days as though to represent the future penitence of Israel.

The two accounts can be merged into a single coherent narrative of a personal experience of the prophet, illustrating the unhappy history of Yahweh's betrayal by his people. Hosea banished his wife, then ransomed her, hoping that the painful experience would not prevent them from resuming a happy relationship. In the same way, Israel betrayed God, who banished her but now is ready to take her back in the hope that she will repent. Another interpretation of Hosea's marriage is that Gomer's misbehavior triggered his prophetic mission. Through his experience, he came to a new understanding of the love of God and of the injury that Israel had inflicted by its faithlessness. This seems to be the case with other prophets whose theological insights and accompanying pronouncements were sharpened and focused by their personal, often painful, experiences.

(b) The second section of the book, chapters 4–14, contains short separate oracles whose arrangement and connection are not obvious. Although they are mainly judgments against Israel, Hosea's message is not limited to impending disaster. Words of comfort are interspersed among prophecies of doom.

PART VII

FIRST ISAIAH

Isaiah lived during the reigns of Kings Uzziah, Jotham, Ahaz, and Hezekiah of Judah. When he was called to his ministry about 742 B.C., Judah was a flourishing state, thanks to the aggressive policies and energetic activities of Uzziah, who reigned for over fifty years (791–739 B.C.). His father, Amaziah had reconquered Edom (2 Kings 14:7) with its copper and iron mines, and for the first time Judah had completely subjugated maritime Philistia. But the days of plenty passed as Judah was subjected to invasions that depleted her power and prestige. The first significant threat was the Aramaean-Israelite invasion of 735 B.C., described below.

Isaiah saw that greed and covetousness divided the nation into the possessors and the dispossessed. As urban life expanded rapidly, the nobles built up large estates and, with the help of some corrupt judges, piled up wealth in houses and land; meanwhile the oppressed and dispossessed peasantry sought legal redress in vain. Extremes of wealth and poverty, impossible under the older biblical system of land tenure, were now quickly appearing. Indeed, the prophetic writings provide evidence of land accumulation and the emergence of a royal tenantry. Landless farmers, who flowed into the cities in search of a livelihood, were surrounded by wealth, luxury, and vice, while they lived in poverty, misery, and squalor. Nevertheless Isaiah foretold better days, when settlements would extend through the lowland and the farmer would prosper without interference (32:15–20).

Isaiah stands at the forefront of the prophetic tradition. In fact, the sixty-six chapters collected and canonized under his name represent the prophecies of at least two different men: Isaiah ben Amoz, who lived in the eighth century B.C. and to whom most of chapters 1–39 of the book are attributed, and an anonymous prophet, now designated Second Isaiah, who lived in exile in Babylon on the eve of its fall in the mid-sixth century B.C. and to whom the bulk of chapters 40–66 is usually ascribed.

The prophecies attributed to Isaiah ben Amoz were not collected into a single anthology until long after his death. There are indications in the book of smaller collections that may have existed in independent form before the book as a whole was assembled.

1. CONTENTS

Although the composition of the book has resulted in a loose collection of pronouncements originally unrelated, the following groups are fairly distinct: chapters 1–12 are generally autobiographical and deal mainly with Judah and Jerusalem; chapters 13–23 contain oracles against the nations;

Hittite version of the "heavenly court," a symbol met with in Isaiah's vision

chapters 24–27 are eschatological prophecy; chapters 28–33 deal primarily with the relationship between Judah and Assyria; chapters 34 and 35 consist of two eschatological prophecies; and chapters 36–39 contain historical narratives and can be regarded as an appendix.

a. *The Call and an Ancient Image*

Isaiah's career may have begun with his call, which he describes in chapter 6. In a vision he finds himself in the heavenly court, in the very presence of Yahweh on his heavenly throne and surrounded by his heavenly host. Yahweh then purifies Isaiah and commissions him to carry the divine message to Israel.

The concept of the heavenly court has antecedents in Canaanite mythology. The Ugaritic texts present vivid descriptions of the meeting of the gods in the court of El. This image was adapted in Israelite tradition so that Yahweh is pictured as the king, surrounded by his divine entourage of counsellors and servants.

b. *Archaeology and Isaiah's Call*

Many scholars associate the seraphim of Isaiah's vision with the winged serpent or four-winged uraeus, a well-known symbol in the ancient Near East. There is a uraeus rising vertically from the two back corners of the seat of the throne of Tutankhamen (fourteenth century). The four wings of the Egyptian uraeus represent the pharaoh's rule extending over the whole earth. The winged seraphim chant: "The whole earth is full of his glory" (6:3). Archaeological evidence reveals that this symbol was known and used by the Israelites, especially in connection with royalty. Numerous scarabs from Megiddo, Gaza, Beth-shemesh, Lachish, some with inscribed Hebrew names, bear the Egyptian uraeus; two-winged or four-winged uraei were well known in the time of Isaiah, a period when Egyptian motifs were common in Palestinian art. An ivory handle in the form of a winged uraeus wearing the double Egyptian crown came from the floor of Ahab's courtyard in his palace at Samaria.

In the third quarter of the eighth century B.C., Judah faced political circumstances that altered her status permanently and decisively. Following

150

the war with the Aramaeans, Assyria regained the strength and energy to
rebuild its empire. Samaria fell before the Assyrian expansion in 722/21
B.C. Though Judah managed to survive for another century and a half (to
587 B.C.), she was not to know sustained political independence again. Our
major sources for this period are the books of Kings and 2 Chronicles.

While it is true that neither religious decay, including wholesale apostasy, nor extreme social deterioration had gone as far in Judah as they had
in the Northern Kingdom, Judean society was not free from these diseases,
as we learn from both Isaiah and Micah. This was particularly the case
during the reign of Ahaz, who paid homage to the Assyrian emperor in
return for the help he asked. This meant burning offerings to the gods of
Assyria along with the sacrifices for Yahweh on the great altar of the
Temple. There was a swell of popular discontent, inspired by dissatisfaction with national policies and promoted by the oracles of Yahweh's
prophets.

2. ISAIAH AND ARCHAEOLOGY

The records of the Assyrian kings illuminate the biblical narrative at
many points and are cited extensively by modern historians. In addition,
the Dead Sea Scrolls copied in the first century B.C. have yielded texts of
Isaiah that are nearly a thousand years older than the earliest extant copies
of the Hebrew Masoretic text of the ninth and tenth centuries A.D. One
scroll is a complete text of Isaiah; the other is fragmentary but in good
condition. The second is practically identical with the Masoretic text, but
the first, which is older (dating to about 100 B.C.), varies somewhat more
and is written with much fuller spelling, characteristic of the Maccabean
Age.

3. THE PROPHECY OF ISAIAH 7 IN HISTORICAL PERSPECTIVE

Isaiah 7 is one of the key chapters of the Old Testament, and it has
been the subject of a great deal of scholarly debate and difference of opinion throughout the long history of biblical interpretation. It is now possible
to set the record straight with the help of the new data at our command.

Two-winged scarab with the
owner's name in the lower
register. Scarab seals were used
to stamp the clay sealings that
protected letters and containers

An Aramaean prince or king. Ivory carving from Arslan Tash

Aramaean mounted soldier; from Tell Halof

The first twenty years of Isaiah's career were spent during the reign of Ahaz (735–716 B.C.), namely the period of the last wars with the Aramaeans and the increasing aggression of Assyria. Pekah of Israel and Rezin of Aram wanted Ahaz to join them in a coalition against Assyria. Isaiah had analyzed the balance of forces for the king and his fellow Israelites. However, he did not appear before the king as a political commentator, but as a messenger of God, claiming that he and his children were appointed by Yahweh to be signs for Israel; from their names and his activities people could infer what Yahweh intended to do. Consequently, the "man of portent" asked to meet with the king "at the end of the conduit of the upper pool" (Isa. 7:3). This was an outer open-air conduit running from the Gihon spring along the Kidron valley floor to a pool at the southern end of the city. It was later abandoned during Hezekiah's reign and replaced by the tunnel leading to the Siloam pool. The visible traces of this conduit mark its termination at the dry upper pool, a mute witness to the dramatic encounter between Ahaz and Isaiah.

a. The Facts Involved

Isaiah was sent there to expose a plot of the kings of Israel and Aram to unseat Ahaz of Judah, thus ending the Davidic dynasty. They meant to install on the throne the son of Tabeel of the house of Tobiah, which possessed vast estates in Transjordan. Another descendant of this house would appear on the scene in Nehemiah's time; still later, a third Tobiad was known as a leading Jewish Hellenizer on the eve of the Hasmonean period.

The point of Isaiah's message was that the solution offered by the coalition with Pekah and Rezin would not prevent Assyria's eventual aggression, which was inevitable. But Judah would be saved in the end, and as a sign, a son named Immanuel would be born. The symbol Immanuel, "God is with us," assures that Yahweh is still the God and protector of Israel. The fact that the boy "will eat curds and honey when he knows how to refuse evil and choose good" (7:15) means that the fortunes of Judah will be reversed by the time he reaches maturity so that there will be feasting in the land. The promise that a remnant will be preserved is contained in the name of the son whom Isaiah brought along: Shear-jashub, "A remnant shall return" (7:3).

The proper sense of Isaiah 7:14, which has been seen as a prediction of the virgin birth of Jesus and is cited in this connection in Matthew 1:22–23, can now be elucidated on the basis of Ugaritic texts. The term 'alma refers to an adolescent woman of marriageable age, not necessarily to a virgin. In Ugaritic the goddess Anat is referred to as both glmt (Hebrew 'alma) and btlt (Hebrew betula, "virgin"). Anat is described in the texts as both a virgin and a courtesan; she is the sister and consort of Baal. The mistranslation of the Hebrew 'alma as "virgin" may be traced to the Greek Septuagint, which rendered it by parthenos. Whatever may be behind that rendering, there is no historical or exegetical connection between

this passage and the birth of Jesus. The connection rests rather on a spiritual and messianic interpretation, an approach to Scripture popular among different sects of the first century B.C.

Two Assyrian scribes record the spoil taken from Israelite Ashtarot, as women and children are carted away

b. *The Political Consequences*

Events proved Isaiah correct as the pro-Tabeel plot failed. Ahaz's enemies made a joint attack against him in 735, but he enlisted Assyria's help against Aram and Israel. In about 733, Tiglath-pileser III marched to the west, conquered Philistia, and devastated Israel and Aram. Judah maintained its position only by becoming an Assyrian vassal state. These events are confirmed by the Assyrian royal chronicles. The episode is further illuminated by a letter written by a certain Assyrian official, which has been found in Nimrud, advising the court that an emissary from the house of Tabeel was bringing an important message to Assyria. It must be noted, however, that when Ahaz turned to the emperor for help he also had to pay the price—official recognition of the state religion of the Assyrian overlord, along with a heavy burden of tribute. Thus Ahaz, against the prophet's vehement opposition, introduced an Assyrian-type altar into the Temple as well as other Assyrian cult practices (2 Kings 16:10-16).

44. KING HEZEKIAH

After the fall of the Northern Kingdom in 722/21 B.C., Merodach-baladan, king of Babylon, tried to form a coalition with Judah and organize

Captured cities invariably brought tribute to the Assyrian invaders as shown by the carving at the foot of a statue

western Asia to defy Assyria (Isa. 30:1–5; 31:1–3). Again Isaiah came forth and warned Hezekiah, son of Ahaz, that he too would be trapped in the middle of a bitter struggle (39:6–7; 2 Kings 20:16–18). He was joined in this protest by the prophet Micah. Isaiah was equally critical of any alliance with Egypt.

Hezekiah, notwithstanding the risks involved, undertook meticulous preparations for the ensuing conflict. He dug the Siloam tunnel to divert the waters from the Gihon spring to a point inside the city walls in case of siege. He also built warehouses to store extra food. He hastily reinforced the walls of Jerusalem by using stones from buildings nearby (22:8–11) and strengthened his chariot forces.

Isaiah opposed a rebellion against Assyria based upon an alliance with Egypt and other neighboring kingdoms, both in 714–711 and 705–701 B.C. He regarded Egypt as a "broken reed" and argued that the kingdom of Judah could not successfully pursue a policy based upon human cleverness without trust in Yahweh (29:15; 30:1–7; 31:1–5).

a. *The Siloam Epitaph*

Many scholars relate an Isaian verse to an intriguing epitaph found on a tomb in Jerusalem. The passage in Isaiah 22:15–25 begins: "Come, go to this steward, to Shebna, who is over the household, and say to him: What have you to do here and whom have you here, that you have hewn a tomb for yourself, you who hew a tomb on the height, and carve a habitation for yourself in the rock?"

The epitaph that was discovered on the facade of a tomb dating to the days of Isaiah and Hezekiah reads: "This is [the sepulcher of] ——yahu, who is over the house. There is no gold and silver here but [his bones] and the bones of his slave-wife with him. Cursed be the man who will open this." The owner of this tomb "who is over the house" must have been one of the notables of Jerusalem, possibly Shebna, but the beginning of the name "——yahu" is missing because of a hole in the surface of the tomb. It is difficult to decide whether this could be the termination of the full name Shebnayahu. The letters of the Siloam tomb inscription are very

Inscription carved in the rock wall of Hezekiah's tunnel (late 8th c.) describing the exciting moments in the hewing of the conduit as two groups of borers were about to meet each other in the middle of the tunnel

154

Assyrian king holding enemies by ropes (see 2 Kings 19:28-Isaiah 37:29). Carved on the "broken obelisk" from Nineveh (10th c. B.C.)

Prism of Sennacherib describing his campaign against Judah (701 B.C.)

similar to those of the famous Siloam tunnel inscription, which belongs to the reign of Hezekiah. Both may be dated around 700 B.C.

We have mentioned and illustrated above the tombs of the aristocrats of Jerusalem in the days of the Monarchy, discovered by B. Mazar near the Temple Mount. The burial places of ordinary people who could not afford to prepare closed rock tombs or epitaphs have been more difficult to locate archaeologically. They are referred to in Jeremiah 26:23 as the "burial place of the common people," which B. Mazar believes was situated in the Kidron valley below the cemetery of the Mount of Olives.

b. *Sennacherib's Invasion*

The accession of Sennacherib to the throne of Assyria in 705 B.C. occasioned a series of rebellions throughout the empire. He set out on a vast campaign in 702, conquering most of Judah, including Lachish, and besieging Jerusalem, where Hezekiah found himself imprisoned. This was the occasion of Isaiah's mockery of Sennacherib (37:21–29), "I will put my hook in your nose and my bit in your mouth ..." (37:29), which is consistent with contemporary custom. The threat has been illustrated vividly in an Assyrian engraving of the tenth century showing a victorious king holding his defeated enemies by ropes tied to rings fixed in their noses. While it is true that Hezekiah paid a heavy tribute to the emperor, Jerusalem itself was not conquered. Though the prophet first opposed a rebellion against Assyria, he now set out to encourage and sustain the morale of the people in the beleaguered capital. His oracles express the calm assurance that Zion would be saved and the Assyrians broken by Yahweh's power.

Sennacherib's inscriptions on clay prisms describing his campaign against Hezekiah and the Philistines in the year 701 B.C. are the most detailed Assyrian accounts of an episode related in the Bible. Sennacherib boasts: "As for Hezekiah the Judahite, he did not submit to my yoke. I laid siege to forty-six of his strong cities, walled forts, and to countless villages in their vicinity, and conquered them ... I drove out over 200,000 people ... Hezekiah himself I made prisoner in Jerusalem, his royal residence, like a bird in a cage."

155

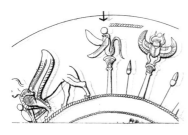

A "copper serpent" from a Mesopotamian temple, similar to the one King Hezekiah cast away from the Temple (2 Kings 18:4)

These were not empty boasts, for scenes of the Assyrian siege of Lachish were carved in the imposing panels now exhibited in the British Museum.

c. *Ahaz's Sundial*

After the siege of Jerusalem and Lachish, the aged prophet drops from view, but before this we read of Hezekiah's illness and Isaiah's suggested cure for his boils: a dried fig cake. The medical use of fig cakes is attested in an Ugaritic text describing the preparation of a plaster pack for a sick horse. When Isaiah predicted that the king would live for another fifteen years, the king asked for a sign and Isaiah replied: "This is the sign to you from the Lord, that the Lord will do the things that he has promised: Shall the shadow go forward ten steps, or go back ten steps? . . . and he brought the shadow back ten steps, by which the sun declined on the dial of Ahaz." (2 Kings 20:9–11). By relating this passage to a former reference to an "upper chamber" of Ahaz, Y. Yadin hypothesized that he built an upper chamber that had two stairways leading up its sides to the roof. This served as a sundial. The angle of the walls threw a shadow onto the steps; it moved down one stairway as the sun rose in the sky and moved up the second as the sun set.

Graphic illustration of Ahaz's sundial

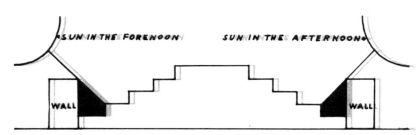

PART VIII

SECOND ISAIAH

There is a scholarly consensus that chapters 34–35 and 40–66 of Isaiah do not date to the eighth century B.C. but rather to the sixth century, the period of the Babylonian Exile and after. The clearest argument for this is the two references to Cyrus (Isa. 44:28; 45:1), but there are other indications. Assyria, the enemy in Isaiah ben Amoz's day, is mentioned only once in passing (52:4); Babylon fills that role in Second Isaiah. The Exile has already taken place; the Jews are awaiting their release (40:1–11). Jerusalem and the Temple are in ruins, but hope for the restoration runs through the oracles of this later prophet. Since his name is unknown and his teachings have been incorporated by tradition into the book of Isaiah, he is conventionally called the Second Isaiah or Deutero-Isaiah.

The issue of the composition and authorship of Second Isaiah is further complicated by certain important differences between chapters 40–55 and 56–66. The major theme of the latter section is the division between the two components of the community: the genuine and the spurious Israel. Chapters 56–66 may have been composed at a later time, for they suggest that the Jews had already returned to Israel, and the Temple had been rebuilt, although the walls of Jerusalem were still to be restored (60: 10). Many scholars have suggested that the last section was composed by still another anonymous prophet, termed Third Isaiah. It is also possible that the twenty-nine chapters were written by a single prophet over a long period of time, covering both the Exile and the earliest stages of the restoration. We will leave this question in abeyance and proceed with the archaeological evidence for the division of the book of Isaiah.

1. EVIDENCE OF THE DEAD SEA SCROLLS

Of the two parchment scrolls of Isaiah found at Qumran, J. T. Milik points out a significant detail in the former, more complete text (1QIsª): "Chapter 33 comes to a close toward the foot of column XXVII. The three ruled lines which follow are left blank. Furthermore, the sheet on which it is written has only two columns instead of the four that are used in this roll. Chapter 34 begins on a new sheet of leather, and the text thereafter continues without further interruption until the end of the book. This oddity may indicate that there persisted a memory of two different collections of prophecy (corresponding roughly to the modern distinction between Proto- and Deutero-Isaiah) although the two collections had been already combined in one book by the time of the copyist." There are, furthermore, differences in grammar and orthography between the two parts, and the material disposition of the text in the roll is not the same. We may explain this division by the fact that there is no material in the book of Isaiah beginning with chapter 34 that can be attributed to First Isaiah.

Chapters 34–35 are exilic or postexilic in date and chapters 36–39, while a historical summary of the period of First Isaiah, are closely related to 2 Kings, which itself was part of the Primary History, probably published in exilic times.

2. NABONIDUS, THE FIRST ARCHAEOLOGIST, AND CYRUS

The Second Isaiah, who proclaimed his message from about 546 to 538 B.C., witnessed Cyrus' meteoric rise to power in the Near East. Beginning with his defeat of the Medes in 550 B.C., Cyrus never experienced a serious setback on the way to building an empire that would eventually include Asia Minor, Syria and Palestine, Mesopotamia, and lands to the east. After the subjugation of the Median empire, he turned to the west, defeating Croesus, king of rich Lydia, and captured Sardis and the Greek cities on the coast of Asia Minor. He was now prepared to turn back and confront the mighty Babylonian empire.

Cyrus was able to enter Babylon without resistance for several reasons. The Babylonian government had been unstable since the days of Nebuchadnezzar II (605–562 B.C.). This instability dramatically increased under the last Babylonian king, Nabonidus (555–539 B.C.). From a number of inscriptions that have been found, including one written by his mother, we learn that Nabonidus was an antiquarian and a religious fanatic. He estranged himself from the priests of Marduk, the major Babylonian god, with his zeal for Sin, the moon god. He spent long years away from Babylon, mainly at the remote oasis of Teima, southeast of Palestine, a major junction on the caravan routes of Arabia. He was absent from the New Year Festival (*akitu*) for ten years, which further enraged the powerful Marduk priesthood. He had left as regent in Babylon his son Belshazzar, whom we meet in the book of Daniel, which describes the fall of that kingdom. Strangely enough, a scroll found at Qumran shows that the

Nabonidus states on this stele that Sennacherib was assassinated by his sons because of the god Marduk's wrath over his destruction of Babylon. This historiosophy stands in sharp contrast to Isaiah's concept of the "Day of the Lord" when all the proud and lofty rulers would be humbled

Section of Isaiah scroll from Qumran (Isa. 47:1–49:8)

dream of Nebuchadnezzar (Daniel 4) was a story originally told of the errant Nabonidus, who is not mentioned in Daniel.

Nabonidus' other passion was for the past. His scholars sought out and read ancient cuneiform inscriptions. When he had a temple rebuilt, he directed his scholars to search for the foundation of the earlier temple: "To the right and the left, in front of and behind the chambers and in the sanctuary I made an excavation." He used a verb that elsewhere means "to dig a ditch," specifically of digging to find ancient remains. He uncovered a temple foundation that he attributed to a Sumerian king who had lived 2220 years earlier. Although his chronology was inaccurate (by almost 500 years), Nabonidus' find still qualifies as the first extant archaeological report.

In the Persian Empire Cyrus the Great established a new policy regarding the treatment of subject peoples. The Assyrian system of maintaining domination over conquered peoples involved the wholesale transfer of populations, to break local ties and generate a common loyalty to the empire. This practice was continued by the Babylonians. The Persian policy, on the other hand, was to treat their subjects kindly, allowing them to remain in (or return to) their land and to worship according to their own religion as long as it did not interfere with the political authority of the empire. Because of this more lenient policy, the Israelites welcomed the advent of Cyrus, and Second Isaiah even refers to him as "his [Yahweh's] anointed" (45:1).

3. THE CREATIVE SIXTH CENTURY B.C.

The sixth century, which has been remarkably well illuminated by archaeology, saw the eclipse of Egypt and the passing of world power to Babylonia. The Babylonian Exile was a major turning point in Jewish history and religion. Under new circumstances, Israelites had to reinterpret much of their earlier tradition. Long-standing doctrines had to be rethought: there was no king, no land, no nation, and Jerusalem and the Temple lay in ruins. This period was also a time of great literary activity, including the collection and composition of the bulk of the principal parts of the Hebrew Bible: the Primary History consisting of the Torah (Pentateuch) and the Former Prophets (Joshua, Judges, Samuel, and Kings); most of the Latter Prophets including First Isaiah and at least parts of Second Isaiah, Jeremiah, Ezekiel, and many of the Minor Prophets. Books like Psalms and Proverbs undoubtedly existed, though probably in an earlier form than is now preserved in the Bible. Other books, such as Ruth, Lamentations, and very likely Song of Songs, were in circulation.

4. CONTENTS

Second Isaiah may be divided roughly into three sections. The first two, 40–48 and 49–55, express the hope for the end of the Babylonian Exile. In the first section, the prophet relates this hope to the figure of Cyrus and also expresses deep hostility toward false gods and idol worship. They are contrasted with Yahweh, sole ruler of the universe and Lord of history. In the second section these themes, particularly the first two, are dropped and the central theme becomes the rehabilitation of Zion-Jerusalem. The four "Servant Songs" interspersed in these two sections (42:1–4; 49:1–6; 50:4–9; 52:13–53:12) deserve special attention. The last section (56–66) contains admonitions and predictions, often in a different literary style from that of chapters 40–55. Especially in chapters 60–61, there is a message of comfort and confidence in Israel's future glory.

55. SYMBOLISM AND THE ANCIENT ARTS

In his eloquent use of imagery, Second Isaiah often made reference to ancient crafts that his contemporaries would readily have understood but are accessible to modern readers only through archaeology. In his succinct picture of the "metalworker" (44:9–20), Second Isaiah describes the process of plating metal over a wooden core to produce idols. He alludes, likewise, to the smelting furnace (48:10) and the testing of metal. At high temperatures, the ore melts and the heavier lead and other impurities sink, while the lighter silver floats on the surface.

Except copper, which was mined in the Arabah, other metals such as iron, tin, silver, and gold were imported in bars and transported on heavy cargo ships (Tarshish ships) from Spain, Cilicia, and other lands. These ores were refined locally. Crucibles for smelting iron and copper, usually made of clay, have been discovered at several places in Palestine. Gold and silver were smelted in closed crucibles to prevent the loss of any of the precious metal. These crucibles were placed in a beehive-shaped furnace, with air holes at the bottom to create a draft, or so that bellows could be used. The pure metal was cast into molds, which were made in two symmetrical halves and provided with holes or small escape channels so that the excess metal could flow out. Molds for making weapons, figurines, and jewelry have been found in excavations.

In one of Second Isaiah's poems the stained clothing of the person treading out grapes in the wine press is a metaphor for the appearance of the wrathful God on judgment day (63:2). The whole process of wine production is illustrated abundantly by the numerous examples of wine presses found in excavations. The Gibeon press has a broad surface for treading the grapes by foot, squeezing the liquid from them. The liquid flowed down through a drainage channel into collecting vats in which the precipitates settled at the bottom. From there the clear liquid flowed to a second vat where it was collected. The new wine was then transferred to vessels that were sealed and put in a cool place to stand until the juice fermented and became wine. The wine was poured into liquid measures,

Left:
Furnaces for metal casting at
Tell Qasileh

Margin:
Clay shields that protected the
mouths of bellows at Timnah's
primitive copper works

Center:
Metal ingot from a furnace

Right, below:
Diagram of a copper casting
furnace, Tell Qasileh

Left, below:
Stone mold for the casting of
weapons

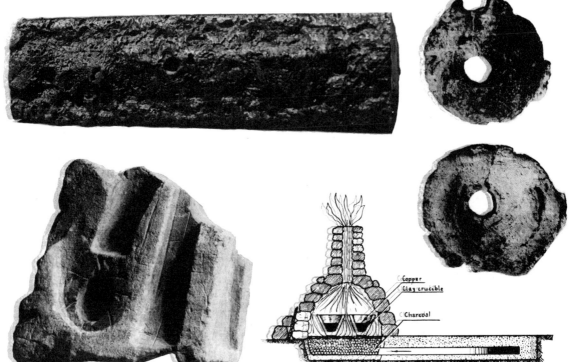

Copper
Clay crucible
Charcoal

Underground wine vats and storage cellars at Israelite Gibeon. The wine filled wineskins and jars, which were stacked in the cellars. Some 100,000 liters could be stored there

the *bat* and the *hin,* forty and six liters respectively. Then these were stored in the wine cellars of the wealthy, including royal and noble families, and sealed with their stamps.

6. THE FALL OF THE BABYLONIAN GODS

One of the beliefs common to most of the ancient Near East was that battles on the human scale were reflections of battles in the divine world between the gods representing the two warring nations. Thus, when the Babylonians attacked Judah, Marduk, the chief Babylonian deity, was simultaneously attacking Yahweh. The notion that Yahweh leads both the divine and human armies of Israel into battle permeates the military traditions of the Bible. The implication of this belief was that the god leading the victorious army had defeated the god of the conquered people. According to this traditional wisdom the Babylonian destruction of Jerusalem signaled Marduk's ascendancy over Yahweh.

Second Isaiah rejected this thinking unequivocally and argued repeatedly against any notion of theomachy (war among the gods) or even the existence of other gods. This is the occasion of his wholesale ridicule of idolatry in 40:18–20; 41:6–7; 44:9–20; 46:1–7. In Babylon the Israelites were confronted with a multiplicity of shrines, each of which contained at least one and often a number of idols. These idols were regarded as divine beings by the priesthood that served them. They were awakened in the morning and put to bed at night; they were royally dressed and fed. At least once a year, during the New Year Festival, all the gods, that is, the idols, were brought out and paraded through the city in a major procession led by the idol of Marduk. This is illustrated by a striking image whereby Second Isaiah draws a contrast between the pagan idols, which

Wine vat from Gezer

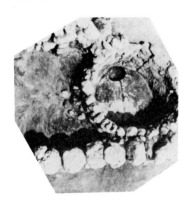

cannot move unless carried, and Yahweh, who has carried Israel from its
origins: "Bel bows down, Nebo stoops, their idols are on beasts and cattle;
these things you carry are loaded as burdens on weary beasts. They stoop,
they bow down together, they cannot save the burden, but themselves go
into captivity" (46:1–2).

A procession of gods mounted
on animals: A striking
illustration of Second Isaiah's
sarcasm against the idols (see
also 2 Kings 23:11). From an
Assyrian relief

7. ISRAELITE MONOTHEISM

The second line of argument used against the belief that Marduk had
defeated Yahweh was Second Isaiah's explicit ethical monotheism. Yahweh
is God alone, unique and incomparable in power and majesty, the Creator
of heaven and earth, and the Lord of all human history. In expressing this
faith, the author produced some of the most beautiful poetry and profound
theology in the Hebrew Bible.

To be sure, this theology was not a radically new development at the
time of the Exile; rather Second Isaiah only made explicit what was im-
plicit in earlier Israelite tradition. In the prevailing religious climate in
Palestine in the days of the monarchy, Yahweh was thought of as the one
national god for Israel, powerful beyond imagination in the land he had
chosen for his people. At the same time, the doctrine of Yahweh's control
of the universe was already present in the Creation story (Gen. 1:1–2:4).
The ramifications of this seminal belief were often overshadowed by concern about the unique relationship between Yahweh and Israel, but with
time they became more evident in the prophetic writings.

The ethical monotheism now formulated by Second Isaiah carried with
it the assurance that the people could have confidence in Yahweh and his
power and authority anywhere in the world. He meant to convince his fellow exiles that the Babylonians and their gods were not the real victors

over Judah and Yahweh, but that, on the contrary, these heathen were no more than the rod of his anger and punishment: "I am the Lord, that is my name; my glory I give to no other, nor my praise to graven images" (42:8).

8. ISRAEL'S MISSION AND DESTINY: THE WIDESPREAD DISAGREEMENT OVER THE "SUFFERING" SERVANT OF YAHWEH

Seal impressions on store jars or wine jars denoting the place of origin of the wine or identifying them as taxes paid in kind to the state. The impressions bear the seal "[Belonging] to the king/Hebron" and "[Belonging] to the king/Mmsht"

The most striking passages of Second Isaiah are found in the four "Servant of Yahweh" poems (42:1–4; 49:1–6; 50:4–9; 52:13–53:12). The Servant, to be elected by Yahweh, will proclaim the message of truth and of righteousness to the world, helped by the divine spirit to overcome obstacles set in his way. Though he first will meet with failure, the Servant will be helped by God to become the savior of his fellow Jews and of the whole earth. The last poem depicts him as a martyr and outcast who lays down his life for others. No concept in the Bible is stronger, more elusive, and more movingly profound than this. Its interpretation has evoked widespread disagreement among scholars.

Who was the Servant? Was it Israel as is suggested in 49:3? However, in 49:5–6 the Servant clearly has a mission *to* Israel, so it has been proposed that he represents a smaller group within Israel. On the other hand, many theologians and scholars believe that the Servant was an individual and not the personification of a group. The question then arises as to whether he is a historical figure or someone still to come. It is suggested that the Second Isaiah himself accepted his undeserved suffering meekly and thereby succeeded in sparing his contemporaries from the punishment that was their due for their transgressions. Numerous other figures from the period of the Exile have been proposed as the model for the Servant.

Finally, many have seen in the Servant passages the promise of a suffering and saving messiah to come. The messianist followers of Jesus saw in him the suffering servant of Second Isaiah and the royal messiah of Israel combined in one person. This interpretation is already present in the New Testament, as can be seen in Matthew 26:24, Mark 9:12, and Luke 18:8. While such an interpretation may be debated, there can be no doubt that the message of Second Isaiah had a profound effect on the formulation of Christian doctrine. At the same time, the message had a contemporary impact and effect, since it was addressed by the prophet as a warning and a comfort to his fellow exiles, and it proved to be a motivating force in normative Judaism in the following centuries.

It is clear throughout these passages that the Servant's mission did not stop with Israel but extended to all the nations. This universal concern is a corollary to Second Isaiah's explicit monotheism. On the basis of the latter he sounded a note of promise, for the God who created the cosmos had also committed himself to the survival and success of his people Israel and could not rest until he had accomplished all. Thus Israel, through its service and suffering, could triumph, and the whole world would share in the salvation of God.

9. THE INSCRIPTION ON THE WALL

Evidence that later generations saw in Isaian prophecy hidden promise of redemption beyond the immediate future is a recent discovery in the excavations of the Temple Mount: a large Hebrew inscription carved in the stone was found in the course of uncovering the Western Wall. It quotes a passage of Isaiah 66:14: "You shall see, and your heart shall rejoice; and their bones shall flourish like the grass." The inscription reads, "and their bones," while the Massoretic Text has "and your bones," which is more likely correct. This was the conclusion of the passage: "As one whom his mother comforts, so I will comfort you; you shall be comforted in Jerusalem. You shall see. . . ." The allusion illumines an obscure phase of 4th century A.D. Jewry. This inscription was made in the days of Emperor Julian "the Apostate," who had promised the resettlement of Jerusalem by Jews, whereupon work on the restoration of the Temple was begun and the inscription carved. But when Julian died in A.D. 363, the hope and the dream had to be abandoned.

Carved inscription on an ashlar of the Western Wall of the Temple Mount, quoting Isaiah 66:14

165

The Israelite wall surrounding the 7th c. B.C. fort-palace of King Jehoiakim at Ramat Rahel is seen in the foreground. The structures in the background were Byzantine halls

PART IX

JEREMIAH

Jeremiah is an invaluable source for the historical background of the period leading up to the Babylonian Exile, as are the books of his contemporaries—Zephaniah, Nahum, Habakkuk, and the young Ezekiel. Jeremiah's career began in the year 627 B.C. during the reign of Josiah and lasted for over forty years, until sometime after the destruction of Jerusalem in 586 B.C. He was active during the reigns of Josiah, Jehoahaz, Jehoiakim, Jehoiachin, and Zedekiah, the last king of Judah.

Jeremiah lived in a period when the tottering Assyrian empire relaxed its grip on its former holdings. In the next forty years, under the rule of Josiah and his successors, Judah passed through a period of independence, only to fall victim to the imperial ambitions first of Egypt, then of resurgent Babylon. It was finally overrun by the Babylonians in two campaigns, in 597 and 586 B.C., as a result of Judah's futile attempt to throw off the yoke of Nebuchadnezzar. Every act of the tragic drama is reflected in Jeremiah, with all its pathos and anguish.

1. GENERAL CONTENTS

The book of Jeremiah, consisting of fifty-two chapters, makes extremely difficult reading, yet it is replete with historical material that can be illuminated by archaeology. This book, as we know it today, is not a single composition but is composed of three shorter "books" that at one time circulated separately. These shorter sections are themselves collections of oracles, which are sometimes arranged chronologically but often according to subject matter. As with the other prophetic books, the completed work is the result of a long and intricate process involving the gradual coalescing of various streams of the Jeremianic tradition. The major sections are:

(a) Chapters 1:1–25:13a; 34–35 is a collection of oracles, dictated to Baruch (cf. Jeremiah 36), uttered between his call (627 B.C.) and the days of Zedekiah; 1:4–6:30 are from the time of Josiah; 7:1–20:18, 35 are from the time of Jehoiakim; 21:1–25:13; 34 are from the time of Zedekiah. They contain words of censure, warning, and judgment for Judah and Jerusalem and to a lesser extent, oracles of hope: 3:11–18; 16:14–15; 23:1–8.

(b) Chapters 26–29 and 36–45 relate the story of Jeremiah's suffering. They show Jeremiah's personal anguish as he is confronted with a stubborn people led astray by false prophets and corrupt priests.

(c) Chapters 30–33, sometimes referred to as the Book of Consolation, were originally a separate section, containing many different promises concerning salvation, extending from the time of Jeremiah to the postexilic period.

(d) Chapters 46–51 are oracles directed against foreign nations. The conclusion of Jeremiah, chapter 52, is a historical appendix, like the appendix to Isaiah ben Amoz in Isaiah 36–39.

It has often been pointed out that there are three major types of material in the book of Jeremiah. They are broadly classified by modern scholars into the following categories, each of which has its own history of transmission. Type A consists of poetry. This is primarily the prophetic oracles, that is, public preaching and brief addresses in which the prophet acts as the direct messenger of God, delivering the divine words. Type B, prose biography, comprises the bulk of Jeremiah 26–29 and 36–45. Type C material is prose discourse cast in verbose and highly rhetorical style. This may be presented in an autobiographical framework in which God addresses Jeremiah and tells him what he is to say or do, or as prose sermons (e.g., Jer. 16:1–13; 18:1–12; 33). A rapid perusal shows that the three types of material are widely scattered throughout the book.

a. Ancient Deeds of Sale

The passage in Jeremiah 32:6–15 is of particular interest in that it affords the clearest extant description of the way in which property was conveyed, that is, bought and sold, in ancient Judah (in this case the property was purchased by Jeremiah). Seventeen silver shekels were paid, showing that weighed-out silver as coined money was not yet in use. The deed was written in duplicate on two halves of a single sheet of papyrus or parchment, as we know from one such deed from Elephantine, a Jewish colony in Egypt. One leaf of the sheet was then rolled up, tied with strips running through holes in the middle of the sheet, and sealed; the other half was then loosely rolled for ready reference while the sealed copy protected the document from fraudulent alteration. They then were placed "in an earthenware jar" (32:14) in a safe, dry place. Y. Yadin found some "tied deeds" in the Judean desert caves. This method of securing documents is well known to us from the preservation of the Dead Sea Scrolls in jars hidden away in the caves at Qumran.

b. Jeremiah and Common Pottery

Chapters 18–20 form an editorial unit containing examples of all three types of material: poetic oracles, prose discourse, and biography. They

Right:
Legal document and its clay envelope

were originally independent but probably placed together because of the "potter-pot" motif that runs through them. They all involve symbolic actions: as the quality of the clay determines what a potter can do with it, so the quality of the people determines what Yahweh will do with them.

Chapter 18:1-12 tells how he visited the potter's house, watching the potter working at his wheel. If he was not satisfied with the first pot he could reshape the soft clay into another pot. (The potter's wheel was made with two stones on a vertical axle. The lower stone disk was spun by the feet, while the upper supported the clay that the potter shaped as the wheel revolved.)

The manufacture of pottery was the principal industry of the ancient world, involving a highly sophisticated and advanced technology. It was used in every phase of man's life from cradle to grave. For example, the household items made of clay were cooking pots, bowls, cups, plates, bottles, jugs and juglets (juglets with perforations were used for sprinkling), cruets, pitchers, and larger jugs for wine, oil, and water storage. Pottery was also used for cheap jewelry, gaming pieces, molds, and scoops to carry live coals. Finally, broken sherds of pottery were occasionally used as scratch paper for writing accounts or quick messages and letters. These inscribed sherds, called ostraca, constitute most of the surviving extrabiblical Hebrew texts, such as the Samaria and Lachish ostraca.

Pottery was cheap and easy to make. The raw material, clay, was available everywhere, and the techniques of pottery-making had been well known since at least the fourth millennium B.C. Pottery is both friable and indestructible, ubiquitous, and distinctive in its styling and decoration, thus furnishing the archaeologist with the chief tool by which he can date ancient artifacts and strata. Broken pots were so common that nobody bothered to repair or remove them, so they provide unerring clues to the chronological order of man's occupation.

c. An Archaeologist Corrects a Misconception

In chapter 19:1-12, Jeremiah relates that he went outside the so-called Potsherd Gate and there, before witnesses, smashed a clay jar, proclaiming that so would Zion be smashed beyond repair. This symbolic action is particularly terrifying considering the spot where it was performed: the valley of Hinnom, where child sacrifice to the god Molekh had been practiced in the days of Manasseh (2 Kings 23:10). Tophet, in the valley of Hinnom (renamed the "Valley of Slaughter" in Jer. 7:32), lay just outside the an-

The potter and his wheel

Revolving stone tournette of the potter's wheel. The coneshaped piece fits into the stone base and is turned

Opposite page:
Clay served every household purpose, from a pilgrim flask (bottom) to pottery cultstands (top). Excavated at Tell Zofit and Tell Amal, 11th-10th c. B.C.

Right:
Cross sections of a potter's oven

Left:
Potter's oven at Tell Qasileh

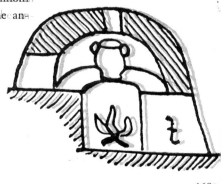

cient gate leading to this southern valley. Some scholars believe that there is some relation between the gate leading to the Tophet, called the Potsherd Gate in Jeremiah, and the Dung Gate (*sha'ar ha-'ashpot*), which is located in the same area in Nehemiah 2:12 and 3:13. B. Mazar has recently pointed out that the word *'ashpot* is derived from the root *sh-p-t,* meaning "hearth" or "burning place," and that it may be an archaic by-form of Tophet. He concluded that the southern gate, erroneously called the Dung Gate, led to the burning place of Tophet in the valley. Furthermore, this gate should not be confused with the present-day Dung Gate, situated on Mount Moriah in the late Turkish wall of the Old City, near the Temple Mount area.

d. *The Abominable Tophet and Josiah's Reform*

The practice of sacrificing children, which surfaced during the reign of King Manasseh but was suppressed by Josiah, was a Phoenician custom. The most important evidence for this ancient practice comes from the sanctuary of Tanit at Salambo, Carthage, built by the Phoenicians; the finds there prove conclusively that the Greek and Roman stories of Punic infant sacrifices to Molekh were only too true. The excavators uncovered thousands of urns containing the cremated remains of small children, mostly under the age of two. The lowest strata of the large sanctuary consisted entirely of these urns of burnt children's bones. The urns were covered by little cairns of stones. At Canaanite Gezer, similar urns were found, dating to the Middle Bronze Age.

2. JEREMIAH AND JOSIAH'S REFORM

Jeremiah's poetic addresses to the people of Judah are filled with his intense hatred of paganizing ritual and of all kinds of cant, particularly the conventional exaltation of the Temple and its sacrificial rites, which were mere lip service at the expense of kindness (*hesed*) and elementary justice (*mishpat;* cf. Jer. 7:21–23). Since he was a contemporary of Josiah, we would expect Jeremiah to have supported Josiah's reform movement, with its emphasis on the election-covenant faith of the Mosaic age, God's love for Israel, the demand for reciprocal love on the part of Israel, and the need for responsible and humanitarian behavior. Unfortunately, it is uncertain whether we have any record of Jeremiah's activity in the years immediately following the reform. It may be that Jeremiah 11 gives an authentic account of Jeremiah's early support for the movement. His general silence, however, suggests that the reform did not appear to have affected the people or to have halted the moral deterioration, and so the prophet dissociated himself from it.

Josiah's revival was made possible by the death of the great emperor Ashurbanipal in 627 B.C. and the subsequent decline of Assyrian power. For a short period of time Judah had a respite from external pressures, allowing Josiah to effectuate a thoroughgoing religious reform in the country and enabling him to eradicate pagan practices throughout the land. This power vacuum was temporary, however, as the Babylonians and the Medes split up the Assyrian empire and the Egyptians sought to become an international power again. The year 609 witnessed the tragic death of Josiah in battle, as he attempted to halt the forces of Pharaoh Necho that were marching north to the Euphrates to assist the Assyrians. Necho deposed Jehoahaz, a son of Josiah, and elevated Jehoiakim, another son of Josiah, to the throne as his vassal, although the latter was utterly unfit to rule.

3. JEHOIAKIM'S PALACE

Having decided that his father's palace in the city was not good enough for him, Jehoiakim set out to build a new and finer one and imposed forced labor on the local population for this purpose. This provoked Jeremiah to one of his most scathing denunciations (22:13–23), contrasting Jehoiakim's desire for a fine house with Josiah's desire for justice and righteousness.

A fine complex of buildings, probably similar to Jehoiakim's proposed palace, was found at Beth-kerem, south of Jerusalem, a site founded during the Judean Monarchy. There was a wide house with large chambers; the facade of the main building was decorated with conspicuous ornamental windows (cf. Jer. 22:14). The imposing palace, surrounded by a lower citadel extending over an area of five acres, resembles the one that was unearthed at Ramat Rahel. The palace walls were constructed of ashlar blocks, like those of Ahab's palace at Samaria. It was decorated with

Right, below:
Urns containing the incinerated bodies of sacrificed children. From the Carthaginian cemetery near Tunis

Left, below:
Entrance to a secret passage found in the Israelite wall of Jehoiakim's fort-palace (see photograph, p. 166)

proto-Aeolian capitals. Among the other finds were window balustrades of the main palace. The remains of the balustrades indicate that the capitals supported cedar beams. Traces of red paint still are visible on the stones. A painted potsherd was also found there, depicting a king seated on his chariot or throne.

4. THE IMPENDING BABYLONIAN THREAT

Jeremiah had become increasingly convinced that the Babylonians were to be Yahweh's agents of judgment upon his people. Some of his oracles telling of the "foe from the north" were uttered as the conquerors swept south to quell the rebellions of Phoenicia, Israel, and Philistia (cf. 46:2–12). By 605 B.C. the Babylonian army had rolled onto the Philistine plain, which they ravaged, carrying off many prisoners. An Aramaic letter found in Egypt contains a desperate plea for help from the king of one of the Philistine cities, probably Ekron, to the Pharaoh. It failed, as we know from the Babylonian Chronicle, for that territory was captured and destroyed by Nebuchadnezzar's army in December 604.

The last years of Judah's independence were overcast by a sense of inescapable doom, as King Zedekiah followed a suicidal pro-Egyptian course against Babylonia. Town after town fell to the Babylonians on the coastal plain and in the Negeb, as we learn from passages in Jeremiah and as is vividly illustrated by the Lachish ostraca. The excavations of Debir and Lachish show how impoverished these cities had become in the last decade before the final destruction in 586.

During this catastrophic period Jeremiah attacked the prevailing view that the physical presence of the Temple brought protection. Belief in the inviolability of Zion had long since hardened into dogma, and the notion that the city could fall and that the Davidic dynasty might end was simply not entertained in many circles in Jerusalem. Yahweh would not allow it! Secure in this confidence, the state marched blindly to disaster. When defeat and destruction came, the popular religion was powerless to explain it. The national-cultic community disintegrated. The state was at an end, and its people scattered. One era had ended and another begun. The idea of Israel, while permanently linked with a land and a tradition, would never again be limited to a political entity or geographic area.

5. JEREMIAH'S ULTIMATE INFLUENCE

If Israelite faith had been no deeper than the popular religion, it never would have survived such a disaster; it would have sunk into oblivion like the religions of the other peoples of the Near East when their states were destroyed by the might of Assyria and Babylonia. And when in turn those great empires fell, their religions collapsed as well. This did not occur in Israel mainly because of men such as Jeremiah, Ezekiel, and the anonymous biblical historiographers who explained the tragedy in terms of Is-

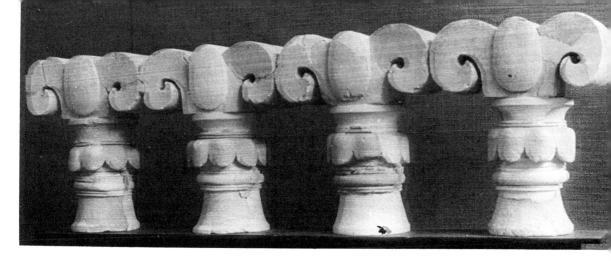

rael's faith. The prophetic oracles enabled the people to survive the dark days facing them and to put their hopes in a brighter if more distant future.

Stone balustrade from Jehoiakim's palace, Ramat Rahel

The characterization of Jeremiah as the weeping prophet is little better than a caricature. He was a failure as the world might judge such matters. His words could not deter the people from the suicidal course that they followed, yet after his death his prophecies served as guarantee and promise of God's eternal faithfulness to even an undeserving people. All that was needed was a genuine change of heart and mind, a renewal of faith and commitment, and a future greater and more marvelous than any past would be their lot. Jeremiah's ultimate and continuing influence can hardly be exaggerated.

6. THE ARCHAEOLOGICAL EVIDENCE OF THE BABYLONIAN VICTORY

The publication in 1963 by D. J. Wiseman of additional tablets of the roughly contemporary *Chronicles of Chaldean Kings* provided a much fuller picture of the course of events in the Near East in the period preceding the destruction of Jerusalem than had previously been available. These clay tablets, inscribed in Babylonian cuneiform, describe the political and military developments in the years 616–595 B.C. They tell of the fall of Nineveh, the Assyrian capital, to the Babylonians and Medes in 612 B.C. and document Babylonian relations with Necho of Egypt. They continue with Nebuchadnezzar's conquest of Syro-Palestine as implied in 2 Kings 24 and list the tribute received from the kings of these lands. Among those giving tribute is Jehoiakim, who remained loyal until the Babylonians were defeated by the Egyptians in 601 B.C. Spurred on by the pro-Egyptian false prophets who saw in this Babylonian setback confirmation of their predictions of well-being, the king of Judah rebelled openly against Babylon. The inevitable response came as soon as the Babylonians were able to settle problems elsewhere in the empire. The fifth paragraph of the chronicle relates the capture of Jerusalem in 597 and the deportation of Jehoiachin (the young son and successor of Jehoiakim, who died during the siege).

The fifth paragraph of the Babylonian Chronicle for 605–594 B.C. relates the first capture of Jerusalem in 597, the exile of Jehoiachin and appointment of Zedekiah as king

Trephinated skull found among the remains of Lachish

Jehoiachin's uncle, Zedekiah, another son of the great Josiah, served as the last reigning king of the house of David.

a. *The Evidence from Lachish*

The archaeological finds at Lachish (Tell ed-Duweir) vividly confirm the upheavals and crises that lay behind Jeremiah's writings. These finds fully support the biblical evidence of the Assyrian campaign of Sennacherib (ca. 701 B.C.) and the Babylonian campaigns of 597 and 586 B.C. As a result of the Assyrian campaign the town of Level III at Lachish was utterly destroyed. In a last effort to prepare the town to withstand the coming assault, the defenders attempted to ensure the water supply by excavating an enormous rock-cut shaft connected to a spring or reservoir. Unfortunately it was not completed at the time the city fell.

The debris that covers Level III shows evidence of appalling destruction. In the gateway, eight feet of burnt debris separated the floor of Level III from that of Level II. The citadel was ruined completely as is shown by heaps of calcined bricks over its stone foundations. The rooms of nearby shops were filled with objects of daily use, storage jars for corn, and the remains of a weaving establishment. Two thousand skeletons with some of the bones calcined were found in a tomb outside the city. Among the skeletons were three skulls from which a square of bone had been removed by a saw to reduce pressure in the head. This rather crude surgical procedure is known as trephination and apparently was a part of recognized medical practice in Judah.

After Sennacherib's withdrawal, the town was rebuilt in the seventh century. Its defenses were reconstructed and the gates were placed so that any intruder would have to pass through an outer gate on the west side of the city and then through an inner gate beyond the outer bastion. In the final Babylonian assault against Judah, Lachish is listed by Jeremiah (34:7) together with Jerusalem and Azekah, "for these were the only fortified cities of Judah that remained."

b. *Tale of the Lachish Letters*

In a guardhouse between the outer and inner gates of the city, in a layer of ashes, a collection of eighteen ostraca was found, of which eight are sufficiently legible to make connected sense. These letters are probably all from Hoshaiah, who was in command of a garrison stationed outside of Lachish, to his superior Ya'osh in the city itself. Letter 4 is particularly interesting in the light of Jeremiah 34:7 cited above. Hoshaiah informs Ya'osh that he has carried out his orders and ends: "We are watching for the fire signals from Lachish, according to all the indications my Lord had given, because we do not see [the signals of] Azekah." This line suggests impending tragedy: Azekah may already have fallen, and as we know, Jerusalem and Lachish will soon follow.

The military correspondence found at Lachish seems to have covered an appreciable period of time. Throughout the letters Hoshaiah insists that he has been carrying out Ya'osh's orders in full. In Letter 3 he tries to

Lachish Letter 4 of the days of the Judean Monarchy (587 B.C.)

justify or excuse himself in the face of insinuations or accusations that he has read some secret documents sent from Jerusalem to the commander at Lachish and revealed their contents to others. The letter then tells of a warning brought by an unnamed prophet from Tobiah, a royal official. Perhaps in relation to this prophet, the ostracon reads "The army commander Koniah, the son of Elnathan, has gone down to Egypt...." This in turn may be related to Jeremiah 26:20–24 where Jehoiakim sent certain men, including Elnathan, to Egypt to bring the prophet Uriah back to Jerusalem.

c. *Letter 6 and Jeremiah*

The best course to avert total disaster, Jeremiah said, was to compromise with Babylon and bow to its yoke, awaiting a brighter day (Jeremiah 27). This was the voice of moderation—the will of God—but the priests and other prophets opposed Jeremiah and treated him as a traitor (Jer. 27:9–22). The royal officials, *sarim,* denounced him to Zedekiah "for he is weakening the hands of the soldiers" (38:4), and demanded his execution. In Letter 6, however, there is a complaint about the messages circulated by the *sarim* because "they weaken the hands of the people." The same expression is used here as in the biblical text, although it is the officials, not Jeremiah, who are accused of sedition.

Excavations at various Judean sites prove that they all suffered total destruction at this time. This is true of Lachish, Eglon, Beth-shemesh, Gibeah, Ramat Rahel, Beth-zur, En-gedi, and Arad.

7. THE AFTERMATH

After the destruction of Jerusalem in 587/6 B.C., the leading figures of the community had either been carried off in exile in the two major deportations to Babylon or had fled to Transjordan or Egypt. The land was in shambles and its economy wrecked.

Gedaliah ben Ahikam was appointed governor. He belonged to a very prominent family in Jerusalem, which had been closely associated with the reform movement in the time of Josiah. According to M. Weinfeld, Geda-

Defenders of Lachish fight from a tower as women remove their belongings from the town. From the vast bas-reliefs found in Sennacherib's palace at Nineveh

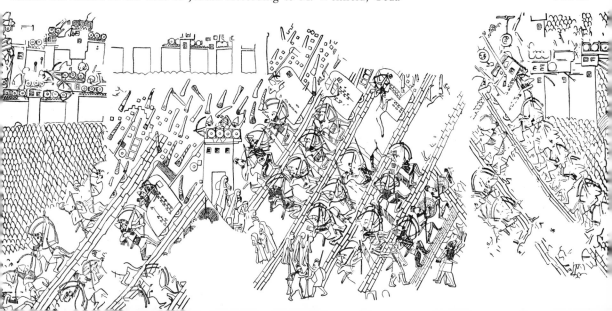

The two standing pillars must have supported the roof of an Israelite house of ca. 800, judging by the pottery found there

Remains of Israelite houses demolished during the siege of 588–586 B.C.

liah's grandfather, Shaphan, was a principal scribe who played an important role in the discovery of the Book of the Law in 622. The family was friendly to Jeremiah and protected him at critical points in his career. It may also have had a hand in the preservation and compilation of some of the prophetic literature, including an edition of Jeremiah's oracles. It has also been suggested that the scribes from this family residing at Mizpah were responsible for the final edition of Deuteronomy. Among the numerous seal impressions found at Mizpah, one bore the inscription "Jaazaniah, servant of the king." This is probably the Jaazaniah who met with Gedaliah at Mizpah according to Jeremiah 40:8. Gedaliah was murdered at Mizpah by a survivor of the royal house, a man named Ishmael, who obviously intended to restore the monarchy. Despite Jeremiah's urging them to remain in Judah, a group went to Egypt taking him forcibly with them (Jeremiah 41-43).

Tablets found in Babylon, dated 595 and 570 B.C., list rations of oil and barley delivered by the royal storehouses to the deposed Jehoiachin and his entourage, held as prisoners

83. JEHOIACHIN IN BABYLON

When Nebuchadnezzar laid siege to Jerusalem for the first time (598 B.C.), Jehoiakim was assassinated and replaced by his son Jehoiachin. Almost immediately he surrendered the city, possibly to appease the pro-Babylonian faction that had killed his father. The Babylonian Chronicle records the capture of Jerusalem and then describes Nebuchadnezzar's deportation of Jehoiachin and his retinue: "The king of Akkad [Babylon] ... laid siege to the city of Judah [*iahudu*] and the king took the city on the second day of the month of Addaru. He appointed in it a new king of his liking, took heavy booty from it, and brought it to Babylon." The new king was Zedekiah. The deposed king, Jehoiachin, was well treated; a list of foodstuffs found in a storehouse near the Ishtar gate in Babylon details the rations issued to his household and refers to him as "Yaukin, king of Judah." This agrees with the biblical account of his treatment in 2 Kings 25:27. Jehoiachin was released by Evil-merodach, Nebuchadnezzar's successor, in the thirty-seventh year of his captivity (561 B.C.).

The search for traces of the destruction of Jerusalem in 586 B.C. has produced scant evidence. One explanation for this is that the same area was thoroughly destroyed by the Romans in A.D. 70. But the remains of homes destroyed by fire have been found on the eastern slopes of the Ophel. Among these was a structure with three halls, divided by partitions made of monolithic pillars resting on their sockets. There is an abundance of sherds and other artifacts discovered on that hill and around the Temple area that date to the last years of the Judean monarchy (see page 176).

LAMENTATIONS

The small book of Lamentations follows directly after the book of Jeremiah in the standard Bibles, because traditionally it was thought to have been composed by him. Actually, it is of anonymous authorship and dates from exilic times. Five successive dirges relate and bemoan the disasters that befell the country at the hands of the Babylonians in the sixth century B.C., including the destruction of the Holy City, the captivity of the people of the land, and the subsequent invasion of the country by its southern neighbors, the Edomites. In this last respect, it is reminiscent of Obadiah 10–14. The book is read to this day in the synagogues on the eve of the date (9th of Ab) when both the First and Second Temples were destroyed. Much of its interest lies in the vivid picture the book provides not only of the devastation wrought in the city but of the soul-searching and agonized questions that the fall of Jerusalem provoked in the minds of the survivors. It seems to have been composed for use in the liturgy for the days of fasting and lamenting. Formally, the poems in chapters 1–4 are composed in an acrostic pattern in which the first verse begins with the first letter of the alphabet, the next verse begins with the second letter, the third with the third letter, and so on through the rest of the alphabet. The poems do not give a connected story of the last days of Judah and Jerusalem, but rather evoke the terrible experience and reflect the agonized thinking of those who were left. The poetic style and acrostic arrangement of the lamentations, which contribute to fixing the text of the poem, ensure effective memorization of the composition. It seems clear that from the beginning the poems were intended for use in public mourning observances.

Hanging above the Assyrian siege-engine are nude figures impaled on poles

The literary type represented by Lamentations is one of the oldest in the repertoire; an excellent example is provided by S. N. Kramer in his publication of the Sumerian tablets of Lamentation over the Destruction of Ur. They were found in the excavations of Nippur in Mesopotamia. This form of ancient lamentation has been preserved for millennia in Babylonia right down to the fourth to third centuries B.C. There is little doubt that the biblical book of Lamentations owes much in this way of form and content to its Mesopotamian forerunners. Thus the expression "He has made my flesh and my skin waste away, and broken my bones" (Lam. 3:4) is typical of the physical sufferings endured by the conquered people at the hands of the Babylonians, who followed the same general policy of the Assyrians, whose atrocities were a byword in antiquity. Their artists proudly commemorated them in stone as shown in the reliefs in the palace of Ashurbanipal at Nineveh.

Lamentations 5:13 draws attention to the fate of young men drawn into forced labor, carrying beams and gravel.

PART X

EZEKIEL

Ezekiel ben Buzi, of the priestly family of the Zadokite line, was exiled to Babylon, probably as early as 597 B.C. shortly after the deportation of Jehoiachin. The Judean exiles were not dispersed throughout the Babylonian empire, but settled in towns like Tell-abib on the river Chebar near the holy and prestigious city of Nippur (Ezek. 3:15), as well as Tell Melah, Tell Tarsha, Kerub, Adan, Immer, and Casfiah. They were able to assemble and to continue a communal life (8:1; 14:1; 33:30–33). They practiced their religion in the first synagogues, and such communal centers helped them maintain their identity. In the course of time, many Jews entered trade and some grew rich.

1. LIFE IN NIPPUR AND TEL-ABIB

Apart from a fragmentary cuneiform record listing rations provided to the exiled Jehoiachin in Babylon and Jeremiah's injunctions to the exiles to establish a normal community in exile (e.g., 29:4–7), little is known of the Jewish Diaspora there. In the course of two generations, some Jews specialized in banking in the rich city of Nippur and are known to have amassed great wealth, laying the foundation for the long-lived and well-

The ziggurat, or sacred temple-tower of Nippur (see "Tower of Babel" in "Genesis")

179

One of the Murashu documents, mentioning two witnesses to an agreement over the cultivation of leased land

educated Jewish community located there in the following centuries (see "Esther"). An archive containing over 700 tablets, known as the Murashu documents, provides a significant glimpse into the social and commercial activities of a Jewish business family in Nippur in the fifth century B.C. The tablets record varied commercial and real estate deals, including business contracts, land leases, and loans and payments. Judging from the non-Hebrew names in this corporation, the Murashu family had adapted itself effectively to the local community, thus fulfilling the commands of Jeremiah, perhaps more thoroughly than he would have wished, since partial assimilation may also have taken place.

2. CONTENTS

The book falls into three major parts that roughly reflect distinct phases of the prophet's varied activity:

Chapters 1–24 are oracles of doom, pronounced between 593 and 586 B.C.

Chapters 25–32 are oracles of doom awaiting the nations that had contributed to Israel's fall: Ammon, Moab, Edom, Philistia, Tyre, Sidon, and Egypt.

Chapters 33–48 are discourses of promise and consolation. Ezekiel's concern is with the revival of the nation through collective action, both in exile and in the land of Israel. Chapter 37 contains the vision of the valley of dry bones, an allegory of the people's resurrection after the exile. Chapters 38–39 describe the apocalyptic wars of Gog of Magog. Chapters 40–48 present an elaborate description of the restored nation, including the future organization of the cult and the plan of the ideal Temple. The basis for this vision of the future was Ezekiel's firsthand knowledge of Jerusalem before the Exile.

a. The Trauma of the Exile: A Coherent Explanation of the Tragedy

The events of Judah's last years sent shock waves through the nation. The popular belief that Yahweh would not under any circumstances let Jerusalem fall had to be abandoned. The reliability of God's ancient promises was put in question. The despair that spread through the people is reflected in Ezekiel 18:25: "Yet you say, The way of the Lord is not just." The leaders had to supply a theological explanation of the national disaster in terms understandable and acceptable to the exiles. They had to resolve this problem or the community would disintegrate from despair. By incessantly announcing the righteousness of Yahweh's judgment against the nation, Jeremiah and Ezekiel gave the tragedy coherent explanation. They viewed it as the vindication of Israel's historic faith, not as a contradiction. The Exile was a merited punishment, but also a purge preparing Israel for a new future. While they demolished cheap or false hopes, they affirmed the ultimate triumph of Yahweh's redemption and provided the people with a hope they could cling to while the future remained obscure.

Ezekiel stood like a watchman over his people (3:17–21), announcing Yahweh's righteous decision with the authority of ancient tradition. Judah and Jerusalem had fallen because the people had trusted in false doctrines and false prophets, thus failing their obligation to God to obey his commands and to listen to the words of his true servants. Knowing that Yahweh's decree of destruction against the city was fixed (chapters 9–11), he likened the prophets who gave hopeful oracles to fools who try to save an old, bulging wall by daubing it with whitewash (13:1–16). Judah had brought disaster upon itself by its political machinations. Henceforth he advised the exiles to submit to the Babylonians and bide their time. God's indefeasible righteousness would bring deliverance to the faithful and observant members of the community.

The Mesopotamian winged sphinx evokes Ezekiel's symbolism of 28:14

There is no inconsistency between Ezekiel's harsh announcements of doom before the destruction of Jerusalem (Ezek. 1–24) on the one hand, and his subsequent visions and messages of consolation and eventual restoration (33–48) on the other. Once the great tragedy had occurred, he naturally turned his thoughts to salvage and salvation. Now hope was the order of the day and steadfast reliance on the divine promise.

b. The Cherubim

In Ezekiel's inaugural vision of the throne-chariot (Ezek. 1:4–2:8) there is a detailed description of the "four living creatures." They are cherubim, guardians of God's throne, symbolizing mobility, intelligence, and strength. The image may go back to the winged deity, called *karibu*, "intercessor," in Mesopotamian texts and represented in art by a sphinx, a griffin, or a human figure. Winged sphinxes and griffins are found in the iconography of the Samarian ivories, as well as at Carchemish, Nimrud, and Aleppo. In Ezekiel's vision, the traditional image of the cherubim is combined with several other concepts, including the wheels symbolizing God's mobility, the all-seeing eyes, and the four faces reflecting God's dominion over the animal as well as the human world.

c. Mimetic Symbols

During the initial phase of his prophecies in Babylonia, which lasted for about two decades, Ezekiel resorted much more than his predecessors to symbolic imagery and mimetic acts. Whether driven to it by inner or outer compulsions, these strange demonstrations underscore the prevailing situation confronting his audience.

Drawing a diagram of Jerusalem on a clay brick, Ezekiel laid mock siege against it (Ezek. 4:1–11). Drawing city maps on clay bricks is a Mesopotamian practice, as is demonstrated by a number of such maps discovered at Mesopotamian sites. In one of his more histrionic actions, he swallowed a scroll on which God's word for his people was written on both sides (2:8–3:3). This would not be a piece of parchment, made of animal skin, since that could only be penned on the side where the hair was shaved. It was probably common papyrus that could be inked on both sides.

181

Ezekiel's mockery of the king of Tyre who identified himself with the god Melkart (Ezek. 28) finds an apt parallel on an incised stone bowl from Sidon depicting the ritual burning of a god. The rite, apparently connected with the Melkart cult, depicts (in scenes 1–4) the "awakening" of Melkart as a solar deity and his resurrection celebrated by burning him in effigy on a pyre

Shaving his head and beard, Ezekiel burned some of the hair in the fire, hacked at some with a sword, scattered some to the winds, and tied only a few wisps in the fold of his robe, symbolizing a similar fate for his people (5:1–4). He once made a hole in the brick wall of his house, passed through it at night, carrying his pack on his back, and thus enacted the role of the wandering exile. This scene also has a Babylonian background as houses there were built of brick, while houses in Israel were built of stone.

3. EZEKIEL'S IMPACT ON LATER JEWISH THOUGHT

Ezekiel has frequently been misunderstood as a strange figure of fantasy, a visionary priest remote from reality, and regarded as a psychologically abnormal person. His prophecy stands at the dividing line between the pre-exilic covenant community of the land and the post-exilic legal community outside of the land. This emerges in chapters 33–48 where he promulgates the principles and program of a restored cult, government, and Temple. The life of the new community was shaped by Ezekiel's representation of the ancient faith.

One of Ezekiel's most interesting discourses, which can be illuminated by archaeology, is against Tyre (28:1–20), still the queen of the seas in the sixth century B.C. The prophet mocks and denounces the king of Tyre because he identifies himself with the god of the city, Melkart, either directly or symbolically. The bejewelled sphinx is the emblem of Melkart in Phoenician art. Perhaps the association between the sphinx and the god explains the reference in verse 14: "With an anointed guardian cherub I placed you...."

Tyre was first built on a narrow coastal strip and subsequently expanded to include an island separated from the mainland by a strait half a mile wide. It reached its zenith in the ninth century B.C. when Carthage was founded as a daughter city. After that period, the Assyrians extended their sway to the Mediterranean coast, and Tyre had to pay tribute to them. Later Nebuchadnezzar besieged Tyre for thirteen years (585–573). While

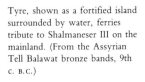

Tyre, shown as a fortified island surrounded by water, ferries tribute to Shalmaneser III on the mainland. (From the Assyrian Tell Balawat bronze bands, 9th c. B.C.)

he was not able to conquer it, he wrecked its commerce, cutting off its sources of trade and wealth. It never truly recovered and ultimately was captured by Alexander the Great.

In the description of proud Tyre riding in the harbor like a great galleon soon to be shipwrecked in the political storm (27:32), Ezekiel draws upon knowledge of the city, its trade, and its monuments. Tyre is portrayed in an Assyrian maritime scene, with Phoenician vessels drawing logs from Tyre and Sidon to Khorsabad. There is another Assyrian relief that depicts the escape of Luli, king of Sidon, from the city of Tyre, an event mentioned in Sennacherib's annals.

Ezekiel was well aware of the great wealth and power of the merchant city and the wide range of its commerce (27:27). In the same passage he refers to the sources of ivory tusks and ebony: "The men of Rhodes traded with you; many coastlands were your own special markets, they brought you in payment ivory and ebony" (27:15). There were two main sources of supply for elephant tusks: one was Africa, the other was northern Syria and Mesopotamia, where a kind of pigmy elephant survived until the eighth century B.C. The latter was apparently the more common source of the small carvings and inlays found in rich homes of Syria, Mesopotamia, Samaria, and Judah.

Finally there is the reference in 28:3 to the claim by the Tyrian king that he was "indeed wiser than Daniel...." We now know that Dan'el was a legendary king and that his wisdom was proverbial. In the Ugaritic texts, *Dn'l* is the hero of an epic cycle in which the central theme is the king's quest for an heir, realized in the birth of Aqhat. There is no apparent connection between this ancient king and the biblical Daniel, reputedly a contemporary of Ezekiel. On the contrary, Ezekiel refers to the ancient Dan'el as a contemporary of ancient figures like Noah and Job (chapter 14).

a. *The Ideal Temple*

Ezekiel stressed the role of the destroyed Temple in the worship of Yahweh. In his picture of the future, the restoration of the people to their land and the renewal of life there were principal features. But at the center was the new Temple, the ultimate symbol and guarantee of God's eternal presence with his people.

An Assyrian scene depicting the escape of King Luli from Tyre (Ezek. 27:32)

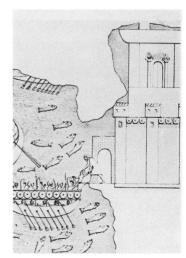

Comparison of the extended descriptions of the Temple in 1 Kings 6–8 and 2 Chronicles 2–4 with Ezekiel's vision of the future Temple (40–48) reveals so many discrepancies and differences that scholars have been hard put to explain the variations. As a young priest in Jerusalem, Ezekiel obviously was familiar with the first Temple, before its destruction. There is a general resemblance between it and his vision of the restored Temple, and while many details of the latter are imaginary, some correspond to the reality of Ezekiel's earlier experience.

b. *Ezekiel's Altar*

In his description of the great altar in 43:13–17, Ezekiel relies on his remembrance of the altar at which he served in his youth. This may well have been the one that Ahaz had copied from a model in Damascus (2 Kings 16:10–16). The impression is supported by the Syro-Mesopotamian influence evident in some of its features, especially the storied structure resembling the Babylonian temple tower. The uppermost tier of Ezekiel's altar was called *har'el* or *arie'l.* The fact that it was to be made of wood suggests that Ezekiel is describing the altar after it had been stripped of its gold by Nebuchadnezzar in 597 B.C. (2 Kings 24:13).

c. *How Did the Priests Dress?*

Phoenician carvings and statuary provide significant clues to the appearance of the garments mentioned in Ezekiel 44:17 and 42:14 as the vestments of the priests. The details, especially for the high priest, are given in the book of Exodus, chapter 28 (cf. 39:1–30): the breeches, robe, waistband, coat, girdle, and headdress. There were four outer priestly garments: the robe of the breastplate, the breastplate itself, the ephod, and the embroidered sleeveless garment falling from the shoulders to the heels. The head of the high priest was covered with a miter decorated by a blue band (Exodus 28:36–38; 39:30–31), while the priests wore a "decorated turban" (Ezek. 24:17).

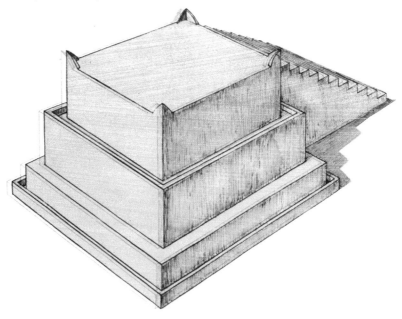

Reconstruction model of the storied altar of sacrifices envisioned by Ezekiel

PART XI

MINOR PROPHETS*

A. MICAH

Micah, as a product of rural Judah, was particularly critical of the urban society that arose in Jerusalem: "What is the sin of the house of Judah?" (1:5). He goes on to place the blame on the leaders of the people, the "rulers of the house of Israel," the priests, judges, and prophets. A century after Micah died, Jeremiah (26:18–19) recalled that the earlier prophet had forecast the destruction of Jerusalem, but instead of provoking angry retaliation by the king, his words inspired a popular repentance led by the king and resulted in a general reformation.

The book has been arranged into four sections that alternate between doom and promise. Chapters 1–3 contain prophecies of judgment and punishment over Samaria, Judah, and Jerusalem. The opening chapter may reflect the prophet's lament over the destruction of the cities of western Judah in the days of Sennacherib's campaign against Hezekiah (701 B.C.), including the siege of Lachish (Micah 1:13), near the prophet's home of Moresheth. Chapters 4–5 consist of promises for the future when "the remnant of Jacob" shall flourish among the nations. Micah 6:1–7:6 is an indictment against the people for not responding properly to God's gracious acts on their behalf. The final poem in Micah 7:7–20 returns to the theme of hope and has affinities with exilic poetry such as Second Isaiah.

THE DOMESTIC CULTS

Micah foresaw Yahweh's violent eradication of idol worship with the accompanying sorcery, images, and pillars (*masseboth*). He was referring in part to the domestic cult performed at home with small images of the goddess of fertility, which were also used as talismans against barrenness. These Canaanite practices were widespread, as is demonstrated by the presence of representations of nude goddesses with elaborately dressed hair in excavations of Palestinian sites dating from the end of the second millennium to the eighth century B.C.

Micah was able to define the essence of biblical religion in a classic question. He asks: "What does the Lord require of you but to do justice, and to love kindness, and to walk humbly with your God" (6:8). He echoes the injunction in Deuteronomy 16:20: "Justice, and only justice, you shall follow. . . ."

Like the other great prophets, he condemned those seers who had become mere professionals and hangers-on at the local shrines. Many of them were interested chiefly in their fee (Micah 3:11) and did not feel impelled to criticize the king and society that were bound by the ancient Covenant.

Sorcery and the "science" of divination, through the inspection of livers, required the use of clay models to guide the adepts. (From Mari, Mesopotamia, early 2nd millennium)

---

*The books of the Minor Prophets are presented in what has been determined to be their chronological order, and not according to the traditional arrangement in Jewish and Christian Bibles.

B. NAHUM

ON THE ASSYRIANS

Nahum of Elkosh prophesied in Judah, probably after the middle of the seventh century B.C., about the impending fall of Nineveh, the Assyrian capital, an event which occurred in 612 B.C. and shook the ancient world. Nahum adopted it as his leading theme to demonstrate the justice of Yahweh (1:2–3), ending his oracle on a somber, almost elegiac note (3:-14–19). The body of the poem is a triumphal ode that recalls Isaiah's mockery of Sennacherib when he failed to capture Jerusalem almost a century earlier.

With a few powerful strokes, the prophet paints a vivid picture of the destruction of Nineveh as an act of vengeance by Yahweh (3:2 ff.). The description of the opposing armies and their equipment reflects the Assyrian annals in which battle and conquest were constant features. The bronze gates of Balawat (ninth century B.C.) show the Assyrian chariot force in action as it destroyed the fleeing army. Only this time it was Nineveh that suffered the fate of all its previous victims.

Additional light has been thrown on the oracles of Nahum by the *Babylonian Chronicle* (published by C. J. Gadd), which recounts the victories of Nabopolassar, founder of the neo-Babylonian empire. It asserts that a decisive part of the overthrow of Nineveh was played by his allies, the Medes who "made a great slaughter of the princes. . . . They took a heavy weight of booty from the city and the temple [and turned] the city into a mound and a ruin. . . ."

The Babylonian Chronicle relates how the Median allies of Babylon defeated Assyria

C. ZEPHANIAH

King Manasseh had gone overboard in complying with Assyrian orders to recognize Assyrian deities. Local shrines flourished where pagan practices were given free rein. Even within Jerusalem followers of Baal were prominent (1:4). In addition, there was a general aping of foreign fashions and ways (1:8) and enormous interest in the occult arts. The inevitable result of this widespread disregard of covenant law was social injustice and violence (1:9; 3:1–7).

Zephaniah's pronouncement of the coming destruction of the Philistine cities, Gaza, Ashdod, and Ekron, reflects the ancient enmity between them and Israel, once more fanned by the attempts of the Philistines to encroach upon Judah in the eighth and seventh centuries B.C. The capture of Ekron by the Assyrians is depicted in a relief from the palace of Sargon II, identifying the name of the city, *Amqaruna,* in cuneiform characters. Zephaniah continues with a curse on the seagoing "nation of the Cherethites" (2:5–7), a synonym for the Philistines derived from an old tradition that attributed their origin to the island of Crete (cf. Ezek. 25:16). There is another archaic allusion in this passage that is misinterpreted easily. In speaking of "Canaan, land of the Philistines," Zephaniah is probably referring to the merchants (Canaanites) of Ashkelon, the leading emporium of the Philistines.

There is a sharp contrast between the dire predictions of the first two and a half chapters and the concluding eschatological vision of the third chapter. In this section (3:8–20) Zephaniah looks forward to a time when the guilt of the nation is removed and Yahweh shall rule as the King of Israel.

Oil press built in a 7th c. B.C. Judahite habitation of the Mishneh, the Upper City of Jerusalem

THE MISHNEH AND THE MAKHTESH

There is an interesting reference in the prophet's predictions of doom to the sections of Jerusalem that have been excavated recently: "On that day ... a cry will be heard from the Fish Gate, a wail from the *Mishneh* [Second Quarter], a loud crash from the hills. Wail, O inhabitants of the *Makhtesh* [the Mortar or Vale]. . . ." (1:10–11).

Several sections of the Mishneh have been uncovered by N. Avigad's excavations of the Western Hill or Upper City, which overlooks the Temple Mount area. It was populated by the upper-class people and lay close to the city's main commercial center, as shown by the finds illustrated here. The Makhtesh is probably the lower area later known as the Tyropoeon Vale that separated the Upper City from the Temple Mount.

D. HABAKKUK

The short book contains no information about the prophet's life. It consists of three chapters, the first two containing a dialogue between the prophet and God about the rule of iniquity in the world. The second chapter also contains a series of five woes against the wicked nation. The third chapter is a prayer in the form of a liturgical psalm. It is quite different from the preceding material, evoking the imagery and style of some of the most ancient Israelite poems.

1. ORACLE

Habakkuk lived during the time when the Babylonian Empire was at the height of its power, in the sixth century B.C. In his oracle he expresses amazement at the doom in store for his suffering and defeated people. There is an interesting pictorial representation in Mesopotamian art of the theme of the net mentioned in Habakkuk 1:15. Pictures of the victor carrying away captives, shown wriggling in a fishnet, are found in murals from the twenty-fourth century B.C.

While Habakkuk's prophecy concerned the Chaldeans (or *kasdim*), it was later adapted to apply to other hated enemies. Thus in the commentary on Habakkuk found at Qumran (from the first century B.C.), the term *kasdim* was interpreted as Kittim, that is, the people of Kition (Cyprus), but really applied to the oppressive Romans, who had moved into the area in force, replacing the equally hated, if somewhat less powerful, Greeks.

The king of Lagash holds a mace and smites the nude figures contained in a net (Mesopotamia, mid–3rd millennium B.C.)

2. ARCHAIC SYMBOLS

The psalm of Habakkuk (chapter 3) contains archaic material reminiscent of the old poetry in the Primary History. For example, the land of Cushan mentioned in 3:7 is probably the ancient name of Gilead in the Late Bronze Age when the Cushites were in possession of southern Transjordan and possibly the Negeb. The Ishmaelites traded and transported goods there in the Late Bronze Age and the Iron Age. The "sons of Sheth" appear in poetic parallelism with Moab in Numbers 24:17 (the Oracles of Balaam), and in like manner Cushan is parallel to Midian in Habakkuk 3:7. Evidently, these passages preserve the ancient names of nomadic peoples in these regions.

Habakkuk 3:10 preserves the memory of the ancient Semitic creation stories in which the world was created out of the body of the conquered god, either from "Tehom" (the primeval Flood) in Babylonian epics or from "Yamm" (Sea) in the Ugaritic texts. Here this pagan motif is used as a metaphor of Yahweh's historical victories over the enemies of Israel.

In Habakkuk 3:5 the prophet alludes to the calamities and plagues to befall Yahweh's enemies. The image still contains overtones of the Canaanite use of the word *resheph,* "pestilence," which was the name of the god of war as he defeats his rivals. This god was also worshiped in Egypt, as is illustrated by a relief from the second half of the second millennium B.C. The symbols help to convey the prophet's message.

Stele of Resheph, god of war
and pestilence. From an
Egyptian engraving

189

E. OBADIAH

Containing only twenty-one verses, Obadiah is the shortest book in the Old Testament. His vision expresses the age-old hostility of Judah toward Edom, its southern neighbor. This feeling was heightened dramatically when Edom took advantage of the Babylonian capture of Jerusalem in 597 to exploit Judah, rejoiced in its plight, and occupied the Negeb (Obad. 10–14; Ezek. 35:10). Edom's territory was particularly attractive to Israel and Judah because the lucrative trade from the exploitation of ore in the Arabah valley passed through Edom. In the final section (19–21) Obadiah promises the return of the scattered Israelite exiles and the restoration of Israel to its former glory, including dominion over Edom. The Judean exiles, who will join the ingathering, will come from as far as Sepharad, most probably the city district of Sardis (Persian *Sapparda*) in western Asia Minor, famous for its great wealth.

F. JONAH

The book relates an episode of Jonah's life, including the well-known incident of Jonah and the great fish, but unlike the minor prophets, it does not contain prophetic oracles. Rather it is a narrative with a message, like the book of Ruth and some of the stories in the historical books of the Bible. It is a parable that illustrates the power of repentance and divine mercy for all living creatures. Here there is emphasis on God's concern for all human beings, not for Jews alone—the universalism so important to Second Isaiah.

1. THE PURPOSE OF THE BOOK

It is important to dissociate the popular concept of Jonah and the fish from the modern historic view underlying our understanding of the book.

There is no need to discuss the physical possibility of the fish swallowing Jonah. The miracle in the parable of Jonah is on the same order as those of the prophets Elijah and Elisha. Few would argue that the book was written before Nineveh's destruction (612 B.C.) or that it is the record of a personal experience of a prophet by this name mentioned in 2 Kings 14:25. It is difficult to date, but there is nothing in its contents or style to suggest a date later than the sixth or fifth century B.C., namely within the range of the Minor Prophets. The author may have chosen the eighth century prophet because he lived when Nineveh was still standing and anti-Assyrian feelings were strong in Israel.

The places that are mentioned in the story have symbolic importance: Nineveh typifies all the great ancient cities filled with iniquity; Tarshish is a remote port at the other end of the Mediterranean. Therefore we do not need to try to associate the allegorical material with any particular archaeological background to place the work in its proper setting.

2. CONTENTS

The narrative consists of three sections. In chapters 1–2 Jonah is commissioned by Yahweh to go to Nineveh and proclaim its destruction. He refuses to commit himself to a prophecy that he does not believe Yahweh will fulfill, so he flees in the opposite direction by taking a ship from Jaffa to Tarshish. As a result of the storm, the sailors throw him into the sea where he is swallowed by a fish. At this point a hymn of praise is inserted (2:1–9) that originally was unrelated to the narrative. At the end of chapter 2 the fish vomits Jonah on an unspecified shore and Jonah proceeds to Nineveh. There he proclaims the city's imminent destruction, but God relents when the people repent. In chapter 4, the prophet argues with God, sulks in a booth, and finally is instructed in the meaning of pity. The metaphor at the end of the book expresses its central theme: God's compassion for all his creatures. Nineveh was not destroyed, because its people repented, showing that it is never too late to repent.

3. THE PARABLE

Although the anonymous author drew on myth and folklore, essentially the story is a moral tale. It says nothing of the fate of Nineveh after it was saved or of Jonah's future career. The book ends with God's question to Jonah, and the audience is left to find the answer for itself. More specifically, this is a parable of two conflicting attitudes, one seeking the punishment of the pagans: people like Jonah would be outraged if they were not destroyed for their sins. The other view is that of the author himself, who contrasts Jonah unfavorably to his Gentile shipmates and conceives of a compassionate God who is willing to forgive even the hated inhabitants of Nineveh if they repent. The author rests his case on the ancient formula attributed to Moses in Exodus 34:6–7 and cited in Jonah 4:2: "I knew that you were a compassionate God, slow to anger...." A further indication of the broad-mindedness of the book is that it makes no mention of "Gentiles" or "the people of the land," terms denoting a sharp distinction between Jew and non-Jew. The New Testament makes further reference to Jonah when Jesus affirms the truth of the story concerning him (Matt. 12:40).

G. JOEL

The first narrative section describes two natural disasters, a plague of locusts and a drought, and then there is a call for repentance (1:13–2:17). It closes with a promise of God's blessing (2:18–27).

Joel then proceeds to describe the coming of the Day of Yahweh. The imagery shifts from the natural in the first section to the supernatural events of the apocalypse. On the Day of the Lord there will be an outpouring of charismatic gifts together with fearful portents (2:28–32). Chapter 3 is full of military motifs in the description of the eschatological conflict between Yahweh and his enemies. God intervenes with terrifying disasters, defeating the foe with great slaughter and establishing his people forever in peace.

As with many of the Minor Prophets, the composition and date of Joel are unresolved problems. Some authorities believe that the material in Joel 2:28–3:21 comes from a later period than the rest of the book although most are satisfied with the essential unity of the book. The question of date has occasioned much speculation by biblical scholars, with opinions ranging from the ninth to the second century B.C. Most indications point to the early post-exilic period when the Temple had been rebuilt. The reference to the Greeks in 3:6 clearly points to a time prior to the conquests of Alexander the Great. Thus a date in the late sixth century or around 500 B.C., corresponding to other Minor Prophets like Haggai and Zechariah, is entirely reasonable.

H. HAGGAI

1. DEVELOPMENTS IN JUDAH

We know little of the conditions of the land during the latter part of the sixth century B.C., when Sheshbazzar, the first Jewish ruler of the Persian province of Judah, returned to Jerusalem to rebuild the Temple and Haggai and Zechariah appeared to exhort the people. The land was in no condition to support a significant restoration. Among those who had never left the land, few evinced great enthusiasm for a return to a way of life since abandoned.

Haggai's prophecies may be dated to the early years of Darius' reign, or some eighteen to twenty years after the edict of Cyrus allowed the return of Jews from Babylonia. Shortly after 522, the Persian empire faltered and some subject provinces revolted. Believing that there was a chance to restore Judah's independence, the Jews named Zerubbabel, a descendant of the royal line, God's chosen one (Hag. 2:20–23). But Darius crushed the rebellion in the empire, and Zerubbabel was not heard of anymore. The glory of Darius' reign is memorialized in huge reliefs and inscriptions at Behistun (Iran), where he is portrayed sitting in judgment over those who had rebelled. The inscription corroborates the date of the restoration of peace cited in Zechariah (1:7).

It was during the time when Judean hopes were running high, stimulated by a change of Persian kings, that Haggai urged the Jews to begin work on the Temple. In his four prophecies, dated to 520 B.C., he accuses the people of being too concerned for their own welfare to help with the Temple. He claims that once the work started, their prosperity would return.

2. CONTENTS

The message of the book is contained in four oracles. The first, following the introductory verses, describes lamentable conditions in Judah and tries to arouse the people from their passive attitudes (1:3–11). The second oracle (2:1–9) speaks positively of the rebellion in progress and the hopes of a new Jewish commonwealth. The third (2:10–19) argues that sacrifices without a central sanctuary would be valueless and that the people would remain ritually impure. The fourth oracle proclaims the overthrow of the nations and declares that Zerubbabel is to be the messianic hero.

Darius' reliefs and inscriptions at Behistun as he is sitting in judgment upon rebels

I. ZECHARIAH

Zechariah was one of the heads of the priestly families that returned to Jerusalem with Zerubbabel (Neh. 12:16). He began his prophetic mission in the same year as Haggai and prophesied over a period of two years (520–518 B.C.). His oracles reflect the situation in Judah when Darius the Persian strengthened his hold over the vast empire. The Jews, however, were left alone and the community stagnated for decades before the arrival of Ezra and Nehemiah.

It is surprising that neither Zechariah nor Haggai mentions the other, as both were active in Jerusalem at the same time, urging the population to begin working in earnest on the Temple. However, they are mentioned together in Ezra (5:1). Considering the breadth of Zechariah's concerns versus Haggai's narrow focus on the Temple, of the two, Zechariah reflects more accurately the important spiritual and historic trends of the time. Messianism is the dominant note in the book, but messianism had become strongly apocalyptic, influencing religious thought in subsequent centuries.

The returnees, as mentioned, found communities of foreigners settled in Judah. Some, like the Edomites, had encroached on Judah's southern territory; others were scattered throughout the land. A ray of hope appeared in the wake of convulsions against Darius' rule, accompanied by the commencement of work on the Temple and rising expectations of the reestablishment of the Judahite commonwealth under the leadership of Zerubbabel. This, Zechariah proclaimed, would entice the Gentiles to join Israel: "And many nations shall join Yahweh" (2:11) and "many nations shall come to seek Yahweh in Jerusalem . . ." (8:22). This is an indication of the readiness of some of the people to encourage the fusion of disparate elements such as the Samaritans, the Philistines, and the Ammonites into the community. Thus, Zechariah seems to be on the side of the proselytizers and universalists. His attitude was countered by the exclusivist trend that we will see in Malachi's writings. Ezra and Nehemiah, a few decades later, would lend their authority to the exclusion of foreigners from the Jewish community.

1. VISIONS

The book of Zechariah has two major sections: chapters 1–8 contain oracles of Zechariah delivered between 520 and 518 B.C.; chapters 9–14 are quite different, but whether they are by Zechariah or date to the same period is uncertain and the subject of much dispute. Much of the material in the first section takes the form of night visions or visual allegories. These eight visions, which are unique to Zechariah, are said to have taken place on a single night in 519 B.C.

The first (1:7–15) and eighth (6:1–8) visions contain numerous references to horses and riders. The use of this symbol may be explained by

the prominent part played by horses in the lives of the Persians, who were great horse breeders; the cavalry was the mainstay of the Persian army at all times. Representations of horses are well known in Iranian art, as the Iranian plateau was ideal for raising horses.

The third (2:1–5) and fourth (chapter 3) visions refer to the rebuilding of Jerusalem and the anointing of Joshua as High Priest. The fifth vision (4:1–5, 10b–14) uses the symbol of the gold menorah (seven-branched candelabrum) of the Temple to represent the omniscience of God. We now have two examples of this symbol before A.D. 96: one appears on the relief of the Arch of Titus in Rome and the other is in a fresco uncovered under the plaster of a priestly house in the Upper City of Herodian times. The sixth (5:1–4) and seventh (5:5–11) visions depict the elimination of evil from the new Jerusalem.

2. ZECHARIAH 9–14

Of the book's fourteen chapters, the first eight can be ascribed without question to Zechariah ben Berechiah, the contemporary of Haggai. There is little in chapters 9–14 to indicate the date of composition or the author, but in view of the general uncertainty it is perhaps best not to speculate. The mysteries of the messianic chapters (9–11) and the heathen assault on Jerusalem (12–14) have not been resolved satisfactorily so far. Much of the difficulty in interpreting and assigning this material may be attributed to the use of apocalyptic imagery whereby historical references are cloaked in obscure symbols.

J. MALACHI

Malachi lived in Judah during the first half of the fifth century B.C., that is, in the Persian period, when the fortunes of Judah were at a low ebb. We are given no biographical material about the prophet and it is possible that the name Malachi, meaning "my messenger," is not a personal name but a title. Unlike the earlier prophets who simply presented the divine message, Malachi states his argument in a question-and-answer method. The prophet picks an opinion that is opposed to his own, making it the basis of a dialectic comment.

1. JUDAH AND THE IDUMAEANS

The hopes for the restoration of the kingdom and the rebuilding of the city had faded in the century after the return from Babylon. Taking issue with the prevalent mood of defeatism and indifference, Malachi endeavored to raise the people's spirit by explaining that Yahweh had not ceased to love Israel any more than he had ceased to despise Edom. The latter had expanded northward and settled at Hebron in the more fertile southern Judah, thus restricting the settlement area of the Jews. The Greek and Roman name for this part of the country, Idumaea, is derived from the name Edom.

2. MALACHI'S ETHNIC EXCLUSIVENESS

Malachi contains one of the most frequently quoted and erroneously interpreted verses in the Old Testament: "Have we not all one father? Has not one God created us?" (2:10). He does not refer to all mankind, as is commonly assumed; indeed he opposed the trends of coexistence between Judahites and their neighbors which would lead to the mutual assimilation of their cultures. It is clear that Malachi directed the question to his fellow Jews only, in order to point out their mutual commitment not to injure the community by introducing foreign ways. This interpretation is supported by the reference to a foreigner in 2:11 as "the daughter of a foreign god." Malachi insisted on exclusivist Jewish nationality to protect the feeble community from disappearing under the twin pressures of hostile threats on the one hand and the friendly danger of assimilation on the other.

PART XII

A. PSALMS

Though Jewish tradition ascribes the composition of all the hymns of the book of Psalms to David, the results of scholarly investigation make it clear that most of them could hardly have been composed by the king. Rather they were attributed to him because he was considered the father of Israelite music. Just as Moses was traditionally the author of the Law (the Pentateuch), and Solomon of Wisdom, so the musical traditions were gathered under David's name.

Recent study has shown that the Psalms were intimately related to the forms of worship in pre-exilic Israel. In the main, they had their origin in cultic circles and are much older than has been assumed by many modern scholars. Originally they were not so much expressions of personal piety as hymns intended to be chanted as part of the ritual of the pre-exilic sanctuaries or high places: Shiloh, Bethel, Dan, Beersheba, Hebron, Gibeon, Arad, and of course, the Temple of Jerusalem. At one time, each type of psalm was probably related to some specific act in the ritual of the sanctuary.

1. THE MORNING RITUAL IN THE HERODIAN TEMPLE COURTS

According to the Mishna, before the break of day, the voice of one of the Levites who attended the altar of Holocausts would ring out: "Out of the depths, I cry to thee, O Lord, Lord hear my voice! ... my soul waits for the Lord more than watchmen for the morning...." (130:1, 6). Early in the morning lots were cast to determine which of the priests would perform the sacrificial rites. The lambs were brought up, examined by the priests, and then immolated while the ninety-three officiating priests stood around the altar and blessed the worshippers in the ineffable name of God: Yahweh. As one priest bent to pour the libation and offer the oblation, another priest raised the standard and signaled ben-Arza, the leader of the Levitic band, to strike the cymbals, and the priests to blow the silver trumpets. The Levites read the prescribed daily psalm and portions of the Law to the accompaniment of musical instruments. As they finished each verse, they stopped and the priests blew the trumpets again, while the worshipers bowed in prayer (Mishna, Tamid 7:13).

2. ARCHAEOLOGY AND THE PSALMS

With the help of archaeology and the resulting epigraphic finds, we now know that the Psalms represent a cross section of Israelite religious life from the earliest period onward (twelfth century to approximately the fourth century B.C.). The discovery of Canaanite hymns and epic poems

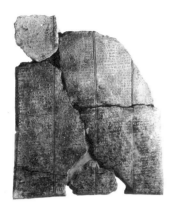

The legend of Aleyan (the mighty) Baal, from Ugarit, is a saga of the mightiest of the gods, scion of Daġan, the primordial West-Semitic deity

Baal-hadad, the god of thunder, illustrated by appropriate symbols, including the might of the bull (reminiscent of "the bull of Jacob" in Genesis)

has proved the antiquity of many of the linguistic forms found in the Psalms, as well as in other poetic books of the Bible. They demonstrate conclusively that there was a well-established literary tradition in greater Canaan (including Syria) before the Israelites settled in its southern region. The earliest Hebrew poets drew upon a highly developed literary heritage as they composed their own works.

3. THE LITERARY TREASURE OF UGARIT

The seventy-acre tell of Ras Shamra on the north Syrian coast concealed the ancient city of Ugarit, destroyed by fire in the twelfth century B.C. In the spring of 1928, a Syrian peasant was plowing his field when his plow jammed against a stone slab that formed a tomb ceiling. As a result of this accidental discovery, some thirty archaeological campaigns were conducted there under the leadership of C. F. A. Schaeffer. The many discoveries at this site, and particularly the thousands of texts uncovered, make this site a rich source of information for the biblical scholar and archaeologist. The discoveries include temples, palaces, private houses, sanitation systems, statuary, and jewelry. As may be gathered from earlier pages, the Canaanite civilization of Ugarit was an outgrowth of the earlier West Semitic culture reflected at Ebla in northern Syria, in the third millennium B.C.

The tablets from Ugarit date from the last two centuries of the city's existence (fifteeenth to thirteenth centuries B.C.), but much of the epic poetry goes back to an earlier time. There are three major compositions that have relevance to Hebrew psalmody. The first is the Baal cycle of poems that describes how the storm-god gained ascendancy over the Canaanite pantheon by defeating Prince Sea ("Yamm") and had his palace built on Mount Zaphon. The Legend of King Keret may be a semihistorical epic, describing the varying fortunes of Keret of Hubur. The third major composition is the Epic of Aqhat, son of Dan'el. Another text worth mentioning is the poem of the Beautiful and Gracious Gods concerning the birth of the twin deities, Dawn and Dusk.

4. THE OLDEST PSALMS IN THE BIBLE

On the basis of recent scholarship, it is altogether likely that Psalms 29 and 68 are among the oldest Psalms. This conclusion is based on a comparison between biblical and Canaanite poetry from Ugarit, which is archaeologically datable. The similarity between the Canaanite and Hebrew poetry is most striking in the use of imagery and other literary devices.

One of the essential features of both is the use of parallelism, symmetry in pattern of both content and form between two lines of poetry. For example, using capital letters to indicate parallel units of each line, we may analyze the opening lines of Psalm 29 as follows:

habu / *layhwh* / *bene 'elim* (ABC)

habu / *layhwh* / *kabod wa'oz* (ABD)

habu / *layhwh* / *kebod shemo* (ABE)

A slightly different example comes from verse 6:

wayyarqid-mi / *kmo 'egel* / *lebanon* (ABC)

wesiryon / *kemo ben-re'emim* (C'B')

Here the second members of the parallel units are marked as being synonymous but not identical. These two patterns are examples of the parallelism found in both Hebrew and Canaanite poetry. The first type is called repetitive parallelism because the terms are identical. This pattern is characteristic of Canaanite poetry and of the earliest Hebrew poetry. Its use decreased with time.

Psalm 29 has so many features characteristic of Canaanite poetry that many believe it was originally a hymn dedicated to the Canaanite storm-god, Baal, that was adapted to Yahweh. For example, according to M. Dahood: "Virtually every word in the psalm can now be duplicated in older Canaanite texts." The antiquity of the poem is also indicated by the use of repetitive parallelism, not only in verse 1 as seen above, but also in verses 4, 5, 8, and 10. The use of imagery in this psalm is also highly reminiscent of that of the poetry from Ugarit. Here Yahweh is described in terms that resemble the descriptions of Baal-hadad, riding the great storm-wind from the sea and giving forth peals of thunder. Another similarity is the invocation of the *bene 'elim,* who are lesser gods in the pantheon at Ugarit, serving the chief god, El. In biblical theology they become the angels who wait upon Yahweh and carry out his orders.

Psalm 68 has many of the same archaic features that are found in Psalm 29. There is repetitive parallelism in verses 8 and 15. Once again the imagery describing Yahweh echoes that of the storm god Baal. The epithet of Yahweh in verse 4 is almost identical to a title used for Baal at Ugarit. There is more archaic material in verse 22, which M. Dahood translates: "The Lord said: 'I stifled the Serpent, muzzled the Deep Sea.'" In the Baal cycle we read: "I indeed muzzled Tannin [in Hebrew, the sea monster], I silenced him; I smashed the twisting Serpent."

These examples are but a few of the thousands of poetic parallels between biblical and Ugaritic hymnody. The discovery of the Ugaritic material has supplied biblical scholars with a standard by which to analyze the grammar and vocabulary of old Hebrew poetry, which is quite different from the standard prose of the Hebrew Bible.

Stele of Baal, from Ugarit, carrying the thunder in his left hand, the mace in the right; flowing water beneath him and horns over his head symbolize fertility; a faithful representation of his designation as the "rider of the clouds," the god of the thunder, the rain, and the fertility of the earth, as he is described in Psalm 68:4 and 33. (14th c. B.C.)

5. THE GRADUAL AMALGAMATION OF THE PSALTER

It is generally admitted that Psalms 29 and 68 derive from a Canaanite background and in their present form come from the earliest period of Israel's history—the twelfth to tenth centuries B.C. It is probable, according

to Albright, that other Canaanizing psalms, like Psalms 18, 45, and 89, were written in the tenth century B.C. In the light of available evidence, it is entirely reasonable to assign a pre-exilic date for most of the psalms, leaving only a few from the period of the Exile or later.

Many attempts have been made to classify the 150 psalms according to their superscriptions, the use of the divine names, or some other principle. But the timeless quality of many of the psalms and the varied nature of the individual poems make it difficult to trace the history of these collections or the process by which they were combined. Nevertheless, it is probable that the various collections had been gathered by the end of the Persian period (fourth century B.C.). The inadequate knowledge of the language and images of the Psalter displayed by the third and second century translators of the Septuagint points to a long gap between the original composition of the psalms and their translation into Greek. Even the later psalms (e.g., 1, 19, 112, and 119) are clearly much older than the second century Hymns of Praise ("Hodayot") from Qumran.

6. THE CONTEXT OF THE PSALMS

a. *Psalms to David:* The superscriptions of seventy-three psalms contain the phrase *leDavid*. In fact, the historical significance of this title is still a matter of dispute. These psalms may have been "dedicated to David" by later composers or they may have been written "in the Davidic manner." The Ugaritic material may provide a significant parallel in titling a number of hymns with *lb'l*, "concerning Baal."

b. *Festivals:* The title of Psalm 92 indicates that it was a psalm for the Sabbath. In addition, the Septuagint notes that other psalms were to be used for certain days of the week: Psalm 24—Sunday; Psalm 48—Monday; Psalm 93—Friday; Psalm 94—Wednesday. Psalm 81 was composed for a major festival, either for the Passover or the Feast of Tabernacles as shown by verse 3: "Blow the trumpet at the new moon, at the full moon, on our feast day." We also know that Psalm 30 was intended for the Dedication of the Temple. Finally, Psalms 78, 106, and 107 are didactic psalms, drawing salutary lessons from Israel's history and composed for use at major festivals.

The shofar (ram's horn)

c. *Liturgical Prayers:* The Psalter is the hymn book of the Second Temple; both Jewish and Christian prayer books are based upon it and have adopted specific passages for use in their liturgy and hymns. It is often hard to distinguish between individual and collective prayers, and between private and corporate liturgical prayers. Psalms placed in the mouth of an individual were sometimes included in the Psalter for use in Temple services; others were adapted for liturgical use by the addition of doxologies (praise of God). Psalm 44, one of the finest expressions of supplication in the Psalter, ends with a fervent appeal for help. Worshipers who presented their entreaty went down on their knees, as is illustrated in our picture, below right.

d. *Pilgrim Songs:* The Songs of Ascent (Psalms 120–134) were used in connection with pilgrimages to sites hallowed in Israelite tradition, such as Bethel, Gilgal, and Jerusalem. Prayers uttered by pilgrims as they entered the holy place are found in Psalms 15 and 24:3–6: "Who shall ascend the hill of the Lord? And who shall stand in his holy place?" (24:3). There are references to the happiness of the pilgrims in Psalms 27; 42–43; 84; and 122. The Songs of Ascent may have been used by pilgrims on their way to Jerusalem. They include archaic material, as can be seen in 132:5, which refers to the "dwelling place of the Mighty One of Jacob." The use of the archaic appellation of God may indicate that this phrase originally referred to the portable tent-shrine in the wilderness. When the pious pil-

"Thou preparest a table before me . . . my cup overflows" (Ps. 23:5). The obscure allusion may bear a relation to the ancient clay cup on its stand. (Exhibited at the Israel Museum)

Left:
The wide stairway uncovered south of the Temple Mount and leading to the Hulda Gates (walled up as seen in the corner) is an apt illustration of the Songs of Ascent. This is the stairway pilgrims ascended on their way to the inner courts of the Temple

Man making an offering

Sistrum with metal bow and jingles

Man and woman playing the tambourine

grims came to the Temple with their fruit offerings, they sang as they deposited their baskets at the foot of the altar: "I shall exalt you, O Yahweh, for you drew me up."

e. *The Musical Guilds:* The superscriptions of the Psalter ascribe psalms to musical guilds named for their eponymous founders: Heman, Korah, Ethan, Calcol, and Asaph. 1 Kings 4:31 refers to Heman, Calcol, and Darda as "sons of Mahol," that is, members of the choir. The names are not typically Israelite. Heman was one of the legendary wise men of Israelite tradition. Calcol is found in an Egyptian inscription from Megiddo as the name of an Egyptian woman from Ashkelon. The name Ethan is apparently of Canaanite origin. R. de Vaux and B. Mazar believe that the first choir singers at the Temple were recruited from among the indigenous Canaanite families who joined the community in David's time (see "1 Kings").

One of the most interesting illustrations reproduced opposite is that of a musician playing a lyre as he marches (eleventh century B.C. pottery from Megiddo). Psalm 150 provides us with a list of the various instruments used by the Levites in the Temple courts: trumpets, ram's horns, drums and timbrels, cymbals, and portable harps. Some of the instruments named are still not identified. Many of them, however, decorate numerous Assyrian and Egyptian reliefs.

f. *Hallelujah Psalms:* In Psalms 105, 106, 111–117, 135, and 146–150 God is praised for his mighty deeds and for his great promises. The Chronicler shows how these psalms were used in the Jerusalem cult: "Hallelujah" is sung as the antiphon by the different choirs of Levitical singers (Ps. 135:19 ff.) or by the congregation (1 Chron. 16:25).

g. *Royal Psalms:* These psalms (especially 2, 18, 20, 21, 45, 72, 101, 110, 132, and 144) belong to the ritual of the Jerusalem sanctuary, since it was the royal shrine. They are rooted in the theology of the Davidic kingship and were sung on the most solemn occasions. For example, Psalm 45 was apparently composed for a royal wedding.

In Psalm 2 Yahweh declares that it is he who has anointed his king on Zion, whereupon the king reads the divine decree (*ḥoq*), a declaration of a covenant between Yahweh and the House of David.

In Psalm 18:37–42 the king's victory over his foes is described as though it were his personal achievement, with no mention of the role of the army. This description is derived from traditional modes of thinking in the ancient Near East. The pattern is reflected in other forms of Oriental art, especially in painting and sculpture. A striking example is seen in Egyptian art, in the stele commemorating the victory of Rameses II over the Hittites, where the king is enlarged to superhuman proportions.

In Psalm 110 Yahweh seats the king on his right hand and declares: "You are a priest for ever after the order of Melchizedek," the pre-Israelite high priest of Jerusalem. This verse serves not only to combine both the priestly and royal functions in the person of the king, but also to legitimate Davidic claims to the city of Jerusalem. These psalms suggest that every king of the Davidic line foreshadows the ideal king and express the hope that the enthroned king might fulfill the promise.

Some Scandinavian scholars have proposed the theory that the royal psalms, including 47, 93, and 96–99, celebrate the mythical enthronement and reign of Yahweh on the pattern of the well-known Babylonian cultic practice. While there are certain similarities, and Babylonian influence cannot be ruled out, they are nevertheless distinctly Israelite, stressing Yahweh's permanent enthronement on Zion, his kingship over Israel, and his promise to David of an eternal dynasty.

Trumpets, stamped on a coin

Below:
Musical instruments of ancient Israel. Cymbals

Left:
Hebrew captives of Assyria playing lyres

"A garden locked, a fountain sealed. Your shoots are an orchard of pomegranates" (4:12–13). A gazelle head, two amphorae, two pomegranates, and two doves are grouped on a ring base found at Megiddo (12th c. B.C.)

Pottery incense burner, with figures of musicians, one playing the lute. From Ashdod, 10th c. B.C.

B. SONG OF SOLOMON

The book is a collection of erotic lyrics that are connected by common themes and characters but do not form an integrated work with a consistent plot line or narration. Part of the difficulty lies in its complex structure and the abundance of sophisticated poetic devices. Tradition assigned the authorship to Solomon, who is mentioned in the work. Its unsurpassed beauty led early rabbinical scholars to present it as an allegory of the love of God for his bride Israel. Early Christians also read it as an allegory, but for them it applied to the relationship between Christ and the Church, his bride. Aside from the tacit agreement among interpreters, there is no basis of support for such an allegorical approach to the Song of Songs.

Most modern scholars regard the material as a collection of Hebrew love poems, including bridal songs, similar to those sung at Palestinian and Syrian village weddings to this day. In the last centuries B.C. and the first centuries A.D., Jewish wedding guests used to dance before the bride (Ketuvot 16; 17a) and sing verses from the Song of Solomon. The early Egyptians serenaded lovers, referred to as brother and sister, and used similes much like those in the biblical book. The pastoral background of these similes also suggests that some of the songs were sung at harvest and other communal gatherings. It is evident that the collection was made at a rather late date (after the Exile) but that the bulk of the material comes from earlier times, reflecting traditions about romantic episodes in the life of Solomon. This nucleus served as the basis for the anthology that grew throughout the biblical period incorporating poetry from both the Northern and Southern Kingdoms. Some of the earlier poetry was reworked in later times and updated so that it would be comprehensible to the post-exilic Jewish community.

1. TIRZAH

One of the poems speaks of the loved one as "beautiful as Tirzah ... comely as Jerusalem" (6:4). The comparison probably reflects the period from the end of the tenth century B.C. when the two cities were capitals of the rival kingdoms of Israel and Judah. In the Iron Age city of Tirzah, which was excavated by R. de Vaux, there are three well-defined strata. In the lowest and earliest of these levels, dated to the tenth and early ninth centuries B.C., the houses erected over the remains of the former Canaanite town were built on a completely different plan: the four-room Israelite house. The plan of this house is nearly square; the inner portion consists of three oblong rooms and another room running along the width of the building. The old city gate was still in use, and close to it a small shrine was constructed. The excavators assumed that Canaanite cults still prevailed, to the chagrin of the prophets. In the later layers of the city gate (eighth century B.C.) a stone bench is visible along the length of the wall. This was probably the site of formal gatherings of the elders "at the city gate," to conduct the affairs of the community. Other buildings attest to the wealth of the fortified city, which remained the capital of the kingdom until Omri transferred the seat of government to the newly built Samaria early in the ninth century. Tirzah was destroyed by the Assyrians in 732 B.C.

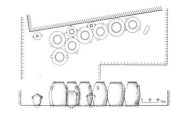

Reconstruction of a perfume workshop at En-gedi

2. EN-GEDI

The oasis known in ancient times as Hazazon-tamar (2 Chron. 20:2) was settled and built up in the later Israelite period, as is shown by the excavations of Stratum V conducted at Tell el-Jurn by B. Mazar and I. Dunayevsky. In antiquity the district of En-gedi was already known for its aromatic plants: for example, "the camphire in the vineyards of En-gedi" (Song 1:14). It became still more renowned for its groves of palms and balsam in the period of the Second Temple.

The earliest period (Stratum V) is attributed to the days of King Josiah and his successors (seventh and sixth centuries). To this period belong several houses in which large rough storage jars were found, as well as a variety of other pottery vessels. There were also metal utensils. The excavators believe that these houses were connected with the perfume industry and that the pottery and metal objects were probably used in the extraction of essence from balm.

Clay barrels from a workshop for the manufacture of perfumes at En-gedi. Israelite period

"The king has brought me into his chambers . . . (Song 1:4). Reproduced here is a section of a relief from the Pharaoh's palace at Tell el-Amarna, depicting the women's house enlivened by music and dance

205

C. RUTH

The book tells the story of Ruth, a Moabite girl who married into a family from Bethlehem. She is widowed in her homeland, then returns to Judah. Ruth is noticed by the landowner, Boaz. As a kinsman, he agrees to act as *go'el,* or redeemer of her late husband's estate, and marry her.

There has been considerable discussion of the date of the book, but no firm decision has been reached. On the basis of recent research, it may plausibly be placed in the time of the Monarchy. In any case, it faithfully reflects the way of life in a provincial Judahite town, which probably did not change greatly from the time of Ruth and Boaz until the time the work was written. The details of the story illustrate village practices from earliest times; the legal transaction before the elders at the gate (Ruth 4) is typical.

A TALE OF COMMUNAL EXISTENCE

It is often suggested that the book was written as a protest against the exclusivist policy of Ezra and Nehemiah in the fifth century B.C.; they forbade intermarriage between Jews and Gentiles and even forced those already married to be divorced. It is possible that the book of Ruth was cited for its remarkable portrayal of a Gentile woman as a model of faith and good works. But the story itself has nothing to say about the question of intermarriage, and Ruth is a bad example of a Gentile wife, since she would qualify as a convert and proselyte to the Jewish faith, which would give her equal standing in the Jewish community with the native-born. Just as Ruth does not deal with intermarriage as a religious problem, so Ezra and Nehemiah do not mention the question of conversion in dealing with the foreign wives of members of the Jewish community. Some believe that it is more reasonable to see in the book of Ruth a story about the royal house of Judah and the remarkable personality of one of the ancestors of the founder of that dynasty, David, the son of Jesse of Bethlehem.

PART XIII

A. WISDOM

The tradition of wisdom literature, which is found in the Bible chiefly in the books of Proverbs, Job, and Ecclesiastes, goes back to patriarchal times, centuries before the Hebrews arrived in Canaan. We learn from the Bible that Israelite wisdom was similar to that of neighboring peoples like the Edomites and the sons of Qedem ("people of the east"). The biblical material also reflects the wisdom tradition in the far older cultures of Canaan (Phoenicia), Egypt, and Mesopotamia. Only fragments of the Canaanite wisdom literature have come to light in Ugaritic tablets from the Late Bronze Age. They must represent an extensive and influential literature, which finds echoes in the biblical book of Proverbs. Ezekiel (28:3) attributes to a Phoenician king a wisdom greater than the prestigious Dan'el, a royal hero of Canaanite legend. Indeed, Sanchuniathon of Tyre and Mochos of Sidon are quoted by later writers as famous Phoenician sages.

The most extensive nonbiblical wisdom literature comes from Mesopotamia and Egypt. The wise men of Egypt are mentioned in the stories of Joseph (Gen. 41:8) and in Exodus 7:11 and Isaiah 19:11–12. A section of Proverbs (22:17–24:11) is based on the Egyptian work *Amen-em-ope*. The international nature of wisdom may also be seen in Esther (1:13) with its reference to the soothsayers and wise men of the Persian court and in the intertestamental book of Tobit (1:21–22) where the Assyrian sage Ahiqar is represented as the nephew of the Jewish storyteller.

Thus, wisdom literature was the product of an intercultural and international school of thought.

There are two major tendencies within the biblical wisdom tradition. On the one hand, the book of Proverbs embodies the practical worldly wisdom of men of wide learning and experience: conservative, didactic, pragmatic, optimistic in spirit. On the other hand, there are the books of Job and Ecclesiastes that express the questioning side of wisdom: they are pessimistic, introspective, independent, and skeptical of traditional values and views.

THE COSMOPOLITAN NATURE OF ANCIENT WISDOM LITERATURE

In Egyptian wisdom writings, the conservative and didactic type predominates and persists from 2600 B.C. to sometime after 500 B.C. Among earliest examples are the *Instruction of Ptah-hotep* and the *Instruction to King Meri-Ka-Re,* both of the third millennium B.C., containing precepts that the sage or ruler passes on to his successor. The *Dispute over Suicide* is more questioning in its dialogue and resembles Job in this attitude. Other important compositions are the *Instructions of the Scribe Ani,* the *Instruction of Amen-em-ope* (eighteenth to sixteenth centuries B.C.), and the *Instructions of Oneh-sheshonqy* (fifth century B.C.).

The wisdom tradition in Mesopotamia had its origin in Sumerian culture and was expanded, but not radically changed, by the Babylonians and Assyrians. In Mesopotamia, wisdom is found in the form of adages and maxims, short fables and illustrative anecdotes, or even in parts of epic cycles such as *Gilgamesh and the Land of the Living,* which deals with the search for immortality. A fragment of the *Instruction of Shuruppak* seeks to explain the suffering of man, much as in the book of Job. Other works that deal with this theme, according to the interpretation of S. N. Kramer and W. G. Lambert, are *I Will Praise the Lord of Wisdom,* (1500–1200 B.C.), the *Dialogue about Human Misery,* a discussion between two sages, and the *Dialogue of Pessimism.* A series of precepts similar to Egyptian and biblical proverbs and laws are contained in the *Counsels of Wisdom* from the Early Babylonian period and the later *Words of Ahiqar* (an Assyrian scribe), known from an Aramaic copy of the fifth century B.C.

In sum, wisdom in Israel was part of a much wider and older tradition that extended throughout the Near East. But biblical wisdom is distinctive in its emphasis on the unitary divine source of all knowledge and comprehension, its ethical awareness, its great breadth, and its accommodation of widely differing and conflicting attitudes.

B. THE BOOK OF JOB

The wisdom movement produced also a second type of literature, more speculative and radical, among which are Job and Ecclesiastes. The former, one of the indisputably great classics of world literature, undertakes a vigorous and vehement examination of the doctrine of reward and punishment and the eternal problem of suffering, as taught by Jewish tradition and by its conservative sages. The book, as we know it today, presents the argument in a unique literary framework: the prosperous, happy and just man, Job, is presented dramatically in a prose introduction or Prologue that tells how Yahweh permitted the hero's piety to be put to the tests of disaster, the loss of his family, and a loathsome and painful disease. The root problem is then explored in a poetic colloquy between Job and three friends, Eliphaz, Bildad, and Zophar, who try to comfort him but anger him as they expound the traditional viewpoints. The dramatic confrontation culminates in the great intervention of God, in which he defends himself against the charges of injustice and indifference proffered by Job. The great poetic interlude ends with a second prose section, Epilogue, in which God restores Job's fortunes and happiness.

The occasion—if not the contrived reason—for these undeserved calamities of Job is Satan's challenge to Yahweh to test the sincerity of Job's faith. It is traditional to refer to Job's patience, but that factor is only in evidence in the Prologue and Epilogue of the book. In the former, Job accepts his ordeal with equanimity as he refuses to blame God. In the Epilogue, he is restored abundantly and his endurance is rewarded. The poetic Job, emerging out of the dialogue, is anything but patient. His complaints crash like thunder: he attacks his creator and accuses him of being insensitive to man's suffering and even the willful cause of it. His outcries raise the question of divine providence and justice, which occupies the greater portion of the poetic dialogue between Job and his three companions.

1. THE TWO STRATA OF THE BOOK

The contents of the book may be summed up as follows as it falls into five unequal parts:

a. The prose Prologue: chapters 1–2
b. The poetic Dialogue or Colloquy: chapters 3–31
c. The Elihu speeches: chapters 32–37
d. The Theophany or the Voice from the Storm: chapters 38–42:6
e. The concluding prose Epilogue: chapter 42:7–17.

We will discuss below the connection with archaeology and the ancient world, but we should precede this by pointing out that the book is a composite, as it is made up of two distinct strata: the prose sections, which are Israelite in origin and date to post-exilic times, and the forty chapters

Miniature model shrine house from Beth-shean

forming the poetic colloquy, where sources are far older, often archaic, and of external origin, as has been demonstrated.

The anonymous poet of this composite work was familiar with the archaic mythological motifs that abound in the poetic sections constituting the core of the book, while the prose sections represent the later stratum, that is, the period of its writing, and the cultural and historical background. What situation in Palestine could account for the acceptance, not to speak of the popularity, of a book so speculative and radical compared to orthodox works that were canonized as sacred literature? Was it written in the period of the classic prophets or after the Exile?

2. THE BOOK REFLECTS A COSMOPOLITAN POST-EXILIC OUTLOOK

We have already seen that the religious and social tenets that animated post-exilic Judaism as exemplified in Ezra and Nehemiah did not reflect solid and monolithic orthodoxy in the days that followed them, when other, far more cosmopolitan views, were aired.

Job, according to A. Schalit, is one of the biblical works that attests to the existence of differing views among post-exilic Jews, namely whether or not the separation of Israel from other peoples was the all in all of Judaism, as was the belief of Malachi, the last prophet, or of Ezra and Nehemiah. In fact, it may be assumed that the general outlook of the book of Job reflected the thinking of people after the reforming attempts of Ezra and Nehemiah. Hence, it is generally assumed that the work in its present form dates to the late fifth or early fourth century B.C. Even if we grant that the poetic colloquy originated in an external and more ancient source, it became popular during the post-exilic period under discussion. The universal human problem that animates it proves not only that it was familiar to the people after the time of Ezra and Nehemiah, but that it summed up their world philosophy. The book deals with neither Jews nor Gentiles; it has no dispute with the God of Israel, but with a universal godhead. Its central problem is that of universal justice and of man's suffering or success, without reference to race and creed. God's answer to Job from the storm (38:1) proclaims its application to one and all throughout the world. The same sentiment is voiced by Elihu, "whether it be a nation or man" (34:29). In this respect the outlook bears comparison with several Psalms that reflect similar views (to cite some among many, 22:28; 24:1; 67:5, 7; 72:11, 17; 82:8; 145:9).

Hence we meet again the two opposing tendencies, exclusivism and communal coexistence, that polarized post-exilic Jewry for centuries. Neither viewpoint finally prevailed, as is evident from a study of the literary products of the later intertestamental period.

3. PARALLEL AND MORE ANCIENT SOURCES UNDERLYING THE BOOK

The problems with which the book of Job is concerned also exercised the sages of Egypt and Mesopotamia. The texts having the most striking affinities with Job are a Sumerian lament excavated at Nippur, and tablets in Akkadian, *ludlul bel nemeqi*, "I will praise the Lord of Wisdom," that describe sufferings even more gruesome than Job's. They date from the second millennium B.C., and there is every reason to believe that a similar story about an ancient Job circulated in Palestine-Syria in pre-Israelite times. The outline, at least, has been incorporated in the biblical work. The locale of the story of Job is in Transjordan, among the "children of the East."

Major assistance in understanding the many obscurities in the book of Job has come from the Ugaritic texts discovered since 1929 and then deciphered and interpreted. Difficult terms, mythological allusions, and archaic usage and construction have been clarified in a remarkable way by these alphabetic inscriptions in a Canaanite dialect closely related to biblical Hebrew.

4. THE REMOTE MYTHOLOGICAL BACKGROUND OF THE POETIC COLLOQUY

As Job's three friends come to console him, he breaks the silence with bitter complaints and curses, evoking the help of the master curser among the gods. By comparison, in Baal's battle with Prince Sea in the Ugaritic myth, the weapons by which Sea was defeated were rendered effective by incantations by the god Koshar, who specialized in magic as well as metallurgy. The versatile Koshar fetched a weapon while pronouncing incantations; then a second weapon toppled Prince Sea (cf. Job 3:8). Eliphaz' response to Job avers that man is born for trouble "as sparks fly upwards," or in better, modern, translation as "Resheph's sons wing high" (5:7). The allusion is to Resheph's mythological children, who fly up from the nether world to plague mankind. Resheph is a god of fertility as well

Representations of gods warring against mythical monsters are found on Mesopotamian cylinder seals. One of the gods is shown thrusting his sword into the mouth of a horned "serpent" while two other deities back him up. This is suggestive of the primeval monsters Yamm or Leviathan of early legend echoed in Job

as of pestilence. In his reply (7:12) Job refers to the mythical Sea, who is closely guarded. In the Ugaritic texts, the conflict between the sea god Yamm and the god of lightning, Baal, results in the defeat of Prince Sea, who is captured and muzzled (like Job in his complaint). The theme recurs in the mythological allusion (38:8–11): "who shut in the sea with doors ... when it burst forth from the womb," clarified in an Ugaritic text that mentions swaddling clothes in connection with the birth of certain bovine monsters. The god El contrives a diabolical plot to undo his enemy, Baal, when he sends divine handmaids into the wilds equipped with obstetrical instruments, there to give birth to monsters called Eaters and Devourers. When Baal goes out to hunt them, he is incapacitated, whereupon drought and infertility ensue for seven or eight years. The great monsters Behemoth (40:15) and Leviathan (41:1) both have mythological backgrounds and identities, the hippopotamus and the crocodile being only pale reflections on earth of their supernatural dimensions and powers. Leviathan is the great sea monster with seven heads (Hydra) whose body girdles the world, while Behemoth is the great Bull of Heaven (*Shor Habar*), of whom the rabbis spoke as comprising the chief dish for the messianic eschatological banquet.

In his reply to Eliphaz (14:16) Job does not admit guilt commensurate with his suffering. His allusion to a count of his steps indicates his hope for an eventual fair reckoning. Light has been shed on ancient methods of accounting by cuneiform documents excavated at ancient Nuzi (Kirkuk) recording that pebbles placed in a shepherd's pouch were transferred to different accounts, that is, "deposited," "removed," or "transferred" in, from, or to various receptacles to represent the actual movements or changes in status of the animals being counted.

Job pleads in his rebuttal of Bildad's second discourse that his words be engraved (probably in copper) or carved in rock for all time (19:23–24). The use of copper or bronze for writing material was fairly common in

Right:
"Worthless physicians are you all," said Job (13:4). Ancient medicine resorted to exorcism, and this Assyrian tablet depicts priest-doctors, masked as fish, trying to exorcise the evil spirit from the supine figure

Below:
A Sumerian medical tablet prescribing treatments. This dates about two millennia before Hippocrates

antiquity. The now famous copper treasure scroll from Qumran is an illustration of what Job is presumed to have had in mind: a record for posterity. Similarly, carvings on rock are a common feature seen along the paths of the caravan routes in Sinai since early Nabatean times.

That passage is followed by another significant image: "For I know that my redeemer [vindicator] lives ..." (19:25). The agent in question is not God, against whom Job rails, but a remote mythological figure, a member of the divine court who acts as legal advocate and defender of accused men before the great god who sits in judgment.

In Bildad's third discourse, chapter 26:7 should be translated "He stretches *Zaphon* [not 'the north'] over the void." Since the discovery of the Ugaritic myths about Baal and his holy mountain, Zaphon (Mount Casius in Lebanon), it is clear that the allusion here is to the storied mountain of the gods, the Mount of Assembly. It is on top of this mountain that the great palace of Baal was erected by the god Koshar-wa-Hasis, who formed it of gold, silver, and lapis lazuli.

In the poem on the inaccessibility of wisdom (chapter 28), a comparison is made with the remoteness of mining operations, whether in or out of Palestine. Such activity has been uncovered at Timnah and in the Arabah near Edom, at the turquoise mines of Serabit el-Khadim in Sinai, and overseas at Ophir, the source of gold.

In Elihu's final speech (37:18), the sky is likened to a molten mirror. Ancient mirrors were made of polished bronze. The sky was thought to be a solid dome-shaped vault, separating the two primeval reservoirs of water.

"Who has let the wild ass go free?" (39:5). Assyrian relief portraying an ass-hunt

213

C. PROVERBS

The book of Proverbs expresses wisdom in brief adages and maxims, or in longer admonitions suited to the instruction of young men in the discipline necessary for a happy and profitable life. The contents range from folk sayings to lofty speculation on the nature of wisdom and its relationship to God, man, and the universe. The first major unit (chapters 1–9) begins and ends with the same summary statement, embodying the essence of biblical wisdom: "The first principle of knowledge is to hold the Lord in awe" (1:7; 9:10). Although Job and Ecclesiastes also speak of the fear of the Lord, the book of Proverbs does not contain the poetic dialogues and theological skepticism that characterize these other wisdom books.

1. GENERAL CONTENTS

The introductory section of Proverbs, chapters 1–9, consists of a series of ten admonitory discourses, two allegorical poems in which wisdom is glorified as the first of all creations, the companion of God, and the true guide of men, and some additional miscellaneous material. In the admonitions, young men are warned to live according to moral standards, to shun evil (personified as a wicked woman), and to follow wisdom, represented as a beautiful woman of sublime virtue.

Chapters 10:1–22:16 present a long series of proverbs, attributed to Solomon. For the most part, they are in the form of a single balanced line with poetic parallelism between the two halves of the line. The sayings revolve around a group of basic practical issues, but shift from one to another without a clear principle of organization. Apparently this section is the end result of a long process of accumulating couplets, derived from the instruction in the wisdom schools.

Chapters 22:17–24:22 form the "thirty Precepts of Sages," a compendium of thirty longer exhortations, modeled on the Egyptian *Instruction of Amen-em-ope,* which contained thirty chapters. The close similarities between this section and the Egyptian work enabled scholars to interpret the appearance of the strange word *shalishom* in Proverbs 22:20 as a corruption of *sheloshim,* meaning "thirty," rendering the proper translation as "Have I not written for you thirty sayings?" This is one of the very few cases of confirmed borrowing in the Bible, and it illustrates the international and cosmopolitan nature of wisdom literature in the ancient Near East.

Chapters 25–29 contain proverbs similar in style to those in chapters 10–22. The heading, however, is of special interest: "These are further wise sayings of Solomon transmitted by the men of Hezekiah, king of Judah."

In chapters 30–31 there are four separate appendices, ending with the famed acrostic poem describing the virtues of the ideal housewife (Prov. 31:10–31).

The book of Proverbs is more than an anthology of wise sayings that circulated in Israel, although the "Proverbs of Solomon" in chapters 10–25 represent this type. It is also a textbook of instructional materials for the young to gain practical wisdom and cultivate personal morality. Many of these aphorisms and folk sayings that were in common use in ancient Israel have passed into current use in Europe and America. We need only cite a few: "A poor man is better than a liar" (19:22b); the antithesis between personified Wisdom and Dame Folly (9:1–6, 13–18), one of the most picturesque figures of the book; or the saying: "A soft answer turns away wrath, but a harsh word stirs up anger" (15:1).

2. MASHAL: A PROVERB AND OTHER CONNOTATIONS

The Hebrew word *mashal* has the basic meaning of "a comparison" or "similitude." It may be simply an extended metaphor or as long as a parable. The English word "proverb" does not cover so much ground, but in general a *mashal* is a wise saying with some special literary feature. It could be said of Balaam's oracle (Num. 23:7), a mysterious comparison backed by effective power, or of a prophetic utterance (Jer. 24:9). Ezekiel's observation: "The fathers have eaten sour grapes, and the children's teeth are set on edge" (Ezek. 18:2) is called *mashal*. Finally, there are lengthy discourses in the book of Proverbs that belong to this category, such as the description of the virtuous wife (Proverbs 31) or the invitation of Wisdom in chapter 7.

In Proverbs 7 and 8 Wisdom is personified as a female figure addressing men on her own behalf. It is true that Wisdom is regarded as a distinct deity in the pagan cultures, as we see in the Egyptian Maat, goddess of truth and order, or Ishtar, the chief Babylonian goddess, the personified genius of life and wisdom consulted by the legendary Gilgamesh. The biblical passages reflect this mythological usage and portray Wisdom as a divine being, though created by and subordinate to Yahweh. It is to be remembered, however, that the passages are examples of poetic imagination and rhetoric rather than serious statements of theological doctrine. Biblical monotheism remains intact.

3. SOLOMON'S PROVERBS

The traditional ascription of the book of Proverbs to Solomon (specifically Proverbs 10–17 and 25–29) is based on the tradition in 1 Kings 4:29–34 and elsewhere, emphasizing his great wisdom, intellectual brilliance, and cosmopolitan culture. Actually, certain sections of the book are ascribed to anonymous sages (22:17; 24:23), to Agur (30:1), or to Lemuel (31:1), mysterious figures of non-Israelite origin.

There is something to be said, however, in favor of Solomon as a great patron of the arts and culture. In the chapter on the historic Solomon, we traced the rapid cultural development of the United Kingdom in his time. The rich cultures of Egypt and Phoenicia (Tyre) made a great impression on Israel at that time, both of these lands being famous for their wisdom

First columns of the papyrus containing the *Instruction of Amen-em-ope* in hieroglyphic script. It was written down in the first half of the 1st millennium B.C., but it dates to the 12th c. or before and is remarkably similar to some biblical proverbs

traditions (cf. Isa. 19:11–12; Ezek. 28:3–5). Although the amount of actual participation by Solomon in the dissemination of wisdom is debated, it is likely that moral instruction of the upper class began in Solomon's day or soon after. It is also probable that wisdom literature, not only royal annals and histories, was composed and compiled at the royal court. The truth behind the Solomonic tradition is that he promoted a school of wisdom teachers on the Egyptian model; it is plausible to think that the pithy sayings contained in a single balanced line that constitute the bulk of the two collections specifically associated with his name were characteristic of the Solomonic period.

4. PROVERBS "WHICH THE MEN OF HEZEKIAH COPIED"

There is extrabiblical evidence of the wisdom movement that is associated with the royal court in the eighth and seventh centuries B.C. W. F. Albright suggested that renewed activity in this respect finds a parallel in a Phoenician literary renaissance of the same period. The fourth collection (Proverbs 25–29) is distinguished by its headings: "These are further wise sayings transmitted by the men of Hezekiah," the king notable for the reformation reported in II Kings 18 and II Chronicles 29–31 (ca. 715–687 B.C.). These "men" must be understood as "professional servants," a school or guild under Hezekiah's patronage. To these men the king assigned the task of collecting and recording the traditional wisdom of Israel. His reforming zeal apparently led him to undertake the great enterprise of assembling, organizing, editing, and publishing the literary legacy of Israel.

5. ANCIENT SCHOOLS

The acceptance of practical responsibility for the instruction of youth characterized the wisdom tradition in the Near East long before the emergence of Israel. From the collections of teaching materials such as Proverbs, R. B. Y. Scott and others infer the existence of schools in Israelite cities. Further and final compilation of older collections of proverbs must have taken place in the Persian period, producing the long prefatory section (chapters 1–9) as a guide to the interpretation and understanding of the remainder of Proverbs.

From later records and the Talmud, we can reconstruct ancient schools: the teacher was seated on the floor or stone bench with his students seated on straw rugs around him. The teaching of the Law consisted of an oral recitation accompanied by an interpretation of the law and admonitions in the general manner of chapters 1–9. The first of the admonitions in Proverbs calls on the youth, when tempted by bad companions into a life of crime as an easy way to wealth, nevertheless to cling to the moral training received at home.

The Audience

Formal education was intended for young adults rather than children. This is shown by the maxims against infidelity, prostitution, the "adulteress," and the foreign woman with her seductive wiles (2:16 ff.). The teacher thus underscores the traditional condemnation of the law against sexual aberration and marital infidelity (Exod. 20:14; Lev. 20:10; Deut. 27:20–23). Similar language is used in the Egyptian *Instruction of Ani:*

"Be on thy guard against a woman from abroad.... Do not know her carnally; a deep water ... is a woman who is far away from her husband.... She has no witnesses when she waits to ensnare thee" (J. Pritchard, *Ancient Near Eastern Texts,* p. 420).

Also condemned were the six, even seven vices hateful to Yahweh (6:16). The use of numerical pairs, in succession, is characteristic of traditional poetry in the ancient world. This pattern appears also in the proverbs of Ahiqar:

"Two things are meet, and the third pleasing to Shamash: one who drinks wine and gives it to drink, one who guards wisdom, and one who hears a word and does not tell" (ibid., p. 428b).

6. THE IDEAL HOUSEWIFE

The last unit in the book is the famous praise of the ideal housewife, well known to many modern readers. It is an acrostic where the initial letters of the twenty-two lines follow the order of the Hebrew alphabet (cf. "Lamentations"). It is interesting not only for the light it throws on domestic activities, but for what it indicates about the extraordinary scope of managerial responsibility assumed by the Israelite wife. The picture of the woman in her role as wife, whether well-to-do or peasant, contrasts with traditional notions of the servility of women in the Near East.

The Aramaic parallel, in the Proverbs of Ahiqar, of the Hebrew proverb 23:14: "If you beat him with the rod you will save his life from Sheol." The text, preserved in papyrus and reproduced here, was discovered at Elephantine, where a Jewish military colony was established in the 5th c. B.C. The Proverbs of Ahiqar, however, go back ultimately to an Assyrian book of wisdom of the early 7th c. B.C.

217

D. THE BOOK OF ECCLESIASTES

Ecclesiastes is the most radical work in the biblical wisdom tradition. It consists of a series of soliloquies on the main theme: man's existence and his struggle to comprehend the meaning of life or to achieve anything of permanent value are futile, for the conditions of life are determined by an inscrutable power. The best course for man is to learn from each experience life affords. The opening verse, "Vanity of vanities, all is vanity," exposes the writer's major thesis. He goes on to consider the question of how men should live in a world where all experiences are fleeting and all efforts produce no lasting result.

1. CONTENTS

Chapters 1:2–18	There is nothing new under the sun; the futility of human effort and wisdom.
2:1–26	The illusory satisfactions of pleasure seeking; the wise man is better off than the fool; death robs man of the fruits of his labor.
3:1–4:3	Everything happens at the time God decrees for it; the existence of injustice proves that man is only a mortal animal.
4:4–5:9	A life of sheer toil is profitless; advice about religious observances.
5:10–6:12	Wrong and right attitudes toward wealth; contentment is life's highest good; man is at the mercy of fate, which is incomprehensible.
7:1–9:12	Short comments: no man can be perfect; the frustration of seeking wisdom; the proper attitude towards civil authority; wickedness goes unpunished; man's mysterious fate.
9:13–12:14	Pessimism about wisdom in practice; the joys of youth; biographical footnotes and summation.

2. THE LEAST ORTHODOX BOOK OF THE BIBLE

The book of Ecclesiastes, dating from the latter part of the Persian period (fourth century B.C.), embodies a different philosophy of life from that set forth in Proverbs. It is openly speculative, far more radical, penetrating, and pessimistic. From the didactic elements of the work, it is evident that

A fragment of Ecclesiastes 6:3–4 found among the Dead Sea Scrolls. On the basis of the script, the scroll can be dated to the middle of the 2nd c. B.C.

218

the author, referred to as *Qohelet,* "one who conducts an assembly," was a renowned wisdom teacher. It appears from the biographic notes (12:9–12) that he won a following among the Jews of his time. The period in which he lived is marked by the impact of Greek thought in Judea, which occurred somewhat later than in the coastal cities of Phoenicia and Egypt. For the latter, there is widespread evidence of Greek influence from the end of the fifth century B.C. There was a dramatic increase in Greek penetration of Western Asia after Alexander the Great's conquests and the subsequent division of his empire into three great Hellenistic kingdoms. Greek officials, merchants, travelers, and soldiers went everywhere, and Jews, for their part, migrated or traveled to foreign lands. Alexandria had such a large population of Greek-speaking Jews that a translation of the Scripture into Greek, the Septuagint, was made for them.

3. THE AUTHOR

The reason for the association of the book with Solomon, the traditional patron of wisdom, is not stated explicitly in the book. The author is identified in the opening verse as "son of David, king in Jerusalem," as though he were the famous successor of the founder, but this is a device adopted by the author for purposes of his argument or for literary effect. The author assumes the role of Solomon, not only because of his wisdom, but also because a king can do as he pleases; he is free from the obstacles that beset ordinary men, and can thus exercise a wide range of options, explore many life styles. The author was a professional sage and teacher, and his precepts and proverbs, which were teaching tools in the schools, were obviously popular. The background of the book appears to be a stable and stratified authoritarian society, engaged chiefly in agriculture and commerce.

4. THE IMPACT OF FOREIGN CULTURES

The book is far more worldly-wise and cosmopolitan than other post-exilic books of the Bible. Its Hebrew is significantly different from the classical Hebrew of the pre-exilic period, with linguistic features resembling the Mishnah (completed by A.D. 200) and the Copper Scroll from Qumran. There are so many similarities to Phoenician inscriptions that M. Dahood has suggested that the author was either a Phoenician himself or living in a Phoenician city. Finally, the use of Persian loan words indicates that it could not have been composed before the fifth century B.C., but before the Greek period. These linguistic arguments point to a date toward the end of the Persian period, when Jews lived in a more cosmopolitan society whose doors had been opened by commerce, foreign conquest, and increased relations with other nations. An example of nontraditional biblical theology is the attitude toward God: in Ecclesiastes Yahweh is not only unknown to man through revelation, he is unknowable through reason,

In his list of the human activities that have preordained times, Ecclesiastes indicates that there is "a time to mourn, and a time to dance" (3:4). Greek art, contemporary with Ecclesiastes, illustrates ancient forms of these expressions of human emotion.

The Attic vase above shows men and women mourning according to prescribed gestures. Below is a statuette of a dancing girl swaying rhythmically with her arms raised and head thrown back

the medium by which Qohelet believes knowledge is attained; this doctrine is similar to the views of the Greek Stoic philosophers and derives from earlier Phoenician thinkers.

The author shares the questioning spirit of the Stoic and Epicurean schools of thought. In common with Ecclesiastes, Epicurus of Samos (340–270 B.C.), an expositor of Hellenistic hedonism, praised physical comforts. The author also has much in common with the Stoics, who maintained that man's strivings are foolish and that for peace of mind one should cultivate virtue instead.

When and why Ecclesiastes was included in the authorized canon has been a persistent subject of debate. The Alexandrian Jews admitted it in their loosely defined scriptures, the Septuagint, and the Mishnah says that it was retained "because its beginning is religious teaching and its end is religious teaching" (Talmud, Shabbat 30b). The book shows that wisdom teachers were individualists and not subservient to orthodox theologians and priests; the same is true of Job, which was written earlier.

5. ECCLESIASTES AND JOB

Ecclesiastes denies the possibility of man's knowing God through revelation or by reason. The author's analysis goes beyond that of the book of Job, because his concern is primarily intellectual, while Job's is moral and religious. Just as in the case of Job, the author denies the traditional dogma that virtue is rewarded, that vice is punished, and that suffering is inevitably the consequence of sin. He breaks away from tradition in understanding God as an incomprehensible power that has determined man's fate and conditions forever.

Clay cylinder of Cyrus (538 B.C.) containing a proclamation similar to those recorded in the book of Ezra

PART XIV

A. EZRA AND NEHEMIAH

1. THE TRANSITION PERIOD DURING THE EXILE

Thanks to archaeological discoveries, it is possible to reconstruct the situation of the Jews in Palestine during the Exile after 586 B.C. Practically all the fortified cities in Judah had been razed to the ground, as we know to be the case from systematic excavations at Jerusalem, Lachish, Debir, Beth-shemesh, Ramat Rahel, and Beth-kerem, as well as a host of others known from soundings and surface explorations. The poor were left to harvest grapes and make wine since they constituted no threat to the ruling power. The Edomites were allowed to settle in Hebron and other centers of southern Judah, while large communities in Samaria and Transjordan, partly assimilated with non-Jewish groups, were able to survive. The former Northern Kingdom towns such as Bethel and Tell en-Nasbeh had remained under Babylonian control, and thus were saved from the fate of the Judean towns that had resisted the onslaught. Curiously, a number of settlements were left intact in the Negeb.

B. Mazar calls attention to the fact that Jews still came down in pilgrimage from the north to the ruined Temple, bringing cereal offerings and incense (Jer. 41:5). A significant archaeological discovery is a contemporary carving on a tomb near Lachish that reads: "I am Yahweh thy God; I will protect the cities of Judah and will redeem Jerusalem." A century and a half later, Nehemiah (1:3) comments with feeling about the Judahites who had not been exiled: "The survivors there in the province who escaped exile are in great trouble and shame." The classic Hebrew tradition paid little attention to them, but their influence persisted as we shall see.

2. SPIRITUAL AND SOCIAL ATTITUDES THAT FACED EZRA AND NEHEMIAH

We have noticed that the Jewish population—both old residents and returnees from the Exile—in the early part of the fifth century had polarized into two camps. One hewed to orthodox ethnic and religious exclusivism; the other was more cosmopolitan in its social attitude and was led by the high priest, Eliashib, the Assembly, and the upper class.

That is the situation Ezra and Nehemiah confronted when they came from Babylon. Ezra's initial efforts were intended to alter the people's attitude and way of life, involving their dealings with their Gentile and Samaritan neighbors and their intermarrying with them. Ultimately, with the backing of the more practical administrator, Nehemiah, Ezra's plan was carried through, and orthodoxy was established firmly in the land. They did resist, however, the attempt of certain Judean fanatics to revive messianic pretensions in a scheme to establish an independent state with a scion of David to occupy the throne, as had been proposed and perhaps attempted in the days of Zerubbabel, who took steps to rebuild the Second Temple with the encouragement of the prophets Haggai and Zechariah. But that attempt, if it was made, failed.

3. CONTENTS

The books of Ezra and Nehemiah were originally one book, then separated. We shall deal with them as a unit concerned with the same historical situation during Persian times.

a. *Book of Ezra*

Chapter 1:1–2:70	The decree of Cyrus in 538 B.C. permitting the return of exiles to Jerusalem eighty years before Ezra's time.
3:1–13	The work of restoration begun.
4:1–24	Progress brought to a standstill.
5:1–6:22	The building of the Temple resumed and completed.

Chapters 7–10 deal with the situation some sixty years after the events described in chapter 6.

7:1–8:36	Ezra comes to Jerusalem and faces the almost hopeless situation described in his prayer of confession.
9:1–10:44	The problem of mixed marriages and Ezra's inquiries.

b. *Book of Nehemiah*

The thirteen chapters of Nehemiah's memoirs constitute the autobiographical account of the governor appointed by Artaxerxes I of Persia (464 –424 B.C.) and his mission to Jerusalem, including his achievements, and passages derived from other sources and inserted in the book.

Chapter 1:1–11	Nehemiah hears of the distress in Jerusalem. His confession and prayer.
2:1–3:32	His arrival in Jerusalem; the king's commission to rebuild the city; his secret survey of the damaged walls; the people's readiness to undertake the work. A list of the builders.
4:1–7:4	The work completed in spite of the mockery of Sanballat and Tobiah; the workmen armed against a surprise attack; social injustices remedied; further attempts to trap Nehemiah; arrangements for the guarding of the city.
7:5–73	An old register of returnees from Babylonia.

4. EZRA

The first verses of Ezra (1:1–2): "In the first year of Cyrus king of Persia, that the word of the Lord by the mouth of Jeremiah might be accomplished, the Lord stirred up the spirit of Cyrus king of Persia so that he made a proclamation throughout all his kingdom and also put it in writing: 'Thus says Cyrus king of Persia: The Lord, the God of Heaven, has given me all the kingdoms of the earth, and he has charged me to build him a house at Jerusalem, which is in Judah.'" This echoes the wording of the proclamation of Cyrus (538 B.C.) sanctioning the return of Jews to Jerusalem, as it was publicly announced by herald and then circulated by royal messengers throughout the new empire. Similar terms are used by Cyrus himself in an inscription on a clay cylinder.

The decree granting royal sanction for the rebuilding of the Temple was deposited at Ecbatana ·(modern Hamadan), and it was found there after a diligent search when, in the reign of Darius I, officials in Palestine questioned the right of the Jews to rebuild. This scroll also authorized a grant from the royal treasury and specified the plan of reconstruction, including the use of cedar timber. These planks were inserted at intervals horizontally into the stone walls to reinforce the structure, as may be seen in walls at Megiddo, Beth-shean, and Masada, where charred pieces of wood were found in the space at the bottom of the stone wall of the palace. Actually, Nehemiah's memoirs mention a letter the king gave Nehemiah ordering the keeper of the royal forest (apparently in Lebanon) to supply him with cedar for the gates and walls of Nehemiah's home (Neh. 2:8).

Ezra had come from Babylonia earlier (458 B.C.) with a contingent of Jews (8:15 ff.) to join the community, strengthen its numbers, and improve its status. Ezra found, however, that many of the established people lived on intimate terms with those outside the fold and with the Samaritans

Charred remains of wood found in the space at the bottom of the stones forming the palace-wall of Masada show that it once contained courses of timber

223

Coin of Judah inscribed YHWD
to the right of the Athenian owl

who followed heterodox Israelite rites as a separate community. Ezra initiated a drastic reform that involved an end of such liberal behavior, especially in requiring that the Jews divorce their foreign wives and religiously illegitimate offspring. This brought on the hostility of those who were excluded, and it became imperative to rebuild the walls of Jerusalem (Ezra 4:13, 21) against the possibility of attack. The effort was nullified by the intervention of Rehum, the governor of Samaria, who reported it as a prelude to rebellion.

5. NEHEMIAH

Shortly after (445 B.C.), Nehemiah, an official in the court of Artaxerxes I, arrived in Jerusalem as *peha* or governor of the *medinta* of Judah. The Persian realm was divided into satrapies, each governed by a Persian commissioner, the biblical *Ahashdarpan*. The satrapies were subdivided into smaller units called provinces in the Bible, which in turn were made up of districts such as Judah and Samaria, each of which was under the direction of a governor or his subordinate.

Of the two districts in Nehemiah's time, Samaria was the larger and more wealthy. Bronze fragments of the lower part of a ceremonial chair were found there, probably that of the governor. The original chair was apparently patterned after the throne of Darius I, found on a relief at Persepolis (illustrated opposite).

a. *YHWD and Y-R-Sh-L-M*

Silver and gold coins first made their appearance in Judah in those days (Ezra 2:69). They were coins issued by Darius I following the example of Lydia, which first issued coins in the seventh century B.C. The Greek states likewise issued coins in the eighth to sixth centuries B.C. The Judean coins were simply copies of the Attic drachma, which was common currency in the eastern Mediterranean in the fifth and fourth centuries. It bore the emblem of the owl of Athens and an imprint of the letters YHWD (Yehud, Judah). Many jar handles were also found bearing this imprint. Furthermore the letters Y-R-Sh-L-M (Jerusalem) were impressed between the points of the star of David.

Impression on a jar handle
bearing the imprint YHWD (4th
c. B.C.)

b. *Which Walls Did Nehemiah Repair?*

After examining the dilapidated walls (which were not completely destroyed) Nehemiah summoned the leaders of the people and inspired them to begin the arduous task of reconstruction, namely the repair of various sections of the wall by different teams of builders. Rich and poor responded to the call, even the high priest Eliashib who had opposed Ezra's reform, and the work was completed in fifty-two days in 445 B.C.—clearly devoted to intensive repair rather than basic reconstruction, as is confirmed by B. Mazar's review of the background (*The Mountain of the Lord,* p. 193 ff.). In any case, this work was restricted to the southeastern ridge (or City of David, unchanged in Nehemiah's time). He reduced Jerusalem's area of

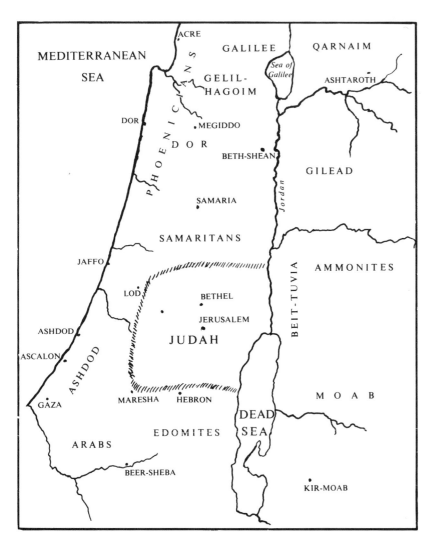

Left:
The *medinta*, "district," of Judah in Nehemiah's time formed a small part of the Persian satrapy of Eber-Nahara (west of the Euphrates)

Above:
Fragment from a ceremonial gubernatorial chair found at Samaria

Below:
The legs of King Darius' ceremonial seat served as a model for that of the Samarian governor

occupation within the walls in comparison to the larger city in the time of the Monarchy, thus leaving the Upper City (the Mishneh) unfortified. His other building enterprises were (a) the Birah, or citadel and seat of civil government, situated at the northwestern angle of the Temple Mount; (b) his own residence, the governor's mansion. This evaluation fits well with the results of recent archaeological excavations. They show that his repairs were concentrated on the western "Ophel" wall (3:24 ff.) of the City of David and, along with it, the Valley Gate. A section of the western wall restored by Nehemiah, later expanded by the Hasmoneans into a fortified complex, is shown in our illustration. Nehemiah 3:8 states that the Jerusalemites abandoned the depleted outer areas as far as the wide wall, this being the wall built by King Hezekiah in former days and recently discovered by N. Avigad in the Upper City.

One of Nehemiah's major achievements lay in persuading a tenth of the population of Judah to move into Jerusalem, thus strengthening the

Right:
Section of the defenses at the crest of the Ophel hill behind which Nehemiah rebuilt the wall. In the foreground are steps, which presumably led to the roof of a house destroyed by the Babylonians.

Above:
The inscription found in Goshen of Egypt settles the debate over the identity of Geshem, the Arab ruler of Nehemiah's time

Persian figurine from the Persian period. Tell Zippor

city in the face of threats and encouraging the growth that made it the metropolis of Judah at the end of the Persian period.

Nehemiah gained considerable popular support among the poor by proclaiming a remission of debts. Again the Samaritans tried to block the reconstruction program. Sanballat, the governor of Samaria, and Tobiah, a powerful noble in Transjordan, led the opposition. Both were connected through marriage with influential Jewish families and were allied with Geshem, the Arab ruler (Neh. 6:6). The identity of Geshem of the Negeb and Sinai and the land of Goshen has been settled by the discovery of an inscription on a silver dish found at Tell el-Mashkuteh (the Pithom of Exodus) in the Land of Goshen. It reads: "Which Qainu the son of Geshem the king of Qedar brought as an offering to Han-Ilat" (fourth century B.C.). Qainu's father, Geshem, reigned in the second half of the fifth century, in the time of Nehemiah.

c. *Nehemiah's Convocation*

Nehemiah's aim was to enforce the law of Moses; we may single out the following prescriptions: (1) To prohibit business on the Sabbath and on holidays; (2) to enforce the sabbatical year with its remission of debts (a boon for the poor); (3) to have each citizen contribute a third of a shekel head tax to the Temple; (4) to render first fruits and other emoluments to the priests, and tithes to the Levites (cf. Neh. 13:16–22). Acting tactfully but forcefully, as a representative of Persian rule, he achieved his objectives by renewing the ancient Covenant, an agreement between God and his people. On one side were the priests, the Levites, the singers, and the *nethinim,* the temple servants (Neh. 10:1–28). On the other was the God of Israel to whom his people, "the holy seed," owed allegiance (9:5–37). The people as a whole undertook to abide by the written undertaking of their representatives. This agreement confirmed the unique status of Israel before God. In this way also, Nehemiah was able to establish an autonomous community within the larger sovereignty of the Persian Empire, and thus put off for a time the aspirations for political independence and the resto-

ration of the Davidic monarchy. For the time being, Judah would content itself with being a theocratic state, as defined by the historian, Josephus.

6. THE JEWISH COMMONWEALTH AND THE SAMARITANS

It would be erroneous to believe that Nehemiah's reform sealed Judah off from all other contacts. After all, the numerous non-Jews who had adopted Judaism were entitled to the same privileges as the native. Thus a latent liberalism remained and would take on more serious proportions. Nehemiah's work proved to lack sufficient momentum. Before or after his return to Persia in 433 B.C., public laxity set in, and upon his return in 432 he tried to disrupt the family ties between the Jews and the Samaritan hierarchy. This led to a rupture between the two communities that became irreparable. Though the Samaritans observed the same Law, faith, and ritual, they identified God's Holy Mountain as Mount Gerizim, not as Jerusalem's Temple. The temple on Mount Gerizim enjoyed the favor of foreign suzerains from Hellenistic times (second century B.C.). Nevertheless, Samaritan Shechem was destroyed and rebuilt four times, the last time by the Hasmonean John Hyrcanus (128 B.C.). The site was not occupied in the Roman period. Its ruins were covered by a Roman temple, and ultimately by a Byzantine church.

The history of the Jewish people, shaped largely by the reforms of Ezra and Nehemiah, and by the priests during the rest of the Persian period, was soon to enter a new stage in the Hellenistic period that followed, when the theocratic community was replaced by a commonwealth in the early third century B.C. and the rigid Torah precepts were reinterpreted by the liberal rabbis (Pharisees) in accordance with later conditions.

7. THE TOBIADS SPAN THE INTERTESTAMENTAL PERIOD

Though the Bible, the books of Chronicles in particular, provides lengthy genealogies of important families or clans, few have left physical remains that archaeology can identify. A notable exception is the promi-

227

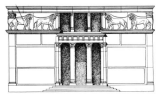

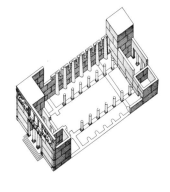

nent house of Tobiah, known since the days of the Judean monarchy. In the days of Nehemiah this house was represented by Tobiah the Ammonite (fifth century B.C., cf. Neh. 2:10; 13:4–8). Later princely Tobiads of the third and second centuries B.C. are mentioned, before and during Hasmonean times. The epigraphic remains found in their ancestral domain at 'Araq el-Emir about eleven miles west of Amman suggest a continuous occupation of the site from before the Exile until the second century B.C., when the Tobiad John Hyrcanus was governor of the area (187–175 B.C.). In the papyri of the Egyptian Zenon, who visited Palestine in the third century B.C., the Tobiad center is referred to as *Birta* ("fortress" in Aramaic). Further chronological data are supplied by inscriptions carved on the rock in the caves above 'Araq el-Emir, where the name "Tobiyah" appears twice, as illustrated. When John Hyrcanus fell out of favor in Jerusalem, he retired and built himself a splendid castle called *Tyros* in the heart of his principality. The castle's remains are located at Khirbet esh-Shar, a high point some ten and a half miles west of Amman. The most interesting find of the excavations was a fountain carved in the rock with a relief of lions and tigers in the lower part of the eastern wall of the fort. Excavations in nearby 'Araq el-Emir in 1961–62 by P. W. Lapp have confirmed that the ruins of the large building on top of a hill (Kasr-el-'Abd) are those of a Jewish temple erected by Hyrcanus early in the second century B.C., as shown in the reconstruction. It is of white stone and decorated with colossal figures of lions in relief. It is rectangular in outline with four corner rooms, one of which was a staircase tower opening into a gallery and leading to a terrace. The portico is near the tower; then follow the entrance porch, the shrine (*naos*), and a storehouse at the rear of the temple.

Below:
Priest holding a Samaritan scroll of the Law

Right:
Samaritans at prayer before the paschal sacrificial rite

B. ESTHER

The book of Esther is a vividly told story about the miraculous deliverance of the Jews of the Persian Diaspora from extermination. Though it does not lack touches of satire at the expense of the natives, the story illustrates the insecure position of the Jews living at the mercy of arbitrary princes; they depended for their very existence on the good offices of influential courtiers. The first two chapters relate Esther's success in winning the king's favors. A certain Haman, a high official in the empire, persuaded his master to hand over to him for spoil ("and destruction") the Jews of Susa and the empire. He pointed out that they were unassimilable, their laws totally different from those of other people, and therefore not to be tolerated (chapter 3).

In spite of Ahasuerus' compliance, Haman was thwarted by his rival for the king's favor, the new Jewish Queen Esther. Under the guidance of her astute cousin, Mordecai, she outwitted Haman and brought about his downfall. He was hanged from the gallows he erected in order to hang Mordecai, and his henchmen were killed as well (chapters 4–8). The Jews, the book says, "did not lay hands on the spoil" of the Persians (cf. 9:15–22; 3:11, 13) in fulfillment of the law of Holy War, showing that they did not fight for material profit, but only to preserve themselves and their religion.

The book, as most critics have pointed out, is too neatly organized and contrived to be accepted as historical. Nevertheless, it is known that Jews achieved positions of wealth and influence throughout the Persian empire, and this prominence no doubt provoked the envy and hostility of the Gentile population, thus providing the background and setting for the story of Haman, Mordecai, and above all, Esther.

Nevertheless, although no confirmation has yet been found in Persian sources of the historicity of the events related in the book of Esther, the descriptions of court etiquette and the actual setting accord with what we know of the imperial court of Susa (the summer capital) and its parallel winter capital at Persepolis (Parsa). Ahasuerus is identified with the Xerxes of Greek tradition (485–465 B.C.), known as a temperamental sovereign ruling over a vast empire and still greater wealth. His figure is sculptured in stone on reliefs of his second capital, Persepolis.

1. THE ABUNDANT WEALTH INVOLVED

The palaces of the Persian emperors were renowned for their splendor and magnificence. Though very little has survived of the brick palace at Susa at the eastern end of the empire, archaeologists have unearthed at Persepolis an elaborate complex of stone palaces dating to those times, among them the Hall of Pillars or *apadana* and its seventy-two pillars, the royal throne rooms, the harem, and the treasury.

One of the most piquant and historically significant elements in the

229

Compared to the splendors of Persepolis, the winter palace of the Persian emperors (right), little has remained of the summer palace at Susa (left) beyond the tiled floor and the bases of many columns

story is the reference to the sum of 10,000 silver talents paid by Haman in return for the royal assent to the destruction or despoiling of the Jews. A talent is the equivalent of 125–130 pounds of silver, and the sum offered approximated a ton and a quarter of silver, an important share of the total revenue of the Persian empire. (Herodotus estimates Darius' revenues at 17,000 talents; Alexander carried off 50,000 talents of silver from Susa alone and 120,000 from Persepolis, the richest city on the face of the earth; the treasury of Persepolis was a vast fortified structure.)

2. ANOTHER VIEW OF HAMAN

The usual explanations of the story and its background are rooted in the traditional motives of Haman's intrigue. It is also worth considering another theory suggested by G. Cornfeld. The key to this is the offer of a large sum by Haman to be paid into the king's treasury for a concession to despoil the Jews as an ethnic group. Shorn of its anti-Semitic trimmings, this could well have been a transaction between the emperor and one of the powerful "tax-farmers," who bid the large sum for the privilege of bleeding the Jews and whom the latter regarded as extortionists and enemies.

A procession of lions on the multi-colored tiles was discovered outside the *apadana* (audience halls) of Susa

It is known that in this and the following centuries, the system of tax collection during the rule of the Hellenistic Ptolemies in Palestine (or their predecessors) was based on the system of tax-farming by concessionaires. The right of collection was farmed out to the highest bidder, usually a man from the upper classes who would pay an annual lump sum to the central authority and then proceed to extract as much as possible from the populace. The difference between what he paid the king and what he got out of the people netted him a substantial profit.

The Haman intrigue may well have started along such conventional lines, later encountered bitter opposition in Jewish ranks, and then flared up into the threat of pogroms, averted by the clever diplomacy of Mordecai and by Esther's wiles, consummate artistry, and bravery.

PART XV

DANIEL

A. WRITING UNDER AN ASSUMED "CLASSIC" NAME

Stone capital of a column topped by two bulls joined together to support the roof beam (center) at Susa

It was general practice in the intertestamental period for writers to cast history in the form of prophecy by attributing a contemporary account of the past to some great figure from earlier times noted for his piety and vision, who thus "foretells" the events from his standpoint until the time of the actual author. In this way the writer accomplished two goals. First, he achieved status and authority for his work by attaching a highly re-garded name of the past to it, and second, the reliability and accuracy of the "foretold history" established the credibility of the new prophecy about the actual future that the writer himself wished to contribute, still in the name of the ancient hero.

The writer of Daniel did not invent the setting of the stories, but took well-known traditions of saints and martyrs that had originated in the time of the Babylonian and Persian empires and been handed down for centuries. By the time they came to the writer, they had already been fixed in tradition in the days of the Babylonian Exile. He then adapted the stories to his own situation in the time of Greek Seleucid rule in Palestine (second century B.C.), retold the history of the world and his people from those days to his own disguised in the form of visions with all kinds of animal and cosmic symbols, and wove them into an account of the career and prophecies of Daniel.

Daniel himself is presented as a hero of faith, a wise man favored by God, who interprets dreams and foresees the future according to the plan of God. By appealing to the authority of such a figure of the past, the au-thor could show how Daniel was able through faith in God and loyalty to him to save himself, his people, and the nation that ruled over them. In addition, by combining stories of miraculous deliverance with visions of historical fulfillment, he could convey not only a solemn message of warn-ing in times of great trouble, but also one of great hope for the future if the hearers and readers would only emulate the faithful obedience of the godly Daniel and his true-hearted companions.

Bas-reliefs of winged sphinxes on colored tiles. The winged disk was a Persian emblem

231

Bronze mask of Antiochus IV
found near Susa

B. CLANDESTINE ANATHEMA OF HELLENISM

We have noticed in "Malachi" how the exclusivist strain in post-exilic Judaism expressed by some of the last prophets combated the more tolerant stream favoring coexistence. The struggle between exclusivism and cosmopolitanism flared again as Hellenism became fashionable among the upper classes in Jerusalem early in the second century B.C. Contemporary literature refers to overt acts against hallowed Jewish tradition on observance of food laws, deportment, and worship. Then intercommunal tensions between the groups increased and culminated in the ferocious persecution of the orthodox by the Greek Antiochus IV, who sided with the Hellenizers. His atrocities provoked the armed rebellion of the faithful Maccabees, who attacked Hellenists and Hellenizers with equal fervor. A protest by the orthodox, veiled enough not to arouse police action, had to be written and circulated among the faithful. This is the credo of the anonymous author of the book of Daniel, who tells how his hero and friends avoid impure food, refuse to bow to idols, and live apart from Gentiles or those who befriend them (meaning the cosmopolitan Jews), 1:8; 11:32; 12:3, 8–13.

Hence, Daniel, which is chronologically the last book of the Old Testament, is in its present form a product of the second century B.C. It tells a dramatic story of the purported career of a Jewish youth and his companions living in the Babylonian Exile in the days of Nebuchadnezzar, a period that represented the depths of despair, but it actually concerns the even more desperate period of religious persecution by Antiochus IV (ca. 167–165 B.C.).

C. THE BOOK'S CONTENTS AND ARCHAEOLOGICAL BACKGROUND

The book of Daniel falls into two parts that, while distinct in form, i.e., stories and visions, nevertheless are linked by a common theme and common subject matter.

Chapters 1–6 relate Daniel's early career in the Babylonian court and his symbolic dreams, with veiled allusions to the persecutions of the Jews in the days of Antiochus IV.

Chapters 7–12 follow, in the form of apocalyptic visions of the end of days. Thus the two phases refer in a dramatic manner and a literary rhythm all its own both to the fate of Babylon (which occurred in the sixth century B.C.) and to the impending divine victory over Antiochus IV of Syria about 165 B.C., with the consequent establishment of the eternal kingdom of God.

The framework of later history, with the passing of the Babylonian empire already in the remote past, is apparent in the text from the accurate descriptions of administrative and historical data pertaining to the Persian empire, that is, the division into satrapies, 3:2–3, 27; 6:2–7, and from the use of animal imagery to describe the emergence and dominance of the Greeks. Thus Daniel 8:21–22 refers to Alexander the Great and to the divisions of his empire. It is interesting to note how the prestigious figure of Alexander was treated in ancient art and legend. He was called "Alexander of the double horns," and a Ptolemaic (Egyptian-Hellenistic) coin portrays him as a god, with a covering of elephant's hide over his head and "horns" protruding from his forehead, as from the forehead of the ancient gods of Mesopotamia.

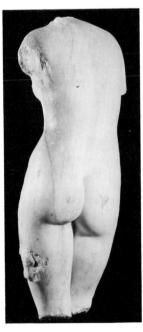

Right:
Marble statue of Aphrodite found in the fields of Tell Dan, probably belonging to the last days of the use of the High Place in Hellenistic times

Left:
Head of Alexander the Great on a Ptolemaic (Hellenistic) coin, portrayed with a covering of elephant's hide and horns protruding from his head

D. THE PRESUMED BABYLONIAN PHASE

In comparison with the Persian shekel, the Israelite stone shekel weight (11.4 grams) was used for weighing silver and gold of the corresponding weight. The stone was incised with the sign 𐤀 signifying 1 shekel, or by another numeral such as 𐤀𐤀 , 4 shekels. Most of the marked weights date to the 7th c. B.C., the period of the *lamelekh* seal impressions reproduced earlier, indicating a standardization of royal weights and measures

The heterogeneous composition of the book becomes apparent from its peculiar stylistic patterns. It starts in classic but stilted Hebrew, breaks off at 2:4 into idiomatic literary Aramaic, then resumes (chapter 8) in Hebrew until the end of the book. It seems clear that the author's language of preference was Aramaic, but that he felt obliged to use the classic language of Scripture (Hebrew) for the opening and closing sections of the book. The language division does not correspond exactly to the organization of the book into stories and visions, leaving some unanswered questions as to the author's purpose and objectives.

1. SYMBOLS AND DREAM INTERPRETATION

Chapters 1–5 relate how Daniel and his friends, presumably Judean exiles, were trained in the lore of "wise-men" or diviners, termed "Chaldeans," and show his growing reputation as an interpreter of dreams. Throughout the years the exiles remained steadfast observers of Jewish law though living in the seductively pagan Babylonian court. Daniel rose to power through his interpretation of the king's fantastic dream of the fallen statue (chapter 2) by an accepted system of correlation, similar to Joseph's interpretation of Pharaoh's dreams in Genesis. Thus, the statue represented a succession of kingdoms: the head of gold was the Babylonian empire, to be followed by the Median, Persian, and Greek empires, represented by the lower parts of the body, until the last one would be destroyed by a great stone that symbolized the kingdom of God and his saints, which would endure forever (2:36–45).

For a contemporary Jewish audience, living in what were believed to be the last days of the Seleucid kingdom, the principal message was in the form of an eschatological vision: in the end of days, God's kingdom will smash the tyrants of this earth and abide forever. Apocalyptic expectations were fostered in Jewish circles, especially in times of persecution, to comfort and encourage the faithful.

2. THE WRITING ON THE WALL

Toward the end of chapter 5, the familiar story of Belshazzar's feast, there is the ominous account of the handwriting on the wall. The words are interpreted by Daniel as a prophecy of doom on the kingdom: The Aramaic "*Mene', mene', teqel upharsin*" may be rendered "Counted, counted, weighed and divided," to signify the approaching end of Babylon; that is, God has counted out its days, weighed the king in the scales, found him wanting, and divided up his dominions. On the other hand, the words taken literally are simply various weights that were employed as units of exchange before the introduction of coinage and subsequently gave their names to coins: *maneh* or the Babylonian *mina,* weighing sixty shekels (*shekels* both a basic weight and coin); *peres*—half of any previously mentioned weight, or a shekel as shown in the illustration of Babylonian measures. These weights or coins then refer to the kings of the Babylonian dynasty: possibly Nebuchadnezzar, Nabonidus, and Belshazzar.

Persian shekel

3. THE FATE OF BABYLON—NABONIDUS' ARCHAEOLOGICAL INCLINATIONS

When Nabonidus of Haran seized power in 556 B.C., he challenged the religious monopoly of the priests of the god Marduk by devoting himself to the revival of ancient gods, especially the moon-god Sin. He was an early antiquarian and archaeologist. When the danger of Persia became acute, he moved his capital to the oasis of Teima on the Arabian border, where he stayed until 545 B.C., while his son Belshazzar managed affairs at Babylon (Daniel 5) until its capture by Cyrus in 539. The biblical text errs factually by naming Belshazzar the son of Nebuchadnezzar, but this slip has been clarified by one of the Dead Sea Scrolls closely related in style and content to the biblical cycle of Daniel. It relates that Nabonidus contracted a "dread disease by the decree of the Most High" and was "set apart from men." The biblical source transfers this affliction of madness to Nebuchadnezzar, and the change of names may have come about during the course of the transmission of the tradition. Hence Nabonidus apparently belongs in the cycle and has been inadvertently displaced by Nebuchadnezzar in Daniel 4–5.

The Babylonian *mína* (which brings to mind *mene', mene', . . .*) was the equivalent of sixty shekels in weight. Metal ingots served as currency before the advent of coins

235

E. THE HISTORIC MEANING OF THE BOOK

The second part of Daniel includes many veiled references to the persecution of Antiochus. The Seleucid kingdom is represented by a horrible beast (7:7–24) that devours and tramples everything. From it ten kings will arise, beginning with Seleucus I, and coming down to the present time. According to the usual analysis of the last verse (7:25), the tenth horn in the vision, with human eyes and a boastful mouth uttering blasphemies, is none other than Antiochus IV.

On the river of Ulai, near Susa, Daniel has a vision of the struggle between Persia and Greece. The first is represented by a ram (a favorite subject of Persian art) with two horns (Media and Persia) and the Greeks by a he-goat. The symbolism of the visions is based on an established ancient pattern. The he-goat charges the ram and tramples him (8:7), an allusion to Alexander's victory at Issos in 333 B.C., described in the illustration.

In the vision of chapters 11–12, Daniel foretells the later history of the two Hellenistic successor kingdoms of Alexander's empire, which were of most concern to the author, Ptolemaic Egypt and Seleucid Syria. They fought intermittently over the territory between them with first the Ptolemies and then the Seleucids controlling Palestine. The ultimate fate of both kingdoms and of the Jews caught between them is the subject of these chapters, a remarkably detailed account of the period down to 165 B.C.

F. A FORERUNNER OF APOCALYPTIC WRITING

The book of Daniel with its dreams and visions, its stories and exhortations, became the model for apocalyptic books, supernatural revelations, which appeared first in Jewish, then in Christian literature. In the present instance the inspiring tales of faithfulness under duress and of miraculous deliverance from tribulation were intended to strengthen the resolve of the faithful Jews, so that they would not collapse under pressure or abandon their religion, since in the end God would save them and destroy the wicked enemy.

In Daniel the angels, who are anonymous agents of God in the stories of the earlier books of the Bible, have names, ranks, dominions, and duties, constituting a complicated hierarchy in heaven. They were destined to play a major role in Judaism, Christianity, and Islam, along with belief in a final judgment for all men, resurrection and eternal life for the just, and damnation for the wicked.

PART XVI

A. INTERTESTAMENTAL PERIOD

1. THE GAP BETWEEN THE OLD AND NEW TESTAMENTS

In spite of the many historical and theological links between the Old and New Testaments, there are significant divergences and differences, many of which are attributable to special developments during the period between the Testaments. The recognizable gap between the two was caused, on the one hand, by the process of canonization of the Hebrew Scriptures and, on the other, by the emergence of a varied extracanonical religious and historical Jewish literature. Though they represented important trends in Jewish life between late post-exilic times (fourth to second centuries B.C.) and the first century A.D., they were not canonized by the rabbis and sages of that period. These were the apocryphal, pseudepigraphical, and apocalyptic writings, to be described briefly below. Yet these writings exerted an important influence on early Christianity and left their mark on the New Testament, especially in respect to its apocalyptic eschatological expectations.

a. *Canonization*

The canonization of the Old Testament was the end result of a process that lasted throughout post-exilic and Second Temple days and produced in effect two different but overlapping bodies of Scripture, one Hebrew and Palestinian, the other Greek and Alexandrian, both entirely Jewish. They incorporated most trends in Jewish life, exclusivist and cosmopolitan alike, as is evident from the inclusion of writings as diverse in spirit as Ezra-Nehemiah or Malachi, and Job, Jonah, and Ecclesiastes, not to mention the additional books in the Greek canon. The canon of biblical books initially included the Torah, to be followed quickly by the Prophets, Former and Latter. The scope and status of the writings were a matter of discussion for many years, not finally resolved until the Council of Yabneh around A.D. 100. The process by which the Greek canon was established and the organization of its parts are somewhat different, since the Greek Old Testament included all of the books in the Hebrew Bible, plus some others composed in Persian and Hellenistic times. The only such work included in the Hebrew Bible was the book of Daniel, all others being relegated to noncanonical status. The Greek canon was more extended, and when the Christian Church was established, it adopted the Greek Old Testament as its Scripture, to which were added later the books of the New Testament. It should be added that for all Jews the Torah (the five books of Moses) was paramount, and *halakha* ("rules of practice") had to be based on it.

b. *The Apocrypha*

The Apocrypha are books that were rejected by the Palestinian rabbis and scholars as not manifestly inspired works and written mostly by unknown men. Fourteen of these were included in the Greek canon, among them such works as 1 and 2 Maccabees, Ecclesiasticus (Ben Sira), Judith, Tobit, Wisdom, and additions to Esther, Daniel and Jeremiah. They constitute the core and cream of the literary production of this period of persecution and ferment in the life of the Jewish community in Palestine and the Diaspora.

c. *Pseudepigrapha*

The Pseudepigrapha were composed under assumed names, the choice of which was affected by theological considerations. To give these books both the aura of divine sanction and the patina of antiquity, the actual authors assigned their work to great heroes of the faith, known for their piety and intimate relationship with God, for example, Enoch, Moses, Baruch, Ezra. These books purported to be forecasts of the future delivered by these ancient worthies, but were thinly disguised historical works, interlaced with moral warnings, and exhortations to hold fast to the traditional faith.

d. *Apocalyptic Literature*

The apocalyptic literature consists of the revelation of secret information about God's plan for the world in general and Israel in particular. The revelation is couched in colorful often bizarre imagery and is set down as a series of extraordinary visions, the meaning of which is revealed only to the visionary, and by him to the faithful. The book of Daniel in the Old Testament is a prime example, as is the book of Revelation in the New Testament. Using symbolic language full of fantastic figures, the texts allude to mysteries beyond the reach of man but revealed and explained by God through helpful angels to his chosen few. It seemed to the authors that the present world was passing while the new eschatological age was about to begin. The details are worked out with an agonized blending of history in this world and idealized pictures of the world to come, recapturing the vision of the Garden of Eden and combining it with that of a heavenly paradise. The present crisis would be resolved in a final Day of Judgment when the worthy could inherit eternal life and the wicked corresponding damnation. These ideas are reflected in New Testament writings, particularly the book of Revelation. Strikingly similar literature, before the New Testament, has been found among the famous Dead Sea Scrolls. Other apocalyptic works are: Enoch, Testament of the Twelve Patriarchs, Second Baruch, Fourth Ezra, The Assumption and Testament of Moses, and Third Baruch.

2. THE JEWISH HISTORICAL SOURCES

The fullest description of the period from 175 B.C. to the first century A.D.—including the rule of the Greek Ptolemies in Egypt, the Seleucids in

Syria, and the Hasmoneans in Palestine—that ended in Roman domination and the puppet reigns of the Herods is found in *Antiquities of the Jews* by the Jewish historian, Josephus Flavius (in Books VII–XX of this monumental work). His work in turn is dependent upon older accounts in 1 and 2 Maccabees. First Maccabees traces the growth of Jewish independence from the revolt of Judas Maccabaeus to the reign of John Hyrcanus. Its author was a devout and patriotic Jew and, while the book reflects his commitment to the Maccabees, it is one of the most reliable sources for the intertestamental period. Second Maccabees covers a briefer portion of the same period, ending with the death of the Syrian general, Nicanor (161 B.C.). It is a digest from an older work by Jason of Cyrene (North Africa), who wrote in Greek and stressed the supernatural aspects of the deliverance of his people by Judas the Maccabee. Nevertheless, it supplements 1 Maccabees at a number of points where the latter is deficient and corroborates it at others. There are many differences in detail, but these are rarely of significance, except for historians.

3. DIVERGENT SPIRITUAL AND SOCIAL TRENDS—FOURTH CENTURY B.C. TO FIRST CENTURY A.D.

a. *Israel and the Nations*

Several of the biblical works already considered reflect a basic problem of post-exilic Judaism, namely the sharp division between Israel and the nations and varying views on its position in the world. The two groups were in opposition from the time of the Babylonian Exile, and that tension persisted throughout all the days of the Second Temple. Whereas the prophets Zechariah and Haggai saw no harm in peaceful coexistence with non-Jews, Malachi hewed to the line of strict exclusivism. Two principal social trends appeared in these times, but while Ezra and Nehemiah were dominant in their day, exclusivism did not win out. A more liberal view, evident in Job and Jonah, and a more cosmopolitan outlook, as in Ecclesiastes, were preserved through public recitation and reading and, finally, in canonical Scripture. Thus the two attitudes continued side by side for centuries without either completely dominating the other. The tolerance Jews enjoyed in the world impelled them to adopt a more cosmopolitan outlook, akin in some ways to Hellenistic philosophical thought, which was popular among the educated and sophisticated circles in the Near East, and not unknown in Judea (as southern Palestine became known in post-exilic times).

b. *Hellenism and Judea*

Hellenism swept the East through the conquests of Alexander the Great, which extended from Greece to India. His empire was split into three powerful kingdoms after Alexander's death in 323 B.C.: the Ptolemies in Egypt, who also controlled Palestine until 200 B.C., the Seleucids in Mesopotamia with headquarters in Syria, and the European domain centering on Macedonia.

Right:
King Darius at Issos (333 B.C.)

Left:
Alexander at Issos

The high priest of the hereditary house of Zadok presided at the Temple in Jerusalem. He was also the leading political authority and levied taxes for the Egyptian overlord, though the actual collection was delegated to local tax-farmers, usually recruited from leading Jewish families. A prototype of such a tax-farmer was Joseph ben Tobiah in the mid-third century B.C., a scion of the powerful dynasty that had established itself in Transjordan as far back as the days of Nehemiah. By that time (early third century) Greek and Macedonian settlers had come to Palestine, forming islands of Hellenistic civilization complete with all the architectural, social, and political forms of the self-governing *polis* ("city") and the polytheism to which it was bound. Their rulers encouraged mutual exchanges between Greek and Semitic civilization, and their interpenetration created a symbiotic Hellenistic-Oriental culture, characterized by the graceful Greek styles in art and architecture, but affected as well by traditional Oriental spirit and manners.

Judea proper was surrounded by a ring of such states and modelled its own municipal governments on Greek patterns, including their elected town councils, clearly an innovation in oriental cultures. The more exclusivist and pious Judeans looked upon this as a necessary evil, while the more cosmopolitan-minded Jews prospered in the new climate; this was particularly true of the class to which the Tobiads and their contemporaries belonged, as well as the powerful priesthood. The Tobiads provide a classic example of the attraction and advantages of Hellenization, which was a useful and effective instrument in the drive for greater wealth and power. Contemporary conditions are described graphically in the non-Jewish Zenon papyri (late third century B.C.).

c. *New Western Institutions Come to Jerusalem*

As the Hellenistic way of life first infiltrated and then shaped urban life in Judea, the people of Jerusalem and other cities became familiar with the ubiquitous Greek institutions for the physical and moral training of young men. Many attended the gymnasium and *ephebeion* (for athletic games). The first to endorse the new culture were those already in close contact with the authorities: the landed gentry, rich merchants, officials, and the priestly aristocracy. Large elements among the masses did not become Hellenized, and the more traditional and exclusivist elements bitterly resented the new cosmopolitan way of life.

d. *The Hellenistic Reform*

In spite of growing tensions within the Jewish community, the situation remained relatively calm at the end of the third century B.C. But in 198 B.C., Judea—heretofore under Ptolemaic rule—was annexed by Antiochus III, the Great, the Seleucid king. While autonomous Jewish life was not disturbed under the new foreign ruler, strife intensified when the Tobiads, now loyal to the new overlords, succeeded in deposing the high priest, Onias, and replacing him by his pro-Hellenistic brother, Jason. Onias retired to Egypt with many other refugees who fled from the distasteful religious and social climate. He then built a Temple at Leontopolis in northern Egypt to rival that of Jerusalem.

One of the halls of the 2nd c. B.C. Hellenistic gymnasium, part of the *Xystos* place of public assembly in Jerusalem. It lies underground, close to the Western Wall bordering the elevated Temple esplanade. The upstanding column supported the roof of the hall

241

Unlike the ancient prestigious *soferim*, the present day *sofer* or scribe is a professional copyist of Torah scrolls

The right of succession to the high priesthood of the house of Zadok had never before been challenged. It was almost as sacrosanct as the tradition of the house of David. Now the usurper Jason gave the Seleucids the privilege of appointing future high priests when it suited their political or financial needs. From 2 Maccabees we learn that Jason established a gymnasium and ephebeion in Jerusalem, virtually turning it into a Hellenistic *polis*. This construction, identified by Josephus with the *Xystos*, seems to have been an open-air porticoed plaza paved with large polished flagstones, and used for public assemblies. It faced the Temple Mount on the west and lay therefore in the busy Tyropoeon Vale, the busiest thoroughfare of the Lower City. One of the halls of this complex has been uncovered, as described. By that time cosmopolitan Jews began to adopt Hellenistic names, either by Hellenizing their Hebrew names or by coupling their own with a Greek-sounding name.

4. THE HASSIDIM

Thus far, Hellenization trends had not directly affected the religious faith of the people. Its real purpose, according to 1 Maccabees, was to end the exclusiveness of the Jews and to open their way to membership in the commonwealth of Hellenistic peoples. But the erection of the gymnasium was a radical and treacherous step, in the opinion of the orthodox; this explains the hidden meaning of Daniel 11:30–33, as well as 1:5; 12:3, 8–13; 7:13–14, which refer to the underlying resentment and ground swell of protest. Its apocalyptic viewpoint reflects the appearance of a new movement in Judaism led by the exclusive Hassidim (or Assideans). They believed that secular rule was granted by God to the nations according to a predetermined plan that controlled the course of world history. Israel, the chosen people, must also conform to this plan and be subject to pagan empires until the end of time, when God would destroy the kingdoms of the world and replace them with his own kingdom, made up primarily, if not exclusively, of the faithful among his people. According to the Hassidim and the author of Daniel, that day was fast approaching, and therefore it was all the more important for Jews to cling to their faith in the face of enticements and persecution. This secret was known to the elect, the apocalyptists, and such other pious people who adhered to a strict observance of the priestly Code of Holiness and Levitical purity.

Besides being strict upholders of the Law, the Hassidim also instructed the people in its observances. Many illustrious scholars belonged to the group, including the *soferim* (scribes), who were responsible for the transmission of holy scripture. First Maccabees (7:12) refers to a company or synagogue of scribes involved in a conflict with Alcimus, another usurping high priest, in the days of Judas Maccabaeus.

According to historic Jewish sources, the early Hassidim split up later into the sects of the Essenes and the Pharisees.

5. THE HASMONEAN WAR OF INDEPENDENCE

Antiochus IV, who acceded to the Seleucid throne in 175 B.C., was a firm believer in an ecumenical Hellenistic religion that would embrace all the peoples in his large kingdom. A few years after his accession, in 171 B.C., the Tobiads and their allies in Jerusalem successfully promoted Menelaus, a relative of theirs and an extreme Hellenizer, to the high priesthood. He used the appointment, obtained through bribery, for political and material ends. He supported Antiochus IV's disregard for Judaism and plundered the Temple's treasure on the king's behalf. His unrestrained personal behavior, coupled with growing class conflicts between the wealthy Jewish Hellenizers and the masses, resulted in riots and street fighting. Two years later, when Antiochus suffered reverses in Egypt, the priest Jason returned from exile and executed a number of Menelaus' followers. Antiochus then occupied Jerusalem with his troops to suppress the civil disturbances and in the process massacred 80,000 people. He profaned and pillaged the Temple and took away a treasure amounting to 1800 talents (approximately seven million shekels of silver). The king instructed his officers to carry through the Hellenization of the Jewish religion. In 167 B.C. he forbade the observance of the Jewish faith, a religious policy hitherto unknown in Hellenistic annals. Instead, he ordered the worship of the Greek Zeus in his Oriental form, Baal Shamem ("the Lord of Heaven").

The process of identifying similar gods in different pantheons had been going on for millennia in the Near East, and it was accelerated by the introduction of Greek and Roman deities during this period. Thus Melkart of Tyre was identified with Heracles; Baal Shamem was represented in Baalbek in Lebanon as Jupiter Heliopolitanus. For Antiochus the equation of Yahweh with Zeus-Jupiter-Baal was entirely appropriate, though utter blasphemy to all but the most radical and emancipated Jews. Though Menelaus was reinstated as high priest, the Temple had been so desecrated that pious Jews avoided worshiping there, even before it was officially closed to them.

a. *Restoration of the Kingdom*

Fidelity to the Law of Moses finally led to rebellion. Holy war against Hellenism was proclaimed in 166 B.C. by the Hasmonean priest, Mattathias, and his sons and bands of valiant men who rallied around him. Judas, surnamed Maccabaeus, the third of the five sons, took strategic command. He was killed after six years of fighting. Under Jonathan and Simon (165–135 B.C.), who secured the high priesthood, the territory of the Jews was recognized as autonomous and was greatly extended north and west to include Samaria and the coastal plain. By the time of Simon's violent death, the dynasty was firmly established. During the reign of Hyrcanus, Simon's son (135–104 B.C.), Antiochus VII led an army against Jerusalem; he imposed a tribute on Judea and took John Hyrcanus as hos-

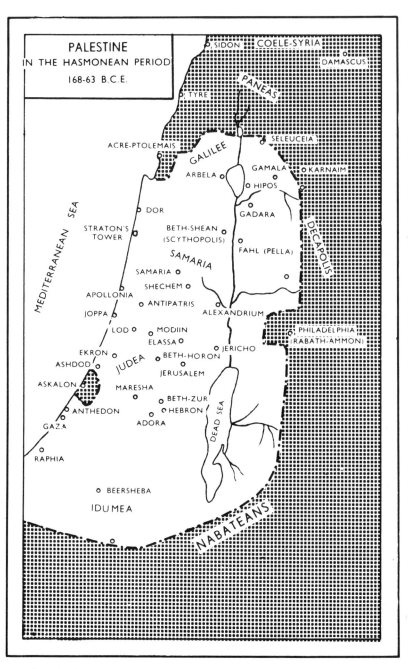

PALESTINE
IN THE HASMONEAN PERIOD
168-63 B.C.E.

SIDON
COELE-SYRIA
DAMASCUS
TYRE
PANEAS
ACRE-PTOLEMAIS
SELEUCEIA
GALILEE
ARBELA
GAMALA
KARNAIM
HIPOS
DOR
GADARA
STRATON'S TOWER
BETH-SHEAN (SCYTHOPOLIS)
FAHL (PELLA)
MEDITERRANEAN SEA
SAMARIA
DECAPOLIS
SAMARIA
APOLLONIA
SHECHEM
JOPPA
ANTIPATRIS
ALEXANDRIUM
LOD
MODIIN
ELASSA
PHILADELPHIA (RABATH-AMMON)
EKRON
JERICHO
ASHDOD
BETH-HORON
JUDEA
JERUSALEM
ASKALON
MARESHA
ANTHEDON
BETH-ZUR
HEBRON
DEAD SEA
GAZA
ADORA
RAPHIA
BEERSHEBA
IDUMEA
NABATEANS

tage, but the latter escaped and succeeded in restoring the independence of his country (and even considerably enlarged its territories).

b. *Conflict with the Hasmoneans*

The Hasmonean leaders, once independence had been won, began a process of secularization of national life. This seemed to the Hassidim, their allies in the struggle, a betrayal of their faith and commitment to God. When Jonathan assumed the high priesthood in 152 B.C., he compounded the offense with a disavowal of Hassidean tenets of priestly succession, as he was not of the ancient priestly house of Zadok established since the days of Solomon. When this office became hereditary in the Hasmonean line under Simon, the act displaced the Zadokites from their pre-eminent position. The Hassidim had expected the eventual restoration of the ideal kingdom, but the historical success of the Hasmoneans only alienated them. After political independence had been gained, the Hassidim broke away from the Hasmoneans, giving up their participation in political life and emphasizing instead religious observance and faithful adherence to the ancient ways. They became rigorous critics of the Hasmonean establishment but preferred prayers to protests and rather than fight against the Maccabees chose nonviolent forms of resistance. A group of Essenes, an off-shoot of the Hassidim, went out into the Judean wilderness, there to build a new society based strictly on the most ancient traditions of the Bible, to be the nucleus of a new pure Israel that would one day inherit the kingdom prepared by God for his elect. This event was never recorded in contemporary annals, and it would have been lost forever but for a chance discovery by a Bedouin shepherd of one of the greatest finds of modern times. The discovery of the Dead Sea Scrolls at Qumran and nearby localities—so essential for the study of contemporary Judaism and early Christianity—has identified a religious and social group of Covenanters associated with the Essenes, if not the central group of Essenes themselves.

Syrian Jupiter Heliopolitanus
(from Baalbek)

c. *The Pharisees*

On the other hand, larger numbers of the Hassidim chose to unite, instead, in active opposition to the Hasmonean dynasty, because its claims and behavior ran counter to their theological outlook. In time they were organized as the powerful Pharisaic party backed by the masses and eventually became the dominant force in normative Judaism.

d. *The Sadducees*

Unlike the other sects, these supporters of the Hasmoneans, devout, conservative, and committed to the strict observance of the Law of Moses, were bent on consolidating the new independence of the nation. They were quite willing to maintain contact with their neighbors in Palestine and Transjordan and, as the occasion warranted, to negotiate with them or fight against them and forcibly Judaize them. This pragmatism, coupled with their support of the new Jewish power, kept them busy with mundane matters and led them away from eschatological visions of the Day of Judgment. Organized as another sect around the Hasmonean hierarchy, the Sadducees were represented in the main by the aristocracy, the numerous and rich priesthood, and their own scholarly leaders.

6. THE PHARISEES AND THE HASMONEANS

The early Pharisees, concerned with the practical interpretation of the traditional Law in relation to everyday problems, also took an active part

245

in teaching the people. They shared the Hassidean contempt for secular politics and for years maintained the same objection to Hasmonean usurpation of the high priesthood. Later, as members of the Assembly of Notables, they supported the new government out of patriotic motives. However, as King John Hyrcanus' international status grew, so did the pomp and ceremony of his court, as when Hyrcanus appeared before his people in splendid imitation of a Hellenistic Oriental monarch. Though Hellenization had lost its potency in the country, the Hasmonean monarch behaved like a secular dynast. Although theoretically restricted in his authority by the Assembly, his rule became increasingly autocratic. Disaffection stemmed from the Pharisees, who up to then had been inclined to support the government. Their deepest wish was to let Hyrcanus exercise only civil authority, and even that on an interim basis, until "a priest descended from Zadok and a savior or king from the house of David could be reinstated." Eventually their insistence turned Hyrcanus against them and he adhered firmly to the aristocratic Sadducee party. It must be noted, however, that his reign was a period of prosperity and expansion of Jewish interests in Palestine, so no serious opposition could crystallize (see below: "Numerous Remains in Jerusalem of Hasmonean Times"). In fact Josephus speaks glowingly of him, saying that in John the roles of prophet, priest, and king were combined.

a. *Rise and Fall of the Hasmonean Dynasty*

John Hyrcanus was succeeded by his sons, Judah Aristobulos (105–104 B.C.) and Alexander Yannai (Grecized as Jannaeus), who were bidden to make peace with the Pharisees. Judah died after a year and was succeeded by Alexander, who adopted the royal title and reigned until 75 B.C. He assembled a professional mercenary army and conquered Transjordan, Idumaea in the south, and the coastal plain, carving out a large kingdom. His antagonism to the Pharisees, who opposed his expansionist war policy, led to civil rebellion, which he suppressed after a bloody struggle. His cruelty was notorious, and he was remembered for his practice of crucifying his enemies. Nevertheless, the Pharisees gained influence and power during the reign of his widow, Salome Alexandra (76–69 B.C.). Hasmonean rule began to decline with her death, due to the strife between her sons, Hyrcanus II and Aristobulos II. This led to the intervention and eventual domination of the state by Antipater, a Judaized Idumaean, and his son Herod, who were abetted by the Romans, the new superpower on the scene. The Roman general, Pompey, who had invaded the country, captured Jerusalem and entered the Temple precincts in 63 B.C. The last Hasmonean princes had frittered away the remnants of their power and authority through internecine feuds. Hyrcanus remained a puppet in Antipater's hands. Meanwhile, the efforts of Aristobulos II and his sons, Alexander and Antigonus Mattathias II, proved unsuccessful. The latter disappeared after his defeat by Herod and the capture of Jerusalem in 37 B.C. This spelled the end of the Hasmonean dynasty.

b. *The Tomb of Mattathi, Son of Judah*

A rock tomb was uncovered in recent years on Mount Scopus, east of Jerusalem. It bore a monumental inscription and contained a sumptuous ossuary. The inscription proclaims that Abba, descendant of the High Priest Aaron, who had been persecuted, had brought back the bones of Mattathi, son of Judah, and that he buried him in his cave tomb. The discovery has aroused considerable speculation, as Mattathi is presumed by some to be the last Hasmonean prince, Antigonus, who was deposed by Herod. No conclusion has been reached as yet, however.

The startling inscription over the loculus where the bones of Mattathi had been buried

7. NUMEROUS REMAINS IN JERUSALEM OF HASMONEAN TIMES

The Hasmoneans effectively ruled in the land for one hundred years (163–63 B.C.). Herod took the throne from the last Hasmonean prince, Antigonus, and killed off most of the surviving Hasmoneans to insure that there would be no political threats from that quarter. Then he embarked on a vast building program in Jerusalem and other urban centers in Palestine.

Regret is often expressed that very few Hasmonean buildings and monuments have survived, especially since theirs was the last Jewish kingdom in the Holy Land and they devoted a great deal of time and effort, and much of the royal exchequer, to reconstructing the city of Jerusalem that served as their capital. But this is a misreading of the available evidence, produced by a series of archaeological discoveries during the last century, and more particularly in the decade since 1967. These remains are not less important than those surviving from the days of the Monarchy and are second in significance only to those dating to the Herodian period.

The monumental remains illustrate how the Hasmoneans fortified the expanded area of Jerusalem and built its walls and palaces and how this expansion and increased population encompassed the commercial centers to the east and north, particularly the Upper City (the present Jewish Quarter). The evidence consists of massive walls, monumental buildings, stone carvings, and rock-tombs and of small finds in great quantity, including pottery and coins.

a. *The Walls and Fortifications*

Beneath the ramparts constructed by Herod or later builders, archaeologists have uncovered in various locations solid Hasmonean foundations and stretches of massive wall that help to explain the ancient plans underlying Jerusalem's defense. Let us examine them at the west, south, east, and north. The excavations at the Citadel on the west (and since 1976 along the entire length of the western wall of the Old City, which faces modern Jerusalem) have uncovered the thick walls apparently built by John Hyrcanus and Alexander Jannaeus. The line of walls and adjacent towers at this lower level interlock with the massive Herodian walls and

Above:
The base of the Herodian Tower of Phasael (in the Citadel) built into the former Hasmonean city wall

The two top, right, and bottom, right:
Foundation layers and fortifications of the Hasmonean western city wall, excavated in 1976

towers built above them. It is not difficult to distinguish the different styles of stone carving and jointing throughout the length of the walls. This is one of the most spectacular discoveries in Jerusalem, along with those made at the Temple Mount and on the slopes of Mount Zion—Magen Broshi's dramatic excavations since 1976.

One of the key achievements of the Hasmonean kings was to fortify various sections of the capital so that each could stand on its own in time of war. The Hasmonean wall of Jerusalem is built mostly of large rocks, squared roughly and uncarved, in contrast to the characteristic finely chiselled and embossed Herodian ashlars. The earlier line of walls was built hastily under military pressure and threat of imminent attack.

The second most imposing fortification was erected on top of the Ophel, the site of the ancient City of David, in later times the Lower City, about 220 feet west of the Gihon spring and several hundred feet east of the Temple Mount. This wall was flanked by two towers and protected on the eastern side by a sloping ramp faced with stepped masonry to prevent the approach of besiegers trying to scale the walls and of siege engines to batter them. The fortifications were erected by the Hasmoneans during the second century B.C. and rested on an earlier wall and houses

Below:
A section of the southeastern wall of the city (right) as it dovetails into Herodian layers (left)

erected in the days of the Judean kings (ninth to eighth centuries B.C.). The earlier wall had been repaired by Nehemiah; a section of it is still visible in the rear of the structure illustrated here. It is one of the oldest surviving structures of biblical Jerusalem, which has suffered more than its share of attacks and destructions. Another segment of Hasmonean wall has been located near the southeastern corner of the ramparts of the Temple Mount esplanade. This section, made of roughly cut square stones, stands out in sharp contrast to the abutting larger ashlars carved in characteristic Herodian style.

Pediment of a 40-foot column (Attic style) in the Upper City

b. *The Upper City and the Akra*

A large number of Hasmonean remains have been uncovered in the Jewish Quarter through excavations conducted by N. Avigad on the occasion of its reconstruction. It is now definitely identified as the Upper City described by the historian Josephus, the aristocratic quarter of the capital in which the Hasmoneans erected their palace and where the elegant homes of the nobles, military leaders, and high priests were built. It overlooked the Temple Mount esplanade, the scene of solemn daily ritual and the great festive occasions. The settlement and expansion of this quarter followed the capture of the Akra, the last stronghold of the Hellenizers. The exact location of the Akra is disputed, some scholars holding that it was in this quarter, while B. Mazar, in charge of the excavations of the Temple Mount, believes that it stood further south, on top of the Ophel ridge facing the southern gates.

Evidence of extensive Hasmonean construction in contemporary Hellenistic style is offered by broken columns and the Corinthian or Ionian capitals that topped them. They were scattered about in the wreckage, but some have been reset on their bases. The standard size was about forty feet high and six feet in diameter, used in the construction of large and impressive buildings. The excavations carried out have uncovered, in addition, vast quantities of pottery and other ceramic remains dating to the third and second centuries B.C. Some of their handles bear the *Yhwd* impression in archaic Hebrew letters characteristic of Hasmonean ware.

Under the floor of one of the contemporary houses, a rich treasure of coins was found, some attributed to Alexander Jannaeus or Antigonus, and others to Herod. The excavation of a lower layer revealed only Hasmonean coins. Another important find in this building was a stone relief of a cornucopia and pomegranates, a motif found only on Hasmonean coins and familiar as the emblem of the royal house.

The Hasmonean fortifications of the Ophel, with ramp and glacis on the right. The ramp meets a square tower at the left

Right:
Corner of the Hellenistic
Gymnasium in the Xystos
center. The small outline of a
lion is seen at the upper center
below the vault

Above:
One of the arches that
supported the aqueduct over the
Xystos and the Tyropoeon Vale

The name of Jonathan
(Alexander Jannaeus) is spelled
between the horns on the
Hasmonean coin

Below:
Stone relief of cornucopia
depicting a pomegranate
between the two horns of
plenty

c. *The Gymnasium, Xystos, and Wilson Arch*

Another fascinating relic of Hellenistic and Hasmonean days is a small hall found in the Tyropoeon Vale facing the western ramparts of the Temple Mount, with the remains of a column that supported the roof and the carving of a winged lion at the upper corner. The underground hall lies below the present level of the Old City of Jerusalem. According to B. Mazar, it is related to the Xystos, the site of the Hellenistic gymnasium famed for athletic games and other entertainment held there before the Hasmoneans banned them (*The Mountain of the Lord,* p. 215). The site abuts on the lower ruined arch (named the Wilson Arch after its discoverer) supporting an aqueduct that brought water to the Temple Mount from distant springs in the south.

d. *The Stairway and the Pools*

A further reminder of the times was a cache of weights dating to Hasmonean times. It was found at the top of a long stairway, beginning in the grounds of the Church of Gallicantu, which connected the western quarter on Mount Zion with the Siloam Pool situated at the outlet of the underground aqueduct dug by King Hezekiah.

e. *The Hasmonean Pool of Bethesda*

This double pool, which has since dried up, was discovered just beyond the northern end of the Temple Mount esplanade. It was about 400 feet long, 200 feet wide, and 33 to 50 feet deep. At least a section of the pool was cut in the rock in Hasmonean times. Five rock-cut rooms in Hasmonean style were found there, to which access was gained by a flight of stairs that led to immersion rooms. A monument in honor of Alexander Jannaeus had been erected near the Bethesda pools. These pools, lying just

outside the Temple area esplanade, adjoin a large number of other underground pools, passages, and corridors to the south under the upper esplanade, on which stands the Moslem shrine (the Haram esh-Sherif).

f. *Family Tombs in the Kidron Valley*

Further evidence of the city's splendor, as attested in 1 and 2 Maccabees and Josephus, are the underground family tombs, cut into the bedrock of the Kidron Valley east of the Temple Mount, and the monumental mausoleums surmounting them, such as the priestly Bnei Hezir tomb. It consists of a porch and sepulchral chambers decorated with motifs borrowed from the Greco-Oriental (Hellenistic) art of the time. The facade is decorated with Doric columns and a Hebrew inscription on the upper panel, identifying it with the distinguished priestly house.

g. *Extent of the City in Hasmonean Times*

These extensive finds attest to the rapid growth of Jerusalem in Hasmonean times and its economic prosperity. Greek historians who visited there say that its population exceeded 120,000, and that it was protected by three city walls. Its streets were paved and its markets packed with people and merchandise, a far cry from its diminished state in Nehemiah's time. The population estimate may be too high, however, although in the opinion of B. Mazar, it would suit the still greater city in the time of Herod the Great.

Above:
Lower reaches of the Pool of Bethesda, dating to Hasmonean times

Left:
The columned part of the Bnei Hezir rock-tomb in the Kidron valley (left) over the burial chambers

Ancient stairway descending from Mount Zion (Upper City) to the Ophel

B. HEROD'S PERIOD

1. DEVOUT AND RUTHLESS

Antipater's ascent to power, with the direct help of Julius Caesar, was accompanied by a division between the religious establishment under the Hasmonean Hyrcanus II, who bore the title of "High Priest and Ethnarch," and the civil government with power vested in Antipater the Idumaean, who was named Epitrophos (Procurator). After the defeat of Mattathias Antigonus, Antipater's son Herod was enthroned king in 34 B.C., with Mark Antony's backing. The Jews labelled him the "King of the

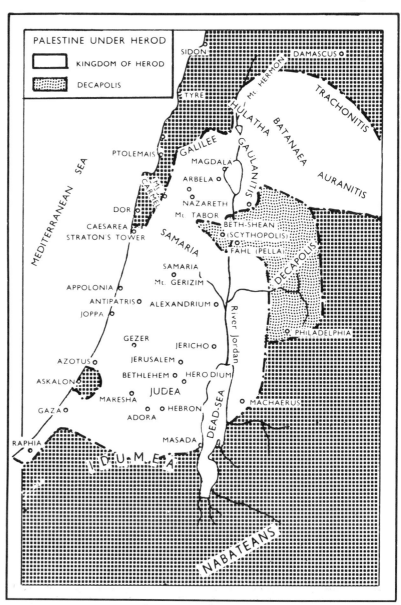

Jews," to distinguish him from a "Jewish King." His reign was immensely successful by the standards of the day, being long and prosperous; but his character, made up of ruthlessness, cunning, and courage in equal parts, left something to be desired, and those who wrote about him reflected the fear and hatred he inspired in his people along with grudging admiration for his magnificent achievements, which included the greatest building program in Jewish history. He favored the Hellenizing elements in Jerusalem society and the Jewish Diaspora for administrative, diplomatic, and military purposes. At the same time, he observed Jewish ritual closely and devoted great efforts and sums to the renovation of the Temple, his most notable accomplishment. His purpose, apparently, was to win over the disaffected rabbis and scribes who rejected his royal claims because he was not a descendant of David, or even of Jewish descent. Like his illustrious predecessor, he was a great leader and complex personality, whose commitment to the Jewish faith should not be discounted simply because his hands were stained with blood and his crimes so great. He safeguarded his position as a faithful vassal and ally of the Roman empire and maintained close cultural and commercial ties with the countries of the eastern Mediterranean world. Ambivalence in his loyalties met different responses among the people. The more orthodox, and certainly the Essenes, distrusted him (as attested in traditional Hebrew writings and the Talmud), while the most cosmopolitan circles, who were exposed to Hellenistic cultural influence, as well as the wealthier classes and the Pharisees, appeared to appreciate both sides of the complex picture. He strengthened his ties with patrician Jewish families in the Hellenistic Diaspora and appointed successive high priests from such families as the House of Boethus. The period from his death in 4 B.C. until A.D. 70 witnessed the rivalry of two great priestly houses—Boethus and Hanan. It appears that Joseph Caiaphas, who collaborated with Roman authority, was the son-in-law of Hanan the First (cf. John 18:13–14). Herod's family life was a disastrous combination of lust and jealousy, intrigue and suspicion, resulting in the murder of his sons and the execution of his favorite wife. In his last years the alienated maddened tyrant wandered from one mountain fortress to another seeking peace and respite from a host of real or imagined enemies. He then retired to the beautiful winter palace he had built on top of the mountain-rock of Masada (whose monumental structures were revealed by Y. Yadin's excavations) or sought water cures in the elegant baths of Calirrhoe, east of the Dead Sea.

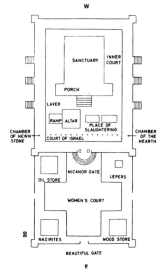

The Courts of the Temple and the Sanctuary

2. HEROD'S MONUMENTS AND CITIES

By the second decade of his reign, Herod had expanded his kingdom to northern Palestine and large parts of northern Transjordan. Having secured his borders and increased his revenues, he undertook a vast building program. Around 20 B.C. he began the reconstruction of the Temple. He enlarged the esplanade by building new retaining walls of huge

trimmed ashlars, still visible at the lower levels of the Temple Mount on its western, southern, and eastern contours. He rebuilt the fortress at the northwestern end of the Temple esplanade and named it Antonia in honor of Mark Antony. He also erected a great palace on the western side of Mount Zion that consisted of two main structures resting on a large podium, surrounded by elevated gardens and courts, and flanked by three massive towers. This royal administrative complex was also the headquarters of government throughout the Herodian era, and later it became the seat of authority of the Roman Procurators during the first century A.D. This is the actual site of Pontius Pilate's Praetorium referred to in the Gospels (though Christian medieval tradition places it at the head of the Via Dolorosa on the opposite side of the city).

South of the palace area rose Jerusalem's richest quarter, already known to us from Hasmonean times. It expanded south and east over the slopes of Mount Zion, as is revealed in excavations conducted since 1976 by M. Ben-Dov. The clearing of the lower slopes of the western walls of the Old City by Magen Broshi has exposed the enormous walls recon-

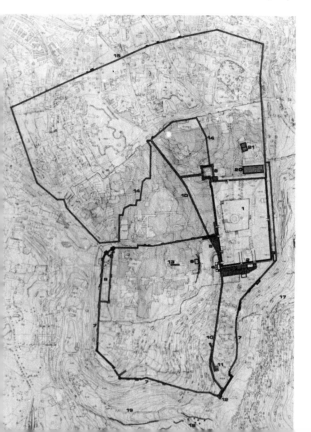

structed in Herod's time. The city itself contained an amphitheater, a hippodrome, a theater, public squares and new paved streets, and colonnades that covered acres of ground, all of which still await the spade of the archaeologist. During the period in question, Jerusalem doubled in size and population as a result of Herod's building operations and the increasing prosperity of city and country. In addition, tens of thousands swelled the population of the city at the annual festivals, especially Passover. In all respects, the remains and small finds in the Upper City (Mount Zion) of Hasmonean levels are surpassed in wealth and extent by the Herodian materials. Furthermore, a number of magnificent mausoleums were erected by priestly and patrician families in the Kidron Valley, and the increase in family tombs around Jerusalem created an ever widening necropolis. These are uncovered constantly as bulldozers clear the ground of expanding modern Jerusalem.

Herod enlarged the city of Samaria (which was called Sebaste, Greek for Augustus) and built in it a temple to Augustus Caesar. He dedicated other monuments to the Emperor and paid an annual tribute estimated in millions of dollars in silver and gold pieces. He reconstructed a sumptuous winter palace at Jericho. At a former Phoenician town on the coast, called Straton's Tower, he founded the city of Caesarea and formed an artificial harbor with breakwaters surmounted by towers. He built a great aqueduct to lead spring water into the city; he also improved the aqueduct that brought water to the reservoirs in Jerusalem. He fortified his borders with castles and strongholds and donated funds for public buildings in many cities outside his own realm, including Antioch, Rhodes, and Pergamum. Both his winter palace and his summer palace at Jericho were marvels of architecture, as the excavations by J. L. Kelso and R. de Vaux have shown. The synagogues at Herodion and Masada, both constructed under his orders, are the oldest so far discovered.

3. HERODIAN STRUCTURES UNCOVERED BY THE EXCAVATIONS SINCE 1968

The excavations conducted by B. Mazar since 1968 around the Temple Mount—the most important archaeological undertaking in Israel—have

Above left:
Herodian columned street and ruins of monuments at Samaria

Above:
Section of the aqueduct, Caesarea

Opposite page:
Below right:
Lower sections of Herodian and later constructions in the Upper City (Mount Zion). The wall at the left is of later, Turkish, origin, which left most of the Upper City and lower Ophel outside the walled Old City of Moslem times

Below left:
First century Jerusalem. 1. Temple area 2. Southern Gates 3. Archway to "Solomon's stables" 4. Archway to Royal stoa 5. Xystos 6. Citadel Antonia 7. First wall 8. Royal palace 9. Hasmonean palace 10. Tyropoeon street 11. Siloam pool 12. Ashpot Gate 13. Remains of Herodian street 14. Second wall (acc. to Vincent) 15. Third wall 16. Monumental tombs 17. Kidron Valley 18. Necropolis of Hanan priestly family 19. Hinnom Valley 20. "Israel" pool 21. Sheep pools

255

Above:
The Temple facade, commemorated on a Bar-Kochba coin (ca. A.D. 135)

Above, right:
Reconstruction model of the southwestern corner of the walls (left) and stairway leading up to the gate of the southern Royal Portico (the columned structure which included the Hanuyyoth halls). The southern wide stairways (right) led to the Hulda gates

Below, right:
Section of the pavement of the Tyropoeon main street which ran at the foot of the western retaining walls of the elevated Temple esplanade. The street is bordered by a curb to help rainwater flow downhill

Below:
Rainwater sewers beneath the Tyropoeon street

helped to reveal many unsuspected aspects of life in first century Jerusalem before its destruction by the Romans. In addition, they have confirmed the extraordinary accuracy of architectural and topographical details reported in Josephus' *Antiquities of the Jews* and *The Jewish War*.

The Tyropoeon and the Lower City

The Tyropoeon Vale that crossed the lower part of the city west of the Temple Mount and the paved road uncovered in sections amid remnants of municipal institutions, shops, and arcades were at the center of the daily life of the capital city, teeming with crowds and commerce of all kinds. The Tyropoeon road skirted the gigantic supporting walls of the high Temple Mount esplanade and the gates that led through rising ramps to the Temple Mount courts. The road then ran under the aqueduct that passed over the Wilson Arch, branched south to the other gates, and descended southeast to the ancient City of David or the Ophel built over the ancient Millo terraces. It then reached the Siloam pool at the southern end of the city, in the valley. Contrary to what was believed for a long time, this road did not pass under a viaduct that spanned the Tyropoeon Vale from west to east, that is, from the Upper City to the Temple Mount; instead, it led to the foot of a great stairway that rose to the so-called Robinson Arch and entered the Temple esplanade through a wide gate facing the southern Royal Portico or Hanuyyoth built by Herod.

The paved road that turned and rose eastwards to reach the southern gates met the southern approaches to the Double and Triple Hulda Gates, the plaza at the top of the Ophel, and the great stairway (since reconstructed) over which the worshipers and pilgrims flocked daily, in greater numbers on the holidays. On the way up the worshipers performed their purification rites in the numerous *mikvehs* or immersion baths carved into the rock of Mount Moriah.

Many sewers, gathering rainwater and refuse from the Temple grounds, have been uncovered at the lowest levels, and several underground passages have been found in the lower levels under the esplanade. The network of ramps leading to the other Porticoes has been analyzed along with its relation to the vast underground stores of the Temple built by Herod over the southern slopes of Mount Moriah (illustrated by the cover picture of this book). Several inscriptions, stone fragments, and ritual artifacts, as well as thousands of coins and other artifacts, attest to complex activity relating to the formal acts of worship at the meeting places on the Mount (*The Mountain of the Lord*).

Below, left:
Subterranean chambers that lay beneath the wide stairway to the Hulda gates (the walled triple gate)

Below:
Ritual slaughter of a heifer

C. THE DEAD SEA SCROLLS

1. THE SETTLEMENT AT QUMRAN

The Dead Sea Scrolls are one of the most dramatic archaeological discoveries of the present century. The first seven scrolls were found in 1947 above the banks of Wadi Qumran near the northwestern shore of the Dead Sea, as a Bedouin shepherd chased a goat up the marl hill into a cave containing half-buried jars and scroll fragments. Several scrolls were acquired by E. L. Sukenik (father of the famed archaeologist, Y. Yadin) for the Hebrew University during the War of Independence in 1948; the rest were taken to the United States and ultimately acquired by the government of Israel. They are all kept in the Shrine of the Book adjoining the Israel Museum of Jerusalem. Shortly after the first discovery several scholars and larger numbers of Bedouin began the hunt for other scrolls; some were found in other caves to the north of that site, along with large numbers of fragments, and the largest single collection turned up in Cave IV, in the vicinity of Khirbet Qumran, the ancient settlement established by the sectaries who wrote and guarded the scrolls.

The site of the settlement was excavated by R. de Vaux in 1951–56. It is situated on the terrace of marl facing the wadi and caves. The 250 square foot enclosure and buildings used by the Qumran sectaries from the second century B.C. had been incorporated into earlier remains of an old Judahite fort, built around the time of Josiah in the seventh century B.C. and abandoned after the destruction of the Judean state by the Babylonians. It seems to have been part of an ancient town, "the City of Salt" (Josh. 15:62).

The Qumran enclosure was entered from the north, protected by a massive three-story tower; a narrow court led from the gate to various parts of the enclosure. The other important rooms lay south of the tower. One hall is identified as the *scriptorium,* where the scrolls were copied. To the east was another small court, and around it were the kitchen, laundry, and some large reservoirs made watertight by several coats of plaster. A dam was built across the wadi from which an aqueduct and channels led to each cistern. South of this complex was the assembly hall, measuring 67 by 35 feet, a pantry (which was found still containing sets of dishes), more reservoirs, and a potter's workshop with two kilns, one for firing large jars of the kind used to store the scrolls, the other for small vessels for daily use. The western part of the settlement contained workshops, stores, silos. Separated by a stone wall, a cemetery with at least 1,100 burials lay to the east of the settlement.

Qumran was resettled in the days of John Hyrcanus (135–104 B.C.) by the Dead Sea sectaries, probably a branch of the Essenes. It was destroyed and burned as the result of an earthquake in 31 B.C., then rebuilt in 4 B.C., and finally destroyed by the Romans in A.D. 68 at the time of the Jewish Revolt. A Roman garrison occupied it for another twenty years. The sec-

taries raised their own food and tanned skins for leatherware or parchment at Ein Feshka, one and a half miles to the south.

The Covenanters were ruled by a council of twelve "princes," or lay leaders, and three priests. Their affairs were administered by a *mebaqqer* or *paqid* who was regarded as the shepherd of his flock and performed many of the same duties as the bishops of the early Church. The Essenes rejected private property in favor of the communal sharing of goods. The central group practiced celibacy, but other adherents of the community did not.

2. THE SCROLLS

Most of the scrolls were made of animal skins; their smooth sides were written on in the Hebrew square script with ink made from charcoal or iron. A few papyri fragments also have been found. One scroll consisted of copper sheets riveted together, with the letters incised on the metal. Some were written in pre-Hasmonean, others in Hasmonean times, and the last date to Herodian times. A number of documents, including the books of the Pentateuch and Job, were written in the paleo-Hebrew script imitative of pre-exilic writing and Phoenician. The largest single document in this script is a partial manuscript of Leviticus. In a number of manuscripts in square script the word YHWH (the Tetragrammaton or sacred name of God) is written in the old script. About a quarter of all the manuscripts and fragments are biblical texts that date between the middle of the third century B.C. and the middle of the first century A.D. They are earlier by a millennium than any previously known copy of the Bible (the Aleppo Codex of the ninth century A.D.) and as a group are an invaluable witness to a much earlier stage in the transmission of the biblical text.

In addition to the Old Testament books in Hebrew, all of which are represented at Qumran with the single exception of Esther, many of the Apocryphal and some of the Pseudepigraphic books are also present, including The Wisdom of Ben-Sira, Tobit, Jubilees, Enoch, parts of the Testaments of the Twelve Patriarchs, and so on. Known heretofore from translations, the Apocrypha copies are in the original Hebrew and Aramaic. In addition to these, there are commentaries such as the Habakkuk *Pesher* and elaborate paraphrases such as the Genesis Apocryphon (in Aramaic).

Ruins of Qumran, home of the Essenes. Some of the caves are seen above

The Aleppo Codex dates to the 9th c. A.D. and was written on parchment a thousand years after the Dead Sea Scrolls

259

3. THE WRITINGS OF THE DEAD SEA SECT

For information about the sect itself and its organization and life-style, the best source is a collection of their manuals, hymnals, and other edifying works, which may be classified as follows:

The Manual of Discipline from Qumran

a. *The Sectarian Scrolls*

Of all the sectarian works, the most important is the "Manual of Discipline." The first part contains prescriptions for the annual ceremony at which the Covenant between God and the sect was renewed, the ideology of the Covenant sect, its laws and regulations, its principles of religion and law and rules of conduct. It concludes with a hymn of praise. The second composition in the Manual is a Rule for "All the Congregation of Israel in the Last Days," with an eschatology peculiar to the people of Qumran.

b. *The Damascus (Zadokite) Document*

A book similar to the Essene manual had been found in 1896 among ancient texts preserved in the *genizah* (depository of old and worn-out manuscripts) of the Cairo synagogue. It is commonly called the Damascus Document and indicates that there was a community in Damascus affiliated to the sect, with the same general rules. However, some prominent scholars feel that the mention of Damascus is a disguised allusion to the Qumran community. This document, containing exhortations to the people to return to the true faith, is interwoven with the history of Israel, while it alludes also to the history of the sect. It reiterates many of the principal stipulations of the Manual of Discipline and formulates rules for the government of urban and rural societies, both of which were affiliated with the central group. The document avers that it was written by pious Jews who remained more faithful to tradition during the Exile in Babylon. It mentions three classes: the priests, the Levites, and the sons of Zadok, the traditional line of high priests. The "priests" were those Jews in Israel who repented and departed from the land of Judah, the "Levites" were their associates, and the "sons of Zadok" were the Elect of Israel who were designated for the exercise of authority in the last days. They firmly believed that while prophecy and direct revelation from on high had ceased, they, the *elect,* were blessed with a continuing revelation. The conviction that they were the elect remnant of the people of God gave them an enormous self-confidence and a dynamic optimism about the future, in spite of present hardship and suffering. The document ends with rulings that correspond generally, though with important exceptions, to standard *halakhot* ("ruling") of the Mishnah. Fragments of the so-called Damascus Document have turned up in the Dead Sea Scrolls, confirming the linkage between the groups mentioned.

c. *The Commentaries*

Once the biblical books were canonized, it was imperative to have an authoritative interpretation for the use of later communities, and each of

these naturally interpreted the biblical oracles as it saw fit, using a variety of methods to arrive at the applicable truth. Thus at Qumran there were found a number of *pesharim* ("commentaries") that provided contemporary applications of prophetic and poetic passages of the Bible. There are similarities between the sectarian approach and that of the early Jewish Christians (see Parts XVII–XVIII). Both groups believed that they were living in the times of fulfillment of Old Testament prophecy and interpreted the older materials accordingly. There were distinct differences as well. Normative Jewish exegesis of a later period differed from both in important respects. Each of the scrolls begins with a biblical passage followed by its commentary, then the next passage from the Bible is quoted and another comment added. The ancient history of the original text is brought up to date by allusion to contemporary circumstances. So the background and experience of the sect and its principal leaders can be recovered to some extent.

The Commentary on Habakkuk is the most important among these works and accords in general with the allegoric rabbinical style that attempts to translate the obscure oracles of this prophet into terms of the contemporary conflict between the faithful remnant and the unbelieving world. The oblique references to the "wicked priest," his arrogance and materialism, are too vague to pin down the identity of that figure, though they apply only too well to the Hasmonean high priests from Jonathan, the brother of Judas, to Alexander Jannaeus.

The Nahum, Hosea, and Micah Commentaries are fragmentary and ambiguous, but their pattern of interpretation is similar.

d. *The Teacher of Righteousness*

This dominant but enigmatic figure in the community is described in the Habakkuk Commentary as having unique divinely given powers to interpret Scripture and reveal the true meaning of the message of the prophets (like Habakkuk). While it is clear that the Teacher was in direct opposition to the then high priest and his Jerusalem establishment and suffered along with his fellow Covenanters as a consequence of the persecution carried out by the former, there is no justification for identifying the Teacher as a messianic figure, or in speaking of a crucifixion or resurrection in connection with him. There are similarities with the figure of Jesus in the Gospels, but they have been exaggerated by sensation seekers. The correspondences can be explained in terms of their common background in the Jewish community and their instruction in the Old Testament. The differences are pronounced: Jewish Christians and Essenes shared this common heritage, but parted company over the difference between Jesus and the righteous Teacher and diverged from that point.

e. *The Thanksgiving Scroll*

This scroll is a collection of hymns expressing the conviction of the Covenanters that in spite of their imperfections and sins, they belong to the elect of God and in the great division between righteous and unrighteous will be saved from the fate of the wicked. The religious lyrics resemble the Psalms of the Old Testament and often interweave words and phrases, sometimes whole verses from the earlier anthology. The Qumran Psalms are a link between the biblical Psalms and the poetic elements of the New Testament, though no direct link between the Jewish Christians and the Qumran sect can be demonstrated. The Teacher has been identified as the author of the hymns, and they have been interpreted autobiographically by some scholars. It is more likely that, as in the case of similar usage in the canonical psalms, the use of the pronoun "I" is representative of the group, or simply collective.

f. *War of the Children of Light against the Children of Darkness*

For the Qumran sectaries, the world was divided in a cosmic struggle between the forces of good and evil, in which men and angels were ranged on both sides. This composition contains a prophecy of the coming war to be waged between the nations that rule the world, called *Kittim* of Ashur and of Egypt, the Children of Darkness, and the people of faithful Israel, the Children of Light. While the original setting, as in the book of Daniel, reflected the precarious position of the Jews in the time of the Ptolemies and Seleucids in the second century B.C., the present form of the composition points to the Roman period, because the description of military equipment and tactics seems to be derived from the manuals of the Roman army rather than any of its predecessors in the Near East. This is followed by regulations for the enrollment of the warriors in the Holy War, the strategy and ritual of the war, supplemented by a timetable indicating the vicissitudes of the Children of Light until they are triumphant over all the forces of darkness. Specific details are provided about the trumpet calls, the signals to be given to the troops, and the arms and tactics to be used in the great battles. Its extant part concludes with prayers to be said before, during, and after the battle. The end is missing.

g. *The Copper Scroll*

Two rolls originally riveted together were discovered in another cave (III), one of the few finds made by archaeologists in the scroll hunt. The scroll consists of a list of hiding places containing fabulous treasures with instructions for reaching them. It is the opinion of most scholars that the treasures are imaginary and that the list belongs to a genre well known in Jewish and pagan tradition in which great treasures of the past are described in elaborate detail, with descriptions of their hiding places. In the present instance, no reference is made to heroic figures of the past, and the treasure itself is not identified. But the amounts of silver and gold and precious garments seem exorbitant, and the locations, while identifiable in part, are too vague to permit actual search. The date of the Copper Scroll can be fixed around the middle of the first century A.D.

Perhaps the most important of the sectarian writings so far discovered is the famous *Temple Scroll,* which has been published by Y. Yadin (in Hebrew, while the English version is now in press). It presents the sect's views on cultic and ritual matters, especially with regard to the Temple, that is, a new Temple to replace the present one in Jerusalem. In this respect it resembles the last chapters of the book of Ezekiel with its visions of a new Temple, but the picture is both complicated and different. Another important find was a complete phylactery, which differs in important respects from the standard type.

The outer sides of a leather phylactery box after opening. The boxes were fastened to leather straps laid around the arm and forehead and contained portions of the Pentateuch written on parchment

4. BIBLICAL AND APOCRYPHAL BOOKS

Complete scrolls or fragments of all the books of the Old Testament were found, except the book of Esther. Cave I contained the most complete scroll, almost the entire book of Isaiah; another copy of Isaiah, less complete, was also found. In Cave IV was found a copy of the two books of Samuel (in a single scroll) but in very dilapidated condition. Since its text differs significantly from the standard Hebrew text, but resembles the Greek translation, it is regarded as perhaps the most important of the biblical manuscripts at Qumran. On the basis of its readings it is possible to recover an earlier and more reliable form of the text than hitherto has been possible.

D. OTHER BRANCHES OF THE ESSENE MOVEMENT

1. IN THE REGION OF DAMASCUS

Before leaving Qumran, let us mention other groups of a similar nature. First of all, various similar groups and their beliefs are described by Josephus and the Alexandrian Jewish philosopher, Philo, but these authors seem not to have known of the writings of the Qumran sectaries and their specific way of life. Another important group may have retired to the region of Damascus between 31–4 B.C., living in camps or in the city. The region south of Damascus was fairly densely settled by Jews in the Greco-Roman period, and until the fourth century A.D. many Jewish, Jewish Christian, and Gentile Christian groups were to be found there.

Prescriptions concerning family life in the Damascus group, their Sabbath rest and ritual purity, are characteristics that reveal religious links with the Pharisaic groups or *haburot* ("fellowships"). There are some differences between the rules for organization and practice of this group and the sectaries of Qumran, but they can be attributed to the historical development of the groups and their geographical displacement.

During this period there was also a lessening of eschatological tension in the Qumran community, superseded by a greater emphasis on the daily observance of the Law, as determined by the sect's priestly specialists. The apocalyptic community continued to wait for the Messiah of Aaron and the Messiah of Israel, the anointed ones who were to preside over the banquet of the end of the age that was prepared for the congregation. The presence of so many sets of plates and pots in the storerooms of Qumran indicates that outside devotees came there on pilgrimages.

2. OTHER HETERODOX SECTS OF SPLENDID ISOLATION

Besides the Syro-Palestinian branches of the Essene movement, we learn from Philo and Eusebius of Caesarea (fourth century A.D.) of the Therapeutae, whose way of life was analogous to that of the Essenes. They were Jewish solitaries who lived in the region of Lake Mareotis near Alexandria. They had a religious feast of an unspecified type every few years, no doubt similar to the Covenant renewal festival of the people of Qumran. In addition, the Ebionite movement had developed as another offshoot of Essenism. From its modest beginning in the second century B.C. the Essenic movement and heterodox forms of Judaism spread throughout the Jewish world, reflecting the power of the "splendid isolation" that gave rise to the Hassidean movement. They and associated and derivative groups served as catalysts in each crisis that developed under religious and political persecutions (by the Greeks and later the Hasmonean princes). Being born out of an intense ideological crisis posed by the Hasmonean priest-kings, they persisted through the power struggles that followed the fall of the Hasmoneans and the Herodians. They were caught up in the great independence movements of the Jewish people in A.D. 66–70 and 132 –135, and suffered the same fate as their counterparts. Only remnants survived, and these ultimately disappeared, merging back into various Jewish or one or another of the Christian groups. After the suppression of Jewish resistance in Jerusalem in A.D. 70 and at Masada in A.D. 73, and the utter destruction of the short-lived independent Jewish state established by Bar-Kochba in A.D. 135, the rabbinic successors of the Pharisees alone enjoyed authority in the religious and social sphere and were active in stabilizing the form of Judaism that persists today.

3. THE DEAD SEA SCROLLS AND THE NEW TESTAMENT

a. *Are There Any Links Between Them?*

Pharisaic Judaism and early Christianity represent different offshoots of Old Testament religion. The one emphasized the Law of Moses, but in terms of oral tradition and the adaptability of ancient revelation to contemporary conditions. The other placed stress on prophecy, on the fulfillment of divine promises in the messianic figure of Jesus and his judicial sovereignty in the last days. It is clear that some Jewish Christians, along with the Essenes of Qumran, stressed obedience to the Law of Moses as much as any other group of Jews, whether Sadducees, Pharisees, or Zealots, and in fact adhered more closely to the written code than the Pharisees, who combined oral and written tradition and exhibited remarkable flexibility in applying the Law (Torah) to given situations. At the same time it is clear that the Essenes were closer to the Jewish Christians in terms of messianic expectation and eschatological fulfillment, although they were at different points in the timetable. Thus the people of Qumran awaited both royal and priestly messiahs, while in the New Testament the term "Messiah" clearly refers to the Davidic king. At Qumran all is still future; only preliminaries have occurred, and the major events and people are yet to appear. For Jewish Christians, the process of fulfillment is in full tide. The Messiah has appeared; he has been put to death and raised from the dead. Resurrection is not just a hope, but a reality.

Another historical line of development from the Old Testament is represented by Pharisaic and Rabbinic Judaism as the contemporary Mishnah and Talmud passages depict it. It is true that eschatological theology is already becoming stronger in the later books of the Old Testament. We are aware that Old Testament apocalyptic writings share the specific Essenic doctrine of the end of days as well as the dogma of the *Gzera Kedumah* ("foreshadowed fate") whereby God ordains the fate of every man for good or for evil. Finally, the Pharisaic establishment respected and tolerated the visionary mystics and Essene sectaries, for they too believed in the eventual coming of the messiah. They deprecated, however, the extreme hopes of the visionaries and criticized those who "hasten his coming." They believed that the Kingdom would come when the people obeyed in spirit and in truth the Law and the Word of the Prophets.

b. *Conclusion*

There does not seem to be a direct derivation of early Christian doctrines or rites from the sectaries. Many of the parallels between Qumran and early Christianity can be explained from the apocalyptic materials in the Old Testament and the intertestamental literature. Both early Christianity and Qumran had something in common with the early Pharisaic *haberim;* like the Hassidim, they accepted the authority of Moses, were messianically inclined, and believed in the resurrection of the dead and final judgment. The Qumran Teacher, however, made no claim to messiahship.

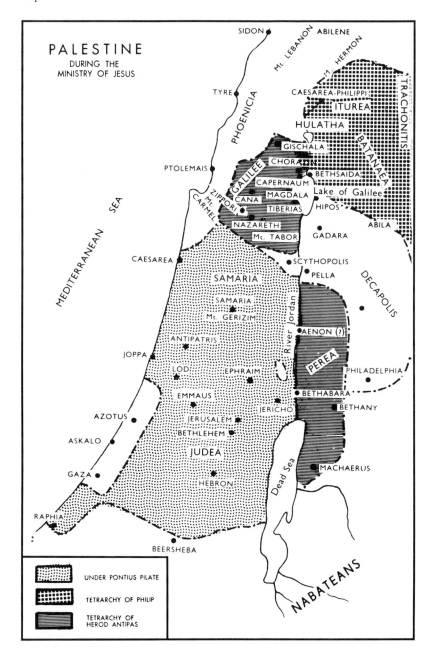

PART XVII

NEW TESTAMENT

A. INTRODUCTION

The emergence of the Christian community in the first century is a distinct historical, cultural, and religious phenomenon for which the great bulk of the available evidence is to be found in the New Testament. The writings of Josephus and other historians provide useful background information, and occasional inscriptions shed random light on the movement in various parts of the Roman empire. The Jewish literature of the intertestamental period, as we saw, yields substantial links between the Old Testament and the New Testament writings and shows how Jewish experience and thought produced significant modifications in traditional beliefs and patterns of practice, thus opening the way for the even more radical departures of Christianity. In this respect a significant forerunner of the Christian community was the Qumran settlement on the shores of the Dead Sea. The former, however, had advanced beyond that stage to the moment of truth, when the Messiah had come and his kingdom had appeared, consisting of disciples and followers of the way he had enjoined and by which he had lived and died and been raised again to life. In addition to the new literary evidence for the background and origins of Christianity, recent archaeological excavation has brought to light a great deal of data bearing on the Jewish Christian community in Palestine, its emergence, differentiation, and ultimate separation from the parent body. Eminent Franciscan and Dominican scholars have corrected earlier misconceptions and have contributed much to an understanding of the beginnings of the Christian movement in Galilee and other parts of the country. Recognition of this development and the information about it now available is indispensable for a comprehension of Christianity as the more radical offshoot from the trunk of post-exilic Judaism, the other being Pharisaic and Rabbinic Judaism, which represented a creative version of a more orthodox line.

1. THE LIFE SITUATION AROUND A.D. 1

Herod's kingdom was divided among his sons (4 B.C.–A.D. 6), but this seeming independence was short-lived. Herod's son Archelaus, who ruled Judea, was disgraced and deported, and the government was transferred to Roman procurators in A.D. 6. Their autocratic and arbitrary treatment of the Jews only emphasized the dramatic change in fortune that had overtaken the Jewish community since the days when they were an independent nation, ruled by a man of their own stock.

Restoration of the position in which an unknown first century Jew—with the legs adjacent—was crucified. This was determined from the skeletal remains found in his tomb in the northern necropolis (Giv'at Hamivtar)

Stone bearing the inscription mentioning Pontius Pilate, found in the Roman theater at Caesarea

267

Right:
Northwestern side of the Lake
of Galilee (top left), scene of
many Gospel stories

Above:
Remains of the pagan shrine at
Caesarea-Philippi devoted to the
pastoral god Pan

No Gentiles could pass beyond
the low balustrade (soreg) that
encircled the inner Temple
courts. Warning inscriptions in
Greek were set there to that
effect

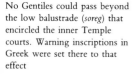

The only Jewish princeling who held out was Herod Antipas, another of Herod's sons, whom we meet in Jesus' story (cf. Luke 3:1, 19; 9:7, 9; 23:7–15). He ruled in northern Palestine. The general political situation outlined in our map is the background of the events related in the Gospels. On the whole, Roman rule was regarded as the ordeal preceding the advent of a messiah. While the Pharisaic and Sadducean majority maintained a shaky balance and prevented an explosion against Rome—which came a few decades later under the leadership of the Zealots—a minority of people, inspired by Hassidean and Essene ideals, faced the future in a different way. The present world had to be endured, but their commitments, hopes, and expectations were in the world to come. Again the eschatological visions of the "End of Days" inspired many to repentance and a renewal of vows of obedience to God and his revealed will. A movement of this type was led by John the Baptizer, who preached in the Jordan valley (ca. A.D. 27). It was a significant development as events proved, and though this activity was not of a revolutionary type, it provoked the last of the pro-Roman Herodian rulers and their Jewish allies to persecute its leaders, John and Jesus, both of whom were put to death, and their adherents.

While these people suffered at the hands of their fellow Jews as well as of the Romans, they evoked and expressed a feeling shared by most against the established authorities, a deep unhappiness with their present lot and an irresistible longing for the days of the messiah, when everything that was upside down would be righted. This was no less true of Palestine than of the Jewish multitudes in the Greco-Roman Diaspora.

2. JESUS

These conditions provide the ideological background of Jesus' youth and subsequent career. Though he was a fervent lover of his people and his country and would rather die than hurt the national interest, as the Gospels and Paul show, he was not a revolutionary or Zealot. Jesus was

born in Bethlehem, according to the Gospels, sometime before 4 B.C., during the reign of Herod the Great. His home was in Nazareth of Galilee, where he grew to manhood. His baptism by John was to transform his life, and he retreated to the wilderness near Jericho (no contact with nearby Qumran is known). The following years of his career in Galilee, as described in the Gospels, were central. Though revered by some and rejected by others, he was both prophet and healer, the leader and teacher of a band of followers. His travels outside of the country or to Caesarea-Philippi in the north were apparently intended in part as escapes from the persecution of Herod Antipas' agents. When he ventured in his last journey on a pilgrimage to the Temple, he traveled through Peraea, east of the Jordan, to avoid setting foot on Samaritan territory, so as not to have any contact with the Samaritans, customary practice on the part of the Jews. He proceeded from there to Jericho and came to Jerusalem, where he was met by an admiring crowd, who provided a triumphal welcome.

a. *Jesus at the Royal Portico and Hanuyyoth*

Jesus stayed in the house of Annas on the Mount of Olives and went down to preach in the southern Royal Portico. The majestic halls created by Herod were built, according to Josephus, of 162 monolithic columns, each 4.6 feet in diameter, with a Corinthian capital and rows of acanthus leaf decorations. The columned structure was three stories high and served several functions. It housed the section of the Hanuyyoth ("halls") to which the Sanhedrin moved in the days of Rabbi Gamaliel (known as Paul's teacher). Other public halls of the Hanuyyoth were used by money changers and dealers in ritual objects. These auxiliary precincts were probably differentiated, in the public eye, from the truly sacred areas within

Left:
The earliest vestiges under the church of St. Joseph are remains of a Byzantine cathedral built over cisterns (right), stairs, and a baptismal font (center) situated in the ancient crypt. It was apparently used by the early Jewish Christians for the mystic initiation rites of neophytes (see "Part XVIII: Jewish Christians")

Above:
Ancient underground cave and silo situated under the Church of St. Joseph built over the biblical village of Nazareth

Left:
Reconstruction model of the Temple facade, seen from the historic Women's Court (The Holyland Hotel)

Below:
Before entering the gates Jesus probably immersed himself in one of the *mikvehs* (ritual baths) situated nearby

the *soreg* ("balustrade"), beyond which no pagan was allowed to pass. Jesus, like other puritanical Jews, regarded their presence there as an intrusion of commercial affairs into places dedicated to the service of God, so he drove away the dealers. Christian tradition maintains that James, the brother of Jesus, was an ascetic Nazirite (not to be confused with Nazarenes or natives of Nazareth, which he happened to be, along with the rest of the family). He spent his days in devout seclusion, prayer, and study in the Temple precinct (though not in the inner Temple where the daily rites of sacrifice were conducted).

A large number of decorative columns and architectural fragments recently uncovered in the excavations of the Temple Mount attest to the magnificence of the Hanuyyoth, which have been replaced by the vast El-'Aqsa mosque and its substructures.

b. *The Crucifixion and Site of the Praetorium*

In connection with the Passover festival, Jesus partook of the ritual supper with his disciples in the house of a notable on Mount Zion in the Upper City. It was the place of residence of the wealthy burghers of Jerusalem, as the excavations in progress there have revealed. He was betrayed and arrested shortly afterwards in the garden of Gethsemane, the site of olive groves and oil presses in the valley east of Mount Zion. The high priest refused to try him as a rebel and transferred his case to Pontius Pilate, the Roman procurator, then resident in Herod's former palace in the Upper City. Jesus was tried in the Praetorium hall for sedition as the alleged "King of the Jews" and ordered by the procurator to be crucified, the manner of execution prescribed for crimes against state and emperor.

Unbiased scholarly opinion, convincingly presented by Père B. Benoit, maintains that Herod's palace, situated in the Upper City, was the official residence of the Roman procurators in Jerusalem. Hence Pilate's Praetorium referred to in the story of the Passion of Christ was situated here. The street along which he carried the cross must have started from that point and led to the site of the crucifixion outside the city walls (John 19:20b; Heb. 13:12). However, medieval Christian tradition placed the *Via Dolorosa* at the opposite, eastern end of the Old City, and reinforced the choice by instituting the annual procession along the Way of the Cross for the benefit of the pilgrims. In view of the conflict with the archaeological evidence about the location of the Praetorium, questions have been raised about the traditional site of the crucifixion on the rock of Golgotha.

c. The Burial Site at Golgotha

According to the Gospels, Joseph of Arimathea, a member of the National Assembly (*buletheros*) in Jerusalem and a believer in the "Kingdom of Heaven," removed Jesus' body from the cross and buried him in his family tomb. His followers, the first Jewish Christians, believed that Jesus was raised from the dead the third day thereafter and appeared to his disciples around Jerusalem, at Emmaus, and at the Sea of Galilee. They also believed that sometime after the Resurrection he ascended into heaven. This event was represented by inscriptions and art found in contemporary graves in Jewish cemeteries.

d. The Debate about the Burial Site

Regarded from the viewpoint of historical and archaeological data, the following is to be said: from early times Christians regarded the Holy Sepulchre as the site of Christ's crucifixion and burial. The place was desecrated by the Romans, who erected there a statue of Jupiter Serapis, thereby making it impossible for believers to come there and worship, as had been their practice. Though they kept away from the place, the Jewish Christians preserved the memory of the site until the time when

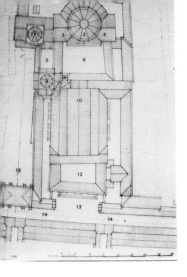
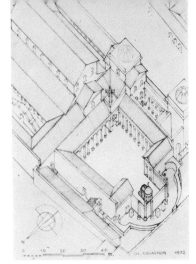

Left:
Roof plan of the fourth-century
Holy Sepulchre: (1)
Ambulatory; (2) Rotunda; (3)
and (4) lateral vestibules; (5)
southern atrium; (6) courtyard
of the Rotunda; (7) Baptistry;
(8) Church of Golgotha; (9) the
Cross; (10) Basilica of
Constantine; (12) eastern atrium;
(13) entrance; (14) Cardo
Maximus; (15) site of Hadrian's
Forum

In the middle:
The basilica that Constantine
erected prior to the construction
of the Anastasis (Rotunda). An
adjacent tomb venerated under
the open sky preceded the
Rotunda

Right:
Reconstruction of the 4th-c.
Rotunda

Constantine decided to erect a shrine to mark and protect the place of
Christ's burial. The tomb was exposed during A.D. 326/7 and work on the
Church of the Holy Sepulchre began. In the course of the church's reconstruction in recent years, excavations conducted by V. Corbo uncovered a
number of important artifacts. They shed new light on the edifice erected
there by Constantine and his successors (fourth century A.D.) and put an
end to a century of debate over the true nature of the original shrine, the
Anastasis (in Greek, "resurrection") and the Rotunda over Christ's tomb.
However, apart from authenticating the fourth-century building, the question of the burial site and of the crucifixion remains unsettled.

It is known that in the days of Constantine the tomb stood uncovered
in a court and only was covered towards the end of the fourth century, by
a *Rotunda,* or circular church, 37 feet high and 40 in diameter. Indepen-
dently of this, Constantine erected a *basilica* over the bare rock of Golgotha. The two construction sites stood apart until the tenth century.

A remarkable discovery in the excavations at the foot of the Temple
Mount deserves mention. A golden ring was found, with what appears to
be a representation of the dome of the original tomb shrine, the Anastasis.

As Jesus' crucifixion took place outside the walls, the identification of
the site depends, first of all, on locating accurately all the city walls then
in existence. No final agreement has yet been reached on this subject.

In conclusion, the different approaches of the traditionalists and the
scholars on the debated points may be summed up as follows:

1. The traditional view identifies the medieval "Via Dolorosa" in eastern Jerusalem as the "Way of the Cross" to the place of crucifixion and
burial. The place of Golgotha and the tomb of Jesus were memorialized
by the Church of the Holy Sepulchre.

2. One scholarly view, taking into account the presence of the Third
Wall of Jerusalem several hundred yards east of the Church of the Holy
Sepulchre, regards the traditional location as doubtful at best.

3. A rival of the Catholic Golgotha is a rock-tomb or the "Garden
Tomb" that was "discovered" near the Damascus Gate, but still within the

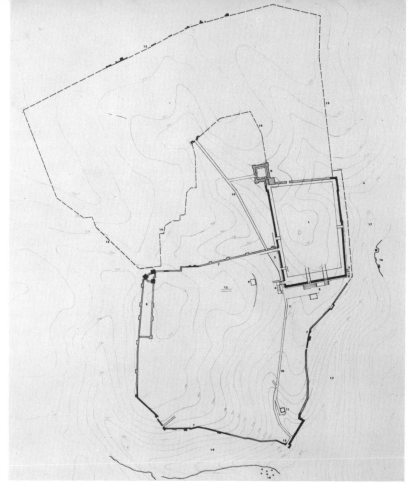

In this map of Jerusalem, the Third Wall (No. 15, built in A.D. 41) stood far north of the ancient Second Wall (No. 14) near which stands the traditional site of the Tomb of Golgotha. Scholars argue over the relevance of these two walls to the point at issue: was the Second Wall the northern limit of Jerusalem at the time of Christ? It must be observed that the city had expanded far north in Herodian times and King Agrippa I built the Third Wall only a decade after the Passion. The problem cannot be resolved to the satisfaction of all

Left:
The excavations of the Third Wall proved conclusively, from finds at the foundations, that it was built in A.D. 41 as the northern city wall

Below:
Representation of the dome of the Anastasis on a gold ring discovered in the excavations at the Temple Mount (4th c. A.D.)

273

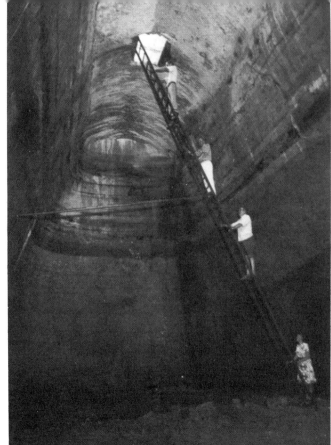

area circumscribed by the Third Wall; this is in all likelihood a Jewish family tomb dating to the days of the Second Temple or possibly the days of the First (see Map of Jerusalem; diagram of the Third Wall, overleaf).

4. The most recent discovery bearing on this subject is that of a large group of cave-tombs, dating to the time of the Judean Monarchy, underneath the Dominican cathedral of St. Etienne, which was built in the Byzantine period outside the Old City. These tombs seem to be part of the Jewish necropolis outside the walls of the city. As new evidence piles up, none of it decisive, traditionalists and skeptics will continue to argue these various points. It is not likely that the problem will ever be resolved to the satisfaction of all.

B. THE GOSPELS

1. THE CANONICAL TEXT OF THE NEW TESTAMENT: A SUMMARY

The only significant direct source for the beginnings of Christianity, apart from isolated references in contemporary literature and the rudimentary archaeological data cited above, is the text of the New Testament itself. It is also the main source of our knowledge of the relationship between the Jews and the Jewish Christians (the primitive church).

The four basic classes of literature in the New Testament are: the central message in the four Gospels; the history of the early church: the Acts of the Apostles; the Apostolic correspondence: the Pauline and other letters; and apocalyptic literature: the book of Revelation. This grouping corresponds to the order of books in the New Testament, but it does not reflect the chronological order of composition. While the Gospel traditions go back to earliest experiences of the disciples, the canonical Gospels did not appear in their present written form until a generation or two after the events they describe. It is generally agreed that the earliest documents of the New Testament are the Pauline Epistles, dating from the 50s and 60s of the first century.

a. Of these assorted documents the four Gospels deal with the life, death, and resurrection of Jesus, called the Christ.

b. The book of Acts is an account of the early Christian movement, emphasizing the missionary achievements of the followers, chiefly Peter and Paul. It closes with Paul under house arrest in Rome, awaiting trial before Caesar.

c. Thirteen books of the New Testament are letters attributed to Paul. Of these, the four great epistles, Romans, 1 and 2 Corinthians, and Galatians, are universally regarded as being authentic, while opinions differ about the others. Many scholars accept ten as genuinely Pauline, excluding the three Pastoral Epistles (1 and 2 Timothy and Titus), which seem to have been compiled by a follower on the basis of Pauline ideas and attitudes. Varying degrees of doubt are expressed about Ephesians, 2 Thessalonians, and Colossians, but Philippians, 1 Thessalonians and Philemon are almost certainly genuine.

d. The general or catholic epistles number seven and are attributed to various disciples and followers: John (3), Peter (2), James, the brother of Jesus (1), and Jude, the brother of James (1).

e. The epistle to the Hebrews has traditionally been assigned to Paul, but there is no basis for this opinion, as the work differs markedly from all of the Pauline letters. It is an anonymous work of the latter part of the first century stemming, as does the book of Revelation, from Jewish Christian circles.

f. The last book of the New Testament, like Daniel, is an apocalyptic work that forecasts the sequence of events in the last days, which are now

Opposite page:
Below, left:
Entrance to the "Garden Tomb," presumed since 1882 to be the tomb of Christ, according to General C. G. Gordon's theory

Below, right:
The inner tomb. This may also be part of the northern necropolis ringing Jerusalem since the latter days of the Judean monarchy. Notice the bench on which the body was laid

Above, right and the two, middle, left:
A cistern and wine press discovered near the site by Dr. Schick in 1890, dating to Second Temple days. The cistern, marked by a cross, may have been used as a meeting place of early Christians

Above, left:
One of the tombs of Jerusalem's necropolis, dating to the end of the Judean monarchy, found near the St. Etienne cathedral. Notice the characteristic stone bench and "pillow"

coming upon the world. The great struggle between the forces of good and light and the forces of evil and darkness will culminate in a complete triumph for God and the Lamb, the crucified and risen Lord.

2. THE SYNOPTIC GOSPELS

The principal source for the life and ministry of Jesus is the four-fold Gospel. These documents in turn were dependent on older sources and represent a series of reworkings and restructuring of the earlier traditions.

a. *Sources*

What led to the writing of the books that are called Gospels, meaning "good news"? Modern Bible study stipulates the existence, prior to the written Gospels that we now possess, of comparatively early Palestinian and other tradition-cycles, some oral, some written, of the "Sayings of Jesus," the so-called Q source, and stories about Jesus, especially the narrative of his last days on earth. Their purpose was to bear witness to Jesus Christ. Hence, they told the story of the coming of Jesus among men, his words and deeds, his suffering and death, his resurrection and exaltation. The word Gospel became established in the vocabulary of the early church as the technical term for the message of salvation proclaimed by the evangelists.

b. *General Plan*

Due to the marked similarity of the subject matter, the order in which their material is presented, and their language, the first three Gospels of the New Testament are generally referred to as the synoptic (Greek, "having or taking the same point of view") Gospels. If the data in these three Gospels were to be arranged side by side in parallel columns so as to be seen at a glance, the interrelationship among them would be clearly visible. The agreement among them can extend to the smallest details, as for instance:

Mark	12:36–37	Matthew	22:43–45	Luke 20:42–44
	6:41–43		14:19–20	9:16–17
	2:10–12		9:6–7	5:24–25

In fact, practically all of the contents of Mark can be found in Matthew, and much of it in Luke, because they share some common sources. Equally impressive, however, is the element of divergence. For example:

Mark	10:17	Matthew	19:16	Luke 18:18
	8:29		16:15–16	9:20
	10:46		20:29–30	18:35
	1:12–13		4:1–11	4:1–12
	6:8–9		10:10	

The distinctive style and special purpose of each Gospel caution one against superficial blending or harmonizing of the three synoptics. The differences are at least as important as the similarities in analyzing and evaluating the material and in determining such questions as date, authorship, provenance, and objective.

While most of Mark can be found in Matthew, the material is handled differently because of their different traditions. Each author recorded the material either in the words that were handed on to him or in his own words so as to express more clearly his understanding of the tradition. In addition, the material has been transferred from a Semitic context in which Aramaic and Hebrew were used to the Greek language common to the Mediterranean world.

For well over a millennium, the opinion expressed by St. Augustine, that the canonical order of the Gospels likewise reflected their order of composition, held sway in the scholarly circles of the church. However, as the synoptic Gospels were subjected to closer scrutiny, their parallelisms analyzed, and their relative contents compared, it became increasingly evident to many scholars that the Gospel of Mark predated those of Matthew and Luke. It was argued as well that both Matthew and Luke were acquainted with Mark and adopted or adapted his material in their Gospels. Since Matthew and Luke have material in common that is not found in Mark, it was deduced that they used another source, Q (which consisted mostly of sayings). Finally, Matthew and Luke each has material not found in the other Gospel, and these are regarded as deriving from separate sources or the evangelist himself. The four-document hypothesis—1) Mark; 2) Q (material not in Mark common to Matthew and Luke); 3) M (Matthew, special source); 4) L (Luke, special source)—is still held by the majority of New Testament scholars, but in recent years especially, there have been numerous challenges. Different scholars argue for the priority of Matthew and the independence of Luke; but nothing has yet displaced the Markan-Q synoptic hypothesis.

c. Differences Between Mark and Matthew and Luke

There are, nevertheless, certain significant differences between Mark and the other two, mainly in relating the words of Jesus. Matthew's Gospel is arranged around five discourses, the best and most familiar being the Sermon on the Mount. There is a similar discourse in Luke, but not in Mark. Accordingly, most scholars have distinguished in the Gospels between the narrative and the discourses (what Jesus *did* and what he *said*). It is an accepted tenet of New Testament scholarship that the Gospels are not intended as a biography of Jesus in the modern sense, but rather reflect the apostolic teaching of what Jesus did and what he taught (Acts 1:1). They are a statement of the faith of the early Christians, founded on the historical fact of Jesus and preached as a lesson to the world.

The generally accepted assumption that Mark preceded Matthew and Luke is, however, only a partial solution of the synoptic problem, for Matthew and Luke have some two hundred verses of material in common that are not contained in the Mark Gospel. These passages consist largely

Luke twice attempts to provide a chronology for his story. He names "Lysanias the tetrarch of Abilene" (3:1), one of the contemporary governors, identified by a votive inscription found near Damascus. He mentions also Cyrenius, governor of Syria (2:1–2), apparently identical with Quirinius referred to in the broken Roman inscription

A page of Papyrus Bodmer II
containing John 11:31–37

of the sayings and teachings of Jesus, including, for instance, the Sermon on the Mount (Matthew 5–7). The fact that this also appears in Luke (in a different form and arrangement) but not in Mark points to the existence of another literary source aside from Mark. Though the source is no longer extant in an independent form, it is commonly referred to as Q, as mentioned above. Another significant difference between Mark and Luke has been noted by D. Flusser in determining the origin of the so-called synoptic apocalypse in Luke 21:20–24 (paralleled by Mark 13:14–26 and echoed by Matthew). This will be discussed below.

Eusebius (*Ecclesiastical History* iii. 39, 15; fourth century A.D.) quotes Papias,' Bishop of Hierapolis, ca. A.D. 140, as reporting that Matthew composed the *Logia* (source or tradition) in Hebrew (i.e., Aramaic) and that "everyone interpreted them" (i.e., translated them into Greek). For some time it was assumed that these Logia represented the Q document, but modern scholarship is growing increasingly skeptical of this theory. The Logia (words about rather than of Jesus) may be an original Semitic Gospel of Matthew. Scholars today are also inclined to believe that the language behind Matthew was probably Hebrew, not Aramaic, and they accept Papias' statement as literally exact, although it is still not certain just what the Logia were.

d. Mark and John

The relation of the fourth Gospel to Mark is more difficult to assess; John has a different outline. Where there is common ground with the three Synoptics, there are some striking phrases not in Matthew and Luke, but common to Mark and John, for example, loaves costing 200 dinarii (Mark 6:37; John 6:7); pure nard (Mark 14:3; John 12:3); pallet (Mark 2:11; John 5:8).

The accidental discovery of Christian papyrus fragments, namely Papyrus 52, Egerton Papyrus 2, John Rylands Fragment, Bodmer papyri, has shown that the Gospel of John circulated in Egypt early in the second century A.D. It is once again acceptable to hold a comparatively early date for the composition of the Gospels, especially Mark and Luke, though it is generally agreed that the evangelists were not themselves apostles or directly involved in the events described.

e. Christian Writings of the Second Century

We find in extant Christian writings of the first half of the second century A.D. many indications of knowledge of the Gospels, especially the teachings recorded in them: in the period A.D. 90–120, Clement of Rome (96), Ignatius (ca. 115), Polycarp (ca. 115); in the period A.D. 120–150, the "Didache" (which has many primitive elements and in its original form is much older), "Shepherd" of Hermas, and Papias. At mid-century Justin Martyr probably refers to Peter's "memoirs which, I say, were composed by His apostles and those who followed them." Tatian (ca. 170), in his "Diatessaron," made a harmony of the Four Gospels, while with Irenaeus (ca. 180), Clement of Alexandria (ca. 200), and others begins the period of clear citations and quotations from the four canonical Gospels.

C. RECENT DISCOVERIES AND THE GOSPELS

1. THE MYSTIC GROTTO OF BETHLEHEM

For purposes of worship, the Jewish Christians of Palestine not only availed themselves of the synagogues, but also developed their ritual in certain "sacred and mystic grottoes," as reported by the ecclesiastical historian, Eusebius of Caesarea. In their worship in this "Lord's house" in Bethlehem, carried on there until the fourth century, they celebrated two of the "three mysteries": Mary's virginity and her bringing forth the Christ child; the third mystery was the death of Christ. Because of its mysteries, this Bethlehem grotto, though itself dark, was bound up in the minds of the Jewish Christians with the concept of light, the effulgence that filled the place at the birth of Jesus. They had a deep devotion to the grotto for yet another reason, as it represented the incarnation or first descent of Christ to earth from heaven.

The mystic grottoes were associated with their doctrine of the "descent" and "ascent" of Christ and his initiated ones. He descended from heaven and rested in Bethlehem under the earth. For them the Bethlehem grotto became a symbol of the passage of the soul from darkness to light. Bethlehem also came to stand for the Church of the Gentiles, in the per-

Inscriptions found in Peter's house. 1–6 name Jesus and Peter. 7–8 derive from an eschatological citation of 3 Baruch

The octagonal Byzantine church (foreground) standing on the site of Peter's house (1st c. A.D.) was used as a cult place in the second century. It is related historically with the Capernaum synagogue mentioned in the Gospels. Remains of the hall of the later third-century synagogue appear in the background

279

The Bethlehem grotto. The niche on the left is the birthplace of Jesus, and the manger is on the right. The grotto became a symbol of passage from darkness to light

son of the Magi, to whom the star appeared. On the other hand, Jerusalem was the symbol of the Church of the Circumcision, as the Jewish Christian community was known. Hadrian profaned the site by planting a wood over the grotto, but this helped to maintain the tradition of the birthplace of Jesus.

2. CAPERNAUM AND ITS REMOTE TRADITIONS

a. *Peter's House*

Considerable material has been brought to light at Capernaum, some of which bears on the location of Peter's house and his association with the mission among his fellow Jews. The house was built about the first century B.C. It became a center of religious activity, a house-church or meeting house, already in the second half of the first century A.D. *Minim* (as the Jewish Christians were later called) were numerous and lived continuously in Capernaum and kept alive this tradition; their graffiti on the plastered wall of the place of worship testify to their faith in Jesus, the Christ, the Lord, the Most High and Good, and to their veneration for Peter, the local saint. Non-Jewish Christians took over the sanctuary in the middle of the fifth century and built the splendid octagonal church with baptistry, which was uncovered in 1971 and 1972. A Spanish pilgrim, Aetheria, states "that the house of the chief of the apostles has been turned into a church." The pilgrim of Piacenza (ca. A.D. 570) also relates that the house of Peter has given way to a place of worship.

Rooms south of the house of Peter with stone pavement (1–2). Foundations of the octagonal church (3–4)

b. *The Synagogue*

The well-known synagogue of Capernaum was built in the third or fourth century as a rectangular basilica, as attested by a hoard of some 3000 coins found under the mortar of a pavement and another of 6000 found in the courtyard. It has been restored in recent years by Father G. Orfali, with additional work in progress or being planned.

Though Capernaum is a holy place for Christians and not for Jews nowadays, it may be noted that Jewish and Jewish Christian communities had lived side by side and constructed their religious buildings in the same quarter. The two Jewish communities differed in personality and spirit and had different "committees." There is no written evidence of any rivalry.

3. THE ROCK OF CALVARY AND THE MYSTIC GROTTO

What, archaeologists ask themselves, was the rock of Calvary in fact? It is almost completely enclosed by the existing Byzantine monument, but Father C. Couasnon gives us some new clues based on the 1961 excavations conducted by V. Corbo. A quarry bed was found below the mystic Adam's Chapel west of the rock, with an ancient cistern nearby. This suggests that the rock of Calvary was an isolated vertical block in the ancient quarry. A cavern that communicated with the underground cistern could, in relation to the vertical block, have been a tomb. Couasnon suggests that the vertical block was the *nephesh* ("funeral monument") of a Jewish tomb similar to those erected in the Kidron Valley in the second and first centuries B.C. In time, a mound was formed through the accumulation of earth around the rock, and only a bare rounded tip emerged, like a skullcap or Golgotha. A stone's throw away, the tomb of Joseph of Arimathea had been cut into the rock face of the quarry.

4. THE MYSTIQUE OF THE TOMB OF ADAM

In the second century or possibly before, mystical speculation born of the Jewish Christian milieu of Jerusalem had transferred the legend and site of the presumed "tomb of Adam" from Mount Moriah to Golgotha. The crack in the rock below the top of Calvary, still visible and venerated today, the belief that Jerusalem was the hub of the world, the siting of Adam's grave there, and the localizing of the deeds of the Patriarchs all contributed to the formation of a mystique centering on the spot. The second Adam was to make good all the damage brought about by the first Adam, even to triumph over death. This tradition is not far removed from Paul's theology that saw in Christ the "New Adam," taking the place of the former Adam and atoning for his original sin (Rom. 5:12 ff.).

This train of thought around Calvary was far earlier than the neo-Christian fervor of the fourth century that caused and witnessed the exposure of the tomb of Christ and the erection of a shrine over Calvary by Constantine's orders. On the other hand, this idea of Golgotha as the place of the skull of Adam, pleased the Fathers of the Church and the devout penitents and pilgrims to the Holy Sepulchre. In any case, without regard to the Jewish Christian mystique of the cosmic ladder, the legendary myths about the grotto of Calvary have been preserved by Catholic and Eastern churches to this day.

D. THE EVANGELISTS: EDITORIAL STAGES AND ARCHAEOLOGICAL BACKGROUNDS

In the process of the formation of the Gospels, two distinct stages must be recognized: (a) the transmission of the oral tradition by the early religious community and (b) the editorial redaction by the evangelists. In the earlier stage, the community provides the setting in which the different units of tradition are shaped, in terms of its needs and purposes, while the role and impact of the creative individual are diminished. In the latter stage, the community tradition is reworked by the evangelist, who, while bound by the common creed, the common commitment, and the common interpretation and by being a member in good standing of the group, nevertheless exercises his own judgment, puts his own stamp on the material, and formulates the essential "good news" in his own way and with his own words. Comparison of the resultant Gospels shows the range of divergence resulting from the differences among the communities by which the Gospel tradition was given form and the discretion exercised by the individual evangelists in setting down their versions of the message.

Distinguishing the effects of the different stages of development is not easy, but the particular contribution of the evangelists can be identified in terms of interpretive comments, selection, modification, omissions and additions of material, summaries, and conclusions, reflecting a long process of editing and revising.

The limited compass of this book does not permit a detailed analysis of the Gospels, and we must limit ourselves, therefore, to recent discoveries bearing on the interpretation of the Gospels and new assessments emerging from recent investigation. We will see below ("Jewish Christianity") that the material remains provide authentic background for the central tradition of the Gospels and the life of the early church in which it received its basic shape.

1. MATTHEW

In relation to the Gospel of Matthew, we have selected the following topics for discussion:

a. *The Sermon on the Mount*
The three chapters (5–7) that make up the Sermon on the Mount are not considered the transcript of a discourse delivered all at one time by Jesus, but rather a collection of sayings pronounced at different times and under varying circumstances drawn from a number of partly written and partly oral sources. In spite of its heterogeneous origin, it constitutes a remarkable compendium of the ethical teachings of Jesus, giving a very clear impression of the style and content of his message. The end result is the work of Matthew, who was not simply an amanuensis, but an imaginative and creative editor, concerned to present the tradition in a specific way to a specific audience. According to W. D. Davies, it was the

church that "took what was radical, modified it, and made it regulatory," and this process "is contained and continued in the Christian-Rabbinism of Matthew, where we see slowly emerging a neo-legalistic society" (W. D. Davies, *The Setting of the Sermon on the Mount,* New York, p. 701). Moreover, in support of his doctrine of messianic fulfillment, Matthew cites the Old Testament at every turn, often quoting verses out of context or imposing a meaning upon them that seems forced, to illustrate and emphasize the central idea that in Jesus Christ all the lines of prophecy and promise have come to fruition. The Old Testament is understood to be predictive in all its parts, everything in it (explicitly, implicitly, or presumptively) pointing to the figure of the Messiah: Jesus. While from the point of view of scientific, historical, and linguistic exegesis, such an approach gives a distorted picture of the material in the Old Testament and derives from Old Testament passages meanings and implications that the authors did not intend, the purpose of Matthew and the community must be understood and respected. Once it had been established that Jesus was the Messiah (chiefly because of the resurrection attested by eye witnesses apart from scriptural references and arguments), then it was both permissible and desirable to read this datum back into and out of the Scripture upon which they relied as the bedrock of their faith: the Old Testament. In short, the Old Testament was not used to prove Jesus' messiahship, which was established on other grounds, personal and group experience, eyewitness testimony; but once it became an article of belief, then the Old Testament was ransacked to illustrate, elaborate, and articulate that conviction.

b. *Matthew Modifies the Older Source*

As an illustration of this tendency, modern scholarship has noted that Matthew took liberties in changing and modifying the Old Testament Scriptures quoted. But he went further by using an ever freer hand in modifying and rearranging documents not protected by Jewish scriptural sanctity, namely sources of a popular character like Q and Mark, in putting together his Gospel. His account of the triumphal entry changes Mark's record. The result is that Jesus rides on two donkeys into Jerusalem. In the sequel Matthew changes Mark's account (Mark 11:1–11) of the return to Bethany, in which Jesus comes back the next day to drive the traders from the Temple. Matthew, on the contrary, states that Jesus drove them out immediately after his arrival at the Temple (Matt. 21:12–17; Mark 11:15–19; Luke 19:45–48). In his account of the resurrection (Matt. 28:1–10 in contrast with Mark 16:1–8), Matthew says the women ran and told the disciples what they had seen, while Mark recounts that they came to the tomb early that Sunday and were frightened when they found it empty.

2. MARK

In the Gospel of Mark, the following historical and archaeological items deserve notice:

a. *Nazareth, from the First to the Fourth Century A.D.*

What do we know concretely about first century Nazareth? In the first two centuries A.D., it was a modest village built on rocky soil in a valley far from the main trade routes. By the third century, however, there was a revival of interest in the town on the part of Christians, who knew it as the hometown of the family of Jesus, where mementos and memorials were preserved. Two excavations, one led by Father P. Viaud, the other by Father Bagatti, have led to the discovery of the traditional site of the Annunciation to Mary and the places that Jesus frequented as a growing lad. Other discoveries included a large complex of caves, silos, cisterns, oil vats, and wine presses; mosaic floors; numerous graffiti, inscriptions, drawings, and symbolic signs. These constitute important evidence of the religious life of the Jewish Christians, preserved beneath the foundations of the two later shrines in Nazareth, as they were described in a report to Constantine. Ancient inscriptions and archaeological discoveries at Nazareth bear witness to a Jewish Christian cult of Mary there, at a very early time. The primitive shrine was erected by Jewish Christians who used it for worship. They were natives who remained in the area, holding on to the property and preserving the traditions about the family of Jesus and the shrines of Nazareth. They were followed in the third and fourth centuries by the faithful of Gentile origin. The magnificent basilica of the Annunciation is late Byzantine.

b. *Interpreting the Last Supper*

According to the synoptic Gospels, the Last Supper was the Jewish Passover meal, while according to the Gospel of John, it preceded the Passover by one day. While there has been considerable debate as to which tradition is correct and no final resolution has been reached, there can be no doubt about the paschal overtones of the meal. While none of the accounts provide details of the Passover celebration and the correlations between the Last Supper and the Passover meal are inexact at best, there is a strong emphasis on Jesus' role as the mediator of a new covenant who offers himself as the paschal lamb. It is a witness to the "Christ, our Passover sacrifice for us."

c. *Genuine Holy Places and Later Christian Monuments*

It has been observed that the early Jewish Christians (until the fourth century A.D.) marked sites sacred to them by modest monuments, rather than impressive buildings. Examples of this practice are found in the oldest foundations of the Church of the Holy Sepulchre in Jerusalem, in Nazareth, in Bethany, and in the Tomb of the Virgin in Jerusalem. The erection of a modest baptistry without a church structure identified it as a holy place.

Other topographical points of reference have been preserved in the traditions surrounding the "holy places" in Israel. They were "rediscovered" by the official church during the era of Constantine. Previously, the information and traditions about them had been kept by the native Jewish

Christians. Among them, the mystic grottoes very early became places of worship: Eusebius lists Bethlehem, the Mount of Olives, and Calvary. These were not Christianized pagan shrines, but ancient Jewish-Christian sites associated with memories of the life of Jesus. Some of them were profaned by Romans who had used them for their own cults and were then "rediscovered" at the time of the Constantinian restoration. Since that time the Christian monuments have been embellished, extended, and restored by different groups at different times. Since the Middle Ages especially, competing Christian communities have attempted to control the holy places and thus benefit from the steadily increasing flow of pilgrims to the Holy Land. As a result, identifications of sites became confused, sacred traditions were transferred from place to place, and in the process authentic memorials and attested locations were lost. Had it not been for the emergence of modern scientific archaeology, the confusion of conflicting claims and the multiplication of spurious sites and manufactured traditions would have been complete and permanent. Thanks to controlled excavations and dispassionate evaluation of data, it has been possible to sweep away the cobwebs of prejudice and sentimentality and to recover authentic data from the earliest days of the Christian community in the Holy Land.

d. *The Jewish-Christian Character of the Pre-Constantine Era*

The Jewish-Christian nature of these and other sites has not been widely recognized, because the data have been available for a relatively short period of time, have been treated in piecemeal fashion, and have been the object of study by a very limited group of Jewish and Christian scholars. Moreover, pilgrims and tourists are usually shown the more spectacular post-Constantinian "holy places," thus perpetuating the errors of earlier times. The archaeological discoveries, however, have been confirmed by literary sources that attest to the existence in these early times of Jewish-Christian culture, as shown by J. J. Danielou, L. Bagatti, and Father Testa in their research. A comparison of the symbols drawn on the ossuaries and those found in the literary texts of the early church shows that they belong together: for example, the cosmic ladder, the eight-pointed "ogdoad" stars, the plow, and the palm. The strange sects described by Epiphanius, Eusebius, and Jerome were Jewish-Christian communities living on the fringes of the "Great Church."

3. LUKE

a. *What Kind of Jew Was Jesus?*

Let us begin by asking who the synoptic Gospels suggest by their general content to have been the audiences, what the prevailing interests were to which the words of Jesus were directed or responded, and how these words define the person who uttered them or convey his central thoughts. Among them certain statements and expressions of attitude stand out.

b. *Luke's Attitude to the Gentiles*

In Luke 4:25–27 there is an anticipation not simply of the Gentile mission, much less of God's rejection of Israel and turning to the Gentiles, but rather of Jewish-Gentile reconciliation, that is, the consecration of Gentiles that will make it possible for faithful Jews and Gentiles to live and eat together in the new age. How does this passage fit with the painful Nazareth episodes and, incidentally, with Luke's attitude to the Jewish-Gentile question? In his treatment of the problem, Luke takes the position that despite what happened at Nazareth and the continuing hostility between Jew and Gentile, the destiny of both groups is bound up with Jesus; it is God's intention to save and heal both together through him.

c. *Jesus' Attitude to His Fellow Jews, and the Eschatological Discourse*

In the eschatological discourse, Jesus prophesies with deep anxiety about the impending destruction of the Temple (Luke 21:20–28). This discourse, in fact, provides one of the most important clues to the significance of the Gospels and Acts, as it illustrates the social and religious situation of the groups who are at the center of the New Testament.

The suggested attribution of Luke to an earlier date (before the destruction of the Temple) stems, among other things, from the eschatological discourse cited above. In the view of R. S. Lindsey and D. Flusser, Luke's rendering is more original and much nearer to the earliest written sources than that of Mark. (R. Lindsey, *Novum Testamentum* VI, 1969, pp. 239 and 243–444; D. Flusser, *Israel Exploration Journal,* 1971, pp. 226–236). There is reason to believe that, in essence, passages about the eschatological deliverance of Jerusalem represent Jesus' own words. Even in its earliest stages, the Lukan discourse was apparently a collage of various "sayings" of Jesus. Jesus is quoted as saying that "Jerusalem will be trodden down by the Gentiles until the times of the Gentiles are fulfilled ... when these things begin to take place, look up and raise your heads, for your redemption is drawing near."

For Jesus and Paul nothing less than the total salvation of their people was in mind, as the New Testament documents show. The word "redemption" is to be understood in the specifically Jewish sense of liberation from Roman rule and the restoration of sovereignty to Israel. In Jewish eschatological thought the idea that the darkest hour must come before the brightest was deeply rooted; before the Messianic Age must come the messianic woes. Jesus' disciples shared the same hopes and fears as other Jews of the period. Jesus himself felt closely bound to the emotions of his compatriots. His disciples were committed to him personally and to the Jewish people. Thus, the prophecy seems to fit the Jewish context and adheres to the scheme of similar prophecies in the Old Testament. It also has a parallel in Revelation 11:1–2. In Acts 1:6–8 the hope for the restoration of the kingdom of Israel is also expressed. The resurrected Jesus there states that it is not possible for his disciples to know the time of the national liberation; their impossible mission is simply to bring Christ's message "to the end of the earth." Behind Luke's story lies the hope that the kingdom will yet be restored to Israel. But until that happens "this gospel of the kingdom will be preached throughout the whole world, as a testimony to all nations; and then the end will come" (Matt. 24:14).

There are good grounds to believe that Paul was aware of the Lukan form of Jesus' words concerning Israel's doom "until the times of the Gentiles are fulfilled" and that he and his contemporaries understood Jesus to be saying that Israel would at last attain complete salvation, after the Gentiles had been converted to the message of the Gospel. Hence his famous words, "A hardness has come upon part of Israel, until the full number of the Gentiles come in; and so all Israel will be saved" (Rom. 11:25–26). In this way, apparently, the original prophecy of the final liberation of Jerusalem from the yoke of the Romans and the eschatological redemption of the people was eventually interpreted as a prophecy of the acceptance of faith in Christ by both the Gentiles and Israel. This is essential to an understanding of Paul's thesis.

d. *The "Witness" Function in Luke*

Why did Luke expand the travel account from Galilee to Jerusalem, as compared to Mark's brevity? A principal reason can be inferred from the speech attributed to Paul in Acts 13:16–41: the witness function attested in verse 31. Mention is made of those who went up with him and to whom he appeared for many days. This accords with Acts 1:21 ff. for the prerequisites for selection as an apostle, that is, "all the time that the Lord Jesus went in and out among us, beginning from the baptism of John until the day when he was taken up from us" (Luke 24:6 ff.; 23:55; Acts 10:37–43). Thus for Luke, the Christian witness was based on the testimony of those: (1) who were present during Jesus' Galilean ministry, (2) who followed Jesus on the trip to Jerusalem, and (3) who witnessed the Resurrection.

4. JOHN

For John the following points are noted:

a. *Prologue*

The book of John begins with the well known Logos prologue on the Incarnation, which sets the tone for the whole book and presents Jesus as the heavenly messenger and transcendental Messiah, a part of the Godhead itself.

It is basic to the concept of the Logos as a divine personality that the spirit received by the believers is to be identified in one way or another with Jesus himself. Paul attests to such a doctrine by assuring the Galatians that their adoption as sons of God has been secured through the indwelling of the Spirit, the Spirit of God's son, in their hearts. From where does this stem? The origins and elaborations on the theology of the "name" found in both orthodox and Gnostic Christian writings are ultimately rooted in Jewish esoteric speculation (as shown by G. Scholem and J. Danielou).

b. *His Theology*

The Gospel of John differs markedly in language, concepts, and theology from the three Synoptics. As the reader proceeds from them to the fourth Gospel, he finds himself in another world. For example, the Synoptics place the ministry of Jesus mostly in Galilee, whereas the Gospel of John divides it between Galilee and Jerusalem. The cleansing of the Temple is dated at opposite ends of Jesus' ministry: John at the beginning, the Synoptics, initiating Holy Week. They have different interpretations of the Lord's Supper, and John's presentation of the resurrection appearances diverges widely from that of the other Gospels. John reveals or reflects an earlier tradition that the first followers of Jesus did not understand him as royal messiah, at least not in the same way that later ones did.

c. *The Earlier Date of John*

While the differences between the Synoptics and John are striking, basic elements in common also should be recognized. The story of Jesus' ministry, culminating in his trial, execution, and resurrection, is basically the same, though details vary. The conviction that Jesus was the Christ, the son of the living God, and the commitment to him as divine leader are essentially the same as well. But why the drastic difference in tone and style, in vocabulary and in articulation of doctrine? It has been supposed widely that John was not interested in historical and chronological accuracy, and also that he wrote the Gospel at a much later date than the Synoptics. These views can no longer be taken for granted; distinguished scholars have defended an early date for the Gospel of John, at least the initial composition, and reconsideration of the narrative details indicates that he had reliable information about matters of fact. It is true that his vocabulary and ideas show the influence of Philo, the Hellenistic Jewish philosopher of Alexandria who tried to harmonize orthodox Jewish thought with Greek philosophy, or at least that they originate in the same world of discourse. It is noteworthy that similar ideas and terms have turned up at Qumran among the writings of the sect there.

A fragment of an Egyptian codex containing John 18:31–33, 37–38 was found in 1935, dating to the first half of the second century A.D. This is the oldest extant fragment of the New Testament and tends to support an earlier date for John, in the first century.

5. ARCHAEOLOGICAL CONTEXT FOR UNDERSTANDING JOHN

a. *Encounter with the Samaritan Woman*

Some ruins on Mount Gerizim would have been visible to Jesus when he talked to the Samaritan woman at Jacob's well in Sychar (John 4). These have been identified through archaeological research. The woman was pointing to Mount Gerizim where the Samaritan temple had stood. It was destroyed by John Hyrcanus in 128 B.C. In the time of the emperor

Hadrian (A.D. 117–138) the Romans built a great temple to Jupiter on the same site. The Samaritans maintained their faith and their existence, and to this day worship and celebrate the biblical festivals. They still perform their Passover sacrifice nearby. Elsewhere on the mountain is the fortification of Justinian enclosing the octagonal Theotokos church.

b. *The Twin Pools of Bethesda*

The authenticity and significance of the twin pools in John 5:1–9 are highlighted by the excavations at the back of Saint Anne's Church on the northern edge of the Temple Mount courts. The rectangular pools were surrounded by porticoes in the account of John. In the process of excavation, remains of a fifth-century Basilica of the Paralytic (traditional site of the cure by Jesus) were uncovered. According to B. Mazar, the ancient pools at the lowest level originated in the days of Simon the Just in the early second century B.C.: "In his days the great water reservoir was dug, a deep pool as extensive as the sea" (Ben-Sira, in the deuterocanonical Ecclesiasticus). We have already discussed the pools in "Part XVI: Remains of Hasmonean Times." According to Père Benoit, the pools are identical with the Eshdatayim ("twin pools") mentioned in the Copper Scroll; treasure is reportedly concealed in the smaller of the two. The Romans who

Marks of Roman games are visible in the flagstones. The Antonia has been erroneously identified with Pilate's Praetorium, as explained above

289

were garrisoned in the nearby Tower of Antonia in the early second century A.D. built a ritual bath there dedicated to Jupiter Serapis (as they did
at the Holy Sepulchre). This was under the vaulted halls of the pool, over
the original Jewish site. The ancient pools, on the other hand, had been
abandoned as a reservoir when the nearby larger installation, the Pool of
Israel, was dug, apparently in Herodian days, to service the Temple area.
Hence, Jesus' miracle of a later time must have occurred at the cave situated east of the twin pools. A small pool forms there from a nearby
spring; the water's reddish color was credited with curative power. This
factor was secondary to the main object, which was to have pure fresh
water in the vicinity of the *mikveh* ("immersion purification bath") conven-
iently placed in the immediate neighborhood of the Temple Mount. Several mikvehs were excavated by B. Mazar along the ascent leading to the
southern gates of the Temple Mount. They were a major facility provided
for worshipers and pilgrims entering the holy precincts.

c. *The Feast of Tabernacles*

John 7:37–39 suggests an organic relationship between the Feast of
Tabernacles (Succoth), which occurs around the beginning of the Jewish
calendrical year (September or early October), as observed by the Jewish
Christians, and ancient messianic associations reminiscent of the eschatological visions of the prophet Zechariah. In fact, Zechariah 14 is probably the
background not only for John 7 but also for Revelation 22. Tabernacles
was the occasion for mass pilgrimage to Jerusalem and the autumn harvest
week-long festival. It was characterized by solemn but joyous ceremonies.
Processions went down to the sacred Gihon spring, whose waters led to
the Siloam Pool. A priest filled a golden pitcher with water and the choir
intoned Isaiah's song of the water (12:3); then the procession went up to
the Water Gate as crowds carried the symbols of Succoth, the palm
fronds, myrtle, willow, and citron, as signs of the harvest.

R. E. Brown also deduces from the story of Jesus at Tabernacles that he remained a long period in the Jerusalem area between Tabernacles and the following Passover, in contrast to the crowded Synoptic picture of the Passion, in which Jesus comes to Jerusalem a few days before his capture.

d. *Caiaphas and the Trial of Jesus*

The high priest Caiaphas (A.D. 18–36), who held office when Pilate was procurator, lived in the aristocratic quarter on Mount Zion. The remains of his house were excavated in very recent times. Some vaulted rooms have been exposed and several interesting artifacts uncovered by Magen Broshi.

With reference to the trial (John 18:31) there is a Jewish tradition that about the year A.D. 30 the Romans took away from the Sanhedrin the right to impose capital punishment; this is substantiated by John, though the other New Testament writings do not mention the point. In any case, Caiaphas, with an acute sense of political expediency, was anxious to be rid of a troublesome messianic figure in time of tense revolutionary agitation. Anything was better than an uprising that would jeopardize the lives of the multitude in Jerusalem; therefore he placed the decision in Pilate's lap. He could hardly have foreseen that Jesus would become a martyr on behalf of the "true Israel" of which his sectarian followers regarded him as king.

e. *The Grotto and the Lazarus Tomb*

A grotto at Bethany was found in 1950 near the Franciscan olive grove, marked with graffiti. The place must have been sacred to Jewish Christians, where they commemorated the Last Supper of Jesus and his disciples. The nature of the grotto is established by the symbols employed: the cosmic ladder, the triangle, and various eschatological designs on the walls. The cosmic ladder symbolizes the journey that the soul must make from the grave to God, and it appears often in the writings of and on monuments related to the Jewish Christians. The grotto was abandoned about the fifth century A.D., when the Jewish-Christian communities also disappeared.

The tomb of Lazarus in its natural state was pointed out by the faithful at the beginning of the fourth century. It was quarried out of rock and composed of a vestibule and a burial chamber faced with stone or marble-work in the Byzantine period.

6. THE CHRISTIANIZED VERSION OF THE MESSIAH

Among the shifting views of the royal messiah in Judaism, there were three constant elements: that he was human, that he was a scion of David and that he would rule a political kingdom. Such a view falls short of the apocalyptic hope in the cosmic Son of Man who will establish an eternal heavenly kingdom. Both kinds of expectations were present in the Jewish community and are reflected in the New Testament. Although Jesus was no Zealot, and though he never aimed at establishing a political kingdom, he was condemned as Messiah in the basic sense of that title, i.e., royal pretender. Accordingly, the political concept of kingly messiah was avoided by the oldest Jewish-Christian community. They adopted instead a spiritualized version of the messiah, whereby the exalted Lord was already seen to be ruling as king, and the authoritative acts of his earthly ministry could be attributed to him as Messiah on earth. Jesus was believed to be of the Davidic line, so that it was a simple matter to ascribe to him the messianic title, even though that created a tension between worldly messianism and Jewish apocalyptic hope. The resurrection of Jesus marked the temporal turning point from humiliation to exaltation. This two-stage Christology aided in the transformation of the "Son of God" from a messianic designation in the Jewish sense to its meaning in the Hellenistic-Jewish church, where the title is used of Jesus as the Lord, the all-powerful agent of God's will during his earthly ministry. Finally in the Hellenistic-Gentile church, Son of God is conferred upon Jesus as a divine title. This development culminates in the doctrine of pre-existence and incarnation.

In the Palestinian Jewish-Christian community, *kyrios* was used as a title for Jesus, not as divine, but as a man of authority, in keeping with the Old Testament connotations of *'adon*. Later, this became a true Christological title by virtue of the unique authority of Jesus. This view was then extended to his coming manifestation in power and finally transmuted under Hellenistic influence so that Jesus is thought of as divine, superior in potency to the gods of the mystery religions and the deified emperors.

PART XVIII

THE ACTS

Another important source for primitive Jewish Christianity is in the Acts of the Apostles, which preserves central traditions of the apostolic age. The value of the accounts given there can be demonstrated by comparing and integrating them with those in the other sources: the Gospels and the material remains of Jewish Christianity.

A. HISTORIC BACKGROUND OF THE ACTS OF THE APOSTLES

Acts offers the extant "official" account of the beginnings of the new Christian church, as seen by an early witness of the movement. It is a chronicle of events in the biblical pattern, with a broad historical perspective based partly upon personal reminiscences of the author who, according to unanimous tradition, was Luke, the contemporary and companion of Paul.

1. THE EARLY JEWISH-CHRISTIAN COMMUNITY OF ACTS

As is shown by the preface to the book of Acts, the history of the first Jewish-Christian community is a sequel to the Gospel of Luke. It carries on the story of the disciples and followers of Jesus from the time of the Resurrection and Ascension, describing the community in action, and the principal events of those early creative, formative, and decisive days: for example, the replacement of Judas to reconstitute the Twelve; Pentecost; the emergence of Peter as the leader of the community; and the martyrdom of Stephen, the ardent preacher and leader of the "deacons." Then the scope broadens: Philip, on a journey, meets and converts a eunuch. Peter's vision and the conversion of Cornelius and his household represents a further dramatic step in the same direction. It is with the appearance of Saul of Tarsus that a fateful turning point in the story is reached.

Acts can be divided into two main sections. Chapters 1–8 describe the growth of Jewish Christianity in Palestine under the leadership of Peter. This was the early church, "the Way" or the Nazarene sect in Jerusalem and elsewhere in Palestine. Chapters 9–28 describe the spread of Christianity, Jewish and Gentile, throughout the Mediterranean world through the efforts of many missionaries, the most important of these being Saul/Paul and his close associates. The author seems intent on showing that the propagation of the gospel was accomplished without hindrance from the Romans.

2. THE SYNAGOGUE-CHURCH ON MOUNT ZION

It was in the "upper room" that Jesus celebrated the Last Supper, instituting at the end of the meal a solemn covenant with his followers, which (as the Eucharist) became the central rite of Christian worship. Beneath this chamber is the Jewish holy place identified erroneously since the Middle Ages as the Tomb of David, which was once a church-synagogue. This has been demonstrated by a close examination of its masonry, especially the details of the apse behind the present cenotaph of David. Equally important are some inscriptions on the walls, one of which connects the homage to David with the memory of the Patriarch, illustrating the meaning of the reference in Peter's first sermon after the Pentecost: "Brethren, I may say to you confidently of the patriarch David that he both died and was buried, and his tomb is with us to this day" (Acts 2: 29). It has been noted that the organization of the early Jewish-Christian group, as it appears in Acts and the Pauline Epistles, shows striking resemblances to the structure adopted by the Essenes at Qumran. Thus, in the summary of the activities of the first Jewish Christians (Acts 2:42–47), we find reference made to the "community of property," "prayer," and "teaching." Likewise, the Qumranite sacred meals, especially the liturgy for the messianic banquet, have notable affinities with the meal fellowship described in Acts and with the ordinance for the *eucharistia* and the *agape* (the joyous communal meal connected with the eucharist), reported in 1 Corinthians by Paul and in the Didache.

The activities of the apostles aroused the opposition of the Jewish establishment of Jerusalem, mainly of the Sadducees, who had opposed Jesus. His followers were brought before the Sanhedrin (Supreme Council), but opinions there were divided. Rabbi Gamaliel defended them judiciously. He was a scion of Hillel the Babylonian, a notable Pharisaic thinker and leader, to whose party Paul originally belonged. He held firmly to the tradition of humility and leniency in the application of the Law as advocated by the school of Hillel. The decision of Gamaliel that the community be left alone (5:33–40) initiated a period of more tranquil relationship with the Sanhedrin and allowed the Christian group to increase its membership and solidify its position. It is true that Acts 8:1 reports a persecution against Hellenistic Jewish Christians who voiced their opposition to the Temple. There were isolated acts of violence like Herod Agrippa's execution of James, son of Zebedee, and his imprisonment of Peter, but otherwise the Jerusalem community seems to have lived in peace with the Jerusalem authorities. In A.D. 58, when Paul came to Jerusalem (Acts 21:18 ff.), it was still customary for Jewish Christians to offer sacrifice in the Temple. The subsequent execution of James, the brother of Jesus, marked the opening of a new period of hostility.

Although the Sanhedrin had refused to condemn the apostles, the zeal of Stephen, the deacon, especially in condemning the Temple and its worship, aroused the congregation of one of the more fanatically orthodox

Recess or apse of the 2nd c.
A.D. synagogue on Mount Zion
and a cenotaph that is
erroneously identified as the
"Tomb of David"

synagogues to prosecute him for blasphemy and to stone him, as prescribed by the ancient legal sanctions (Lev. 24:14).

3. CONTEMPORARY SYNAGOGUES

Although we are inclined to think of the synagogues as primarily institutions of the Jewish Diaspora, the truth is that they were very numerous in Palestine. One example is the synagogue of the Freedmen mentioned in Acts 6:9, whose existence has been authenticated by a dedicatory inscription in Greek, reproduced here. It was discovered in the Ophel, the southeastern part of the lower town. This is the inscription of Theodotus, son of Vattenos, the head of the first century A.D. synagogue. The synagogue was founded by freed slaves repatriated to Palestine and still linked to the Diaspora. While the national ritual was performed at the Temple, congregations attended the synagogues for their morning and evening prayers. There was also a *bet midrash,* or school, to instruct the young and to provide refresher courses for adults. Hebrew and Aramaic were the basic languages, but Greek was also used by Jews both abroad and in Palestine.

Two other contemporary synagogues have been discovered—at Masada, Herod's private desert resort, and at Herodion, Herod's summer palace. Both are distinguished by their simplicity. The small Masada edifice, in its original Herodian phase, had two rows of three columns, which supported the roof; the main entrance was on the east side. Benches were built along the walls in later years by the Zealots who took refuge at Masada during the revolt against Rome (A.D. 70–73). An auxiliary room was built into the northwestern corner during the revolt.

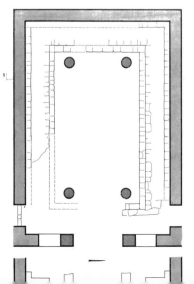

Cross sections of the synagogue of Masada built in Herodian times (right) and that which Herod erected in his palatial summer retreat at Herodion (left)

4. THE HISTORICAL PROCESSES OF JEWISH CHRISTIANITY

Since the author of Acts is primarily interested in describing the rapid spread of the Gospel throughout the Roman empire and brings his story to a climax with Paul's arrival in the capital city, Rome, after devoting the better part of his life to other missionary enterprises, it is understandable that the author passes over many interesting and important aspects of early Christian history. His account of Jewish Christianity is largely limited to the earliest period in Jerusalem, for which he provides excellent data; but once Paul enters the scene, the author follows him on his travels and adventures in the empire, touching home base in Palestine and Jerusalem only on the rare occasions when Paul does. As a result, the story of Jewish Christianity during and beyond the remaining decades of the first century has not received the attention it deserves, either in Acts or in subsequent studies down to the present.

5. THE MOVEMENT OF "THE WAY"

The people of "the Way"—the Jewish Christians—remained part of the larger Jewish community during the decades following the death of Jesus. The men of "the Way" still were faithful to Judaism and engaged in the traditional forms of worship (Acts 3:1; 21:20; 22:17; 23:1; 24:11–18).

The picture preserved in Acts of the early Jewish-Christian community in Jerusalem manifests significant differences from first century Jewry, long before the separation of the two communities confirmed the fact publicly. The Jewish Christians proclaimed that Jesus was Messiah and Lord and that salvation for the individual and world was available through him (2:38–40). The adherents attended the Temple, but they also had their own meetings; they celebrated meals that commemorated the Last Supper, to which only those who had been baptized were admitted; and they developed their own system for caring for the poor (2:44–46). What differentiated them theologically from the other Jews was their expectation of the coming of the crucified and risen Jesus in glory as the Royal Messiah and the Lord of the world. Nevertheless, they regarded themselves as Jews and were considered so by others. They met publicly in "Solomon's Porch" and their numbers grew daily; actually this site was the Royal Portico or the *Hanuyyoth,* mentioned in connection with Jesus' experience there. Then, concurrently with Paul's appearance on the scene, the missionary zeal for the movement of "the Way" resulted in the conversion of proselytes, God-fearers, and pagans and their incorporation into the community, thereby producing additional strains between it and traditional Judaism. Acts describes in rapid sequence the steps by which "the Way" was separated from the parent religion and set out to conquer the world "in the name of Jesus."

B. PAUL'S LIFE AND MISSION

According to Acts, Paul studied under Rabbi Gamaliel, the great Pharisaic leader, in Jerusalem, and he became an active supporter of the Jewish establishment in the growing controversy between the Sanhedrin and the Jewish Christians, which ended in the trial and stoning of Stephen, in which Paul is said to have participated. Shortly thereafter Paul led a punitive expedition against the pernicious Christian movement that had appeared in Damascus; on the road to Damascus he underwent a dramatic conversion experience, and from having been a vehement persecutor he became an ardent follower of "the Way" (cf. Acts 22:6–16; 26:12–18). We have noted the presence of an Essene messianist movement in Damascus that doubtless was related to the contemporary community of Essenes of Qumran. The group in Damascus may have provided recruits for the nascent Christian community there. Following his extraordinary experience, Paul retired into Arabia, that is, the Nabatean kingdom in the arid parts of eastern Palestine, an area in which another form of messianism is also attested by recent discovery. He returned to Jerusalem and was accepted by the leaders of the Jewish-Christian community (Gal. 1:18 ff.); at the same time he asserted the independence of his message, saying that he did not derive his gospel from their instruction. He was certain that he received it from Jesus himself.

1. RESURRECTION AND THE JEWS

Jesus was sinless, had suffered and been crucified in atonement for the sins of mankind. Jesus' resurrection was the guarantee of salvation for mankind, which is extended to Jews and to Gentiles equally. It has been said that for Paul, the Resurrection had the importance that earlier sectarian thought had attached to baptism. It also supplied the vital element in his eschatological teaching. In the life of the risen Christ he saw the prototype for the future life of all who were "Christ's" (Phil. 3:21). In his mission to the Gentiles, it became the beginning, the goal, and the manifestation of the new life (Romans 6). Paul joined the Christian community in Antioch, apparently the first Gentile Christian group to be affiliated with the Jewish-Christian community with its headquarters in Jerusalem. The leading figure of the Antioch church was Barnabas, an early adherent and dedicated supporter of the faith. He enlisted Paul as his associate, and together they served as apostles and missionaries for the church there. They were sent to Jerusalem to take a donation to the leaders of the movement and to confer with them. Following this venture, the Antiochians commissioned them to preach the gospel abroad. Their first journey took them to Cyprus, Perga, Antioch in Asia Minor, and finally the cities of Lycaonia (chapters 13–14), where they met with open hostility. At this phase of the story, the basic controversy concerned the obligation of the converted Gentiles to observe Jewish law. Paul endorsed the posi-

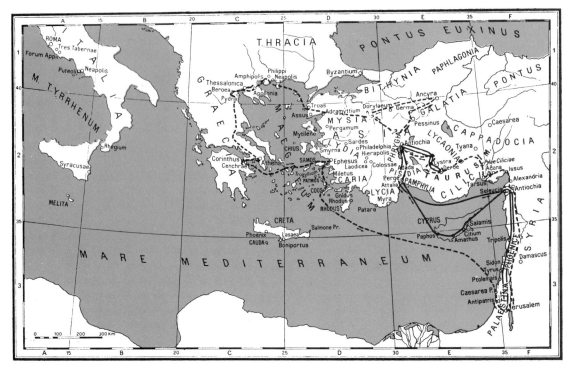

Paul's overland journeys
through Syria and his second
journey by sea to and through
Asia Minor

tion that Gentiles did not have to become Jews (that is, be circumcised
and accept the burden of the Law) in order to become Christians. This
decision was appealed to Jerusalem, but Paul was able to win the approval
of the Jerusalem leaders to his tolerant outlook. James issued an edict in
the name of the Jerusalem church that exonerated and confirmed Paul,
though at the same time urging compromise and good will on all parties.
From Paul's Epistles (which precede Acts in date of composition) we learn
that the ruling was not universally approved and that many Jewish Christians in the Diaspora resented both the argument and the arguer.

Paul's second and most significant journey was begun shortly after
the return to Antioch (15:36–18:21). After passing through Cilicia, Lycaonia, Phrygia, and Galatia in Asia Minor, Paul preached the gospel on the
continent of Europe, in the Macedonian cities of Philippi, Thessalonica,
Beroea, Athens, and Corinth, where serious clashes ended in his arrest and
trial.

2. PAUL AND THE JEWISH CHRISTIANS OF PALESTINE

According to C. H. Kraeling, the Jewish Christians of Palestine in the
first century "did not make the death of Jesus on the cross as central a
factor in their interpretation of his significance as Paul did, for instance.
For them, Jesus was the bringer of the New Law, the Holy One who
taught the higher righteousness that exceeded but did not abolish the
Mosaic ordinances. We can still sense the differences of outlook that existed between the Jewish-Christian communities of Palestine and Paul on
this matter, in Galatians 2:21 where Paul says for the benefit of those un-

der Jewish-Christian influence, 'If righteousness comes by the Law, then Christ is dead in vain.' "

3. SALVATION FOR GENTILE AS WELL AS JEW

Paul's liberal approach earned him the opposition of the old guard of the Jerusalem church, who still refused to make concessions on the question of Jewish observances. A good deal of the opposition to Paul among the Jewish-Christian communities of Palestine apparently was rooted in bitter memories of the part he had played as a persecutor. Although the leaders accepted him, there were many who remained skeptical about his conversion. The "Judaizers" with whom he came into conflict were an extremist group who did not belong to the central party in Jerusalem. Paul saw much more clearly than they that it was impossible to require slaves and hired workers in the Hellenistic world to keep the Jewish Sabbath and festivals, or to abide by the food laws. Nor could grown men, however close to Judaism, accept circumcision. Paul did not deliberately seek a solution for them. He had no desire to make things easy. He himself had been a strictly observant Diaspora Jew and, with certain exceptions related directly to the mission to the Gentiles, continued to be so. But he was concerned with questions of theology, and it seemed to him that with the coming of Jesus, the Messiah, a decisive change in the nature of the holy community had taken place and that with it, the place and function of the Law had also changed drastically.

In his travels in the Roman province of Asia, Paul worked mainly in cities where there were Jewish communities, and through them he may have reached sympathetic Gentiles, "godfearers," who were interested in biblical religion, sympathized with Jews, and frequented the synagogues. Modern pilgrims and tourists hoping to follow in the steps of the apostle through Asia Minor (modern Turkey) or Greece find very few authentic traces in the Hellenistic towns in which he preached. All that is left in most of them are the remnants of temples, forums, and theaters, and occasional traces of ancient synagogues. Excavations have been conducted in a number of important cities such as Ephesus, Sardis, Pergamon, Lystra, Derbe, Perga, Iconium, and Antioch.

Elevated porch at Ephesus, somewhat similar architecturally to the Royal Porches around the Temple

299

Ruins of Pergamon

A glance at the map shows the great distances covered by Paul and his companions. Paul seems to have been equally at home with Jews and with Gentiles and was one of the most cosmopolitan figures of the Bible, entirely at ease in the cities of the Mediterranean where on occasion he also earned his living as an artisan (usually but not certainly described as a tentmaker). There is a sharp contrast between the rural and village quality

of the Gospels and the urban atmosphere of Paul's Epistles, which reflect the hustle and bustle of the cities that he visited and in which he lived.

4. THE CONTEMPORARY ANCIENT SYNAGOGUES

What interests us particularly are the synagogues and communities of Syria and Asia Minor. Outstanding examples are Antioch in Syria, Sardis, and Dura-Europos. The earliest Jewish-Christian community in Antioch, one of the great cities of antiquity, dates approximately to A.D. 40 and numbered among its leaders Barnabas and Paul. It was there that the Jewish Christians became known by the Greek name *Christianoi* (Messianists) and it was from Antioch that the mission to the Gentiles began. The city rivaled Jerusalem as the center of early Christianity.

The beginnings of Jewish Christianity in Asia Minor are bound up closely with the numerous and wealthy Jewish communities and their elaborate synagogues. The most striking example, verified by archaeology, is that of Sardis. Built in the third century A.D., the synagogue was a beautifully ornamented basilica with two ritual focal points: a permanent place for the Torah shrine (Ark) in front of the central entrance in the wall facing toward Jerusalem and, at the other end, a raised *bema* ("altar") from which the Torah was read and the sermons preached. In this manner the congregation seated on the benches lining the long walls could see both the Ark and the altar.

The synagogue was established in the area of the public buildings of

Main hall of the Sardis synagogue (right) and eastern end of the hall (left) and site of the Ark

A gold and metal artificer at work

the city, and was next to the gymnasium and Roman bath. The influential Jewish community maintained the synagogue along with their civic privileges even during the centuries that followed the establishment of Christianity as the official religion of the Byzantine empire.

5. PAUL'S THIRD JOURNEY

The third journey was begun shortly after a stopover in Antioch, with a visit to Phrygia and Galatia and the establishment of a church in the large and important city of Ephesus. Ephesus was the chief city of the Roman province of Asia, a wealthy, highly cultivated metropolis with a temple to Artemis (Diana), one of the seven wonders of the ancient world. The town boasted a number of silversmiths who specialized in pagan images. One of these, Demetrius, provoked a riot against Paul, who ridiculed his craft as part of a biblical polemic against idolatry (Acts 19:29). His hostility was provoked by his loss of business as a result of Paul's success in undermining popular confidence in the efficacy of idols and the religion associated with them.

6. PAUL'S TRIAL

Paul's experience in Corinth (18:12–17) is characteristic of the difficulties that he encountered, important because it came to an end in a way that distinguishes it from the Jerusalem pattern. The Jews were the persecutors (9:22–25, 29–30; 13:50–51; 14:2, 4–6, 19), and the conflicting statements and bitterness led to a break between Paul and the synagogue and to his making plans for an intensive mission among the Gentiles (18:6). But the Roman court refused to interfere with long-standing Jewish privileges.

After the third journey, Paul returned to Jerusalem, where he clashed openly with the Jews on the Temple Mount. He took refuge in the Antonia Tower that Herod had built, which was garrisoned by the Roman troops. The cliff on which this historic fortress was built can still be identified, but the only vestige of the building are parts of a wall in and near the Arab Ommariyeh school at the north end of the Temple Mount. Ultimately Paul was arrested and brought to trial on a variety of charges, chiefly that he had attacked the established order and violated the basic laws of Judiasm.

With Paul's trial in Jerusalem and in Caesarea, and his later appeal to the court of Caesar in Rome, the account in Acts reaches its climax. The book closes with Paul awaiting trial before the emperor, and in the meantime proclaiming the gospel even to the limited audience available under the terms of his house arrest.

7. PAUL, MESSIANISM, AND NATIONALISM

As the center of gravity of the new church shifted from Palestine to the Diaspora and eventually to the great cities of the Roman empire, east and west, the messianic ideal on which Palestinian Jewish Christianity was based underwent a change. Traditional Jewish expectations had been of a purely national "Messiah of David." But the humiliation of Jesus' crucifixion made it essential that any idea of Davidic kingship or suspected political rebellion must be removed from the picture of him as a messiah. In a brilliant tour de force, Jesus' submission became the mark of his messiahship, and instead of the reigning monarch, he was perceived as the "Suffering Servant of the Lord" (as in Isaiah 53). Only when he had borne the sins of the world and endured its wickedness could he be raised to power and glory as the triumphant Son of God. Of fundamental importance in shaping the message of the gospel was the attitude to foreign rule over the Jews. For a long time after the Exile it was accepted fact and doctrine that God had transferred sovereignty to a foreign empire and that the Jewish community must submit patiently and penitently until God acted in some decisive fashion to change the situation and re-establish an independent Israel or bring the empires of the world to an end and reign as Lord over all. The alternate view, expressing the longing of many, was politically oriented and aimed at seizing territory and independence and reviving the ancient Monarchy.

A Jew of the Diaspora, Paul was inclined to ignore nationalist elements in messianism and the details of Jesus' life in the land (which were preserved nonetheless in the traditions of the local Jewish Christians, as is seen below). Instead, he concentrated on the universal aspects of Jesus as the "Son of God," the pre-existent eternal instrument of divine revelation. According to W. D. Davies, "Christ has become for Paul the 'locus' of redemption here and in the world to come. The 'land' has been for him 'Christified.' It is not the land promised, much as he had loved it, that became his 'inheritance,' but the Living Lord, in whom was a new creation. . . . And once Paul had made the Living Lord rather than the Torah the center of life and in death, once he had seen in Jesus his Torah, he had in principle broken with the land. . . . His geographic identity was subordinated to that of being 'in Christ' in whom he was neither Jew nor Greek" (W. D. Davies: *The Gospel and the Land,* 1975).

In any case, the final break between Judaism and Christianity did not come in the late first century A.D., but only in the late second century or even after, depending on the place as well as on local social and economic conditions. By that time the Jewish synagogues began to force Jewish Christians out of their precincts, as may be seen from the fact that among the "Eighteen Benedictions," an obligatory synagogue liturgy, is a curse on the *Minim* or Jewish Christians. As Jews who believed in Jesus refused to recite such a prayer, they could be identified and driven away. Thus they began to worship in their own synagogues. This is probably the origin of the prayer-house built over Peter's Capernaum house in the second century A.D. in the quarter occupied by Jewish Christians.

C. FIRST CENTURY A.D. JEWRY AND JEWISH CHRISTIANITY

The early Jewish-Christian community came into existence after the life and death and resurrection of Jesus, and lived side by side and in conflict with the rest of Judaism, including Sadducees, Pharisees, Essenes, Herodians, and Zealots. It was also the era of the great teachers (rabbis) who flourished before and after the fall of Jerusalem in A.D. 70.

1. THE DIFFERENT ASPECTS OF JEWISH CHRISTIANITY

Hence, Jewish Christianity during this period manifested itself in a variety of forms. There was the basic Palestinian stratum, close to Pharisaism and adhering to rabbinical legalistic *halakhot* ("rules"). There were also apocalyptic and messianic groups in Asia Minor, tending to zealotry. Reflecting a more contemplative or mystical community were written compositions like the *Shepherd of Hermas* (Rome) or the *Ode of Solomon* (Antioch of Syria). The common link among these groups is the original Christian theology expressed in Jewish or Semitic terms. They are postbiblical, belonging in the main to the sub-Apostolic period, and are described in the extant writings of Irenaeus and Clement of Alexandria; they are represented in such works as the Ascension of Isaiah and the Epistle of Barnabas. Material remains of these groups have survived and have been discovered in recent archaeological excavations, as presently described. It is important to define the term Jewish Christian:

a) It may designate the Jewish-Christian community of Jerusalem led first by Peter, then by Jesus' brother James. It was the mother church, with the prestige and authority of the Twelve Apostles and the family of Jesus. It was in the main an orthodox group, described in Acts 2:42–47, worshiping at the Temple and observing Jewish law, and recognizing no mandate to propagate their faith among the Gentiles. It retained primacy until the 60s, even when the gospel had spread through the Roman empire and churches had been founded in the principal cities. There was continuing tension between Paul, the great missionary to the Gentiles, and the central Jewish-Christian community in Jerusalem, but no resolution was achieved until the principals all died in the decade before the fall of Jerusalem (A.D. 70). Before the Jewish-Roman war broke out, the Jewish Christians fled to Pella in northern Transjordan for safety and settled there temporarily. Many of the exiles returned to Jerusalem afterwards and stayed there; later evidence locates them on Mount Zion. The community was led by Simon, son of Cleophas, who was related to the family of Jesus. The bishops who followed, according to Eusebius, were all of the Church of the Circumcision, the so-called Judaizers. The term is used to distinguish the Jewish-Christian community from those early Christians who did not practice circumcision or observe the laws of Moses.

b) It may designate Jews who recognized Jesus as a prophet or even Messiah, but not as the Son of God. They constitute an intermediate group between Jews and Christians, like the Ebionites, the "poor," who did not accept the divinity of Christ. They are not an isolated case, as witness the influence of revolutionary and messianic Jewish propaganda, which spread throughout the Jewish world and affected the young Jewish-Christian communities during the period between A.D. 40–70. Among them were the groups with whom Paul clashed in Corinth, Colossae, and Galatia. The Jewish-Christian communities, living side by side with strictly observant Jews, were syncretistic in nature, influenced by native Asiatic cultures, which we meet in the person of Simon Magus and the like. These communities flourished in Palestine, Transjordan, and Syria. Here and there, they came into touch with churches founded or influenced by Paul, and the resultant conflict over issues such as circumcision (of Gentiles) and observance of the Law brought angry responses in the Pauline Epistles, warning his followers against the Judaizing zeal of his opponents.

Other branches disappeared after the fall of Jerusalem. Their spirit is reflected in the Epistle of Jude, and they are the source of the Gospel of the Hebrews, originally written in Aramaic. Unable to return to Jerusalem, they assimilated with other sects in the Near East, probably in Egypt or in eastern Syria, where remnants persisted for many decades.

c) Finally, one can define Jewish Christianity as a pattern of Christian thought that does not imply a direct link with the Jewish community but which expresses itself in a religious framework borrowed from Judaism. This definition has a wide scope and would comprise the former two categories as well as groups that broke away from the Jewish community but continued to think along the same lines. This would be the case with Paul and other leaders of the early church. Such Jewish Christianity is identical with early Christianity, the origin of which was Jewish, but which had moved away from Judaism to accommodate large numbers of Gentile converts.

2. COMMUNITIES OF JEWISH AND PAGAN ORIGIN

In the course of the second Jewish revolt against Rome, led by Bar Kochba in A.D. 132 and crushed by Hadrian in A.D. 135, the Jewish Christians who did not recognize Jesus as the Messiah were forced to flee. The leadership of the Jerusalem "church" and probably of Jaffa, Lydda, and Pella, founded after A.D. 70, passed to converted Gentiles, who became Jewish Christians. It appears that they wanted to change certain rules such as the date of the Passover celebration. Endless discussions were held between Jews and Jewish Christians, termed *Minim;* the most important of these took place in Caesarea and Tiberias. Constant friction led to the eventual separation of Christians of Jewish origin from those of pagan origin. Churches made up of the latter were established in Caesarea and Acre, Ashdod, Neapolis (Shechem), Bosra, and Philadelphia (Amman of today). These grew rapidly and spread, reaching a peak in the third century A.D. when there were Christian communities in most Palestinian cities

The Amwas "lamella" (metal-foil inscription) placed under the head of the corpse. The idea behind this practice was that the soul came out by way of the mouth and was in need of help. The Aramaic characters and designs (serpent as a snare laid by a demon) suggest a talisman, together with exorcisms of the demon Shamadel. The designs were obscure, and it was assumed that only the initiates would grasp them

Jewish-Christian symbols: the fish, the anchor, the cross

with the exception of the thickly settled Jewish areas of Galilee, Zippori, and Tiberias. The Council of Caesarea, in 196, decided that the Passover should be observed on Easter Sunday. This was one of the signs of the eventual separation of the Jews and Christians; Jewish Christians maintained their identity for two centuries or more, as is shown by material evidence they left behind.

3. JEWISH-CHRISTIAN LITERATURE

There is close historical connection between the Jewish Christians and a large group of extracanonical writings attributed to them and considered apocryphal (heterodox or of doubtful authorship) in Apostolic and sub-Apostolic times. The only one that was included in the New Testament is the Epistle to the Hebrews. It expresses the thought of new Christians involved in the Jewish milieu. The Jewish-Christian *Gospel According to the Hebrews* was popular in Egypt; it is to be distinguished from the *Gospel of the Ebionites,* a later heterodox work. These are apocryphal works that deal with celestial mysteries and the end of days. In imitation of other Jewish pseudepigraphic writings, which were attributed to great figures of the past like Noah, Enoch, or Abraham, these are accredited to prophets and apostles, for example, the Gospel of Peter and the Apocalypse of the Twelve Apostles, or liturgical works like the Ascension of Isaiah, with its doctrine of the seven heavens leading to the eighth that is Christ's domain and of *sheol,* the realm of the dead. The *Didache,* the *Ode of Solomon,* the *Epistles of Ignatius* and of *Barnabas,* the *Pseudo-Clementine Homilies* all date to the first and early second centuries A.D. The second part of the Didache consists of ecclesiastical regulations regarding baptism, the Eucharist, and worship, as well as the appointment of bishops and deacons along with prophets and teachers. The book is of special interest, since it comes from an early period when rules of faith and practice were just being adopted by the Gentile church. Few extracanonical books are more important than the Didache, since it contains an early and alternate version of a group of dominical sayings, compared with the canonical Gospels, and the first instructions on the sacraments and early church procedures.

4. DISCOVERIES OF CHRISTIAN ARCHAEOLOGY

The diligent work of B. Bagatti, E. Testa, and I. Mancini has provided archaeological documentation of such Christian symbols as the cross under the axe, the six-pointed star, the Christ-angel, the plow as a sign of Christ, and other examples.

a. *Sacred Letters, Numbers, and Cross Signs*

There was a secret language expressed in mystic Hebrew letters and words and in special numbers that had a symbolic and theological meaning (e.g., 1000 meaning a period of prosperity); seals that consist of designs (plow, tree, etc.); the sacred names of God and Christ, which were be-

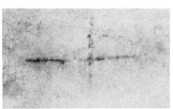

lieved to have miraculous power and were written in the form of mono-
grams; the drawing of the trinitarian sign (a triangle); the *waw* cross; the
cross with two, three, or six horns as dynamic signs, developing the Jewish
Christian teaching on the angels as outward manifestations of the power
of the Trinity; prophetic signs derived from the Old Testament and transmuted into eschatological terms, such as the Ark of Noah, Jacob's Ladder,
the bloodstained lintels of Jewish homes on the eve of the Exodus from
Egypt; the serpent of Moses mentioned in Numbers; the star of Jacob; and
the tree of life.

The Jewish-Christian theology glorified Christ and his cosmic power;
this is related to the mystery of the cross. On the one hand it evokes the

Graffiti on the wall of a tomb at
Bethphage near Bethany

crucifixion of the historic Jesus on earth; on the other, its symbolic double form, †, and the sign × emphasize Christ's redemption and the realization of the eschatological drama. The other symbols include, for example, the luminous cross of the Apocalypse, which represents the attributes of God the all-powerful creator.

b. *Graffiti as Symbols*

In the burial ground of Dominus Flevit on the Mount of Olives, the WAW in the form of a monogram is the sign of the cross. Other signs denote the "centenarian" Abraham, mnemonic substitutions for Christ, the Dove (corresponding to the symbolic 801), and the Fish, symbolized by the number 29. Such graffiti have thrown new light on the buildings used by the Jewish Christians, such as the church-synagogue of Nazareth and the one on Mount Zion, with the signs and symbols used to express their religious beliefs and initiation rites.

The letters XE MARIA, "Hail Mary," and a second graffito, "holy place of M," attest to the worship of Mary in Jewish-Christian times. The symbols found around Nazareth and on the ossuaries of Dominus Flevit were identical. The signs of the triangle on amulets discovered near Hebron have the same meaning; graffiti on the wall of a grave at Bethphage can be compared with Jewish-Christian belief in the future life or in the journey that the soul had to undertake to gain heaven. That journey is symbolized by the cosmic ladder sketched in the tombs and in an ornate building at Beit-Hashitta.

There is other evidence: the tablets of lead or "lamina," copper, silver, or gold refer to the oil of Faith, whose meaning only the initiated could understand. They consisted of magic formulas and strange symbols with mystical interpretations (suggestive in a way of cabalistic signs). They are Jewish-Christian amulets.

5. CONCLUSION

a. *The Church of the Circumcision and the Church of the Gentiles*

In most parts of Palestine, mainly in the mountain areas, the Church of the Circumcision led an active life until the end of the fourth century A.D. and continued in a state of decline for more than another century. For a long time Jewish Christians existed side by side with the orthodox Jews, worshiping in the same synagogues, until they were forced to leave. The Jewish Christians had their own liturgy, expressive of Christian teaching with its roots in Judaism, their own literature, buildings, worship, and customs. Archaeological evidence from neighboring countries shows that their influence was widespread, especially in Asia Minor and the famed cities of the Seven Churches of the Apocalypse (see Rev. 1:12).

This background throws light on the origin of the recognized holy places. The documentation of the tradition helps to trace them back to the beginning, thus bridging the gap from the period of the Apostles to Constantine, when Christianity became the official religion of the empire. A striking example is Nazareth with its Jewish-Christian worship of Mary already in the very first centuries. On the other hand, these discoveries help us to understand some obscure New Testament passages of the Apocalypse. There, the five elements of the Jewish-Christian system of symbolism appear together.

In the course of their history, some Jewish villages and towns of the second to the fourth centuries are referred to as "swallowed up" by the Jews, that is, lost to the land of Israel. Some of them were occupied by the Jewish Christians. From information provided by the historians Epiphanius and Eusebius and the debates between *Minim* (Jewish Christians) and the rabbis in the Talmud, it is possible to draw up a map showing the centers where Jewish Christians lived. They lived in the same places as Jews but, because of their *habdalah* ("separation"), they dwelt in a separate quarter of the town, apart from those faithful to the synagogue. Traces of this separation were evident, until recent centuries, in the village of Bei'na in Galilee, as well as Kfar-kana (ancient Cana) and el-Jish (Gushhalab), where two synagogues served the separate communities.

Bloodstained marks of a slaughtered lamb on a wall to protect the house against evil

b. *The Lesson of Archaeology*

These observations should therefore be borne in mind as a proper guide to the historical background of New Testament literature and, more specifically, as a help in understanding key passages and events in the Gospels, Acts, and Pauline letters and the social and religious situation out of which Christianity in its various forms and types arose.

c. *The Christian Holy Places and Archaeology*

Another question arises in trying to connect the obscure and forgotten traces of primitive Christianity, described above, with over two hundred churches (many of them already in ruins) that arose presumably over or near the ancient sites of early Christianity. The most important were built in Byzantine times or later, hiding what lay beneath. With the possible exception of the lower reaches of the Holy Sepulchre (built in the fourth

Below, left: Facade of the synagogue of Baram

Below, right: The cosmic cross on a mosaic of the Jewish-Christian synagogue at Nazareth, symbolizing the celestial abode

Graffito XE MARIA, "Hail, Mary," discovered in the lower levels of the Church of the Annunciation, Nazareth, indicative of the worship of the mother of Christ

century), the prayer-house over Peter's house at Capernaum, or the chapel of Dura-Europos, they have no more archaeological significance than "David's tomb" on Mount Zion. Tourists, however, are not aware of the facts, and the voluminous illustrated literature on the Christian Holy Places is of no help in trying to guide the innocents abroad in the steps of Jesus.

d. *The Post-Apostolic Age of the Synagogue*

Traditional Jewish life survived the Bar Kochba debacle and continued in a dynamic development throughout the second century and afterwards. There was a renaissance of the Jewish community and its culture in Galilee, the heights of Golan, Transjordan, and other parts of Palestine where remains of dozens of magnificent synagogues have been discovered: Capernaum, Meron, Chorazin, Baram, Hamath (Tiberias), and Beth-shean, to mention a few.

The style of the synagogues and neighboring patrician homes derives from classic Hellenistic-Syrian architecture of late Herodian times, but with the addition of decorative motifs that are plainly Jewish, for example, the palm and bunch of grapes (symbols of fecundity), the acanthus, and rosettes. Traditional motifs are found in the mosaic floors, on tombs, sarcophagi, and ossuaries, as in Beth-shearim and in eastern and northern Jerusalem. Where the same motifs, as in Shafaram, also bear symbolic invocations of Christ, they indicate both continuity of the same culture and distinctive Jewish-Christian elements. Galilee has provided the most numerous examples. Kaukabe ("Star") in Syria was a village inhabited by Ebionites and Nazarenes (a community whose name is derived from Nazareth), according to Epiphanius.

e. *Older Synagogues*

The best evidence of dynamic Jewish culture was the synagogues spread over the whole country between the second and eighth centuries A.D. The early type—besides the Herodian synagogues found at Masada and Herodion and an inscription from the synagogue of the Ophel—was mostly in Galilee during the second and third centuries. The main characteristic was the decorated facade flanked by three portals facing Jerusalem. As worshipers were not allowed to have their backs to Zion, they sat on benches stretching along the walls and facing each other. Only the elders and the *hazan* (cantor who stood before the Ark) faced the Holy City. The main hall was divided by two rows of columns along its length and one row along its width. The building was faced with wide stone slabs, and its walls were decorated by reliefs at times representing animals and, occasionally, human beings. The outstanding inner decoration was the frieze of the balcony. A court or portico stood outside the synagogue. The celebrated synagogues of Capernaum and Chorazin belong to the third and fourth centuries A.D.

310

PART XIX

A. PAULINE LETTERS

The most important source for relations between the Jews and the Jewish Christians outside of Palestine is Paul's Letters, as they were written at almost the same time as the events with which they deal. They are also the earliest literature in the New Testament canon. The letters were of a practical and occasional nature, responding to specific situations in the mission churches, affirming essential truths of the gospel, explaining mysteries of the faith, coping with problems of policy and practice, answering critics, and exhorting the faithful. Paul had established the legitimacy of Gentile Christianity at the Council of Jerusalem (ca. A.D. 48) and subsequently had spread the gospel in Galatia, Asia Minor, Macedonia, and Achaia in Greece. Whether Jewish Christians or Gentiles, these new converts were often in need of guidance about basic issues, for example, the proper observance of the Lord's Supper, the return of Jesus, organizational matters, and lines of authority. The letters actually served a wider audience and larger purposes than originally intended and were saved, circulated, and ultimately assembled as a vivid witness to the life of the churches outside of Palestine and the genius of the great missionary apostle. They are historically of the greatest value for the light they shed on the life, customs, and problems of the early Christian communities. In them are defined the major theological issues confronting the church—the conflict with Judaism over the status of Jesus and the place of the Law in the emerging community. While Paul's views are definitely his own, and he makes no effort to give a balanced treatment of the issues, the great debates in the early church come alive in his letters.

The letters can be grouped by their approximate dates, between A.D. 50 –64, as follows:

1 and 2 Thessalonians, in which Paul defends his mission against Jewish opposition. The setting is Corinth between A.D. 50 and 52, after his second journey.

Galatians, written to his followers in Iconium, Lystra, Derbe, and Antioch in Pisidia. Again Paul is mainly concerned to defend himself against the claim of the "Judaizers" (Jewish Christians of Jerusalem) that Gentiles must be circumcised to become Christians.

1 and 2 Corinthians, written from Ephesus during Paul's third journey. Paul rebukes the Corinthians for their divisions, calls on them for unity, and gives them instructions regarding belief and practice.

Romans, written to the church at Rome before he ever visited there, is more in the nature of a theological treatise or formal presentation of his understanding of the meaning of the Gospel and the significance of Jesus Christ.

Philippians, Colossians, Philemon, written during Paul's imprisonment (perhaps in Rome, perhaps in Ephesus, ca. A.D. 60–64, though scholars are

Chester Beatty papyrus of Galatians 6:10—Philippians 1:1; early 3rd c.

311

divided as to the exact dates). The letter to Philippians describes his condition and his hopes for release, and in Colossians Paul sets out his philosophy of religion.

Ephesians and the Pastoral Epistles—1 and 2 Timothy, and Titus—traditionally have been attributed to Paul, but the attribution is questioned by many scholars. E. J. Goodspeed has suggested that Ephesians was written by a follower of Paul, taking the letter to the Colossians as a model and giving a summary of Pauline thought. The Pastorals, a later collection of letters, show the influence of some of the other letters. E. F. Scott believes that they were edited by a Paulinist from some genuine fragments and published under Paul's name.

1. THESSALONIANS, THE EARLIEST DOCUMENT IN THE NEW TESTAMENT

Paul's oldest surviving letter (and so the earliest document in the New Testament) is 1 Thessalonians; the point of origin probably was Corinth in the early 50s A.D., after his second journey. On his second campaign, Paul had crossed over from Troas to Macedonia and then preached in Thessalonica (modern Salonica), Beroea, and Athens. He had been joined in Athens by Timothy, who had brought a report from Thessalonica. Paul's letter is in response to that situation. He praises the Thessalonians for their constancy and warns them against faintheartedness, fair-weather loyalty, and sexual immorality of the kind popular in Greece and condemned by Judaism. He defends his mission against the Jewish-Christian opposition and closes with a word of encouragement for those who were bereaved and are in mourning.

Another letter to the Thessalonians, 2 Thessalonians, is included in the New Testament canon, but many scholars question its authenticity.

2. GALATIANS

The most spirited of Paul's letters was addressed to the Galatians, his Gentile followers at Iconium, Lystra, Derbe, and Antioch in Asia Minor. Some Jewish Christians from Jerusalem had come among these Gentile converts, claiming that Paul's gospel was illegitimate and that he discouraged his converts from observing the traditional Jewish Law. They claimed that a Gentile had to be circumcised before he could be accepted as a follower of the Messiah, Christ.

In defending himself against these "Judaizers," whose doctrine differed from his, Paul explained that his own apostleship was "from God and not man." Then, in chapter 2, he described the conference at Jerusalem that he and Barnabas had attended, accompanied by Titus, an uncircumcised Gentile. In his debate with the apostles Peter and James, Paul used Titus as a test case of a bona fide Christian though uncircumcised. If Titus was accepted, and it was impossible to deny his qualifications and the manifest presence of the Holy Spirit in his life, then concerns about adherence to

Jewish Law, especially circumcision, were irrelevant to the main issue, the new creature in Christ. While agreeing with Paul in principle, the church leaders attempted to smooth over the differences between Paul and those who insisted on adherence to the Law of Moses on the part of all Christians and imposed a compromise solution (Acts 15) requiring minimal observance on the part of Gentiles, so as not to offend the sensibilities of the Jewish Christians. As a temporary expedient the decision may have been successful in keeping the diverse groups under one roof, but the dynamics of the situation did not favor compromise. Given the potential for Gentile conversions and the extraordinary skill and drive of Paul and his associates, the issue was bound to become more and more acute for the Jewish-Christian component of the church, and the ultimate triumph of Pauline doctrine on the subject could hardly have been in doubt. No hindrance should or could be placed in the way of the Gentiles for whose salvation Christ had died, and their entry into the church in large and increasing numbers was evidence of the overriding power of the Holy Spirit in bringing new things to pass, but it also shifted the balance of power and decision away from the original Jewish-Christian community to the new Gentile majority. For a while they lived side by side symbiotically and sympathetically, but in the end the Jewish Christians were engulfed.

3. CORINTHIANS

When Paul reached Ephesus on his third journey, word came to him of trouble in Corinth due to factional disputes. He had apparently addressed the Corinthians earlier (2 Corinthians is thought to contain parts of more than one letter), and he now rebuked them for their divisions and spelled out the official doctrine of the Lord's Supper and the apostolic testimony to the Resurrection, along with personal advice on the subject of marriage and private morality. The letters reveal the acute problems of the community and Paul's methods in handling them (1 Cor. 1:10 ff.).

The statements in 1 Corinthians 15:3–8 and Galatians 1:11–17 reflect essential components of the apostolic preaching, which may be culled from the Gospels and Acts. The proclamation of the Good News included the following points: (a) the age of fulfillment has dawned; (b) this has taken place through the ministry, death, and resurrection of Jesus; (c) by virtue of the Resurrection, Jesus has been exalted at the right hand of God; (d) the Holy Spirit in the church is the sign of Christ's present power and glory; (e) the Messianic Age will shortly reach its consummation in the return of Christ; and (f) an appeal for repentance, the offer of forgiveness, and the promise of salvation are extended.

4. BACKGROUND

a. *An Inimical Graffito*

The Christian doctrine that the Son of God became the means of salvation of mankind through his crucifixion was unacceptable both to the

Jews, to whom it was a "stumbling block" (1 Cor. 1:23), and the Gentiles, to whom the idea of God suffering the ignominious death of a felon appeared ludicrous. Statements to this effect appeared in polemics against Christians. A graphic illustration of the hatred evoked at times by the new faith was found in one of the guardrooms of the Roman imperial palace, the Palatine, in Rome—a crude third century A.D. graffito showing a man kneeling to a crucified figure with an ass's head, worshiping his god. Similar calumnies regarding the worship of an ass had already been uttered by the enemies of Judaism in the Hellenistic period.

Bronze mirror from Azor; 11th c. B.C.

b. *Mirrors*

Before glass, backed with tinfoil, began to reflect a clear image in later centuries, common bronze mirrors were used in Palestine, and they reflected imperfectly the features of those looking into them, as expressed in Paul's immortal metaphor: "For now we see in a mirror, darkly ..." (1 Cor. 13:11–12).

c. *Aretas*

The Aretas referred to in 2 Corinthians 11:32 is Harethat IV, well known from coins and inscriptions bearing his name, found at Avdat in the Negeb. Paul hid from the Nabatean rulers of Damascus, whose kingdom extended from the Negeb to Syria.

5. PHILIPPIANS, COLOSSIANS, EPHESIANS, AND PHILEMON

The Epistles are also known as "the letters of the captivity," because they were written during Paul's imprisonment. In general, there are two views of their composition date, one which associates them with his imprisonment in Rome from A.D. 60 to 64, and the other which looks to an earlier imprisonment in Ephesus, which lasted for two years.

The first three letters contain some of the loftiest teaching in the New Testament as they define once and for all the nature of the Christian life. Philippians is the most intimate and affectionate of them, as Paul tells his friends of his condition and his hope of release. He then describes his experience of oneness with Christ and admonishes them to preserve their unity: "for me to live is Christ ..." (Phil. 1:21; 2:1; 3:7, 13–14).

Roman calumny suggesting the worship of an ass; drawn in a palace guardroom

Colossians, Ephesians, and Philemon are linked together by the mention of Onesimus and Archippus in Philemon and Colossians, and Tychicus (the Messenger) in Ephesians and Colossians.

Ephesus was the center of one of Paul's most extended and successful campaigns. He established a firm, loyal community there and made many friends. Nevertheless, the Epistle to the Ephesians is a general tract and does not reflect Paul's close attachment to the church there. It should be noted that the best and earliest manuscripts do not have the word "Ephesians," and it is widely believed among scholars that it was not originally addressed to the Ephesians but to another church; or it may have been a circular letter that was passed from church to church. Many scholars also feel that the letter was written by a follower of Paul, rather than by the apostle himself.

Colossians is similar to Ephesians in many ways, emphasizing Christ's role and status as *Kosmokrator* ("ruler of the universe") and as head of the church, but there is a special emphasis in the latter on false Gnostic teaching that has penetrated the church at Colossae. Paul opposes the esoteric, elitist pretensions of the Gnostics with the true knowledge of God revealed in Jesus Christ. He points to the central experience of the believer, who achieves reconcilation with God by dying and rising with Christ. This pattern reflects the vocabulary and some of the teachings of the mystery cults, including those of Jewish Christians.

Paul authenticated his letters by adding a "salutation in his own hand," as did other letter writers whose epistles have been preserved on papyrus. An example of a letter written in two hands is one dated 24th August, A.D. 66, on behalf of a peasant to a governor; the main part is written in a formal scribal hand, with additions in another less elegant script.

The letter to Philemon, while very short, is an important and intriguing document. It is the only personal letter in the Pauline corpus, being addressed to the owner of a runaway slave, Onesimus, whom Paul had converted in Rome and whom he was now sending back to Philemon with this message. Paul has no revolutionary political objective such as abolishing slavery. On the contrary, he insists on obedience to the law; Onesimus must return to his master. At the same time, a new element has been introduced into the relationship—Christianity—that should effect a profound change in attitude and behavior on the part of both men. The operative words are love and brotherhood. While ostensibly they remain master and slave, in fact they become brothers in Christ and must demonstrate this fact in their lives.

6. THE NEW TEMPLE

The wide diffusion of the idea of a new temple as an early Christian theme is indisputable. There are many passages in the New Testament that identify the new temple with the Jewish-Christian community. Paul lectures the Corinthians about the new temple as if it were a basic well-known feature of early Christian theology (1 Cor. 3:16; 6:19; Eph. 2:21). Moreover, the first Epistle of Peter expresses a similar viewpoint (1 Pet. 2:5). Similar allusions to this doctrine appear in extracanonical Christian literature that reflects the Jewish-Christian theology. The Ephesians are addressed by Ignatius, bishop of Antioch, as "temple-bearers." The extracanonical Epistle of Barnabas devotes chapter 16 to the way in which the Jewish-Christian community has taken the place of the old temple by becoming a spiritual temple being built for the Lord. Another of the early witnesses to the new temple is the Didache, whose allusions to the theology of the new temple amplify the material in 1 Peter; that is, the eucharist of the Didache community is a sacrifice for which new rites of spiritual purification are required.

7. ROMANS

Romans is unique in the Pauline canon in that it was written, probably from Corinth about A.D. 56, to a church neither founded nor yet visited by the apostle. It falls into three major sections: Chapters 1–11 comprise a treatise on the need for salvation through Christ. Chapters 12–15:13 give practical directives for living a Christian life. Chapters 15:14–16:27 consist of personal messages and salutations.

According to Paul, sin and death entered the world through the first man, Adam (5:12–14), but righteousness and life have been brought into the world through Christ (5:15–21). The central importance of Adam in the development of Christology is characteristic of Jewish-Christian thought, as we saw in the symbolism of Adam's Chapel at the Church of the Holy Sepulchre.

The term "righteousness" is used by him in the special sense of a satisfactory relationship with God: a righteous man is one who will be found "not guilty" (*saddiq* in Hebrew) at the Last Judgment. This, in a quintessential way, illustrates the unbroken line of thought that runs through Hassidean doctrine, Essenism, the Dead Sea Scrolls, and Jewish Christianity, as shown in the previous chapters.

Throughout the Pauline letters two Pauls seem to be revealed: Paul the practical preacher of the gospel and Paul the theologian. Romans is not a manual of Pauline doctrine. It is an attempt to clear up the main problems of the Jewish-Gentile confrontation within the early Christian church and the friction between synagogue and church or, put into other words, the relationship between Jew and Gentile in the new dispensation and the conflict between ancestral Jewish Law and faith in Christ as a means of achieving "righteousness."

8. THE LOGIA AS COLLECTIONS FOR THE "SAINTS"

The core group of early Christians in and around Jerusalem symbolized the whole movement in their lives of devotion and faithfulness. Their coreligionists in the Diaspora recognized it as their duty to supply the needs of the mother church in Jerusalem. Paul went to great lengths to raise funds for the support of the Jerusalem community, which, in his time, was small and living in hostile surroundings. Collections for the "saints" in Jerusalem are referred to in Romans 15:26 and in 1 Corinthians 16:1, where they are called *logia*. The same term is used in the ostracon dated 4th August, A.D. 63, in which a Gentile Greek, Psenamunis, the son of Pekysis, acknowledges receiving four drachmas, one obolus, as a contribution for the worship of Isis. Collections of this type were a common practice in antiquity.

9. TIMOTHY AND TITUS

The three letters to Timothy and Titus are called the Pastorals, because they ostensibly carry instructions from Paul to his two younger associates concerning their work as pastors or bishops of their congregations. General scholarly opinion, however, holds that the letters are not compositions of Paul, but of a later writer who had adopted parts of an authentic letter and adapted and applied them to the circumstances of his own day, using the name and authority of the great apostle after his death. They lack the color and fire of authentic letters by Paul, but they share his outlook and much of his theology. Perhaps the proper conclusion is that they are Pauline in character and spirit, but are not literally by Paul himself.

10. ADMINISTRATION BY THE BISHOPS AND DEACONS

The early church required the appointment of officials charged with the management and administration of the common property of its members for the benefit of the community (Acts 6:1–6). They were called *diakonoi*, "servants," and their qualifications are laid down in 1 Timothy 3:8. The *episkopoi*, "overseers" or "bishops," were appointed in larger communities (Acts 20:17, 28). There were several of them at Philippi and at Ephesus. This organization developed gradually over the years, but all were expected to qualify by holiness of character as well as competence in handling their duties.

11. PHILEMON: WHAT WERE THE PRIMITIVE AND DOMESTIC CHAPELS LIKE?

The chapel in the house of Philemon is reminiscent of those used in the early Jewish-Christian communities. The modest worship centers were located generally in the interiors of private houses. They were grouped around a courtyard in the prevailing Mediterranean style and enclosed on all sides. A third century A.D. Jewish-Christian chapel of this type was uncovered at Dura-Europos on the Euphrates. It was indistinguishable from the houses around it (see diagram) and consisted of a chapel with walls covered by wall paintings (preserved in Damascus), a big room for the love-meal (*agape*) of the community, and an assembly hall with a seat for the bishop.

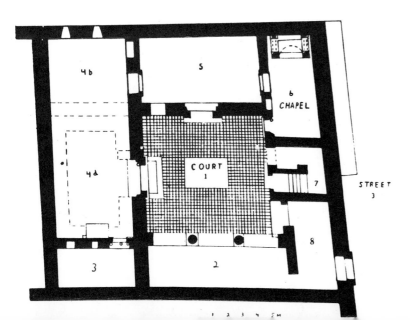

Diagram of the domestic church of Dura-Europos

B. CATHOLIC OR GENERAL EPISTLES

The seven final letters of the New Testament, James, 1 and 2 Peter, 1, 2, and 3 John, and Jude, are more general in character than the epistles attributed to Paul and are generally assigned to the late first century A.D.

1. THE OVERALL POLITICAL BACKGROUND

Postapostolic Christianity (following the days of Peter and Paul) had moved eastward and northward into Asia Minor and Greece, and the congregations were concentrated in that area. At the same time, Jewish nationalism had focused attention on the land and its political liberation, thus drawing Jewish interest and effort back to Palestine. Both church and synagogue had to adjust their thinking in the light of changing conditions and different pressures. Jewish Christians, especially, had to make agonizing decisions about their identity: as they saw the Jewish community move in one direction and the Christian in another, they had to decide to which one they belonged, whereas earlier they could participate in both successfully and be Jews and Christians at once. Now with the Jewish community closing ranks in the face of the great enemy, Rome, there wasn't room for divergent groups like Christians, and with Christianity becoming increasingly Gentile in makeup, the Jewish Christians felt more and more isolated.

During this period, there remained the serious problem of how the primitive church was to define its relations to Judaism on the one hand and the Roman authorities on the other. These difficulties became even more acute toward the end of the century. The religious and social tensions of this period are reflected in the Epistles of James, 2 Peter, and Jude. These writings react against the current surge of Jewish nationalism, and they condemn contemporary revolutionary tendencies. They prescribe instead a policy of submission to the established authorities, not because they approve of them, but because they have been ordained by God, and any change must be instituted by God. Besides, the time is short, and there is no need to engage in seditious or revolutionary activities. God will overwhelm the kingdoms of the world and replace them with his own realm. In the meantime Christians must be obedient and suffer patiently whatever befalls them, as true disciples of Jesus. The inequities of this world are to be rectified by God and his Messiah, not by violence or "zeal" as the revolutionary spirit was called. There is a strong family resemblance to the political quietism of the original Hassidim of the second century B.C., as reflected in the book of Daniel. The success of the Maccabees had changed quietism to activism on the part of most Jews, but the Essenes, for example, remained faithful to the older ideals. Early Christians followed the same pattern, guided by Jesus and his disciples.

It will be remembered that the closest analogy to the new faith and piety taught by Jesus is not to be found in the orthodox tradition, whether in the Temple cult or in the theological discussions of the rabbis. It stems rather from the apocalyptic-pietistic movement that in the third and second centuries B.C. found expression in the book of Daniel and in apocalyptic intertestamental writings and attitudes. These were represented in the days of Jesus by fervently messianic congregations, including the movement of John the Baptizer.

2. CONTEMPORARY SOCIAL AND RELIGIOUS CONSIDERATIONS

The opposition current among the early Christians to the status quo can be traced to a variety of causes and found a variety of expressions:

a. Fundamentally, many felt that the eschatological consummation or "end of the age" had not happened (Paul, who heralded it, had discussed it in his early writings, 1 and 2 Thessalonians). "Eschatological impatience led to social disorder. Dissatisfied believers materialized eschatology, hoping to have final triumph and joy of the faithful realized in empirical forms on earth." The poorer classes wanted the new church, the Jewish-Christian communal group, to improve their status. The groups seemed to be linked with popular fraternities, and hopes of another and better life were understood by many in a materialistic way, here and now.

b. Jewish influence on the Jewish-Christian community was always an important factor. The Jewish presence affected early Christians both positively and negatively for two reasons: (1) The Jewish-Christian movement was invigorated and enriched by new Jewish recruits; (2) Judaism was still a religion officially recognized by Rome. This privilege was not accorded by law to Gentile Christianity, which might be persecuted, and later was, under the severe Roman legislation against fraternities. Hence Jewish Christians could find shelter under the roof of the synagogue where they would not be persecuted. Jews were allowed to affirm "atheism" in the sense of noncommitment to the pagan deities, if they paid the annual tax required by the emperor, but Christians were not. Thus, Flavius Clement and his wife, Domitilla, both relatives of the emperor, were accused of atheism according to the historians, Suetonius and Dio; Domitilla's catacomb in Rome shows that she was a Christian convert.

The existence of nationalistic anti-Roman movements in this period, inspired by the Palestinian situation and waves of zealotry in the Diaspora, is only too evident from extracanonical apocalypses such as Baruch and IV Ezra (so named after historic figures mentioned in the Old Testament).

c. Finally, many contemporary Romans had succumbed to the spell of Stoic and Cynic philosophy with their ideals of freedom and equality.

All these factors were operative among circles in the Roman establishment where strong opposition to Domitian was felt, particularly in the senatorial party. In fact, fraternities and societies, including the Christians, were encouraged by influential Romans. It is true that such corporate propaganda, called *ambitus,* was condemned officially, but it flourished nevertheless. As the conflict between state and opposition grew, the poor Christian community was apparently compromised by its implied connection with the opposition; it could thus be led into unchristian arrogance and consequent persecution. It was the duty of leading Christian personalities such as the authors of the Epistles dealt with in our study to remind their followers of the fact that genuine wisdom is humble, not impatient.

In sum, the General Epistles contain many expressions that bring to mind the Dead Sea Scrolls, as well as the apocalyptic pietism of books like Daniel and the extracanonical works similar to it. Furthermore, while differing from the Pauline epistles in other respects, they agree with Paul in condemning political actions on the part of Christians.

3. CONTRAST BETWEEN THE EPISTLES AND REVELATION

There is a difference in attitude toward the constituted authorities, but neither the General Epistles nor Revelation advocates violent resistance even in the face of extreme provocation or persecution. While the writers of the General Epistles express neutrality or moderate support for the Roman regime (as does Paul), the author of Revelation spares no language in condemning the Roman empire for its blasphemy in usurping the place of God and in forcing the faithful to accord divine honors to the emperor, violating both conscience and truth. Yet his counsel was submission to this ordeal, which would not only win for the martyrs an eternal crown of glory, but also trigger a divine response at the appointed time, when the new age would be consummated in the unending reign of God and the Lamb.

4. THE EPISTLE OF JAMES

The Epistle of James is addressed to the Christian constituency at large, including both Jewish and Gentile components. It is in the form of an allocution from the head of the church to its members and leaders, emphasizing basic Christian virtues and the prime importance of patient endurance (1:21; 5:7–11). The basic theme of the book may be outlined as follows:

a. Patience in the midst of afflictions, which leads to steadfastness and perfection. Wisdom obtained through prayer. Riches are nothing to boast about. Perseverance in tribulations brings blessedness; man's lust is the cause of tribulations. Importance of being a doer of the word (Chapter 1).

b. The impropriety of currying favor with the rich. Worthlessness of a faith not practiced (Chapter 2).

c. Dangers of a poisoned tongue. Humble living (Chapter 3).

d. Combativeness of the recipients. Business ethics. Judgment on the unrighteous rich (4:1–5:6).

e. Patient waiting for Christ's return: a manual of discipline; singing and praying; the healing of the sick. The salvation of apostates (5:7–20).

While the Epistle in its present form and language is to be dated in the subapostolic period, it contains many primitive elements that take us back to the earliest period of the church. Some of the sayings are similar to the teachings of Jesus recorded in the synoptic Gospels and usually assigned to the Q source. The sayings in James derive from the same oral tradition and are in a form that reflects the Semitic original. At the same time, the organization of the community addressed is distinguished by the authority of a committee of the elders, an institution inherited from later Second Temple times, when the elders governed the synagogues. This arrangement conformed also to the organizational chart and operational procedures in the first Jewish-Christian congregations of Jerusalem and Antioch.

5. THE EPISTLES OF PETER

a. *The First Epistle*

The epistle known as 1 Peter is a message to Christians in northern, central, and western Asia Minor, admonishing them to be meek, patient, and ready to endure suffering in time of tribulation. On the basis of the data provided it is not possible to pinpoint the occasion or the immediate circumstances; scholars have proposed dates of composition anywhere from the 60s to the 90s of the first century. Although the epistle is attributed to the apostle Peter as the principal author, the actual writer or amanuensis is said to be Silvanus, an early disciple and companion of Paul.

It is supposed that Peter provided the substance of the epistle, but that the precise language and form as well as the theological nuances were supplied by the secretary. Other scholars hold that it is a "Pauline" composition throughout, perhaps composed by Silvanus, but mistakenly associated with Peter. It is characterized by a shift away from the Jewish-Christian position and toward Gentile-Christian views. It has been suggested further that the epistle was intended to be read to new Christians at baptismal and confirmation services. In this respect, 1 Peter is comparable to the Epistle to the Ephesians, which also appears to have been intended as greeting and admonition to recently baptized Christians.

First Peter calls attention to the incalculable value of the extraordinary gift that his audience has received through the gospel:

(1) This emphasizes the responsibility of those baptized for the grace received (1:1–4:6) and gives admonitions to avoid malice and show loyalty to the authorities; maxims for daily living; fearlessness, evangelical open-mindedness, and readiness to suffer.

(2) The love and steadfastness of the whole congregation (4:7–5:14) in hospitality, cooperation, perseverance in persecution, devotion of the elders to the flock, trust in God, steadfastness, and a wish for peace.

b. *The Second Epistle of Peter*

The Second Epistle attributed to Peter was written by a follower in the name of the Prince of Apostles. In it, the apostle warns Christians to be steady and to avoid corruption in the face of persecution (perhaps under Domitian, ca. A.D. 95); it is addressed to the same churches in Asia Minor that are referred to in the First Epistle, but the Second Epistle is widely regarded as the latest book in the New Testament and clearly belongs to the postapostolic age.

First Epistle of Peter 5:12–14 (Papyrus Bodmer; 2nd–3rd c. A.D.)

321

Its purpose is to admonish the communities to be steadfast and to warn them against deceivers. Of these two themes, chapters 1 and 3 discuss the first and chapter 2 deals with the second. An interesting passage in 1:19 compares prophecy to a "lamp shining in a dark place until the day dawns," a reference to a type of lantern suspended by chains from a handle.

In the second chapter, the theme of deception, of seducers exploiting the Christians, deserves attention. It would appear that senators and other leading aristocrats opposed to the power-hungry emperor, Domitian, used church leaders to gain political adherents among the Christians. This involved political and social propaganda, along with financial remuneration and specious promises of preferment to the naive and unwary Christians. These movements and organizations were vigorously combated by the authorities who, at the same time, persecuted Christians as participants in subversion. To what extent Christians made common cause with the political forces aligned against the emperor we do not know, but the author of the epistle opposes such an unholy alliance. Bad as the emperor may be, Christians are called upon to submit, to obey, and to set an example to all others of perseverance under trials and tribulations, in imitation of the Lord Jesus. Only in this way will the church be seen as true and faithful and be exonerated from false charges. The Gospel must not be perverted or misused for the sake of political propaganda, no matter how great the provocation or the possible rewards of direct action.

6. THE EPISTLE OF JUDE

This short epistle contains warnings by a Palestinian Jewish Christian against deceivers and exhortations to preserve faith, love, and hope. The author of the Epistle is identified as Jude, the brother of James. It would be natural to recognize in James the head of the Jerusalem church and the brother of Jesus. Even if this were the intention of the writer, it is not stated explicitly, and in any case may be doubted. It is generally believed that the work dates around the end of the first century A.D. and is addressed to Jewish Christians. There is a literary relationship between Jude and chapter 2 of Second Peter, but the question of dependence is unresolved. Both may have borrowed from the same original source.

A most instructive element in Jude is the citation of 1 Enoch 1:9. The book of Enoch was not regarded by either Jewish or Christian councils as canonical, yet Jude clearly treats it as inspired scripture. In the pietist schools Enoch the patriarch, the "seventh from Adam," was considered one of the special friends of God, and an authentic prophet. The author of Jude therefore does not hesitate to cite the extracanonical text of 1 Enoch 1:9 in support of his warnings, since he regards the quotation in question as an ancient prophecy of the destruction of the "teacher of heresy" as in 2 Peter.

7. THE EPISTLES OF JOHN

a. First Epistle

The theme of both the first and second Epistles of John is the identity of God and Christ. If one asks what God is like, then the answer can be found in Jesus. The first Epistle of John is close to the Fourth Gospel in style, vocabulary, and thought, and many scholars assume that the author is the same. Some, however, postulate a disciple of the Evangelist or a member of the "Johannine" school.

b. *The Debate with Gnosticism and Its Mysteries*

The epistle is aimed especially against that deviation from orthodox church doctrine known as Gnosticism. The term covers a variety of belief-systems and serves as a catch-all for many different groups, but an essential common ingredient is the possession by an elite of special, secret knowledge (*Gnosis*). The promise held out by different groups to new adherents was to provide this Gnosis, which could only be secured by initiation into certain rites and the practice of an equally secret discipline. Depending upon the teaching of a particular leader, Gnostics might be ascetic puritans or unrestrained libertines. Some of the second-century Gnostics were able speculative thinkers. There was a proto-Gnostic element in Judaism and in Christianity, especially in eschatologically and apocalyptically centered groups. For them the pivotal factor was the secret or mystery of the last days, not only the timetable of divine action, but the sequence of events and the identity of the principal participants. Knowledge of the secret was reserved to the faithful few and was in certain cases unobtainable, that is, according to the Gospels, not even the Son knows the hour when the end comes. Paul also makes much of the special knowledge of salvation that belongs to the Christian. But none of this is Gnosticism in the developed sense of the second-century Gnostic groups that combined dualism (the doctrine of two gods—one good, one evil) and docetism (that spirit and flesh cannot be combined, and that Jesus only appeared to be a man). To the author of 1 John, Gnosticism is the great threat to the life and faith of the church, and he combats it by restating the Gospel in the language of ethical and metaphysical opposites often used by Gnostics, but denying their tenets.

The Gnostics denied the earthly existence of Jesus and, consequently, refused to accept the church's doctrine of Incarnation, that is, that God had appeared in the flesh in the person of Jesus Christ. For his answer to this contention, the apostle turned back to the earliest phases of Jewish Christianity and reminded his readers of the apostolic witness to Christ and, furthermore, of Christ's historical existence and his human roots in the Jewish community. He emphasized the reality of Jesus as the Messiah-Christ and admonished his readers to live in the "fellowship of love."

c. *Contents of 1 John*

The central theme is stated in the first verses of the epistle (1:1–4), which emphasize the writer's personal experience of fellowship with God through his son, Jesus Christ. The development of this theme centers around three main concepts: the "fellowship" between God and Christians within the religious community; "sin," which separates man from God (1:5 –10) and "obedience to God's commandments," which is the only sure way of drawing closer to God. This appears in a number of verses (2:1–6, for example) and is linked with John's reiteration of the commandment to love one's brother (2:7–17). In 2:18–19, the author resumes the discussion, elaborating the threat of the "antichrist," who appears in various forms in contemporary apocalyptic literature and is the antithesis of the Messiah. John bases his refutation of the Gnostics on the argument that to deny Jesus is to deny God. Section 2:26–29 is a recapitulation of the warning against the false teachers who deny this truth.

Chapter 3:1–12 takes up the moral argument. Knowing that Christian salvation is an accepted fact to his audience, the author of John uses the mystical argument that since Christians are God's children and are destined to be transformed wholly into his likeness, they can be sure that they will see God. Christians who have been "born of God" cannot sin. The seal of the transformation is in the Spirit, which is the means and the reward of obedience to God's commandments (3:13–14).

Chapter 4 opens with a paragraph (verses 1–6) on true and false inspiration. The apostolic church believed that prophecy had been revived and that their brethren could be inspired by the Spirit to declare hidden truths. Nevertheless, not all inspiration and all spirits necessarily come from God. The church had found that there was also a spirit of perversity (that of antichrist) abroad in the world, and the author of John explains how to distinguish between true and false spirits (4:6).

Johannine teaching rarely refers to a second coming of Christ. "He who has the son has life" proclaims 1 John 5:12, but that life is something to be lived in the present world. It is not postponed to a "future life" and another world. The believer has received the "eternal life" of Christ, has already triumphed over death and lives in the messianic age.

Second John can be described as a miniature edition (thirteen verses only) of 1 John, for every phrase in it occurs in the larger work as well and the theme is the same: Christian love as the true road to salvation and the need to guard against deceivers and false teachers.

d. *Third John and Diotrephes*

Unlike 1 and 2 John, which deal with doctrinal questions, 3 John is a rebuke to a church leader, Diotrephes, for his insubordination, not his theology. By A.D. 110, the "elders" were no longer the rulers of the church, but had now become the advisers of the bishop who enjoyed a preeminent and all-powerful position. Diotrephes, as bishop, claimed exclusive jurisdiction over the church in Ephesus, whereas John, "the Elder," exercised a traditional authority within the larger district. The title that John uses of himself, "the Elder," seems to have been used at first and for a long time in the sense of one of the original apostolic witnesses. He had authority over the church to which he was writing, although at the time the original pattern of itinerant missionaries was coming to an end, to be replaced by a system of settled local ministries. The writer of 2 John wanted missionaries excluded for fear of their subversive teaching. Third John calls for them to be received and helped. The letter's condemnation was presumably connected with Diotrephes' rejection of these missionaries.

PART XX

A. EPISTLE TO THE HEBREWS

A number of extracanonical writings that date from subapostolic times during the late first and early second centuries A.D. are attributed to the Jewish-Christian community. The only writings of this type included in the New Testament are the Epistle to the Hebrews and Revelation, which express the thought of new Christians belonging to the Jewish milieu.

We do not know who wrote Hebrews. Its doctrine, style, and time rule out Paul. It was apparently written in the latter part of the first century A.D. to encourage Jewish Christians who were enduring bitter persecution and suffering, perhaps at the time of Domitian. Efforts to ascertain the specific community to which the Epistle was addressed have been advanced by the discovery of a third century Greek papyrus of the Epistle. It speaks of the Jewish manner of paraphrasing the Old Testament as a sort of *midrash* (or interpretative commentary on the text), which was also the practice of the Covenanters of Qumran. The Epistle may be understood as a circular letter addressed to Jewish Christians, since its message is worked out in familiar Old Testament terms. Its contents center around the traditional ritual of the Temple, notably the Day of Atonement, comparing its sacrifice of the propitiatory goat to that of Christ, who offered himself in

Greek papyrus of the Epistle to the Hebrews (3rd c. A.D.)

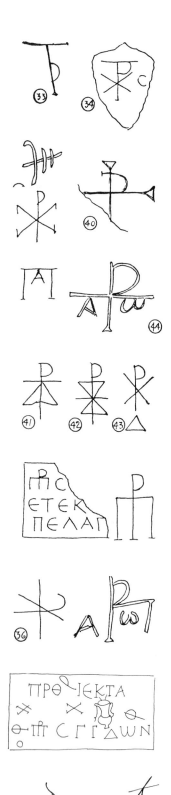

the heavenly sanctuary. The Jewish Christians who were concerned about such priestly and cultic matters needed instruction in the sacrificial role of Jesus, which was different from the usual picture of a royal victorious messiah. Another important emphasis is the transition from the old covenant to a new one, an idea that was emphasized at Qumran. This leads to the climax of the book—the finality of Jesus and his message of salvation.

1. CONTENTS

The Epistle emphasizes the superiority of Jesus over all other beings. In 1:1-2, his superiority over the prophets is affirmed. After that Jesus is placed higher than the angels (1:3–2:18). Jesus, says Hebrews, deserved greater honor than Moses (3:3). Although he was a member of the tribe of Judah, the Epistle does not explicitly mention his descent from David. He could not be regarded as a priest in the ordinary sense (because priests were of the tribe of Levi), but he was a special high priest after the order of Melchizedek, the ancient model of the high-priesthood, which was superior to that of Aaron. He became himself the sacrifice for the sins of the world (chapters 5–7) and thus mediated a new and exalted covenant that

replaced the old and imperfect forerunner (8–10:18). Sacrifices ceased in any case after the destruction of the Temple in A.D. 70. Jesus' sacrifice of his own blood had redeemed men from their sins and made Jewish sacrifices of goats and bulls superfluous. Christ offered his body as a sacrifice, and he himself carried his own blood into the heavenly sanctuary (9:12), thereby reconciling God and his creatures.

The new relationship of the true believer rests on faith (10:12), a matter of belief beyond sight, as in the Johannine Gospel: blessed are those who believe even though they have not seen. The remainder of the Epistle encourages the faithful to endure suffering patiently, illustrating the teaching by examples drawn from biblical and nonbiblical tradition, such as the legendary death of the prophet Isaiah related in the extracanonical Ascension of Isaiah, a Jewish-Christian *midrash*. Isaiah was supposedly put to death by the paganizing King Manasseh of Judah (Ascension 10:19–11:37). Believers are exhorted to live in brotherly love, disdaining immorality or covetousness, loyal to their "leader" (chapter 13).

2. AFFINITY WITH THE DEAD SEA SCROLLS

Y. Yadin believes that the Epistle was addressed more specifically to descendants of sectarian Jews related to the community of Qumran, after

A.D. 70. A fundamental change must be presumed, however, since the Mosaic *torah* remained the foundation of the Qumran community for its faith and practice, along with their codified rules of Discipline, whereas for the community addressed in Hebrews, Jesus as Messiah—regarded as more glorious even than Moses—had already come. The Qumranites expected not only a kingly messiah from the House of David, but also a priestly messiah from the line of Aaron; these hopes were never fulfilled and nothing is known of the fate of the community. Hebrews, on the contrary, opens with the emphatic affirmation that the revelation that God gave in the past was only partial and has now been superseded by the full truth "spoken unto us by his Son."

In Hebrews we find a theological rationale for the termination of bloody sacrifices stipulated in the Law. Jesus' self-sacrifice is the full, final, and perfect offering that makes all further sacrifice futile and unnecessary. Here we have a deliberate break with the traditional Judaism of the Second-Temple period. But the Jewish community itself had to adjust to the termination of sacrifices when the Temple was destroyed by the Romans in A.D. 70. They did not try to maintain or revise such sacrifices but substituted prayers and good work, basing the decision on the words of the prophets who criticized severely the empty worship of the First Temple, with its multitude of animals and its rivers of oil. Thus Judaism and Christianity came essentially to the same conclusion about the proper mode of worship, but by different routes. In the end, Judaism retained, nevertheless, its vision of the Messiah to come, in contrast to Christianity with its crucified and resurrected Messiah.

Selected anchor symbols common to tombs in Palestine, or in the Jewish-Christian Priscilla catacombs in Rome. They were regarded as the sign of hope (Heb. 6:19–20)

3. ARCHAEOLOGICAL CONNECTIONS

We are indebted to Hebrews for one significant statement about the site of the crucifixion: "so Jesus also suffered outside the gate" (13:12). As to the garden where the tomb was, it stood in the immediate vicinity of the gibbet. Taken together with the testimony of the Gospels about the actual burial of Jesus, there seems to be a reliable basis for the traditional site of the Holy Sepulchre. Weighty archaeological questions remain, however, as discussed earlier, and a solution will depend upon further research and new discoveries.

a. *Heavenly Court*

Unlike Paul, Hebrews describes the saving effect of the death of Jesus in terms not so much of resurrection (as Paul does), as of his ascension as high priest into the innermost sanctuary of the heavenly temple, where he performs his act of intercession and enters at the right hand of God. This image is inherited from Old Testament eschatological traditions, among them Ezekiel's vision of the heavenly throne-chariots in chapter 1.

There is also a background in ancient mythological pictures brought to light by archaeological discovery, in which the high god is represented in

Opposite page: Symbols such as the plow, the ladder, the candelabrum, the water spurting from the arms of the monogram cross, seen on early Christian Roman epitaphs, resemble those found on ossuaries and walls of funerary buildings in Jerusalem. They are attributed to Jewish-Christian teachings. Such are the anchor and fish and signs from a Roman catacomb (epitaph of Licinia Amiata) and miscellaneous signs on other Roman catacombs

327

his heavenly palace surrounded and supported by lesser deities (cf. Job 1–2). The Ugaritic mythological texts give us vivid glimpses of the meetings of the gods. They were the members of the ancient pantheon who were transposed in later monotheistic theology into "angels" or servants of God. Yahweh, as king of the gods, holds court in the vision of the prophet Micaiah ben Imlah in 1 Kings 22:19–23, surrounded by his divine entourage of counsellors and servants, who station themselves in attendance upon the king. An echo is heard in Proverbs 22:29:

> "Do you see a man skillful in his work?
> he will stand before kings; he will not
> stand before obscure men."

Above all, the quality of glory in heaven signifies luminosity. In this connection, it is interesting to recall the early Jewish-Christian belief about the divine appearance at Bethlehem. The Bethlehem grotto became a symbol of passage from darkness to light, when a great star shone in the heavens.

b. *A Representation of the Tabernacle*

Hebrews conceives of Jesus as the minister of the true tabernacle (8:2), as opposed to the manmade Tabernacle that accompanied the Israelites in the desert. An early representation of the latter is found in the frieze of the synagogue at Capernaum. Here, as in the synagogue frescoes of Dura-Europos, we have a sanctuary mounted on wheels, suitable for transporting sacred objects from one place to another until it finally comes to rest in the Temple at Jerusalem.

The frieze from the synagogue of Capernaum represents the Tabernacle during its wanderings in the desert, namely, a shrine mounted on wheels. It corresponds to Roman carriages shaped like sanctuaries that served to transport images of the gods from one place to another

B. REVELATION (THE APOCALYPSE)

1. PURPOSE

The book of Revelation, like other apocalyptic Jewish-Christian writings, is optimistic and courageous in tone. The occasion is a crisis in the life of the church and the purpose is to deal with the apparent failure of the cause of God on earth. Confidence in the future is expressed by a forecast of the triumphal coming of Christ, the establishment of the rule of God in the world, and the final Day of Judgment. The general outline conforms to Daniel in the Old Testament, the little apocalypses in the New Testament, and extracanonical intertestamental writing, referred to earlier. Its contents, therefore, mix the terrestrial with the cosmic, the historical with the transcendental, the timely with the timeless, and it is often difficult to distinguish one from the other. Furthermore, the narrative is heavily disguised in symbolism of many kinds, deliberately made incomprehensible to all but insiders. It describes the impending downfall of the contemporary social and political structure, expressing the fervent conviction that the destruction of Roman power, which the author regarded as utterly corrupt, was at hand. The empire is depicted in its death throes, torn by internal dissensions and threatened by enemies without, the participants in the gory drama being presented as either the objects or the agents of divine wrath. In the end mankind will face a final judgment divided between the wicked, who are to perish, and the elect, who will be saved. Apart from the numerous, often obscure, allusions to contemporary politics and the struggle between those trying to hold on to power and those seeking it, the internal and external pressures on the Empire, there are signs and symbols pertaining to the basic convictions and ardent hopes of the faithful, signs which contain and communicate the essential Gospel for those who suffer greatly for their faith. Some of these symbols in graphic form have also been found and preserved in the region of the Seven Churches of the Apocalypse in Asia Minor, where Professors Bagatti and Testa discovered inscriptions, signs, and objects representing the five fundamental elements of the Jewish-Christian system of symbols in association with each other.

The book was written to a persecuted Jewish-Christian community outside of Palestine, most likely after the death of Nero in A.D. 68. The famous number of the beast 666 that is mentioned (13:18) is the numerical equivalent of the Hebrew letters in the words Nero Caesar. Each Hebrew letter has a numerical value, and in accordance with the system known as *gematria,* the number is used to designate the person or event intended so that the secret message will be understood only by the initiated. But Nero's persecution was confined to Rome, and many scholars are of the opinion that the book in its present form comes from a later date, while incorporating earlier material. Irenaeus (ca. A.D. 180) dates the book during the reign of Domitian, ca. A.D. 95, who was a cruel and capricious enemy of the Christians and persecuted them throughout the empire.

The Seven Churches of the Apocalypse in Asia Minor are symbolized by seven golden candelabra. Representations appear frequently on coins, reliefs of synagogues, and Jewish catacombs

329

The author of Revelation was a man named John (1:1–9, 22:8) traditionally thought to be the Apostle, one of the Twelve, who is also credited with composing the Fourth Gospel. Since John was a very common name, and since the book reports only that he lived on the island of Patmos in the Aegean Sea, a place of banishment, there is no way to specify his identity. The Greek of Revelation is quite unusual, bearing unmistakable signs of Semitic thought and imagery and justifying the conclusion that the author was a Jewish Christian steeped in the Hebrew-Aramaic tradition of the Old Testament and intertestamental literature. The book was a product of the tumultuous years surrounding the death of Nero, the disruption of the Empire (the year of the four emperors, A.D. 69), the climax of the Jewish war and the fall of Jerusalem, and the persecution of Christians. Whether it was written entirely in that period (ca. A.D. 69) or was later edited and revised in the light of a more extensive persecution under Domitian are matters to be considered.

2. CONTENTS

In the first chapter of Revelation, God is symbolically described as the *alpha* (A) and *omega* (Ω), the first and last letters of the Greek alphabet, implying the first and last things, as all the secrets of the universe can be expressed by these signs and all else between them.

After the Introduction (1:1–3) the Seer sends greetings (1:4–3:22) to the seven principal Christian churches of Asia Minor: Ephesus, Smyrna, Sardis, Pergamon, Philadelphia, Laodicea, Thyatira. They are described as "priests of their God," a figure used by Levitic sectaries. Their symbols were the seven stars, seven angels, and seven candelabra. These communities, which had existed since Hellenistic times, and their synagogues maintained their Jewish identity although some of them separated in time from the parent synagogue. The seven original synagogues bore the seven-branched candelabrum (menorah) of the Temple, the recognized symbol of Judaism from Herodian times, as well as other symbols since discovered in the excavations of Sardis. Numerous inscriptions in Smyrna attest to the importance and wealth of the synagogue into the third century A.D. In Revelation, however, the menorah is treated as the biblical symbol of divine light (Zech. 4).

Beyond that, these cities possessed splendid palaces, statuary, friezes, temples and other great public buildings, reflecting their great wealth. All these elements are alluded to in the allegorical visions of Revelation.

The Prologue in Heaven (4:1–5:14), clearly dependent on Ezekiel and more ancient materials, is followed by the allegorical vision of the seven seals (6:1–8:1) that can only be opened by the Lamb of God whose blood has redeemed mankind; whereupon he opens the seals and out come the four horsemen who symbolize violence and bloodshed. Then comes the vision of the Seven Trumpets that herald renewed destruction upon earth. The climactic disaster is the fall of Jerusalem, which is predicted. The transition from defeat and suffering to victory and joy is described in terms of the labor pains of a woman in childbirth, a necessary condition of the coming of the Messianic Age (8:2–11:19). The story of the heavenly woman and the child she bears (12) symbolizes the appearance of the messianic community, which is barely saved from destruction by divine intervention, and in turn will be triumphant and usher in the new age.

The vision of the beasts (13–14) underscores the persecution of the faithful (possibly in Nero's time) but is matched by the vision of the faithful in a heavenly choir. Renewed eschatological symbols appear with the Seven Bowls (15–16), the vision of Rome the "great harlot," the visions of Gog and Magog, and that of the Heavenly Jerusalem come down on earth (17:18–22:12).

3. SOME IMAGES OF REVELATION AND THEIR MATERIAL BACKGROUND

The reference to the writing upon the pillars of a temple (3:12) can be illustrated by archaeological evidence from many ancient sites in Palestine, Palmyra, and Asia Minor. Inscriptions on Galilean synagogues often record the donations of benefactors. A column in the synagogue of Capernaum bears such a dedication in Greek ("Herod, the son of Makimos, and his descendants") and another in Aramaic.

The figure of the scroll with the seven seals in 5:1, 6:1–8:5, that had to be broken one by one, is derived from the careful manner in which the ancients protected the contents of written documents from unauthorized eyes. Kings, bankers, merchants, and owners of estates used single or multiple sealings to safeguard their signatures, with the name of the witness recorded beside each. The implication is that the divine judgment against the world, written on the pages of the book with the seals, was to remain a secret until the appointed time and then the seals would be broken by the authorized person in the presence of witnesses.

a. *Accursed Rome*

Although this book expresses a very critical attitude toward the Roman empire, its government and social categories, nevertheless it differs markedly from the political rebellion of the contemporary Jewish Zealots. The roots of Jewish and Christian opposition to Rome were the same, namely Roman interference with the free exercise of religious conscience and the right and duty to worship the one true God. The pretensions of the Roman emperors were blasphemous and had to be resisted at all costs. The difference between Jew and Christian lay in the nature of that resistance and in the objective to be attained. While the Jewish community itself was divided on the subject (generally speaking the Diaspora remained loyal to Rome) and while the Palestinians revolted, the Christians in and out of Palestine were quiescent and suffered without forcible resistance. The Zealots aimed at establishing an independent state; Christians would

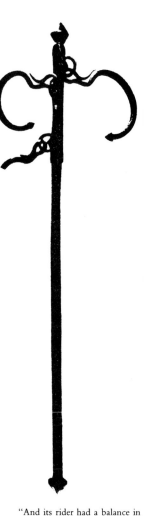

"And its rider had a balance in his hand" (Rev. 6:5–6). The normal balance used for weighing consisted of a bar and tongue and the suspended pair of scales. The balance here is symbolic in terms of measure or weight

A bronze incense shovel of the type found in excavations in Israel (2nd and 3rd c. A.D.)

be content with religious autonomy, leaving to God and his anointed the larger question of the destruction of the empire and the establishment of the divine realm.

b. *The Four Horses of the Apocalypse* (Chapters 6–8:5)

They symbolize the following: first, the rider of the white horse represents the Parthian cavalryman who could humble Rome; second, the rider on a red horse symbolizes the civil war that ravaged the Roman empire in A.D. 68/69, when the Romans would "kill one another" with the *spath,* the great cavalry sword; third, the rider of the black horse stands for famine that would result from the disruption of the economy as a result of the disturbance; and fourth, the last horseman symbolizes death, the summation of the vision.

The golden censer described in chapter 8 was either the closed type, which was swung at the end of a chain and has been adopted by the church, or the open type, which is more ancient and consisted of a small flat shovel on which glowing coals were heaped; the incense was either held in the hand or kept piled up in receptacles attached to upper corners of the shovel, from which it was taken between the fingers and thrown upon the coals.

The sign of the sixth angel pouring his bowls on the Euphrates (16:12) is a clear allusion to the Parthian (late Persian) kings of the East across the river. The prophecy was not fulfilled until much later: in A.D. 260 when Emperor Valerian was defeated after a Persian invasion.

c. *The Day of Judgment*

Armageddon (16:16), as is known, is the symbolic place of the last battle of the kings of this earth. The Greek form of Har-Megiddo (Mount Megiddo), it is one of the main strategic sites of Palestine in biblical times. It was in that area that the Israelites achieved a notable and decisive victory over the Canaanites (ca. 1125 B.C.) that is celebrated in the Song of Deborah (Judges 5). It is where King Josiah was defeated and killed by Pharaoh Necho in the seventh century B.C. and near Lejjun, where Emperor Hadrian established the camp of his Sixth Legion in the second century A.D. A Roman altar, marked "Legio VI Ferrata," was found there.

The appellation of "Babylon the Great" and "the woman on the seven mountains" (17:3–8) is a thinly disguised allusion to Rome, the great enemy of God, and the seven kings of the Empire, culminating in Nero or perhaps Domitian. It was customary to personify great cities of the ancient Greco-Roman world by female deities, such as the majestic Venus of Pompeii riding a chariot drawn by elephants, or the figure of Minerva leaning on a shield. These hieratic figures are reminiscent of the vision of "Babylon the Great." The fall of Babylon-Rome is linked to the failure of shipments of wheat from the granaries of the East, without which neither city nor empire could survive (18:17). The pulping of the grapes in Roman wine presses is a figure of bloodshed (19:15) and symbolizes the fate of those who oppose the will of God.

The overthrow of wicked Rome will be the signal for the inauguration of the thousand year reign of Christ. At the same time, the evil dragon will be chained and locked up in the bottomless pit. The imaginary lock can be exemplified by artifacts of the Judeo-Roman type found in Palestine (20:1).

d. *Jewish-Christian Symbols of Dura-Europos*

Then the Heavenly Jerusalem (21:10-12) will come down and take the place of the desecrated city; the concept is common to the latter days of the Second Temple, as is known from rabbinical sources, the mystic *Yerushalayim shel Maalah,* and, of course, the symbols of Jewish Christianity. Such a vision is depicted in the frescoes of the synagogue of Dura Europos on the Euphrates; they depict the Temple, generally patterned after Herod's monumental structure, with additional walls, gates, and decorations to enhance the splendor of the Heavenly City.

The synagogue of Dura-Europos, or at least its first building phases, dates apparently to the early part of the third century A.D. It was a small prayer-house, apparently Jewish Christian in character, hidden among private dwellings, with paintings of biblical scenes. During the second phase (first half of the third century) the building included a large court with three colonnades and a spacious prayer hall with a niche for the Ark on the southern wall facing Jerusalem. The reconstructed building stands today in the museum of Damascus, with its valuable representations of biblical and allegorical scenes, many of them explained by short biblical quotations in Greek. The paintings show foreign affinities with either Alexandrian or late Persian art, but are of particular interest to us for the symbolism expressed in early Jewish and Christian art. The most interesting representations are the facade of the Jerusalem Temple. Other items of interest are two Hebrew fragments of the second half of the second century A.D. that appear to be liturgical blessings after meals. J. L. Teicher maintains that they were eucharistic prayers (offered to consecrate elements in the Lord's Supper) related to those of the Didache (10:3–4).

The existence of such fragments indicates that Hebrew was used as a liturgical language in the Jewish-Christian church during the first centuries. This finding is corroborated first by the fact that the Hebrew text of the book of Exodus was read in the church at Sardis, and secondly by the fact, already mentioned, that Hebrew was used in early Jewish-Christian symbols discovered at the Jewish-Christian cemetery at Dominus Flevit.

CONCLUSION: NEW TESTAMENT AS SCRIPTURE

At the beginning of the Christian movement, the Church was made up exclusively of Jews and converts to Judaism. Shortly thereafter, Gentiles were admitted to membership without being required to become Jews as well. In time, as the missionary enterprise spread the Gospel throughout the Empire, the Gentile Church became numerically more powerful and ultimately prevailed. The Jewish-Christian church, cut off from the main stream of Judaism and increasingly isolated from the dominant Gentile church, gradually lost ground and finally disappeared, unmourned and un-remembered, surviving only in the remains uncovered by archaeological excavation.

The most significant monument to early Jewish Christianity that we have is the New Testament itself. It was composed almost entirely by Jewish Christians (even if Luke was born a Gentile as is often supposed, he almost certainly was a convert to Judaism as well as Christianity). While it became the Scripture of the Gentile Church, it faithfully reflects and records the origins of the Christian movement completely within the framework of first- and second-century Judaism: Jesus the founder and John the forerunner, who deliberately restricted the mission to the house of Israel. All the key events in the *kerygma* occurred in the same frame-work and were fixed in the tradition by the Jewish-Christian community: Incarnation, Ministry, Passion, Crucifixion, and Resurrection, the gift of the Spirit and the world-wide mission of the Church. In composing the New Testament, the Jewish-Christian community doubtless wrote its own epitaph, but thereby provided the charter of life and success for its inheritor, the Gentile Church.

GENERAL INDEX

Midrash (commentary), 325
Millo terraces, 97, 256
Minim, 280, 305
Mishkan (Dwelling, Sinai), 41
Mishneh quarter, 187, 225;
   Makhtesh, 187
Moab, 35–38; 59, 61–63, 81;
   121–123, 206; Moabite stone, 62,
   123–124
Monarchy, rise, 93–103
Monotheism, 163; cf. Genesis
Moses, 16, 41; Aaron, 6
Music, guilds, 98, 202; instruments,
   202
Mythological figures (Job), 211–212

N

Nabonidus, 158–159, 235
Nahor, 11, 17, 29
Nahum, book, 186; Commentary,
   cf. DSS
Nationalism (Paul's time) 302
Nazareth, 269, 280, 284 f.;
   Nazarean, 55; Nazirite, 270
Nebuchadnezzar, 11, 133, 172, 233,
   235
Nechushtan, 44
Negeb, 25–26, 62, 80, 126–127
Nehemiah, 280–281; book, 222–227;
   237
Nethinim, 226
New Testament; gap between
   O.T., 237; Introduction,
   setting-in-life 267–268; N.T.
   books 267–334, 283; Conclusion,
   334
Nineveh, 186, 190–191
Noah, 7, 22

O

Obadiah, book, 190
Offerings, peace, cereal, sin, burnt
   off., 51
Old Test. period, 237; O.T. in
   N.T. 283
Omri, 119–120
Ophel (City of David), 130–131;
   177; 224–225; 248–249; 256–257;
   295
Oral tradition, Gospels, 282 f.
Oracle, Balaam 50; Haggai, 193;
   Hosea, 147; see Prophets,
   prediction, 137–148
Ostracon, 81, 120–121, 174–175

P

Paschal lambs, 46; Passover,
   haggadah, 46; in N.T., 284
Passion, 270–271, 284 f., 298
Patriarchs, prehistoric 7; Hebrew,
   17–22; traditions, 18–32
Paul, 286, 293; 294; 297–303;
   journeys 299–302; trial, 302;
   Pauline Letters, 311–317;
   Epistles, 294, 298; cf. Gen.
   Epistles.
Pentateuch (Torah), 2–3 f.; 5;
   47–48, 159
Pentecost, 293 f.
Persian period, 158, 159 f.; 196;
   218; 221–230
Persepolis, 229

Peter, 304; P's house at
   Capernaum, 280; 1 and 2 Peter
   318–322; Epistles of, 321
Pharisees, 243–246; fellowships 264;
   265–266 f.
Philemon, 314–315, 317
Philip, 293; Philippians, 314
Philistines, 26, 28, 40, 63; 187. cf.
   Sea Peoples Pentapolis, 81,
   84–88; 93–95
Phoenicians, 80, 88–90; 110–112; 170
Poetry, Heb. 49–50; Psalter,
   197–203; Song of Solomon
   204–205, 211; Job 211–213,
   214–217; see Canaanite, Ugaritic
   literature; see Proverbs,
   Ecclesiastes; see Song
Polis, Hellenistic, 240, 243
Pontius Pilate, 270–271
Pools, 250–251; Bethesda, 289 f.
Post apostolic background, 318–320
Post-exilic Jewry, 193–195, 210–211,
   218; 221–230
Pottery, 81; varieties, 116, 120, 169;
   potter's wheel, 169
Praetorium, 254, 271
Priests; Priestly source 3–4, 51
Primary history, cf. Part 1;
   Primordial sagas, 5–12
Prophets, 83; early 124–125; classic,
   prediction, significance, 137–148
   f.; Former P. 159, 237; Latter P.
   159, 237; Minor Prophets
   185–196
Proverbs, book, 214–217 f.; see
   Wisdom
Psalms, book, 197–203; oldest
   poems, 198; poetry, 198–203;
   prayers, 201; Thanksgiving
   (DSS) 262
Pseudepigrapha (non-canonical)
   238, 259 (DSS)
Purity, purification, 51; Hassidim
   and p. 242

Q

Qumran 250, 259, 297; see
   D.S.Scrolls; 264, 265, 267, 288
Q source of Gospels, 276, 282 f.

R

Rabbis, 237; Rabbinism, Christian,
   283
Rameses I, 13–14; R. II, 35, 59;
   Rameses and Pithom (cities) 36;
   Rameses III, 84–85
Reed Sea, 39–40
Rehoboam, 115–118
Resheph (Job), 211–212
Resurrection, I, 265, 271, 297
Revelation, book and apocalypse,
   329–334; symbols 331–333
Ritual, 54; Temple, 197
Roads, 256–257
Roman empire and Christianity,
   296 (see Gen. Epist.); 331
Romans, book, 316
Ruth, book, 206

S

Sabbath, 226
Sacrifice 45–46, 51; of children, 52,
   170

Sadducees, 245 f.; 265–266; 268, 294
Sages, Proverbs, 214
Samaria, 25, 101–102; 119–122, 151
Samaritans, 227 (Nehemiah); 288
Samson, 69, 76
Samuel, 47; books 83–98
Sanctuary, 41, 42, 56, 80, 93;
   116–118; 126–127; see Temple
Sanhedrin, 294
Saul, 94; see Paul
Shechem, 14, 19, 30, 32, 66, 72, 77
Schism of the kingdom, 115–116
Scrolls, see D.S.S.
Sea Peoples (Philistines), 28, 40, 63;
   84–88
Seals, 31, 94; royal seal impressions,
   132 f.
Seleucids, 231, 236, 239
Sennacherib, 128, 155–156, 174
Septuagint transl. 20, 220
Sermon on the Mount, 282–283
Servant (Suffering) Songs, Isaiah
   160, 164; 303 (N.T.)
Seth, 13, 21, 58
Setting-in-life, 17, 54; 254, 267
   (N.T.); Psalms, 200 f.
Settlement in Canaan, 35, 76–77
Shalmaneser III 122–123
Shekels, 148, 226, 235
Ships, 110–111
Shosu, Shutu, 15, 34, 58–59; Sheth,
   189
Sidonians, 80, 110
Simeon, 19, 30, 32, 73
Snake; serpent, 44, 66, 199
Social changes, 14, 141–146;
   180–181; 221–230; cf. material
   changes
Solomon, 21–22, 53; 87; 104; and
   Song of Songs, 204; and
   Proverbs, 215; Ecclesiastes, 218;
   Solomon's Porch, see Hanuyyoth
Song of the Sea, 39, 47 (Miriam);
   of the Well, 57; of Moses, 64; of
   Deborah, 74; of Solomon
   204–205, 211; see Poetry
Source-critical method, 3
Stele, 13, 14, 21; cf. Inscriptions
Sumer, Sumerians, 5; sources,
   traditions, 7, 9, 11, 12, 17–18, 211
Symbols 181 (mimetic); archaic 189
   f.; visions, 194–195; 238
Synagogues, 295; Capernaum, 280;
   Mount Zion 294;
   Church-synagogue, 294; Post
   apostolic s. 310
Synoptic Gospels, 276–278; sources,
   similarities and divergences
   276–278; apocalypse, 278

T

Tabernacle (Sinai) 41, 45; Feast of
   Tabernacles 290–291
Temple, 36, 45; First, 104–106;
   Ezekiel's ideal, 183; Second T.
   and ritual, 197; 269–270; Temple
   forts, 14
Ten Commandments, 47–48, 52
Teraphim, 23, 52
Thessalonians, book, 311–312
Timnah sanctuary, 10–11;
   copper-mining, 10–11
Timothy, book, 316–317

INDEX OF BIBLICAL REFERENCES

340

INTERTESTAMENTAL PERIOD

NEW TESTAMENT

ACKNOWLEDGMENTS

The publisher and editors are deeply indebted to Professor Benjamin Mazar's books, articles, and views, and to the other scholars quoted in this book for their valuable insights and interpretations.

The editors are grateful to D. R. Burton (Program on Studies in Religion, the University of Michigan) for his comprehensive editing and restyling, to Ruth Elon for the graphic layout and design, and to Hassia Ben Harari for her valuable help.

A List of Illustrations with Acknowledgments

By courtesy of the Israel Department of Antiquities and Museums (5, 13, 18, 23, 51(2), 53, 61, 70, 74, 76, 86, 88, 89, 90, 94, 99, 111, 115, 117(6), 118, 120, 127, 130, 133, 134, 147, 151, 152, 161, 164(2), 168, 174, 177, 200, 204, 210, 226, 233, 314, 329).

By courtesy of the Archaeological Institute, University of Tel Aviv (14, 26, 27(3), 31 (Photo-Credit Abraham Hai), 81, 82, 117, 142, 144, 145, 166, 171).

By courtesy of the Archaeological Excavations in Jerusalem; Temple Mount (108, 127, 128, 130, 132, 176, 200, 201, 224, 226, 247, 249, 251, 256(3), 257, 270, 272, 273).

Benno Rothenberg (10, 35, 42(3), 43(2), 44(2), 56, 213).

Ben Gurion University, Beersheba (87).

Ruth Amiran (Philistines, 69, 83, 85).

Raphael Gibeon (9).

Government Press Office, Photographic Dept. (23, 86, 107(3), 108, 161, 169, 187, 222, 227, 228, 242, 248, 251, 255, 259).

Department of Museums, Cyprus (23, 25, 52, 147).

University of Chicago (45, 69, 70, 73, 230); University of Pennsylvania (180); Bildarchiv Photo Marburg (113, 152); Giraudon, Paris (125, 135, 153); Archives Photographiques, Paris (48, 50, 105, 148, 189, 199, 213); Professor J. A. Calloway (71); State Museum, Berlin (59); Anderson, Roma (240); Musée de l'Homme, Paris (43, 193).

British Museum (4, 6, 9, 108, 110, 112, 123(2), 134, 153(2), 155(2), 178, 182, 195, 220, 331); Schweich Lectures, London (272).

Bureau of Tourism, Ankara (299, 300).

Studium Biblicum Franciscanum (268, 269, 279, 280, 289, 305, 309).

Shrine of the Book (261).

Photo Credits: Garo Nalbandian (14, 77, 78, 96, 97, 130, 241, 250, 254).

The other illustrations in the book are derived from G. Cornfeld's photographic archive.